MOON POWER STARGUIDE 2007

Yearly Edition

Dr. Louis Turi, M.D.S.

Startheme Publications Inc.
4411 N. 23rd St Phoenix, AZ 85016

Copyright 2006 by Dr. Louis Turi

All rights reserved. No part of this publication may be reproduced or transmitted in any form or by any means, electronic or mechanical, including photocopy, recording, or any information storage and retrieval system, without permission in writing from the publisher.

Editing: Laurie Shafer
Illustrations: Madeline Rosenstein
Cover: Martin Hodgson
ISBN: 978-0-9745209-2-6
Published by Startheme Publications Inc.

Visit our websites:
www://drturi.com
Visit : Myspace.com/drturi
E-mail: *Dr. Turi@cox.net*
Tel: (602) 265-7667
Fax: (602) 265-8668

MOON POWER STARGUIDE 2007
Special 2007 Issue Limited Edition
Produced August 2007 in Bangkok Thailand
Printed in the United States of America

STARGUIDE 2007

Table of Contents

Acknowledgments 4

My Story 5

Letter From the Author 18

How to use Starguide 28

The Universal Law 30

Supernova Windows for 2007 51

Predictions For The Century 54

Slow-Moving Planets Predictions 56

2007 Dragon's Head & Tail 64

Your Personal Horoscope 72

Starguide's Day-to-Day Guidance 124

Closing Thoughts 357

Services Offered 359

"He is wise who understands that the stars are luminaries, created as signs. He who will conquer the stars will hold the golden keys to God's mysterious universe."
— Nostradamus

Acknowledgements

Special thanks are given to all my great friends and family, faithful clients, students and readers from all over the world. A special thanks to George Noory and the numerous open-minded people I've known as friends, journalists and worldwide hosts of radio and television program. I am grateful to all of those spiritual men and women who have helped me enlighten their lives and audiences with the knowledge of the stars. I appreciate all those souls who have guided and supported my work. In their common efforts to further the truth, they all are vital participants in the understanding of the human experience. All of you have been invaluable in furthering the truth, and I am infinitely grateful for allowing me to pass on my celestial message to the world.

---Dr. Turi

My Story

"Incredible experiences breed incredible people that have incredible things to offer and to teach others". That is of course, if you pay attention to my predictive work regularly posted on my website and investigate the content of my book with the unfolding daily news. With patience and observation you will realize that I am trustworthy and my work far from being fictional.

For the hundreds of thousands of faithful readers who have been with me for many years there will not any doubt about my predictive ability. My well - documented printed predictions and my numerous televisions and radio appearances made all my premonitions over the years totally unarguable. Especially those of the 911, the Asia Tsunami the Kobe earthquake, the series of deadly hurricanes predicted on Coast To Coast on the George Noory's worldwide radio show and his special "pay per view" television program taped in January 2005. To all of my faithful audience thank you for your support and if you are a new comer to my work, soon you will also bring forth your own cosmic consciousness and realize the Universal Mind impact on all human affairs.

This year I decided to get away from Phoenix and my crazy life in order to produce this yearly book. At this very moment (08/12/06) I am in Bangkok, Thailand, away from all my students, clients, friends, telephone and even the Internet. I have sixteen days to do the task and produce the 2007 Moon Power and it must be done before my return to the US.

Incidentally I watched the BBC news today and again my predictions for "surprises and explosions" for August 12th came true with Scotland Yard thwarting a plot by terrorists attacks directed at many international Airlines. Luckily for me, I made a good use of my wisdom and flew to Thailand before the Full Moon and by flying back to the US in the upcoming New Moon. Doing so, I simply avoided the worse and a lot of frustration.

This is where the hundreds of thousands of people worldwide had to pay the price of ignorance and got stuck in thousands of airports, suffering delays and flight cancellations. Any and all of those travelers would have made a good use of my book, had they heeded my warnings for this Full Moon in Aquarius and the current "Supernova Window" in action. The same applies for all the incredible amount victims of the predicted Asia tsunami. Yes, I was supposed to be in Thailand on that terrible day on December 25th, but I knew about the deadly impact of a Full Moon in Cancer and cancelled my trip. Again my wisdom and intuition saved our lives. This is why it is vital for you to pass on my book to those you care and help them to realize the importance of planning and respecting the Universal rules. Doing so will save money, time frustrations and precious lives.

Further more the "Window" for August 12, 2006 also mentioned devastative forces at work and China suffered the worse typhoon (Saomai) in the last fifty years, killing hundreds of people and forcing thousands of people to relocate. If you have a copy of the 2006 Moon Power, simply open it to page 209 and page 212 for the period of August 2006. Then read what I wrote about Middle East development and the possibility of nature creating deadly typhoon and start to learn how to make a good use of my book. If you don't have last year copy, simply email me at dr.turi@cox.net and request the E-book version.

Sadly enough, my predictions are continuously unfolding as I heard news from Japan in August 2006. A ship named "The Bright Artemis" caused intensive damage to India's coastline of Andaman and Nicobar in the Indian Ocean archipelago after the Japanese supertanker collided on August 12 (on the date I posted on my site) with a Singapore ship that was on fire. The oil tanker approached the burning vessel to rescue the people, when the two ships accidentally collided. An estimated 4,500 tons of crude oil has and is, still leaking from the supertanker.

But this "sea accident" is nothing, compared to the worst oil spill in the history of the southern Asian country, with the sinking in rough seas of the "Solar 1" Super tanker on Friday August 12th (again the window was posted on my website). The ship spilled over 520,000 gallons of industrial fuel ruining the Philippines coastlines and the livelihood of over 10.000 local fishermen. These disasters simply reflect my prediction for 2006/2007 for "serious sea accidents and oil spills".

Even though you purchased this book you <u>MUST</u> occasionally take the time to go to my website www.drturi.com. You need to be aware of some of the worse dates I post there for the current year and read my quatrains. I do this regularly to teach you how to interpret the will of the cosmos and help you to make a better use of my book.

This book is a periodical and indeed my best seller, more and more people used it on a daily basis and recognize the value of my daily guidance and predictions. Over the years I have mentioned that; in order to keep the content as real as can be, I do not let anyone but me edit its content and I am trying really hard to turn my French / English into something readable. Many times people will email or call me pointing out my grammatical errors and I always say that the "editor and proof" have been fired…

I will try to find someone I trust enough to edit my work upon my return to the US. But until then, attempt to teach the Universal laws in a foreign language to millions of foreigners in a foreign language like I do. And unless you can do it as well as I do, be gentle on me. Simply don't miss the forest looking at the tree and once more, you know and I know that my English is bad, so what? Please, get the divine message!

You will be amazed of how many famous authors you read everyday that (unlike me) will NOT take the time to type on a keyboard and still sell millions of copies of their fictional work. Yes, believe me, all that they do is to speak into a microphone and have a transcriber doing all the hard grammatical English editing work for them, so they can look good to your critical eyes. I know so many famous authors out there, who never sat five minutes to type a single word for their book and that is a fact! Of course the book will be translated in many foreign language too, but the full content is still fictional.

It's all about laziness and letting their wild imagination be tempestuous. Especially those writers who "channel"

Nostradamus' predictions. How many of those famous writers who "channels" the Great Prophet' spirit had well documented prediction or any plausible, intelligible way of explaining his quatrains? In all those Nostradamus spiritual writers, I only endorse my good friend and real scholar John Hogue, all others are charlatans and lost in a fantasy world.

Come on people, I am real, my work is factual and demands concentration and solid information and if I screw up with a date or a sentence after seven or ten hours of writing, give me a break! Call me old fashion but at least you are getting the real me, because all about my work and me is real!

Dr. Turi they say, "But professionally editing your book will make you look so good and put more faith in your work". Guess what I say "Look and perceive the divinity in the content of my book and feel my message and not the cold immaculate grammar or the beautiful cover. In the process you may be able to build your own cosmic consciousness that will help you to discern the Divine manifestation of the cosmos in your daily life. I have so many volunteers willing to help me and sad enough, out of the hundreds that have signed up over the years to help me, only one or two has been productive. All the rest of my "volunteers" are much more interested in receiving free stuff from me and never performed when I asked them to submit my articles or my website out there to the Internet world.

Take it from me, the most famous and wealthier authors in this world are not those who promote the truth. Their fictional work is designed to entertain an endless amount of numb minds lost in a world of religion or fantasy, where entertainment is a sure way to escape reality. This is a way of life "escapism" religions, drugs and alcohol brings about the same results, it numbs your spirit I may add. **DON'T** sleep through life! You will have plenty time to do so when you will be dead! You are alive **NOW**, try your best at anything, everything and use your imagination productively and if you are a fictional writer or a movie script writer so be it, I chose a more practical path but I will not endorse Mel Gibson's movie for sure. This deplorable drug and alcohol habit tells you how much promoting Jesus' life really helped him in the depth of his lost soul. Using a priest on CNN to clear his name did not work for me, either.

The same applies for Tom Cruise and his endeavor with "Scientology", or Madonna with her weird spiritual aims. The fact is that rich and famous does not mean emotional or spiritual stability and to me they are very lost souls still looking for the truth. Being actors or in a realm of imagination and deception (or Neptunian) does not help any of them to find true spiritual stability.

The big problem is that the Christians want to convert the world into Christianity. Muslims want to do the same with their faith and so are the Jews. What a mess! To me its like a huge sewer with different pipes and at the end, we all suffocate and drown into stupidity, hate, fears, ignorance, terrorism, unthinkable pain, horrendous suffering and ultimately death.

No intelligent man should endorse, promote or support anything that at the end kills and as I am writing those words, at this very moment again someone dies because of his faith and religion.

In the future when men grow up, all the essence of all the best of all the various religions of this world have to offer will be finally understood and used appropriately to help, love and respect humankind regardless of their race or culture. There is beauty in religious diversity and a true drive to heal and help in any and all religions regardless how weird some may appear to be. This is what the Age of Aquarius is all about to do to this world, uncover its Universal religion so peace and freedom in true brotherhood will replace the present religious despicable carnage the world is suffering.

What is really bothering me is that; none of the secret Agency has yet invested in my methodology or Astro-Psychology and this science is well ahead of both conventional psychology and psychiatry. There are obvious traits in one's natal UCI (Unique Celestial Identity" that produces a indisputable terrorist. Especially when it comes to the Head and Tail of the Dragon or any significant planet in the pious sign of Pisces. This predisposition produces the entire reveille and breed a natural "born" terrorist.

The world's secret services would make such a great use of Astro-Psychology instead of using common facial expressions (traditional psychology) in International airport to detect the physiology and deadly potential of individuals. When will they learn that much of their problem (and your tax dollar saved) could easily be, eliminated? Why the secret services wouldn't use my methodology and cast aside the ridicule and explore true human values through my work is a real mystery to me? I offered my services for FREE to the FBI and the police while taping for the Discovery channel a few years back and none of them honored the very essence of their profession "INVESTIGATION" and missed the very essence of what they are all looking for. Look for all the details of what transpired in and out of the set then with retired Chiefs of police, profilers, lie detectors professionals and even FBI agents in one of my newsletter (read "Taping For The Discovery Channel" in previous newsletters from my home page). The attitude they had with me was simply and absolutely deplorable.

All governmental secret Agencies administrations nowadays are enslaved to uncover anything about terrorism and I have the golden key. Many of these souls are secretly reading my website, but one day once they are ready for me, I will be there to teach them what makes a true terrorist. Until then, the entire world is at serious risk because one day a Neptune's deceiving child will succeed and will kill many innocent people by exploding an airplane; just because the secret services are STILL inadequate in their detective work. Omitting or ignoring any physical or spiritual laws can only bring penalty; for science's purpose is to explore all possibilities, even those laws written in light via the stars.

There is art in the imaginativeness don't get me wrong, but there is a big difference between imagination and divination and my writings are designed to raise my readers' (or the FBI) spiritual vibrations and guide them into a more productive endeavor to save lives.

Dreamer, Slacker, Head in the Clouds, Stargazer, I am sure that we have all heard those terms, but none rang so clear in my head as "Stargazer." I am not in the strictest sense of the word a Stargazer or an astronomer destitute of spiritual gifts. Instead, I do understand the language of the Gods, I perceive the hieroglyphs of the Universe and I translate the almighty God's celestial messages left indelibly across men's souls. Now, I did not start out in life with this intent. No way, I was going to be a big rock-and-roll star. That's right, I did all that I set for myself to do and performing and music became my life for many years. This life style suited me well then; I was young and full of life. I got to travel, meet new people, be creative and all along hurt too many, pretty innocent girls.

My passion for music was very strong and I blessed with a will of steel I had to succeed and when I wasn't working, I practiced my piano until my fingers bled. All the while wishing I still had my guitar, I lost it after a bad fight with a gang that hung out in the Victoria Station metro after dark. These days in 1974 were very hard and surviving was my only full time job. In my new book "You Are God" all my peripheries and incredible experiences are divulged and I am sure, barely believable for some of my readers. In time this book will be turned into a movie. Please sign up to the free "Dragon Newsletter" from my website at www.drturi.com to find out more about my books, projects and all that I do and will do in the future. In each one of my trips including Australia, Hawaii and this one in Thailand, I always take pictures and let all my newsletter' subscribers travel and experience the world with me. I receive thousands of emails thanking me for doing so and it's a way for me to share my "incredible" life with you.

I've been very lucky all along and from homelessness in the street of Los Angeles and San Diego, I made it all the way up to the top and spent time in Malibu and Las Vegas with many celebrities who nicknamed me "The Star of the Stars". Not only did I become a good friend to this famous crowd, but also a personal deeply trusted spiritual guide to all of them. Check some of my famous friends at myspace.com/drturi or in my previous newsletters.

Back in England in 1974 I had set myself to learn piano and become a rock star. However I had to survive in a new country I did not speak the language, and being a Frenchman, English was a real twist. So I started out in the tubes, singing French songs and making a few pence a day to able to eat. Incidentally, my first English words came to me as I went shopping for the first time in a small Indian shop in London. I scanned the shelves in the store until I found the cheapest thing that I could. It came out of a can and was cold and crunchy, but it filled my belly. After eating, I got out my little French-to-English dictionary and looked up to words, "Dog" and "Food." You can imagine my disgust when I found out what this meant, but I was lucky, I got to eat that day. I can laugh about it now and I would not change a thing about it all. When there was a lull in the metro, I would run up the steps and be right at Victoria Station, a huge and busy place with a whole bank of telephones. I would run up and down, listening for someone who spoke my native tongue. I finally found a Swiss man who spoke both English and French, who gave me a job in the hotel in Eastbourne, Sussex.

I started out as a janitor at the five stars prestigious "Grant Hotel" and moved up in two years, to the position of Head Barman at the "Saloon Bar". I was young and wild, full of life and this was the position I dreamed of since I first sat in this bar, loaded with so many pretty English girls. Little did I know about the miraculous creative forces of my subconscious then and the dramatic events that would lead me to become the "Saloon Bar" Manager, months later, I did land on this dreamed of position, totally by accident. But over the years I have learned that there are no accidents and my book "You Are God" will tell you all about the subconscious' incredible ways to make anyone's wish to happen.

After a dangerous knife fight with a drunken ex-convict Scottish man, the management decided to get someone fearless like me, to run this wild place. The crazy man refused to pay for his drinks and tried to stab the young barman instead, when I decided to jump into the deadly situation and saved his life. On my own and in the street since the age of 13 years old, I learned a long time ago how to look after myself. I was wild, but wise and always knew my limitations in many dangerous situations.

Before this unplanned lucky break, I had to work three jobs to survive and pay for my tuition at the Royal School of Music in London. I finished my first job at the "Rumblebelly" restaurant at 1:00 am and I could not afford a car. I had to walk a distance of over a mile in the cold and wet English weather to Saint Marie Hospital, where I worked at night as a switchboard operator. The hospital housed terminally ill elderly people and death was a daily routine, forcing me to take numerous night walks to the mortuary. No one wanted this disgusting position and its appalling duties, but it was part of the job and I did it because I had no other choice. There are so many incredible stories about ghosts, even miracles that took place in this hospital during that time and again in my book "You Are God" many readers would find hard to accept them all.

I was to stay in England for almost ten years, working and studying music really hard. Finally, I graduated at the top of my class ahead of four hundred other students earning the prized "Distinction Cup" and commendation from some Royal family members. This led me to a recording deal with Phillips Phonogram records in my own country in Paris France. I produced several records and then went back to home, to France, glad to leave the harsh English weather behind.

I went through four incredible experiences with UFO and for many years, I was reluctant to mention those encounters to anyone. Little did I know, that much more incredible happenings with extraterrestrial were to happen to me later on in my life. But, I speak the truth and all that I promote is the future and UFO have been with me, since the tender age of seven years old and will always be a big part of my life and mankind's future. In the name of fear, ignorance or jealousy, I also quickly realized that the world was not exactly ready for my unbelievable experiences or my highly spiritual work. After all a magnet will not attract a piece of wood and I do vibrate as such a higher level, that absolutely anything astounding, can and will happen to me (or anyone close to me).

I deal with the future, promote and explore infinity, thus things of an incredible universal futuristic proportion such as the UFO phenomenon are from futuristic in nature and are an intrinsic part of my life and my four incredible experiences with UFO are simply very real.

In those days, my older brother Georges owned a discotheque at the time called L'Interdit or The Forbidden. It was quite the hot spot, and he asked me to come and sing my songs there. I gladly accepted the invitation and we left his farmhouse about forty-five minutes from the discotheque around 9:30 p.m. on November 11th, 1981. We were driving through the nightly deserted roads through the vineyards; not knowing just yet that I was to experience one of the most formidable experiences a human being can have. This night's dramatic occurrence and date will never be forgotten for as long as I live.

Jo was driving, lost in his thoughts when I saw lights flashing out from a distance in the vineyards. Trying to get his attention I asked him, "Hey Jo they're people working out there at night? He looked at me like I had lost my mind, "Louis," he said, "it's

November, all the grapes have been harvested a long time ago!" I then watched the lights come closer and closer until our car was bathed in light so bright that we could not see, and my brother's brand-new Mercedes stalled right there in the middle of the road and would not restart.

We both had our noses up against the windscreen trying to see this thing above in the night sky. It was showering us with brilliant lights but it was still much too bright for Jo or I to see anything at this point. I got out of the car, and then the lights dimmed down in the car, with my brother still in it. This left him scared to death and me outside swathed in a reddish pink light with a pleasing glow. The source of light came from none other than a huge, solid Spaceship or UFO suspended about thirty feet above our heads. It stayed there for at least five minutes, and it made a slight humming sound. It was beautiful, with multi-colored lights all around it that couldn't be seen, while its two main bright white headlights were on.

It just hung there in the sky for our viewing pleasure, just out of reach. We stared in awe, me banging on the car, yelling and cursing for all I was worth for my brother to get out of the car, but he wouldn't. So much for being a big bad powerful guy is he? Or that was his reputation then, big brothers, what do you expect! Finally, the spaceship dimmed its bright beams off allowing my eyes to get used to the darkness and after a short time, I could perceive the contour of the saucer. Then a gentle mixture of red, gold, green, pink, yellow came from its underbelly and enveloped the car entirely. Then the powerful bright lights came on again and the space ship just flew away, careless as you please and we watched as it picked up speed and disappeared. When I got back into the car, my brother swore me to secrecy that "We would never tell anyone about this ever!" When we arrived at the disco that night everything was in full swing. This is very strange because we should have arrived with the crew who was opening; looking back I would say that we had a missing-in-time thing happen, but we didn't know anything about that back then, just that it was really strange. Yet I did not know, that even more incredible UFO experiences were to take place in the US, molding my future and undoubtedly establishing a connection with extraterrestrial and leading to an unusual fate.

The next day, my mother called me and asked if my brother

was okay. I laughed, remembering the secrecy deal and assured my mom everything was fine. Which it was, but my soul had somehow changed and I began to think that there was more to life than singing and making records. Maybe I could make a greater contribution, I didn't know what yet, but I wanted something. It didn't take me long to get the wanderlust again and soon enough, I was back to England. With a dream in my heart just a few short years before, I had written a song about this great land. Now, more than ever I wanted to go. I didn't know anybody and didn't have any money, because it turns out my contract had my music playing everywhere in Europe except my own country, and I couldn't collect my share. This was a solid omen for me to be ready for a new life...

Oh, the trials of youth! But I had high hopes and a business card from a man I met in London who said, "Come to America, I will help you start a new life!" I arrived in Los Angeles, the City of Angels, smoggy and yucky, caught a Greyhound bus to San Diego, gorgeous and green, got out my little wallet with fifty dollars and the business card searching for the business on Garnet Avenue in Pacific Beach, California. I am still looking for this man and his business. Disheartened, I took thirty of my precious dollars and paid for a motel for the night, and then went to a bar up the street. I ordered a drink and then went to the cigarette machine. Weird thing, I never saw one of those before and I couldn't figure out how to work it.

So I asked a man at the end of the bar if he could help me out. He looked at me funny for a minute or two and then showed me how it worked. Later he told me why he had an odd gaze; he thought I was gay and that this was a come-on! This man's name is John Steward and he became one of my best friends. We got drunk and found two beautiful girls soon after, what a start! I thought I might as well, didn't know what the future would hold, but I still held a shiny bit of enthusiasm in my soul. Sadly enough, years later after an accident, fate turned him from a very wealthy attorney, into one of the homeless. I had predicted this for him in Hawaii, upon one of his numerous visits. Life's experiences are dramatic in nature and when the moon resides in a water sign, usually the past, guilt and depression follow. That's why I decided to write this book annually to help those in need to face their challenges.

I had begun to learn the ways of the great Cosmic Clock then and knew that I arrived on American soil during a great trend! When I awoke the next morning, I went up the street with my suitcase in one hand and a purse in the other. In France it is customary for men to carry purses. This may be another reason why John looked at me funny, as that is definitely not the custom here. I smelt the ocean and took off in that direction; the waves crashing against the shore were soothing to my nerves, but seeing the girls wearing tops was more culture shock for me. I spent another dollar or two of my precious money getting a cup of coffee and then grabbed a newspaper, The La Jolla Light. I needed a place to stay and found a section called "Roommates." There was a great ad for a beautiful house on the ocean in La Jolla with a telephone number and an address. I called the lady up and told her that I was on my way. When I arrived with my suitcase, she remarked how fast and eager I was, with a worried look on her face.

She then explained that with two more guys like me, we would all be able to afford a beautiful home on the sea. Wow, new word for me, roommate. I explained my situation and she felt sorry for me, and said I could stay with her and tutor her daughter in French. Housing settled for the moment, I went to find a job. Up the street, I ran into a little restaurant called, "The French Gourmet." Soon I had my first job in America, washing dishes, not glamorous, but a job. Nice guy, my boss then, Michel Malecot. I worked for him for four years, laboring my way to general manager. I also soon moved into my very own apartment and in every spare minute I read and studied my new obsession: Astrology. I inhaled books and knowledge everywhere from the bible to heavy metaphysics. I even painted the apartment that Michel gave me to oversee his catering department with my own astrological chart, the human body and which sign rules each part, as well as other pictures with UFOs prevalent in the bringing of knowledge. As I read, I continually went back to the books about Nostradamus and his works, as well as the books that the great man himself had written. He had a particular way of interpreting the stars that echoed down the valleys of my soul, totally free of mathematical jargon. His methods made much more sense than the other mathematical processes in every way, especially when the great Prophet did not have the luxury of a computer or even a watch then. I dedicated myself to his method for many years, and learned and learned, and then seemed to channel knowledge from the universe itself. When Michel came to collect his rent the first month and found his beautiful apartment all painted, you can imagine his shock, but I sat him down and said, "I want to give you a reading."

He was my first client! He is still a client today and one of my best friends in the US. I began to tell people about my passion and people began to come for readings. I had stopped working for Michel; I couldn't take the stress any longer. I went back to working in engineering, welding and heavy equipment, skills I had learned as a young boy from my stepfather. I worked on San Diego US base then Pearl Harbor in Hawaii then in 1991 my entire life changed following the ultimate UFO encounter with my ex-wife Brigitte. I painted my entire house with UFO drawings and astrological symbols and I could not stop reading and re-kindly the great Nostradamus' Divine Astrology methodology.

Years later with thousands of satisfied clients in all walks of life and hundreds of successful predictions, I am still trying hard to further man's cosmic consciousness and sharpen his intuition by making obvious statements and premonitions in predictive astrology. Some of these were the destruction of the WTC in New York, the fall of Saddam Hussein, SARS break out, the Washington sniper, earthquakes, disasters, NASA failures and the Asia tsunami, hurricane Katrina etc. Note also that the printing process in all my previous books make those premonitions totally unarguable.

Letter from the Author

Happy New Year to All

8/12/2006

Dear Clients and Friends:

One more year has gone and 2007 is already upon us. My predictions of a full restructure of "Middle East has taken its deadly course. Incidentally, the new Dragon's Head moved into the sign of Pisces in June 2006 and sealed the exact moment in time and space when Israel was to invade Lebanon, forcing the UN to take drastic action. This dramatic prediction was put on the air on the pay per view television special produced by George Noory, famous host of Coast-to-Coast where in early 2006, I was a guest. 2006 has unfolded and has undoubtedly been a deadly and very dramatic year for the many people involved in the continuous Middle East conflict. Most of the world's population will be forced by the new celestial order to reevaluate its religious, philosophical and spiritual values following the September 11th WTC destruction by religious fanatics from the Middle East. My predictions of Saddam Hussein's regime, including the full restructure of the FBI and CIA agencies, also came to pass.

The tsunami disaster in Asia and other calamities such as hurricane Katrina made us all also aware of how powerful Mother Nature really is and how vulnerable we really are. America is a great country but also a very young religious country and intercomparable to the Middle East in so many ways. Like many other countries in need to grow spiritually, the new Dragon in the religious sign of Pisces will impose this worldwide religious fanaticism insanity to stop. But how can you alter and redirect two thousands years of religious poisoning to a world gone mad? Wrong information, mental manipulation and dogmatic teachings, lead the Middle East to its own self-destruction and to the demise of so many innocent people through so many conflicts where the entire world is both affected and involved.

The Dragon has its own plan and slowly but surely the deceiving age of Pisces (religion/oil/drugs/deception/the Middle East) must and will be RE-birthing into the more advanced Age of Aquarius and this does mean a few other keywords, such as (technology/brotherhood/UFO/ingeniousity/universality/education/freedom).

The war is also taken place in the heaven (eternal movement of the stars) where the old dogmatic teachings, ignorance and fears will be replaced in time by a more intellectually inclined way of perceiving the manifestation of the divine outside of well established current religions and deities. It will take many years for mankind to raise its spiritual vibration but the higher order is already in motion. Death, fears, ignorance and revenge in the name of a God or a religion will be replaced by life, peace, education hope and respect for all mankind, where all men will master and respect the true will of God through his celestial creation. The promise of the advanced New Age of Aquarius will finally bring true love, respect and ever-lasting peace to this world and other worlds not yet divulged to mankind because of its current low mental predisposition.

In some ways, the dramatic WTC destruction was very symbolic and represents a form of wake up call to many souls, in respect to what any and all religions are about and leads to. But the world is slow to acknowledge any facts but Uranus (the New Age/the future/ the US/technology) is relentlessly battling Neptune (the Age of Pisces/ the past/all religions/imagination/deception etc.). Pluto (death/rebirth/drama/terrorism) is still going through the sign of Sagittarius (codification of thoughts printed rules, books, Bible, ,Koran, foreigners) and adds more fuel to an already very hot subject matter. The negative manifestation of such a murderous celestial recipe will easily affect the uneducated manipulated religious poisoned young souls. Many will fall for the pull of the stars and will become the working force of evil producing the deadly acts (suicide bombers) and the proceeding changes.

The Dragon's Head in Pisces: (Christianity/church) will bring about more damage where the church authorities will have to take drastic actions to survive an approaching "the end of time" (for Christianity I meant). More priests will be exposed with sex scandals while devious financial Christian deals will come to light, bringing more devastative legal suits against the church. The new Pope, unaware of the celestial astrological order, will try to adapt to the changes and already enrolled both gays and Gypsies to the Christian faith. The financial Christian Empire (Church Inc.) is collapsing and all must be done by the last Pope to save the church and the Christians faith. But all will be in vain as ANY humans regardless of their name or position cannot alter the Universal order.

How far will the failing church go and when will the world wake up to reality?

New Hampshire Episcopalians Choose Gay Bishop

First gay Episcopalian bishop The Rev. V. Gene Robinson: "I do believe this is of the spirit."
Laurie Goodstein
New York Times
Sunday, June 8, 2003 Posted: 6:55 AM EDT (1055 GMT)

CONCORD, New Hampshire, June 7 -- Episcopalians in the Diocese of New Hampshire today elected as their leader the first openly gay bishop anywhere in the worldwide Anglican communion, a step likely to roil the church in the United States and England, and deepen the disaffection of the more conservative Anglican churches in Africa, Asia and Latin America.
In all honesty, do the church leaders really think that we are stupid or something?

On May 3 1997, the Pope made an important announcement that

would denunciate for those who can decipher the facts, how desperate the financial situation of the church really is.
VATICAN CITY — When Pope John Paul II makes a choice for sainthood; it's often to make a point. On Sunday, he draws attention to a long neglected and often despised group in Europe, beatifying a Gypsy for the first time in the history of the Roman Catholic Church. Beatification is the last step before possible canonization or sainthood.

DT rebuttal: Note also that; for centuries Gypsies and Gays were persecuted by the church and now the Pope made new rule, Gypsies have "the right" to have saints and now a gay person can also become a bishop. The point I am trying to make is that Men's laws can be changed at will if it "benefit" or justify the goal. These laws are man made and written by men's hands. These translate into the codification of thoughts producing an endless amount of books of laws, used by a priest (the bible) an attorney (DMV/FDA/FAA/FCC etc. or a judge.

But the Universal laws writing in light (via the stars) speak the real truth and CAN NOT be altered by any man (not even the Pope himself). With all the legal battles against a multitude of abusive priests (Pluto/sex) in Sagittarius (law/books/codification of thoughts/bible) the church is desperately looking for new members (any members of our diverse society will do!) to support its collapsing infrastructure and financial abusive empire. Thus after a few secrets meetings at the top the decision was made to grasp money from what ever was left in parts of what Christians have discarded and rejected for centuries or the "lower" disgraceful, immoral members of our society. This decision was a must and an emergency for the church as to avoid bankruptcy. There is a big chunk of wealthy gay people in our society (Elton Jones) for the church to tab on. Don't get me wrong people, I do not really care about the gay society; I have great friends, clients and students of mine that are gay. I know through the stars what create gay tendencies and I can only respect the soul of a person reincarnated with a bunch of feminine tendencies producing this simple fact. I am not judging the gay community knowing that I deal with both male and female homosexuals on a daily base in my practice.

I am simply making you aware how gays are like every one of us, including the Gypsies manipulated by the church authorities for financial purpose. First, realize that anything "organized" is produced by Uncle Sam and like the IRS and any other branches of the government be sure that; the clergy need your money more than God to survive and incidentally much of the church paychecks (billions of dollars) are also exempt of tax!

Well maybe you can also understand that Uranus (the future/shocking news/changes/unification/New Age) just entered the pious sign of Pisces (religion/the church/deception) and will produce some serious changes soon. Unlike the first gay Episcopalian bishop Rev. V. Gene Robinson's remark *"I do believe this is of the spirit,"* **THIS IS NOT** "of a spiritual but is of a monetary affair" imposed by a celestial order unknown to them all. With 99.9 % of the people on this world lacking cosmic consciousness it is not surprising to realize that any and all religious or political leaders in position of power including NASA scientists would be remotely aware on how the stars regiment all human affairs. Try my new book *"And God Created The Stars"* to gather more cosmic consciousness because knowledge is power and ignorance is evil.

Little does the Pope know about the dying Age of Pisces and the True Celestial Order imposing a New World of spiritual changes. A strong spiritual drive and conception for the truth will prevail, while a new wave of information through technology (my website and other light workers' dedication) will reach a less gullible younger generation. In time this new form of divine wisdom will bring about man's spiritual freedom where enlightenment and true information will take over religious fears and manipulative dogmatic teachings.

More shocking news are ahead of us with religion, technology and the US/UK versus the Middle East. This is simply the results produced by the explosive surprising planet Uranus (chocking news/the future/USA/nuclear explosion) passing through the sign of Pisces (religion/the past/deception/Middle East/Oil). Rest assured the difficult task is being done by the universal scheme of things and transpires on this world dramatically on a daily basis.

These classifications of God and its specific "regulations" can only breed differences and animosity. With these differences come hate, death and destruction and all in the name of fear and lack of true wisdom. Ignorance is evil and for all its purposes EVERY SINGLE religion ignores and avoids the teachings of the true manifestation of the creator through its own creation, the stars! And yes, astrology is against my religion I heard, what about those 3 Kings (astrologer?) following a bright Star? And how did the sailors promoting the good words of the Lord in the "Dark Ages" sail the ocean? By and with the help of the stars I presume. And what about the Pope being taught astrology by the Vatican council? Check the picture on my site at www.drturi.com.

All the spirits of this world have been hijacked for too long and are the real victims. 99% of the world' souls are totally religiously contaminated to the point of numbness since childhood. Their true spirit sank into fears and ignorance as planned by a politically oriented and the extremely wealthy and well-organized religion/ church of your country of birth. The true laws of the Divine were cast aside for a group of privileged select motivated by man's folly, greed and thirst for power. The order is for the Dragon to start a chain of events that will reverse all of this spiritual betrayal and bring about a drastic insurrection in man's true spiritual evolution.

Back in 1991 on the Art Bell radio show I had made that awful prediction and said the words, "religious war in the US." But he, the host and his audience did not hear me then. He didn't even believe me with a copy of my book sent to him certified with his name and my predictions printed (Art Bell - OFF THE AIR!) and an upcoming US religious war. It all unfolded as predicted and printed in the book but no acknowledgement of the facts came from this very devout man! Better yet, he even removed our show from his radio archives.

Other souls have had to endure drastic psychological and physical changes. I must admit that the Dragon passage through any sign and house, or its location at birth, will always bring an incredible positive or negative energy to that area and will induce the badly needed changes. Better be aware of its impact by sign and house and most of all get ready emotionally and financially for the imposed challenges. The Dragon took two very close friends away from me in 2006 and like you, I am not immune from its power and I suffered the losses terribly.

But I was prepared and I can only accept my own predictions and be strong, as life is a constant process of changes for all of us. The year 2006 has been nothing less than VERY dramatic for many people and the world at large. The Dragon axis Pisces/Virgo stays nearly two years in both signs. The Dragon's Head entered the religious sign of Pisces in June 2006 and his Tail moved into the sign of Virgo.

More than ever take a chance on me and order your 90-mn Full Life Reading and learn about how this crucial celestial Dragon moves in your own chart, because it WILL change your life. Your very mental or financial survival may well depend on the awareness of how this Dragon's Head and Tail will cause those dramatic changes in your own life. Go to www.drturi.com and order it now and most of all; be patient as I am extraordinarily busy.

Many of our experiences have brought us more knowledge and much more new strength. The firmament of the new millennium is already upon us and with this New Year, various opportunities and new tasks are ahead of us. Whatever you had to go through last year, learn to promote only positive thoughts. There is no room for the sorrows of the past in your future, and whatever you had to go through, the job of building a new life must be done. For every action, positive or negative, physical or spiritual, there will be an equal reaction. So, be aware of your thoughts, as your future starts right there. The reincarnation of your own very "thoughts" will sooner or later, become your reality. **No matter what you've been through, you must let go of the past, refine your thoughts, purify your spirit and keep working towards your goals.**

Whether you realize it or not, progress was made towards some of your objectives. If, after all the hard work you completed, things got messed up, the universe may be trying to tell you something. Either you did not try hard enough, or the people you are working with do not have the same ethical aims as you. Possibly some of your wishes cannot be granted because of your limited working environment, lack of respect for the Universal Law, a limitation from your Astro-Cartography location, or an inappropriate emotional relationship. Therefore, you were first fired or dismissed, allowing the universe to grant you the freedom and opportunity you needed to go in the right direction. Now, knowing it was a blessing that you've lost your job, someone you loved, etc., you must accept the challenge to start all over again with a positive attitude. It might sound strange at first to accept my theory, but subconsciously you actually did set the stage over the years. Look back with an objective mind; after all, those experiences were needed so that you ultimately could do the right thing for yourself. You may also need to educate or trust yourself a bit more, or take more chances. Keep in mind the principle "for every action there will be a reaction," and that's called (good or bad) Karma. Are you willing to initiate the changes? If you do, the upcoming year will be a formidable year of accomplishment for you.

Offensive people may have mistreated you emotionally or financially and left you in a distressed situation. No matter what you experienced, you must go on with your life. This world is a teaching ground, and sometimes we learn lessons that may be harsh to deal with where we must feel the result of all our negative words and actions through pain and suffering. Exacting experiences seem to be the only way for humankind to burn karma and gain real knowledge. It is an inferno of passions and stress, well designed by God, to refine us from ignorance and destruction to the purest form of love and knowledge.

Before reincarnating yourself in this dense physical world, you have chosen a specific time in space. You also picked a set of stars (your natal chart), the country and city of your birth, as well as the souls who ultimately became your parents. You may not be aware of it just yet, but your karmic plan on this "hell" plane was chosen by you. Your soul's aim is to free itself from this low dimension and reach perfection to further its eternal purpose. What you are actually doing is furthering your cosmic consciousness, rising above all earthy vices and becoming a CO-creator with God. Over the years, the experiences you suffered will consume some of that karmic debt and further the awareness of your purpose of immortality. Some precious people whom you loved have left you and moved on while others have been called to the great beyond and are now performing in another reality much closer to God. They will act as Guardian Angels and will always watch over you. By interacting with the Dynamics of our universe and conforming to the dialogue of God's will through the stars, man's karmic journey could be easier. My book, Moon Power Starguide was created for the purpose of assisting you to live your life in harmony with the cosmic will. This book will provide you with a day-to-day celestial guidance and genuine spiritual support.

Its content is healing, informative, entertaining and useful. In times of trouble, this work will touch you directly and give you solid direction and a means of divine support. The daily message of the stars will prepare you for your day and beyond. With patience and investigation, you will notice how much the planets affect you, others and your life in general. In this work, you will find cautionary and specific guidance for certain days. Just be aware of the dates and, most of all, listen and watch those around you. Like robots, your friends, parents, children, loved ones will respond to the tremendous pull of the stars. To the learned man, the daily celestial energy released upon the earth is obvious, and it shapes our thoughts and actions, vices and virtues. Teaching anyone to recognize and respect God's subtle tools is a large task. However, with education, time and observations, those who "ask, shall receive" cosmic knowledge.

The stars do not pick favorites and like anything else in the universal scheme of things they simply do their jobs. As imposed by the Creator in its sublime celestial design, their task is to affect us and make us grow and very often with pain and suffering. Learning to interpret the universal mind will be beneficial to us all in the future. Curiosity and the advanced ever-changing modern technology does bring the golden key to wisdom and further more cosmic consciousness upon the world via the Internet. This fact changes lives, mostly because knowledge means power. The possibility of achieving the best, in promoting education, peace of mind, faith, and love is a certified chance to experience genuine happiness. Over the years, Starguides essence will help you to control the outcome of your destiny. Do not hesitate to offer Starguide to a loved one or a friend in need. You are not just giving a book; you become a contributor of hope and enlightenment. You are empowering someone with a genuine piece of the Divine. You may also help us to set a weeklong crash course in Astro-Psychology, Kabalistic Healing or Astro-Tarot in your area and benefit from a free course for yourself. (See www.drturi.com for more info).

Once more, thank you for your patronage and trust in my work.

Dr. Turi

"Man is superior to the stars if he lives in the power of superior wisdom. Such a person being the master over heaven and earth by means of his will is a magus and magic is not sorcery but supreme wisdom"
—Paracelsus

How To Use Moon Power Starguide 2007

- Universal Guidance and Predictions -

Starguide Universal Calendar of predictions is the result of thirty years of strenuous research into the architecture of our Universe. My findings will help you triumph over your daily challenges by identifying and obeying the Divine will of the cosmos. Starguide offers genuine guidance, positive growth and vital, daily information. Starguide offers the kind of support and direction you are looking for to achieve knowledge. The easy-to-read suggestions for each day of the year will get you started with the right attitude and expectations. Each period of time is empowering you with the Herculean will of the cosmos, thus, the opportunity to synchronize with the creative forces of the universe. Starguide will encourage and guide you to take positive steps to improve your world, and find love, a great career and financial security. This publication will correctly guide you each day of the year. It will give you the opportunity to avoid costly emotional or financial mishaps. Everything you need to know about any and all people's spiritual make up and forecast is in "Moon Power Starguide" and "Nostradamus Dragon Forecast for all Signs." This work will accurately translate the implacable rules of the universe into daily practical guidance. This physical world could not exist without its spiritual counterpart. Starguides purpose is to help you to understand and respect God's universal laws.

You have been taught to drive and respect the physical laws of the road to avoid an accident. Moon Power Starguide will teach you the spiritual laws of the universe and will guide you all along the wonderful road of your life. Breaking the physical laws will bring heavy penalty! The same applies for God's celestial laws. Starguide is specifically designed to teach and remind you of those implacable Universal Laws. Finally, this publication will help you to conduct your life safely in both the physical and spiritual planes.

Important note: Take the time to go now and then to my website and read specific dates and my quatrains. Doing so will help you to make a better use of Moon Power and lead a more productive and safe life. Realize that my work is not for entertainment only and will accurately translate the ultimate will of the cosmos on a daily base. Make sure to sign up for the FREE Dragon's newsletter so you will know all about my moves, television, radio, lectures, teachings and travel the world with me. You are also welcome to ask for a free E-Book copy of the 2006 Moon Power if you need to check on your past. The banner and all information for downloading the book will be on my website www.drturi.com until July 2007. Lastly if you are on My Space become my friend click on the banner on top of my home page. Thank you for your trust in my work.

"When suffering is on all sides and man hungers for the un-manifested mystery in all phenomena: He seeks the reflection of the divine. God's higher truths are cloaked in his creation and the message is in the stars." — Nostradamus

Moon Power - The Universal Law

ANCIENT GREEK BELIEFS ON THE MOON

Our closest satellite has often been linked with spirits of the deceased. The Greek mythology teaches that the moon was the focus point between Earth and Heaven. The ancients believed that spirits going to and from Heaven would stop upon the moon. Before entering the afterlife, the spirits would have their souls purified. On the way back to Mother Earth, through reincarnation, the spirits would go right to the face of the moon to receive their new physical bodies.

The Hindu texts "Upanishads" also states the advanced souls went to the moon after passing away to await reincarnation. Also stated is that the progressive souls who are untied from chain of reincarnation, will go straight to the sun. Many cultures associated the gods and goddesses with the moon and are represented with horns (Moses was a Lunar cult Leader fighting a Sun Stellar group, religious wars started in antiquity.)

Changes and growth are associated with the moon due to it's waxing and waning every 28 days...the moon expires and then is reborn for a new cycle.

The Greek philosopher Plutarch alleged that we have two ends. The first would take place on this world when our physical body expires. The physical body will then turn into dust, while the soul and the mind will journey into the spiritual world. There, the second death takes place, separating the mind and soul. The spirit would then return to the Moon, retaining all of that person life's memories. The mind would then journey to he sun where it was absorbed into the light and then reborn. Lastly, the mind would return to the Moon, rejoin the soul and then journey back to Earth for the eternal reincarnation process.

"There is a tide in the affairs of men which, taken at the flood, leads on to fortune; omitted, all the voyage of their life is bound in shallows and in miseries."
<u>Julius Caesar,</u> Act IV, Scene iii

Every day that God has created, sees the procession of stars across the vault of the sky. They have followed the same regular path through the heavens, tracing the immutability of the cosmos and its constellations, which have spoken to the wise since the beginning of time. This work will explain in detail the subtle energy produced by the Moon's passage through the twelve houses and signs of the Zodiac. These houses govern the twelve facets of our life, and the rhythms of our life's cycle, our emotions, finances, consciousness, home, children, career, friends, wishes, fears, love, personality and all that goes to make our sorrows and joys. Depending on the mystical rhythm of the Moon and her relationship---harmonious or discordant---to the constellation and houses of the sky over which they rule, she will govern our human activity and give birth to our vices and virtues. The infinite and concealed dance of the Moon through the Zodiac is far from affecting only you, but all of us. You are a "microcosm" or a child of the Universe and there is reason for you to be. You are a part of this incredible physical and spiritual structure called a "macrocosm."

Sir Isaac Newton wrote "for every action there is an equal and opposite reaction". We are what we think, having become what we thought. This statement emphasizes that for every thought or action there will be an effect. This is what I call the "Universal Law," the causes and effects of the yin and yang recognized as the law of karma. The Moon is by herself quite responsible for some of the world and people's fate. By tracking the Universal Law and using the Moon Power's information, you will be allowed to see this lunar impact and reaction every day of your life. Obviously, the Waxing and Waning periods of our closest satellite will produce the daily process of tides. Thus, women will have spiritual and physical manifestations (menstruation), and all of us will be responding subconsciously to the word "lunatic." Without a form of opposition such as the Moon's fluctuations, there would be no reaction and thus no life possible on both the spiritual and physical planes.

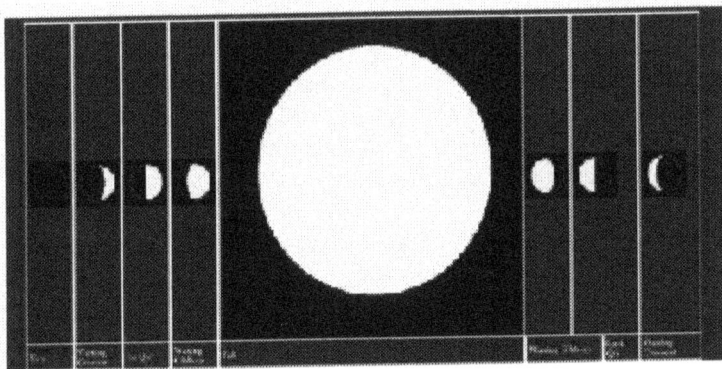

"Our so-called "dead" satellite is very much alive; she is the beating heart of the earth. Vigilantly observing her whereabouts will aid understanding of the psychology of man."
—Dr. Turi

The Changing face of the Moon was revered and understood by the ancients as an aspect of the feminine and idolized as the Lady of the Night who ruled over fertility and magic. Your awareness of the Moon's passage through the Zodiac will enable you to discover a basic structure of energy patterns that underlies the changes and circumstances of your life. This is, indeed, the purpose of a good astrologer, and his main objective is to reveal an order or meaning beneath or within what often appears to be a random or chaotic situation. The Moon's passage through the housing system is one expression of the archetypal structure we call a cycle.

While many of the formally educated scientists have lost their cosmic consciousness, it has remained hidden within astrological values and basic astrological foundations. All of the signs of the Zodiac, the twelve houses, and the numerous astrological aspects are based upon God's higher order in the established, interstellar cycle. Their subtle meanings are derived from a particular place or negative affliction or function to each other's, and all operate within the ordered cycle as a whole. Our lives unfold according to our specific cyclic pattern, interacting with the Universal cycle. Discerning the Universal Mind at work is difficult; those gifted at birth will naturally understand the cosmic mind, using their inborn, intuitional and objective mental tools. However, when properly educated, anyone can learn to further his cosmic consciousness and realize his close relationship with God and the Universe. It often starts with a willingness to expand the consciousness and the simple realization: that which may be invisible to our senses nevertheless still exists. That's what makes a real scientist, investigation! Sadly enough, the majority of these souls fear ridicule or abandonment by their peers or churches.

The obvious structure of the Moon's cycle is derived from the fact that it consists of a beginning, middle and an end. Thus, the monthly lunar cycle suggests by observation that it is divided into two halves. During the first half, the movement is outward, as our close satellite travels away from the area of space occupied by the Sun. As this happens, the powerful light of the Sun increases, "Waxing" (positive) on the white face of the Moon. The Full Moon symbolizes the turning point it reverses motion. The Moon begins to approach the Sun as the reflected light on its surface "Wanes" (negative), until they meet again at the New Moon (new start). Halfway between the New Moon and the Full Moon, we notice another important division point where light and darkness are equal on the moon's surface. At the first Waxing Quarter, the light is increasing, while at the last Waning Quarter, it is decreasing. These simple astronomical observations can only provide the scientist's mind with knowledge for interpreting the physical lunar cycle's phase. Now if the positive cannot be with the negative, and knowing that it takes "Two to Tango" for anything to be, then the scientist should be able to "investigate" the intuitional domain of this work. There was hidden truth beyond to this "lunar manifestation," and I then began to nurture my own critical observations. Later in life I realized that there was so much more beyond traditional star study (Astronomy).

As a child, I always thought of the moon to be something more than a dead satellite orbiting the earth. Many times in the darkness of the night, I found myself staring at her, wondering about her hidden power. She is the swiftest of the planets, passing through the 12 signs of the zodiac in about 28 days. I knew that eventually, I was to uncover her subtle ways and find the answers. To me, all those stars in the sky, shining above my head, were more than bright dead rocks in the darkest night. It does however; take more than our five senses to tap into her subtle manifestation upon our psyches and life in general. Nothing happens randomly in the universe, and the timely return in full each month surely indicates an ultimate order. Month after month, I patiently watched her becoming New and Full, and I learned my first, and one of the most important lesson in metaphysics, "The undiluted truth is not to be found inside man's limited world, but in other worlds and the Universal mind."

Being so close to the earth, the Moon's magnetic pull is so great, that she is solely responsible for the daily process of the tides. Curiosity, observation and comparison become the essential elements to promote anyone's cosmic consciousness. As I met her, becoming full and new, month after month, I slowly began to understand her powers. By constantly watching my environment, friends and family members, she began to speak about her clearly visible impact and control over man's psyche. As the years went by, I realized her uncompromising pull over the sea, and I became more aware of her powerful impact on our daily affairs. I made notes day after day, week after week and month after month, realizing the heavy consequences of either ignoring or adapting to her passage through the twelve signs of the Zodiac. I learned that the farmers of the past followed her fluctuations for the betterment of their crops. Then I carefully put my observations to test in my life and the lives of those around me. I did not take long to realize that by respecting the Universal Law, my life became much more productive. Her positive and negative affect on man's emotions, actions and reactions became so obvious to me that I decided to make it my full time job to tell others about her. As I watched the news in times of a Full Moon, I understood why people became destructive, "lunatic," eccentric, moody and psychopathic. I then named it the Uncompromising Universal Law. Since then, as a professional Divine Astrologer, wherever I am needed, I am teaching the value of this simple and valuable knowledge.

When you first learned how to drive a car, you were carefully introduced to the rules of the road. You learned that you must stop at a red light or follow a road sign, as your very life depends on your doing so. These are the codes that you have learned, and they must be respected anywhere you happen to be in the world. Following established rules will take you safely wherever you have to go. Sadly enough, too many people do not respect these rules, and innocent people have died accidentally. Awareness, knowledge and respect of these rules are desperately needed. However, the spiritual rules established by God, written in the constellations, have been misplaced. Only a minority is aware of the impact produced by the Moon, and the rest, the majority of us are completely ignorant of God's Divine rules. The result is seen during a Full Moon and each time the moon is crossing a destructive sign. This lack of awareness turns into formidable chaos, which produces despair, psychopaths, drug addicts, depression, violence, criminals ... and the list goes on. Know that by ignoring either the physical or spiritual rules leads to a very heavy penalty.

So-called "holy wars" have plagued man all through the ages. Ignorance and fear cast aside God's true Universal message. To my mind, the millions of deaths produced by continuous religious wars all around the world were a good example of the destructive power of fanaticism. I realized that everyone's relationship to God or many gods was deeply personal and that no two people feel the same way about it. My great mother taught me that God is love, beauty, education, responsibility and knowledge, beliefs I have steadfastly clung to. I have noticed the dualistic nature of life, man/woman, front/back, up/down, black/white, yin/yang, positive/negative, the ultimate law of opposition. I soon began to realize that nothing would exist without its counterpart, and this law of opposition was much too obvious to be challenged or ignored. I began to wonder if God would exist without the Devil. One month is made up of two 2-week cycles, one year of two 6-month periods. From the New Moon (black dot on your calendar) to the Full moon (a circle on your calendar), the light is green.

Those two weeks are called "the Waxing time." Then when you see her full, white and round, the light is red. Those two weeks are called "the Waning time." As she starts her positive Waxing time, you should plant your seeds for life. Go out, meet new people, socialize, get engaged, get married, buy a new car, go shopping, sign important contracts, travel, visit family members and generally promote all you can during this positive trend. My Starguide has all the New and Full Moons available for the entire year. Also, Starguide tells you when and in which sign the New Moon or the Full Moon will mature. You can use this knowledge to master the outcomes of all your endeavors. Initiate ideas or projects as she climbs happily through the heavens. When she finally becomes Full, beware of the approaching "Yellow Light," as this signals a time to slow down and reflect. During the day you must work hard and perform your tasks, while nature requires you to rest and sleep during the night. The same rules apply with the Moon. As she is ascending (Waxes) you must dwell with the future, the dense physical world and, as the ancients did, put your seeds in the ground. Again, after the Full Moon (and for two weeks) as the Moon descends (Wanes), you will deal better with metaphysical endeavors, feel like cleaning up, and possibly suffer psychically, as the Moon is the regulator of your inner emotions.

Use your will to fight depression, clean your house, prepare your next move, and write letters but don't send them just yet. Observe and listen to all the people around you. Many will suffer the Waning Moon's power and will become negative, moody and lunatic. Watch the news and see for yourself the dramatic differences in the two periods. However, good things can happen then. This means, officially, that somehow you started "that" situation during her Waxing, positive time, and you are now being paid-off. Bad things can also happen to you when the Moon is supposedly positive. It might only be a tap on your hand, compared to what could have happened. Keep in mind you have been going through your life not knowing nor using the Universal Law. You did not interact with the Moon's fluctuations (the gearbox of our solar system), and many gears (your experiences) have broken down. Apply your knowledge immediately, and take the time to invest in your understanding of Astrology (the dynamics of our Universe). I often use this sample in reference to the respects of the physical and spiritual laws. If you were to travel in China and you could not read, understand or follow the road signs, chances are that you would get hurt. Those laws, even if you are not aware of them, are solid and practical. There is no room for ignorance in this dense physical world, and a heavy penalty awaits those ignorant and skeptical souls.

The Moon also commands women's menstrual periods, and both the Moon and women share the same twenty-eight-day time period. Work non-stop around the Moon's passage, every sign of the Zodiac, and then her deepest secret will by yours. As she travels through the belt of the Zodiac, she will be residing between two to three days in one sign; she will melt your emotions with the energies (positive or negative) found in that specific astrological sign. Never forget that an ultimate higher order has been established, and the essence of our emotional life is within. Learning and adapting to the Moon's power will help you understand what it really means to be human. This cosmic consciousness will lead you towards the understanding of your own strengths, and the ability to use them to further your life, while minimizing your weakness day by day!

MEMO FROM THE PAST – HOW TO USE MOON POWER

The idea is to read between the lines but very often the prediction will be very obvious. Here are a few examples.

From Moon Power 2003 - Prediction: Syphilis and a <u>deadly virus</u> returns to kill thousands in 2003 ~ many will die of sexually transmitted diseases in Africa and Asia during 2003.

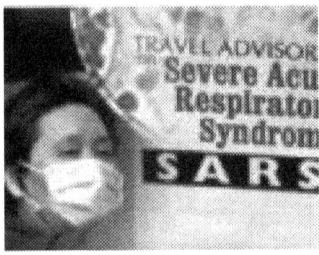

I also wrote about both NASA shuttle explosions but NASA keeps ignoring my heeding.

Again realize that I do not PREDICT anything! I know nature has cycle induced by the movement of the stars and this is why history (or the weather) as a repetitive pattern. Well what about NASA criminals' authorities? There are the worst... I have tried so many times to "advise" them not to send the shuttle during any "Supernova windows" and regardless of my direct requests; none of them have ever had the decency to respond to my emails. Only an insignificant but very smart secretary supported my views and wrote me back to apologize for not being able to pass the thick wall of her superiors' lack of knowledge. Then as I did with the first shuttle disaster, I sent them my dated posts and website warnings accusing them of killing innocent astronauts in the name of their own fear of ridicule and huge ignorance. For God's sake, this crowd deals with the physical aspect of the stars (astronomers) why not try to enter the intuitional domain of those stars (astrology) and save precious lives and money to the tax payers? It amazes me for any of these imbeciles in power at NASA to challenge the true genius of Einstein when he wrote...

"All great spirits have encountered opposition from mediocre minds; a human being is part of a whole, called by us the 'Universe,' a part limited in time and space. He experiences himself, his thoughts and feelings, as something separated from the rest--a kind of optical delusion of his consciousness. The stars are the elixir of life"
- A. Einstein

From Moon Power 2003 – Prediction: Providing NASA had investigated my work a year earlier and realized the values of my research, I wonder if by reading the following if they would have still sent the shuttle during a Supernova window?

Prediction: Moon Power 2003, pages 114-115 First Supernova Window From Wednesday January 1st, through Friday January - 31st, 2003: Many terrible accidents happened under this nefarious celestial energy, such as the Challenger shuttle explosion.... <u>As usual, NASA, which is not aware of the science of Astrology, will waste our taxpayer's money and precious lives with failed missions due to bad weather and/or electronic malfunctions.</u>

Note: Regardless of my expectations posted on my website for the second time and my desperate attempts over the years to make NASA officials aware of dangerous Super Nova Windows, the Columbia was also launched during this window and re-entered the last night of it producing the death of all the courageous astronauts! As a result of ignoring the celestial might, all courageous astronauts are dead - Thanks NASA!

God bless the courageous Crew Members of the shuttle Columbia.

I also made unarguable predictions such as the Washington sniper.

Prediction: From "Moon Power Starguide 2002", pages 235-6 under Events and travel:
Mon, Tues, Wed, Thurs, Fri—Oct. 7,8,9,10,11: Rulers—Pluto (drama) and Jupiter (credulity).

Travel and Communication: Regardless of the New Moon, beware on the road, because with Pluto, absolutely anything nasty can happen to you now. If you are a police officer or security guard, beware of Pluto. The crooks will be active and deadly. Passion may take over, as Pluto will lead a bad young spirit to kill innocent people. Don't take chances now.

KILLER STALKS SUBURBS OF NATION'S CAPITAL

The Washington D.C. area has been on edge since a sniper attack on October 2, the first in a wave of fatal attacks that have occurred with stunning regularity in the subsequent weeks.

Update: In Phoenix AZ another serial killer terrorized the residents since May 2006 until August 2006. I was on KTAR 610 am on the Pat MacMahon radio show in July when I gave him two dates. One was when the killer would strike again (and he did!) and the other for his arrest! I also wrote a newsletter giving those dates and what transpired in that show. Simply sign up for the free newsletter or click on "Read Previous Newsletters" and if you want solid proof of my claim simply look for and read "Serial Killer in Phoenix". More of my numerous predictions are at http://www.drturi.com under "predictions".

There are too many predictions that did transpire to be mentioned in this book such as the Kobe earthquake, the O. J. Simpson dilemma, Bill Cosby's loss, the Rancho Santa Fe mass suicide in San Diego, both Mother Teresa and Princess Diana's passing, President Clinton's legal suit, etc. I have published many *"Moon Powers"* since 1987. I have also written *"The Power of the Dragon"*, *"Nostradamus Dragon Forecast for all signs"*, *"I know All About You"*, *"Asia Dragon Predictions"* and my very latest book *"And God Created The Stars."* I can say that I am not a Stargazer as this is just one who gazes at the stars. You would be, too, if you understood the celestial messages as I do. I believe that everyone, and I do mean everyone, should be educated in this discipline. The mystery of life would be solved.

Realize also that 99.9% of the people walking this earth are robots of the stars and totally unaware of the subtle power affecting their fragile psyches and the impact on human affairs on this dense physical world. Hiding oneself behind a PHD or a doctorate or any academic accomplishment does not means justice to science per se. Keep reading what I wrote about the 9/11 WTC dilemma further on down and see if knowledge can affect any important decisions. When my new book "You Are God" comes out, a full explanation of the supra-conscious and its interaction with the Universal Mind will be explained in great detail. Meantime, never forget that as a human, your will is much stronger than the stars and that "the future is nothing more than the reincarnation of thought."

"L'habit ne fait pas le moine" as we say in French! Or translated a dangerous killer may dress like a priest and fool society'. Just because you graduated from a well-respected institution does not necessarily mean you are intelligent. A talkative parrot can repeat word for word what is printed in the books by the scientific community and because of the bird ability to recall the printed information it will graduate faster than you. But what the majority accepts does not mean its fact, the bird can not and will not think for himself. Challenges and taking chances are things a true scientist should do to HONOR the very words "scientific investigation." It is not a healthy attitude to hide behind a diploma, ridicule my research and dismiss me because the word astrology is used. What really gets me is that some of those scientists do believe in walking on water, yet they don't realize that astrology is a science with solid structures and disciplines. You believe in a religion, astrology is NOT a religion; this means some investigations or studies are needed to bring forth cosmic consciousness into men's awareness and with it the option to see its full manifestation, just as I do.

There is a tremendous difference between education and intelligence by judging the response of the so-called intelligent scientists and my desperate efforts over the years to make them listen and investigate my work. Sadly enough, as soon as the word astrology is mentioned, either a deep-rooted religious fear emerges or the fear of associating with this form of "ridiculous science" scares them to death. Well I have news for you educated mental snobs or religious lunatics-- you can not stop progress and if I am 50 years or so ahead of you, accept it and deal with me without ego or your fears interfering and INVESTIGATE this rare but very real discipline I offer.

Everyone has their own mystery to uncover, and the canopy of stars is what blankets that mystery. They were definitely placed in the heavens for more than the sake of beauty. Through his Divine plan, God enslaved all men to understand the meaning of their existence on earth. You might as well take the easy way and ask someone who knows how to read the universal starlight. Help us to pass on my important message to the world. (See www.drturi.com to help us to set a few days crash course in your area on Astro-Psychology, Kabalistic Healing or the Astro-Tarot).

Pluto's impact on Generations:
Past — Present — Future

Pluto in Gemini: "The hypnotized Generation" Indeed, Pluto is a dramatic planet and its impact on generations is obvious for those blessed with the knowledge of the stars. For good or for worse, the people and leaders of this Era were born with this affliction. Hitler was born on April 20, 1889 and Pluto (power) was located in the sign of Gemini (communication) from 1883 until 1913. Wherever the planet Pluto is located by sign and house in your chart, a sense of power and regeneration will be offered to you. Thus, using his well-known, inborn "hypnotic sound power," it was easy for

Hitler, in his numerous "Plutonic" speeches, to persuade the wise German population to go to war against the rest of the world.

Pluto in Cancer: "The Wasted Baby Generation" the immediate generations to suffer Hitler's manipulation were the young German soldiers and everybody else around the world born between 1913 and 1937 with Pluto (death) in Cancer (family). Thus, the "invaders" and all of the war's victims were the result of an awful Pluto disturbing the basic security principle, homes, families and indeed can be associated with the First and Second World Wars, into the sad historically "Wasted Baby Generation." The entire world and its security (Cancer) were shattered between both deadly (Pluto) World Wars, and millions of children from many different ethnic groups met with their fate.

Pluto in Leo: "The Baby Boom Generation" When Pluto moved from Cancer (security/home) to Leo (love/life) from 1938 to 1957, the world experienced a re-birth of its population. Responding subconsciously to the power of the stars, the unaware masses called the phenomenon "The Baby Boom Generation." Leo (Sun) rules love, the arts, freedom, and the 50's and 60's were good examples of the love and freedom-oriented attitudes with hippie music and drugs (Wood stock) that plagued this generation. Pluto rules sex, and Leo children became a free, sexually oriented generation. Jimmy Hendrix's fate (sex, drugs, rock-and-roll), is a good example of a personal Pluto in Leo that ultimately got the best of him.

Pluto in Virgo: "The Baby Buster Generation" Pluto then moved to the puritanical sign of Virgo (health) from 1957 to 1976, and this generation is next to take governmental power. This generation is fanatic about nature, perfection, work and health. Smokers have already suffered the impact of this "Baby Buster Generation," as this generation must upgrade health and perfection in our society. Unlike Leo (life) Virgo is dry and sterile, thus fewer babies were produced during this era. Since Pluto entered the sign of Virgo, facilities for health programs and exercising boomed to satisfy a generation that craves fitness. The health businesses (body/mind/tools) have started and are still booming with Pluto in Virgo. This generation is banning smokers from restaurants and public places (and they voted the 40-cent tobacco tax increase), and more rigid health oriented regulations are ahead of us. Note-This section and its predictions were written and published in the 1995 Moon Power edition. On a more positive note, this age group will fight hard to preserve nature, animals and the remainder of the rain forest. Many powerful computers and microchips developed by this generation as experienced in Operation Desert Storm, are deadly accurate. Their ideal is very pure in thought and action, but this generation must guard against Pluto's (fanaticism) subtle power for "perfection." If the power of Pluto in Virgo is exaggerated, it becomes as deadly as the poison they try so hard to avoid.

Many of these souls will lose their lives by being too concerned with health (anorexia, hypochondria), turning rapidly to vegetarian diets, thus upsetting their naturally weak digestive tracts. They must understand that cats and dogs were born with strong claws and long, sharp teeth to tear apart raw flesh as intended by nature, while cows, horses, lambs, etc. are herbivores and were designed by God with flat teeth and three stomachs to eat only "salad." They are none of those. They are omnivorous and must eat meat as a vigilant balance for their sensitive metabolism. Some souls who are overwhelmed by Pluto are overly crazy for carbohydrates. They are also protein paranoid. Some starve themselves after 6:00 p.m. Others take their heart rates much too seriously, some have a penchant for pain, and more are victims of the fat-burning syndrome. Worst of all for women is the weight lifting dilemma. It is, genetically speaking, impossible for a woman to take on a man's physical power, and no matter how hard they try; they will never look like Arnold Schwarzenegger. Because of the inborn critical attitude and a strong desire for health and perfection, those natural "puritans" will not find someone good enough for them and many will end up alone in the game of love.

Pluto in Libra: "The Gang Generation." From October 5, 1971 until November 6, 1983, dramatic Pluto (death) moved into the sign of Libra (partnerships). Traditionally Libra rules the 7th house, associations, open enemies, partners and the day-to-day people entering your life. This nefarious combination created a form of regular open-death manifestations as shown by the infamous, daily drive-by shootings. Born with Pluto (death) in Libra (others), those children are willing to die for their inner Plutonic sense of justice (scales) imposed by their partners (gang members). Constantly influenced (bullied) by Pluto or more ferocious souls, they must give in to their high sense of justice for the group. This righteous "die for you/die for me" attitude is now in full operation in our present society and has created "The unbalanced Aggressive Gang Generation." If not for survival or money, then respect, power and justice belong to the group (no matter what), and Pluto is the subtle force behind gang activity. The Plutonic rough initiation principle (beating) is a form of love/hate/submission, a participation and respect found within the sign of Libra in the declaration of peace or war. Then, the ruthless test for security, love, hate, respect and deadly commitment to others (Libra) in the group (gang) has been established. Contrary to what is commonly believed, and to the amazement of psychologists, many children of the gang generation have had perfect upbringings and many are from middle and upper class families.

Early environment plays an important part in how these souls will react to others. If the upbringing happens to be rough and difficult, these Plutonic souls may become the imposing bullies. Negative members of this generation are in constant need of a dramatic regeneration principle-taking place within a group constantly involved in war with others. To those born with Pluto in Libra, it is also a sure indication of a strong inner sense of justice owed to the group for good or for bad. This Pluto (death) generation in Libra (the law) will savagely fight their enemy (authority figures) and other gangs without any fear or regard for the deadly consequences. This problem with the police force has already started and will keep dangerously growing, making some parts of the cities unsafe for the common citizen. This sad situation will continue swelling to a dangerous size and will force the government to take drastic measures. The year 1998 will be a memorable year, as strong efforts will be made to avoid the breaking down of our society. In the process, many youths and numerous police officers' lives will be wasted.

Pluto in Scorpio: "The Death Wish Generation" Pluto then inhabited, from 1983 until 1995, his own daredevil sign of Scorpio. Those very young and wild children have already made dramatic news by executing each other and murdering adults for any reason. Such as in Rachula, Missouri on December 28, 1994, an off-duty police officer had been shot to death by his girlfriend's 9-year-old grandson. The child was born with Pluto in Scorpio on his Dragon's Tail (negative). Many of those "kids" have been reported killing adults for money to buy drugs and guns at the tender age of 10 years. Again in May 1997 a brutal slaying follows a beer drinking in Central Park, New York. Two teen-agers stabbed a real estate agent at least 30 times and tried to chop off his hands so police couldn't use fingerprints to identify him before dumping him in a lake in Central Park. Perpetrators, Daphne Abdela, 15, and her boyfriend, 15-year-old Christopher Vasquez, "gutted the body so it would sink." Both of those young souls are from the dramatic Pluto generation, "The Death Wish Generation." More than previous degrading generations, these children need constant spiritual regeneration and a good reason to be alive.

Note - So far in the United States the "Death Wish Generation" generation produced 700 murderers age 15 or younger in 1995, many of them raised in environments that included abuse, neglect and violence. However, youth violence is neither new nor confined to the United States.

Again, this "Death Wish Generation" is to be taken seriously when threatening to kill others. Their deep and passionate Scorpion nature is so intense that it is practically impossible for them not to follow up by drastic criminal actions. Chances are that none of the army of traditionally educated psychologists will be able to understand the deep motive of the boys. Millions of questions will be asked to the two young souls. But nobody, even the boys, will really grasp the deep motivation produced by vengeful, fixed and passionate Scorpio. Again, unless Astro-Psychology is reestablished in our school system, this type of drama will become current news in the years ahead. Breaking God's Universal Law, either by ignorance, deep religious convictions or pure skepticism will not cut it. There is no room for ignorance and the penalty will have to be paid.

Rest assured that this Pluto (death) in Scorpio (passion) generation is well suited for investigation, planning and acting upon their threats. Imagine the impact of Pluto in Scorpio on the children of the Middle East, and all other unstable countries (astrology has no barrier). Giving their lives for a deadly purpose, is a way of regenerating themselves and their teachers, governments, religious institutions, and even they don't know about it. I seriously hope for the well being of our society to start the cleansing and healing process in educating the masses. For too long now, millions of dollars have been and will continue to be poured into wasteful institutions, feeding your children with fear and ignorance. How long will it take mankind to grow out of its own spiritual limitations, I do not really know, but I am aware of the damage it will bring to its own children in the future. I need your serious understanding and strong help here and I can only hope that this publication will bring enough truth and raise enough questions and answers about what it really means to be human.

Memo: News report that as many as 27 shots was fired. Four girls and the English teacher Shannon Wright, 32, who shielded a student from the attack, were killed in Tuesday's ambush. Ten others -- nine students and a teacher -- were wounded. Officials at St. Bernards Regional Medical Center in Jonesboro said Kim Candace Porter, whom several students described as the boy's former girlfriend, was among the wounded. Gov. Mike Huckabee offered sympathy for the victims of the school shooting and lamented on a culture that would breed such a tragedy.

The dead students were identified as:

Natalie Brooks, 12.
Paige Ann Herring, 12.
Stephanie Johnson, 12.
Brittany R. Varner, 11.

Well, governor. Mike Huckabee you can offer all the sympathy of the world for the victims of the school shooting, and like millions of others lament on a culture that would breed such a tragedy. That is NOT the answer, as you already know that it will happen over again. You, including the educational, psychological, police and governmental system are losing the battle and will soon watch the breaking down of our young society. Scientists from all levels out there are mesmerized and baffled by the awful events that took place on March 25th, 1998 in JONESBORO, Arkansas. Unless you cast aside your fear of the ridicule fueling your academically oriented ignorance and your mental snobbishness, you will not be able to even get closer to the golden key of true knowledge. You might have to challenge your precious books, pass the limitation of your rational mind and realize that the higher truths were never printed by your kind. It's time to look above your head; into the Universal Mind, with a different attitude. If you have any hope what so ever, to provide serious help to this "Death Wish Generation."

Vanoven said the 13-year-old also had pulled a knife on another student Monday. Other students said the boy was specifically targeting one of the girls wounded. "He said he was definitely going to shoot Candace because she had broken up with him," sixth-grader Kara Tate, 11, told the Sun. The two boys, wearing camouflage shirts, pants and hats, were caught near the school with handguns and rifles. Investigators said the boys were running in the direction of a white van found about a half-mile away from the school with more guns and ammunition in it. Police impounded the van. Classmate Erica Swindle, 12, said the younger boy owned a gun and went deer hunting often.

Again, age doesn't matter, and makes the situation even more dangerous. The young soul hasn't yet learned to control the intensity of his desires and his powerful destructive emotions. The incredible passion and deep desires generated by Pluto in Scorpio are somehow unbearable for the soul who has inherited such a celestial legacy. Sending the kids to jail and praying for the souls of the poor victims will not stop future dramas. I seriously hope to be heard before it is too late for all, now and in the future, directly concerned. As imposed by the most powerful planet in Divine Astrology, Pluto (The Lord of Death and Decay) this unaware "Death Wish Generation" regenerates with blood, passion, sex, drama, weapons and murdering others. Let's hope and confederate with me to pass on a message to those children, their teachers, the Educational system and the Government. No one had to die, but they did, and many more will, in the name of ignorance.

Case 3- Again my theory and prediction came true, this time it was to be in April 1998. Unless my message is passed out and understood, more innocent victims will join this mad dance.

EDINBORO, Pennsylvania -- Thousands gathered Tuesday to mourn a popular teacher who was shot to death in front of his students at a school dance. John Gillette, a 48-year-old science teacher and former football hero involved in numerous volunteer, church and business projects, was killed Friday when a 14-year-old student Andrew Wurst allegedly opened fire with a .25-caliber semiautomatic pistol. Students described him as a man who lived by a motto of "Anything that is worth doing is worth giving your best." Several former students paid tribute to him at the service, one of them drawing small ripples of laughter when he told a humorous story about Gillette scolding him at football practice. However, the Rev. John Jacquel, a priest at Gillette's church, Our Lady of the Lake, had a more somber message for the mourners. "Why didn't God do something to protect this man from dying?" He asked. "Why did God let that happen? It seems that faithfulness doesn't guarantee you safety or a trouble-free life."

Some 3,500 people attended the service in the field house at Edinboro University of Pennsylvania, where Gillette's daughter, Abby, is a member of the volleyball team.

Wurst, a bespectacled, aloof student who liked dark-themed music and whose nickname was "Satan," faces homicide charges and remained jailed early Tuesday as the youngest person at the Erie County Prison. Two students and a teacher were injured, none seriously, before Wurst was disarmed by a banquet hall owner with a shotgun. Police and friends said Wurst snuck his father's pistol into the dance and had threatened at separate times to make the dance "memorable," and to kill others and him. He was not taken seriously. State police said they are still trying to determine the boy's motive. Three other school-related shootings since October – in Jonesboro, Arkansas, West Paducah, Kentucky, and Pearl, Mississippi -- left 10 dead and 22 wounded. Mitchell Wright, the widower of a teacher killed in Jonesboro, called

Gillette's widow, Debbie, over the weekend with support and advice. His wife Debbie, and his two daughters and a son survive Gillette.

Continued:
Thus, our society is already witnessing "The Dramatic Death Wish Generation" in action. They are strong-willed, unwavering in thought and action, immensely emotional and totally fearless in front of death. Pluto (sex) is making them very active sexually at an early age, and they will look for a mixture of sex, crime and drugs to survive their harsh young lives. At the tender age of 12 years many of those children have already experienced the use of drugs and sex and some others have committed repellent murders. They are already imposing and displaying their powerful, destructive will on many televised talk shows, where helpless parents complain about their awful behavior. Other much older generations are at bay and baffled, unable to relate to this Plutonic generation.

The passion for self-discovery is extreme and if left without legitimate spiritual food, the worst can only happen to many of these children. They will not react to dogma and common religious teachings as their parents do. Those kids subconsciously understand the principle of life and death and the motivation behind all manifestation. They simply lack the regenerative forces produced by the mystical knowledge to deal with their passionate and rebellious nature. The miserably failing psychological field won't be any help understanding the plutonic motivation behind this upcoming killer generation. Unless the old science of Astrology is reinstated, (Astro-Psychology) in our colleges and universities, there will be either no understanding or therapeutic healing measures available for these children. A few years from now once in power this unyielding generation has the awful potential to destroy the world with the use of irreversible atomic weapons. Let's just hope that the worst elements of this "Death Wish" generation get spiritual guidance quickly, or imperatively auto-destroy themselves, for the sake of all of us. If God's implacable Universal Rules have been broken and ignored for too long, a serious penalty is awaiting mankind. There is no room for ignorance at any level of consciousness or any other worlds above or below us.

Slowly but surely, mankind is witnessing the slow and painful suffocating end of another young generation. Hopefully, our scientists will cast the "ridicule" aside and a solid investigation of "Divine Astrology" will bring it back into the traditional educational system. Only then, the real therapeutic deeds involving Astrology will begin to heal and regenerate the psyches of all of these unquiet spirits. We, the people, in the name of knowledge, love and happiness, still have time to make the change. That's why I am working fervently to produce this work, for the children of this specific generation. For if they get the right spiritual help, and do rebirth from their own ashes, the incredible potential of this Eagle generation can uplift humanity and the world to its highest and most glorious potential.

To all my readers, I need your help to educate the parents first, as the numbers of requests from the concerned parents will make the badly needed changes and save future lives. Start by sending my newsletters to all the people that you know your gesture may help them to grow and perceive my work. My wish is to open my own Astro-Psychology schools if the system is reluctant to make those crucial changes and I need all the help I can get. Any suggestions? Is there someone listening out there? Please do and help me to save the children with education. I need your support.

> *"When men realize the church is the Universe and the twelve apostles are the twelve signs of the zodiac, God's commandments written in light will bring love, respect, and peace to this world." -- Dr. Turi*

Life is not a game of chance; the Creator did not put us where we would be the sport of circumstances, to be tossed about by a cruel fate, regardless of our efforts to save our world.
— George B. Emerson

2007 Supernova Windows

ASTRO WEATHER SERVICE PREDICTIONS

There will be three major negative SUPERNOVA windows in the year 2007. Each destructive "window" is operational for three to four weeks, thus caution is strongly advised during this period. Heavy loss of lives due to nature's devastating forces, aeronautical disasters and structural damage is to be expected. Once more realize that I do not use traditional dates found in popular ephemera. Years of practical observation lead me to extend the Mercury retrograde motion and period of time.

February / March: First SUPERNOVA window - From Saturday February 10th 2007, through Monday March 12th, 2007.

June / July: Second SUPERNOVA window - From Monday June 11th through Friday July 13th 2007.

October / November: Third SUPERNOVA window - From Sunday October 7th through Friday November 2nd 2007.

EXPLANATION OF A SUPERNOVA WINDOW

Concentration of negative celestial energy approaching: Be extremely prudent in driving, and expect chain-reaction accidents. Be prepared for delays, strikes, and nature producing awful weather, including hurricanes and tornadoes. The same energy that produced the Titanic disaster, the Asia tsunami the Northridge Los Angeles and Kobe Japan earthquakes and major other calamities is approaching again. Remember the thwarted terrorist attack of August 2006 in the UK where the BA canceled thousands of flights because the BAA ordered all passengers not to take or check ALL handbags before boarding their planes? Those people did not have a copy of Moon Power and paid the price of ignorance.

Double-check all your appointments, and if you can postpone

traveling and flying during this Supernova "Window". If you must fly like I do very often, simply make sure to purchase your ticket and make your reservation during a Waxing Moon and the stars will not bother you. Remember the Universal Laws do not care for birthday or religious holidays or else, simply think of crossing the street while the light is red or ignore a stop sign, then, see what will happen to you. Those laws are impartial and written by God not men and messing them up will bring about serious penalty. Note that; I flew only a few days before the Full Moon in August 2006 to Thailand during a "Supernova Window" to write this book and I traveled safely and avoided all trouble. Remember; knowledge is power, ignorance is evil!

Communication and electricity will be cut off, and a general loss of power is to be expected. Appliances, computers, telephones, planes, trains, cars, all of these "tools" will be affected by this energy. They will be stopped in one way or another. The people of the past will make the news and will reenter your life. Expect trouble with the post office, education, students, strikes, prisoner's escape, newspapers, broadcasting industries and computer viruses may bother us again. Many a failed mission and expensive electronic equipment (Mars probe etc.) and our tax dollars have been wasted because of the scientist's lack of knowledge of the stars. As usual NASA, which is not aware of the science of astrology, will waste our tax money with failed missions due to bad weather and electronic malfunctions.

In the name of ignorance a few years ago, in the Challenger explosion seven astronauts lost their lives when NASA launched the shuttle under a "Supernova Window".

Note: Regardless of Dr. Turi's expectations posted on his website for the second time and his desperate attempts over the years to make NASA officials aware of dangerous Super Nova Windows, the Columbia was also launched during this window and re-entered the last night of it producing the death of all courageous astronauts. Marine life sharks, whales etc may also beach themselves due to Mercury retrograde affecting their natural inborn navigational systems. All these malevolent predictions and waste of lives and equipment do not have to occur. Those predictions do not have to affect you directly as they unfold. Instead, they are printed to prepare you for setbacks and frustrations, thus advising you to be patient and prudent during this trend. There is no room for ignorance, and those who are not aware of the celestial order, including the NASA space-program management team, will continue to pay a heavy price. In all mankind's affairs, ignorance is true evil. Why any scientists who are against my research do not honor the word science, which is based upon solid investigation, is solid proof of mental snobbery. By omitting any physical or spiritual laws can only bring penalty; for science's purpose is to explore all possibilities, even those laws written in light via the stars.

Earthquake Predictions

Earthquakes tend to occur when diurnal tidal forces are able to release the accumulated strain on a fault. Hard planetary aspects appear able to increase the strain upon a fault. Perhaps the computer-aided Astro-Geologists of the future will be able to do the kind of micro mapping and analysis needed to predict which faults are most susceptible to increased strain. As for the timing, my technique to predict earthquakes seems to be more accurate than all the latest computerized electronic equipment combined! You see why later, keep reading...

Predictions for the Century

Approximately every two thousand years, our planet comes under the influence of a new zodiacal sign. January twelve, 1996 marks the entrance of Uranus (the future) into his own sign of Aquarius (New Age). We slowly begin to explore the possibility of a new consciousness and uncover both the strength and danger of this incredible upcoming age. This liberal sign follows nebulous Pisces. Over the last twenty years, Uranus (the awakened) has advocated more discoveries than have been made during the last 2000 years spent under the illusive power of Neptune (ruler of Pisces). Pisces is the last sign of the Zodiac, and traditionally, it rules the twelfth house. This area governs restriction, sorrow, imprisonment, psychological trouble and secret enemies as well as creativity, dance, high forms of music and works of art. Enclosed and confined places such as asylums, hospitals, churches, prisons, movie theaters, concert halls and theme parks are Neptune's legacy. It is also a mute energy; it has no voice of its own. Submissive by nature, Neptune tends to make those born under its heavy influence pessimists and fatalists prone to addictions and fanaticism. It is a deceiving energy prone to suffering and acceptance. Nuns, evangelists, drug addicts are particularly loaded, for good or for bad, with Neptune's illusive power. Interestingly, the two thousand years that has elapsed during the rule of Pisces started around the time of the beginning of Christianity. For nearly 2000 years, the world has been largely under the influence of Judeo-Christian theology, whose first early chosen symbol was the sign of the fish. Oriental and near-Oriental minds delight in fairy stories, and they are continually spinning such beautiful myths about the lives of religious and political heroes. In the absence of printing, when most human knowledge was passed by word of mouth, from one generation to the next, the illusive power of Pisces opened the doors for myths to become tradition and those traditions to eventually be accepted as fact.

Unmistakably, under the sign of Pisces, Jesus Christ suffered sorrow, imprisonment, restrictions and tortures at the hands of secret political enemies. Also, Christianity has been preaching the blind acceptance of suffering, repentance and sacrifice, if you are to proceed to the paradise of God. According to astrology, Neptune's energy (Pisces) forces the soul towards its opposite sign (Virgo) or the Virgin Mary and its purity principle. This indicates why Christians have subconsciously chosen the symbol of the fish to represent their religion and beliefs. The last 2000 years of Neptunian influence have produced over 875 different religions worldwide, and in the process, millions of people have died and still die in devastating holy wars.

It is well documented that many former civilizations simply worshipped God or gods with the stars, the moon and the sun. The Creator's Divine Manifestation throughout the Universe (Astrology) was well used and understood by the ancients. Whereas Pisces is mute and accepting, Aquarius has a voice. Aquarius rules curiosity, invention, electronics, the UFO phenomena and astrological investigation. Uranus rules the future, electronics, electricity, radio, television, airships and aeronautics. Among its metals are uranium, radium and all the other radioactive elements.

Thus, we can look upon the Aquarian age as a bringer of hope, universal love, and as a promoter of great technological advances and vast increases in man's mental exploration. Uranus rules cosmic consciousness, psychic awareness and the genius quality of man. Uranus is also classified as the "sudden release of energy" and is responsible for nature's devastating forces such as earthquakes, tornadoes, hurricanes and typhoons. Wrongly used, Uranus can be the potential destroyer of the human race through the use of atomic weaponry and as yet undiscovered powers.

We must learn to understand the true message of Aquarius and the awesome power of Uranus. We must overcome the negative forces of this planet, for that is the lesson of the Age of Aquarius, to enjoy an age of great spiritual awakening. We must learn to accept the values and workings of Uranus upon our thought processes, thus creating our own amazing future reality, complete with ETs and UFOs. We must create a universal brotherhood, where love, progress and responsibility become the ultimate goals. If we fail to recognize the awesome power of Uranus, the Aquarius age may be the last age man will live on this planet.

We have twelve months, 12 hours, 12 apostles. The twelve apostles are a hidden representation of the 12 gods of the zodiac. Symbols have survived to this day from very ancient times. In the Catholic Church today, the staff the Bishops carry is a carry-over of the staff held by the Egyptian God Osiris. The symbol of the Christian cross was taken from the Egyptian Ankh, which represented life and fertility. The high pointed hat worn by the Pope was derived from Osiris' tall crown. And even the traditional birthday of Jesus, celebrated on the 25th of December, is taken from the birthday of the Egyptian God, Horus.

2007 Slow-Moving Planets Predictions

October 26th, 2005 - Jupiter in Scorpio: This Universal order brought serious improvement in all affairs related to corporate endeavors, insurance companies, secret services (FBI/CIA) and the police where all foreign countries have been forced by the celestial order to work in harmony with the US to combat terrorism. My prediction of a full-restructure of the US and worldwide secret agencies came to pass.

November 24th 2006 - Jupiter in Sagittarius: Jupiter rules foreigners and foreign lands and the planet of luck and protection in his own sign acted as a serious shield against terrorism. It is because of this international restructure of secret agencies that Pakistan was able to directly contact the US and the UK authorities and thwart the terrorists plot to blow up allied international airliners. The cease-fire of August 2006 between Lebanon and Israel denote also the strengths of the UN but more blood shed is expected before a solid solution would bring peace to the region.

Wherever the lucky planet Jupiter resides in your chart by house and sign you can expect a serious increase in luck and progress. It is important for you to find out where this great impact is, so you can act upon it before the transit is over. Chances are you will succeed if you act with faith. You will succeed providing you aim high and big and involve foreigners or foreign land. Order a full life reading and I will take good care of you. Jupiter the ruler of laws and religions will bring serious changes in the world's religious and philosophical perception. Many ignorant pious souls will lose their lives trying to impose their religious beliefs to others or embark on missions to "save the world" in unstable parts of this world. The drive to travel and teach others will be overwhelming for some and great success is assured for many lucky souls.

July 17th, 2005 - Saturn in Leo: Saturn, "the teacher" has been going through the sign of Leo since Sunday July 17th, 2005. Karmic Saturn is also called, the "Great Malefic" and its gloomy power brings fears, depression by sign and house he resides. In any case, if you are feeling Saturn's gloomy energy you are probably not using this planet structuring power accordingly and feel inadequate or lost in your career accomplishment. Do not give in to Saturn depressive power and use your will: the part of God in you is much stronger than any planet. In the sign of Leo expect a complete and serious restructure of the arts industry, where much work will be dedicated to the children.

Saturn in Leo propagates a subconscious fear of death and diseases or expanding the mind into more advanced topics, such as the study of electronic or New Age matters. Saturn is cold and calculated; Leo is hot and fixed. Make solid plans, stick to them and respect the Universal Law in all your endeavors. On a more positive note, the structural power of Saturn will provide Leo's enterprising spirit, objectivity, discipline and a reasonable approach to any business or writing venture. Many people will feel the urge to "assert" the competitive side of Leo and children involved in the arts will accomplish much progress. Some scientists will bring about incredible inventions that will benefit heart surgery while karmic souls born with an afflicted Saturn (caution) in Leo (the heart) may experience surgery.

Expect the US taxpayer's money to be used for the building of better schools and healthy programs. With the passage of Saturn (re-structure) in Leo (fame) many famous people may lose their position or children. Nature devastating forces may affect France, Japan or Italy (see Supernova windows). In the long run, safer and more solid structures will be erected for the benefit of our youngest members of our society. Avoid the insecurity feeling produced by Saturn in your life and work diligently towards a better health and take care of yourself, as the numbers of heart surgery will rise drastically. A 90 MN taped Full Life Reading will tell you more about the location and impact of Saturn in your celestial make up and how to combat fears.

September 3rd, 2007 - Saturn in Virgo: The planet of discipline and structure moves into the sign of health and service to others. On a world scale expect a full restructure of all that involves the medical field, especially in the area of drugs prescriptions and natural medicine. The "Baby Buster Generation" (See my book The power Of The Dragon) will work very hard to protect Mother Nature and all natural parks. A fierce battle again? Forestry regulations and oil company will rage to save the rain forest and what is left of untamed nature. More on this will be in the 2008 Moon Power.

September 15, 2003 - Uranus in Aquarius: Uranus is the future, be ready to experience a taste of the unbelievable. Uranus in Aquarius has forced the masses to open up to the New Agers' messages. What is now considered eccentric leanings such as: astrology, UFOs, reincarnation, psychic powers, etc., will be approached with an open mind, explored, and in time, finally accepted by the majority. All this will take place soon after the year 2012. Some of the old sciences (including astrology) will be brought back to our colleges and universities and accepted as true and useful disciplines. Soon after this new consciousness, the human race will be prepared for the possibility of exploring the universe with friendly extraterrestrial life form.

Uranus rules the sudden release of energy (earthquakes) and after entering his own sign; the worst of nature's forces will be experienced by mankind and especially in Hawaii, Japan and California. This does not mean the end of the world, but a reminder that old mother earth is still alive and needs to reshape her entrails. Tremendous electronic tools and new discoveries will be brought to the human race. Children born during the passage of Uranus in Aquarius will have sparkling genius qualities and a strong sense of independence. Many will feel the urge to undergo computer studies while others will have to travel far and enjoy their new and exciting careers. Expect more and more electronic breakthrough and a general interest in the new age matters. Many new age schools (Astro-Psychology) will get attention and more will be accredited and recognized as a valuable discipline in our colleges and Universities. Perfect time to apply your will and decide to start a spiritual Astro-Psychology, Kabalistic Healing or Astro-Tarot course (see www.drturi.com or call the office to help us to set a few days-crash course in your area).

Important Memo: This section was written in 2003 years before the deadly Asia Tsunami. Uranus rules the sudden release of energy (earthquakes) <u>and mankind all over the world will experience the worse of nature's forces.</u> This does not mean the end of it all but serves, as a reminder that old mother earth is still alive and now and then she needs to reshape her entrails. Expect tremendous electronic tools and new discoveries will be brought to the Human race. All the children that were born during the passage of Uranus in Aquarius will have sparkling genius qualities and a strong sense of independence. Many will feel the urge to undergo computer studies, while others will have to travel far and enjoy their new and exciting careers. Expect more and more electronic breakthroughs and a general interest in the new age matters.

Neptune will reside in the futuristic sign of Aquarius until April 5th, 2011. When badly asserted, Neptune is known to be the planet of illusion. However, all planets are both positive and negative. Neptune's creative energy produced a wave of evangelists using the "last days" of the Apocalypse, to make fortunes in deceiving the uninformed, God-fearing religious masses. Since its entrance in the futuristic sign of Aquarius (new age) Neptune's illusive power is fading away. However with both Jupiter (expansion) and Pluto (death) in Sagittarius (religions at large/books) both a new crowd of totally psychotic religious fanatics or highly advanced spiritual leaders will roam the world with their teachings fulfilling the Celestial will for a Universal spiritual advancement. You are strongly advised to take the time to go to my home page www.drturi.com, scroll down to the banner titled "SOS To The World" and read all about Neptune's tremendous power over humankind. Doing so will allow you to use your will by understanding and using the positive energy of the planet of deception that has ruled this world for the last two thousands years.

With Neptune, "Poseidon" in the electronic sign of Aquarius, artists of all orders will invest in incredible imaginative resources, and produce incredible movies, some religious some totally ahead of time. Those Neptunian (sea) and Uranian (UFOs) tales will transform into incredible movies. Again my premonition for such a development was written in my 1996 "Moon power" and took place in 1997 with the "Mars Invasion" and "Titanic" the "Matrix" and the latest movie buster "The Passion of Christ". The writers, the actors and the electronic genius of the movie producers in Hollywood performed the incredible Neptunian/Uranian artistically oriented work.

With Neptune's imagination and the electronic sign of Aquarius since 1999 expect more incredible mixture of the future and creativity leading to a solid growth within the cinematography industry.

Important Memo: This section was written years before September 11th 2001 and predicted in April 1991 on Art Bell Coast To Coast radio show.

The full impact has been felt with the 911 WTC dramatic terrorist attacks on the US and the July 7, 2005 London bombing. See predictions at www.drturi.com

Pluto in Sagittarius: Pluto moved from Scorpio to Sagittarius on November 11th, 1995 and will stay in this sign until January 26, 2008. Constrained to face the horrible consequences of his own destructive power, and pay the heavy consequences of mass destruction, man turns to religion for comfort. In Sagittarius (religion) Pluto (regeneration) _will promote a disturbing wave of religious fanaticism that will plague the world. In the US, the impact of Pluto in Sagittarius has already spoken with some religious fanatics, committing serious crimes and many will have to pay the ultimate price for their destructive behavior. Some Middle Eastern residents have also shocked the world, and will keep spawning suicidal bomb attacks, on major European and US cities._ The "contract" they sign with their manipulators, before blowing themselves up surrounded by the highest possible number of innocent victims, promises "the martyrs" twenty or more virgins after an immediate entrance to paradise! After the painful passage of Pluto (expiration) in Sagittarius (codification thoughts), the world will be ready for wiser, new age and religious leaders. Those well-adjusted souls will teach all the higher expressions of all the religions of the past. They will introduce a new image of a God free of fear, full of love and attention. Those futuristic spiritual leaders will combine their religious teachings with a more comprehensive scientific understanding of the manifestation of the Creator throughout the Universe.

Ignorance is evil; when you control someone's source of information or education, chances are that you will control that person's entire life.-- Dr. Turi

Mostly do not worry about anything; it is **NOT** the end of the world. Most of all do **NOT** fall for the "Apocalyptic" times promised by religious lunatics. There are so much more forces above your head in charge of humankind future and you may not know about it. Have faith regardless of what the world is going through because as incredible as it may sound, all will be just fine at the end.

The Dragon's Head in Pisces (oceans) has his own way to REstructure sea life and the oceans and Mother Nature is much more powerful than humans and its technology. Again the same applies for the year 2012 predictions and earth changes lunatics, **DO NOT FALL** in your fears and have faith. God did not put us on earth to die of a terrible death, there is much more beyond your comprehension and those baffled ignorant scientists or religious leaders. None of them possess true cosmic consciousness and can only rely on the "scriptures" or science to give you answers. All of those well-educated scientists did graduate from accredited schools and well-established Universities. Would they be psychiatrists and psychologists from well-known medical institutions or NASA' scientists, mental snobs, USGS geologists or from the Oceanography study departments; don't expect real answers from them. Would they be your political party or your religious organization leaders or even the FBI; they are all at loss and have absolutely **NO** clue about the Universal will or design. They are certainly very good at what they do for sure, but all of them have refused to honor the word science and investigate my work. In the process the very essence of what they are all looking for will never be reached, simply because they have not yet grasped that everything under the stars is under the jurisdiction of the stars and they know **NOTHING** about the stars…

So the scientific community likes solid proof. Here it is again and anything that has ever been posted on the Internet is there to stay forever and with a little search on "Deja New" anyone can trace these posts. Note also that sad enough my newsgroup prophecies. drturi has been totally destroyed where all the young souls have congregated for years to hurt both my integrity and my work. But that is the price anyone has to pay with notoriety. In there, over the years, many young souls have wished me death, in so many forms, but in spite of all the thousands of email of support from advanced souls, I decided ? to stop posting there.

Sample of Proof

WWW -INTERNET - USGS - Message -ID: G1t4Hv@goodnet.com -sender news@goodnet.com (News Administrator) -Dr. Turi drturi @goodnet.com> Newsgroups - sci.geo,sci.geo.geology,ca. earthquakes,hkbu,geog.maps - WEEKLY USGS Quake Report 9/28 - 10/4/95 CA. Seismology Institute - in rticleDG1t4H. v @goodnet.com>   DATE—Oct 6h, 1995 drturi@goodnet.com says...

POSTED (Oct, 6th. 1995) -- >From Dr. Turi - Dear Sirs: - On Oct.8th and Oct.9th a very unusual seismic activity will be noticeable and will produce many quakes above 6.1. More information is available pertaining to my method if requested. <drturi@goodnet.com> Respectfully-- Dr. Turi
SUBJECT: RE: Weekly USGS Quake Report
Results - Full proofs of predictions:
Oct. 8th a 7.0 EARTHQUAKE HIT SUMATRA (INDONESIAN ISLANDS)
Oct. 9th a 7.6 EARTHQUAKE HIT MEXICO.

More Proof
CA. Seismology Institute IDL: 81706 3427.004 400-Received: by / c=us/admd=telemail/prmd= nasa/; converted (1A5-Text; ate: 22 Nov. 1995 10:00:53 -00 from ///el@pl.nasa.gov "drturi@goodnet.com>" Subject: request for 1996 Top Universal Predictions. Content length 603 - Newsgroups - sci.geo.geology, ca.earthquakes, hkbu, geo. Maps -WEEKLY - USGS Quake report   9/28-10/4/95 CA. Seismology Institute -WWW -INTERNET - Message -ID: /// D////v@goodnet.com

Kudos to you Dr. Turi!
I surf the Internet periodically for predictions on forthcoming events, specifically all relating to earthquake activities. You hit the 11/22/95 Egypt/Israel/Saudi Arabia 7.2 quake smack dab on the head, per your earlier prediction. Congratulations again!
E-mail < ////private @ccmail.jpl.nasa.com> Keep up the good work.
Appreciatively, G//

More Proof:
From: /////@mindspring.com
To: Louis a Turi <dr.turi@juno.com>
Date: Fri, 24 Sep 1999 22:31:10 -0400 (EDT)
Subject: Re: Show

I gave you full credit on the show, just after the massive Taiwan earthquake and the Turkey aftershock on Sept 20.... I got a lot of email from people who were watching the date prediction as well. This is marvelous my friend. The nice thing about it is, how you understate these things and never gloat about them when you hit. I had another fine program with John Hogue last night. Be well, my friend.

Jeff Rense

"All I have asked for is a fair scientific investigation of my work for the sole purpose of promoting mans cosmic consciousness, saving time, money and the lives of many people."
--Dr. Turi

Sadly enough your tax dollars is going to those well-established governmental institutions while my valuable research and my obvious findings (and predictions) are not taken seriously or even endorsed. Well, I am well ahead of those scientists and that is the price I have to pay. Once more, HELP me to pass those predictions to all the people and website you know. Please help me in my pledge to educate the world and bring hope to mankind.

Ignorance is evil; when you control someone's source of information or education, chances are that you will control that person's entire life.
— Dr. Turi

⚜ 2007 Dragon's Head & Tail Predictions ⚜

(Date of prediction 8/14/2006)

Memo of the 2004 Dragon's Head and Tail Predictions - (Date of prediction 6/7/03)

"Note: This axis Taurus/Scorpio Dragon will rule upon this world from April 14, 2003 until December 25th 2004. (Note the Asia tsunami took place on 12/25/04).

Scorpio rules life and death, drama, reincarnation, sex corporate endeavors, the police force, the FBI, CIA, Mafia, insurance companies etc. Expect a complete restructure of all the above organizations where secrets will be exposed. Under Pluto's jurisdiction all that is hidden must come to the light. Very often as seen with the church sex scandals, all that is detrimental to the "church Inc" has been kept secret, but some of it came out into the open in 2002, 2003 and in 2004.

Scorpio rules death and rebirth; forcing the world to experience dramatic happenings and wars. The passionate and destructive energy of the Dragon's Tail in Scorpio during those years took many young lives, while terrorist' suicide attacks will increase drastically. Well before Russia made national news about selling technology to Iraq, I wrote in 2003 Moon Power expect Russia and India (Scorpio) countries will be forced to divulge unhealthy secret projects and errors pertaining to nuclear arsenals falling into the wrong hands.

Like all major government institutions, the FBI and the CIA are also unaware of the power of the stars upon their endeavors. Had someone read my forecasts back in 7/7/2002 they would have read the following predictions on page 53 of "Asia Dragon Predictions" and would have anticipated the news of the Russians selling Technology to Iraq: Printed Prediction: Nuclear secrets from Russia and the Middle East will come to light. Under Pluto's immense destructive power, chemical plants explode, airliners crash, nature goes crazy, products are tampered with, and potentially dangerous technology is sold to hostile powers.

2007 Dragon's Head & Tail Predictions

Note: You may download "Asia Dragon Predictions" for free from www.drturi.com."

The Dragon stays about two years in one sign and forces the soul towards his future by imposing world wide karmic work. The Dragon's Head entered the sign of Pisces on Thursday June 22nd, 2006 and will move into the sign of Aquarius on December 15, 2007

Again knowledge is power and ignorance is evil. Raise your cosmic consciousness and enjoy a happier existence; this is why God gave us the stars." To be used as signs so that you can enjoy a more productive life". A progressive or full life 90 MN taped reading would give you all very important information as how the Dragon's Head or Tail will affect your entire life in 2007. Call me at 602-265-7667 for more information.

Thursday June 22nd, 2006 The Dragon's Head entered the sign of Pisces and this is the very important change of the guards! This is the true New Year for the world where very important happening will take place. August 2006 marks the beginning of the re-structure of the Middle East with both the invasion of Lebanon by Israel and the cease-fire on August 13, 2006 (today as I am writing this book in Bangkok Thailand). My prediction of the full restructure of the Middle East has started and it is far from being over.

In the 2006 Moon Power I wrote that; Pisces rules the Middle East and will bring more attacks by terrorists worldwide. August 2006-Scotland Yard managed to defeat a plot against some UK and US airlines and again for those of you who have the 2006 copy of Moon Power, simply read my predictions for these days in August. On my website, I gave a list of all the tragic dates for 2006/2007 pertaining to when terrorists will be active and all that transpired in August was again on the date/window I gave just before flying to Thailand. Make sure to go to my website now and then (even if you have purchased 2007 Moon Power) and make a note of these dates, as they have and will prove me right again and again.

I was approached to do another television show and give a new set of dramatic dates for 2007 and hopefully I will have time to insert those in this book, if time permits. But the predictions I did for 2006 and on the George Noory special Pay per View are still in progress, so I can only repeat myself and add more predictions as I channel them for you.

If you have a copy of the 2006 Moon Power you may refer to the predictions area. I can only add a few more predictions for 2007 as the Dragon is still in the axis Pisces/Virgo.

Serious security decision and new actions pertaining to the war in the Middle East, will have to be taken by the US and British government.

This prediction came to pass following the thwarted August 2006 terrorist plot against major airlines and more security measures have been enforced in both the UK and US airports.

The entire region will ally against the west and will force the US/UK into a much-needed adjustment.

This one too, came to pass with Hizbollah's popularity following its successful missile attacks on Israel. Syria and Iran especially are deeply involved in the conflict and will stop at nothing to destroy the west and its "infidels".

Expect more devastating attacks in both the US and the UK and parts of Asia that could lead to a secret nuclear debate in due time.

This prediction came to pass under closed doors and more planned critical actions are on the agenda and will come to the fore following the Dragon's Head entrance into the sign of Aquarius (nuclear) in December 19, 2007.

This general threat will bring more fears into god-fearing people and this will increase the churches desperate need for subscribers in the last breath of the dying Pisces age.

Certain laws will be passed to stop the proliferation of religious buildings and cities will block zonings, while many protestors from different holy backgrounds will set them on fire.

2007 Dragon's Head and Tail Predictions

Sad enough, this prediction also came to pass in 2006 with direct attacks (bombing) on mosques and churches (killings). More is on the agenda for 2007.

New laws will be established for the shipping industry, to avoid a way for terrorists to bring deadly weaponry and chemicals to the US. A full restructure of the shipping industry will also be imposed by the US Homeland security, to avoid such possible disasters. Secret business sales of gas masks will be uncovered and coastline cities, public dancing places, Sea World and US exotic islands, and Australia, will become new targets for the terrorists.

The new Dragon in Pisces will also force a total restructure of the oil industry. A record capital gain in the history of many oil corporations hit the roof with profit. Those corporations are abusive to the extreme and will take advantage of the situation in the Middle East to ill-treat the American and the rest of the world's population. The price of gas is simply exorbitant and those corporations will squeeze the consumers to its last cent. The greedy abusers are aiming for a $5.00 a gallon of gas within the next few years.

However the Dragon's Head in Pisces (oil industry) is on their side for the time being, but with the restructure of the Middle East (call it karma) they will be forced to be decent with the consumers. But not without losing a few billions dollars in some legal battles in the process. Gas price will be skyrocketing, forcing the population to ask lawmakers to stop the constant rise of oil price.

The need for oil will also justify their need for more drilling plants in forbidden natural US and foreign territory. But their plan to raise the oil price until they are allowed to do so and expand, could work at the expense of the coastlines natural reserve and the ozone layer.

For years those powerful corporations have declined any financial support (or interest) in developing a new, safer and cleaner way to use natural gas or the manufacturing of hydrogen, steam, cold fusion or electrical propelled cars. The technology is there and available and the Dragon's Tail in Virgo (health/nature) will see to it and force them to redirect their colossal wealth in a productive way for Mother Earth and mankind at large. The Dragon's Head in Pisces will impose serious re-structures and the merging of oil giants for business growth or financial protection purposes.

The shipping industry will also see a serious increase for transport but a full restructure of all ports conditions and jurisdiction for security purpose against terrorism will be enforced. Neptune (ruler of Pisces) rules also chemicals and poison and could bring about disaster at sea and on the American and allied soils. Expect serious water damage inflicted by natural disaster such as the latest China Typhoon (Saomai) that killed many people in August 2006. Uranus the planet of sudden release of energy is still in Pisces and will create more natural disasters including hurricanes, serious flooding, dam failures, the possibility of large reservoir of water being poisoned are also on the list.

Neptune rules chemicals and I am expecting some plant explosions or evacuation because of train/ship accident forcing people to evacuate the areas. I am also hoping that all precautions will be taken against sabotage at sea that would spill thousands of tons of crude oil contaminating the coastlines and killing a lot of wild life. The dates of those predictions are in this book but some of them will be posted on my website throughout the year. This is why it is important to go now and then and make note of my premonitions and quatrains. Most of all avoid traveling during any of the three Supernova windows to avoid serious frustration, money even your life.

The Tail of the Dragon in Virgo (rain forest) will impose new rules upon the logging industry. The new regulations will demand replanting trees after deforestation to preserve the ecosystem and endangered species. Activists will also work very hard to save the remaining of the rain forest and stop oil companies to ruin our coastlines.

The cinematography industry will also see a serious progressive restructure, while many famous names will suffer physically and spiritually. Suicide or religious conversion is also a possibility or a way out for some famous people.

A new infectious disease and a very high suicide numbers of people because of abuse and nefarious addictive medical prescriptions will reach the media.

Neptune rules also the pharmaceutical companies, the FDA and movie industry.

Expect some serious legal battle against drug companies that will force a full restructure of the FDA. New pharmaceutical companies will merge under new corporate names to avoid legal battles and future bankruptcy. Expect serious problems with wine exportation due to shortage or drought in productive regions of the world.

Expect also negative news from exotic places, the shipping industry and with food or water poisoning, drugs activity and disappearing people, such as Natalee Holloway dilemma that will become public in time. Neptune rules all affairs involving water and the oceans. Expect a wet year with serious flooding and a series of super hurricanes and tornadoes that will destroy coastlines and some islands worldwide. Accident/terrorism/oil at sea is to be expected, while the hurricane/tornadoes season will bring devastating flooding. The fishing and boating industry will also be restructured, while nerve gas and warfare chemical agents will become a serious threat against many countries allied with the US and the UK. Read the specific set of dates that will be posted regularly on my website throughout 2007.

Expect disturbing news coming from natural reservoirs, oil spills, lakes and rivers. The fishing industry will suffer drastically, due to over fishing and poisoned oceans. Many of my prediction came to pass in 2006 and you can read all details from my website under "predictions". Expect more calamities of this nature in 2007.

I also wrote in the 2006 Moon power to be ready for types of accident involving ships and nuclear submarines during 2006 /2007 Supernova Windows.

August 2006 "the Bright Artemis" caused intensive damage to India's coastline of Andaman and Nicobar in the Indian Ocean archipelago. The Japanese supertanker collided on August 12 (on the date I posted on my site) with a Singapore ship that was on fire. The oil tanker approached the burning vessel to rescue the people when accidentally the two ships collided. An estimated 4500 tons of crude oil has and is still leaking from the supertanker.

But this "sea accident" is nothing compared to the worst oil spill in the history of the southern Asian country with the sinking in rough seas of the "Solar 1" Super tanker on Friday August 12th (again the window was posted on my website before my trip to Asia). The ship spilled over 520,000 gallon of industrial fuel ruining the Philippines coastlines and the livelihood of over 10,000 local fishermen. These disasters simply reflect my prediction for 2006/2007 for "serious sea accidents and oil spills".

The Dragon Head and Tail in Pisces Virgo axis will also bring the highest numbers of incarcerations including serious unrest and riots in jails leading to many deaths and suicides. Expect many prison riots where deadly force will be used, forcing a re-structure of the correctional system. A new drug ring will be uncovered and lead many people to die and to jail. Expect food or water poisoning on cruise lines.

DO NOT TRAVEL AFTER THE FULL MOON especially during a Supernova Window. Save your life and avoid frustrations, educate yourself and don't be like the millions of people who suffered the thwarted terrorists attacks on international airlines flying from the UK to the US in August 2006 and got stuck for days in airports all over the world.

Pisces the sign of religions and deception; is ruled by Neptune the planet that creates illusion and imagination. This celestial body controls also oil and the entire Middle East. This unstable region is totally poisoned with the three deadliest and youngest religions (Christianity/Muslims/Judaism) created by mankind's folly and manipulative governments of the past. Over the centuries myths became accepted as reality by the uneducated fearful working class and spread like a cancer to the masses worldwide.

Expect the entire territory to ally and support the terrorist activity promoting a "holy war" against the West regardless of the UN "cease fire" of August 2006. Expect the worse of the Dragon's Head and Tail to impact the world in March and/or September 2006/2007 especially during the 2006/2007 Super Nova Windows or the given set of dates posted regularly on my home page. It is also important for you to sign up for the free Dragon Newsletter from my home page www.drturi.com as I will in time expose and prove the value of my predictions.

Expect career re-structure and disturbing news involving many famous people including Elizabeth Taylor, Michael Jackson's

"Neverland", Ex-President Bush and Clinton, Governor Arnold Schwarzenegger and famous actors and singers born under the sign of Pisces and Virgo. This prediction touched directly Mel Gibson arrested for DUI and anti Semitic Jewish views including Diana Ross arrested for DUI and Boy George for lying to the police after a dispute with a lover. Drugs were found in the apartment of the famous singer. The same trouble has pestered famous radio host show Rush Limbaugh with his addiction to medical prescriptions that came public. Expect more dramatic news of this nature for many well-known actor, singer and politicians shrinking their public image and career while some unlucky others famous figures will die by accident, suicide or go to jail or seek medical help.

Man is superior to the stars if he lives in the power of superior wisdom. Such a person being the master over heaven and earth by means of his will is a magus and magic is not sorcery but supreme wisdom
— Paracelsus-

Your Personal Horoscope for 2007

Welcome to Each Sign of the Zodiac

Important Note from Dr. Turi: Born and raised in Provence, France, I rekindled and exercise only Nostradamus' 16th-century Divine Astrology method. This formula does not reflect the modern astrology disciplines you may use, study or practice. Realize that over 500 years ago the famous Prophet did not use a watch or any sophisticated computers. Thus like the great Seer, I investigate Outer Space and the Universal Mind with my inborn spiritual telescope. A "microscopic attitude" will not help anyone gain the Golden Key to spiritual wisdom. This limited expletive attitude is for scientists and astronomers alike who have long lost their cosmic consciousness with their stationary scientifically oriented minds. We have all heard of missing the forest looking at a tree. Every one of them is aware of the twelve constellations of the Zodiac; somehow it is still impossible for them to pass the limitation of their five rational senses and enter the intuitional domain of the stars.

To penetrate the clear-sighted domain of those stars is a serious task that demands curiosity and an inborn advanced UCI (Unique Celestial Identity). But entering the archetypal realm of consciousness and decoding the subtle meaning behind the symbols of the Zodiac within the structure of the Universal Mind involves more than a logical mind. At this time, in space some scientists or religious souls are simply doomed and may not be allowed to do so during the course of this incarnation. Not to worry they do have eternity to bring forth their own cosmic consciousness in another incarnation.

Realize that Divine Astrology is an extremely old celestial art and a very complex science and must be practiced as such. Not everyone is blessed with the "gift" needed to assimilate, understand and translate correctly the Divine order of the Creator. That's why a section of the bible clearly mentions, "I will talk to you; but you won't hear me! I will present myself to you; but you won't see me!" God speaks to us within his own celestial creation and manifestation and through his Divine light will the Advanced Soul perceive his will. But the will of man is stronger than fears or skepticism and with education they can expand their own cosmic consciousness and will be able to "perceive and receive" the real manifestation of God. For those born on the cusp of any zodiacal sign, simply refer to the month of your birth, which reflects the exact constellation of your nativity. If you know your rising then read your forecast for your ascendant too. Divine Astrology, as practiced by Nostradamus, is the creation of Dr. Turi and a more accurate and simplistic way of looking at the stars. All students have found it to be incredibly accurate. You may join Dr. Turi Star Student's family by taking the Astro-Psychology course by mail or in person. See www.drturi.com for information.

Philosophical Astro — Poetry
By Brigitte Turi
Copyright 1995

Saturn Governs the Power-Oriented, Structural Constellation of Capricorn

> *Builder of the greatest towers*
> *Holding all the social powers*
> *Striving to climb to the highest peak*
> *For honor has no place for the weak*
> *I am CAPRICORN, child of Saturn.*

- Characteristics For Those Born In January

Saturn rules the practical sign of Capricorn and controls the month of January. You are strongly motivated to succeed and with dedication you will gain a position of power in your life. You are gifted with computers and you possess strong organizational principles. More than any other sign of the Zodiac you strive for respect and accomplishment in your career. Saturn is a karmic planet and rules your life, thus you must avoid nurturing depressing thoughts. The part of God in you is much stronger than the stars you inherited, and you do have the power to master the universal mind. You were born in the middle of the winter when nature was asleep. You must have realized early on, that nothing would come easily to you. Like the goat slowly but surely and against all odds (cold/wind/snow) you must climb towards the top of the mountain. The first part of your life has been a long and painful struggle but Saturn will reward you by giving you a long life and a well-deserved position. You will appreciate old age and solid financial security. You may also marry a much younger or older partner. The fluctuations of the Moon strongly affect your mood and career success. The wise Capricorn soul will use his fish tail accordingly and synchronize his life and business with the Universal tides. Steadiness, organization, patience, and charm belong to you. You have a strong architectural or mathematical ability and your keen sense of observation will help you succeed in life. Karmic Saturn will exact payment for manipulating others for selfish ends and will throw the soul back to a painful start. You are attracted to power and successful people and you may marry into wealth. Emotional and sensitive, you are very responsible and protective of the family circle. However you must learn to openly communicate your deep feelings.

Your real gifts are Astro-Psychology, electronics, and any career supported by Uncle Sam. Your natal Dragon can propel you to the highest position and supreme power. But your challenge is to open up to the intangible world of the spirit and its accompanying Universal rules. Your natural tendency to organize people and business at all times could hinder your sensitivity to others. Capricorns are good homemakers and adept with investments. As a rule you favor a successful business environment where you can apply your tremendous organizational gifts. A word of caution for Capricorn: Be aware of those wild acquaintances willing to help you to climb the ladder of success. Remember to respect the Universal Law (see Moon Power), as your awareness of Moon planning will become a major contribution for happiness and success. The location of your natal Dragon's Head or Tail will seriously alter the strength or weakness of Saturn in your chart. The downfall of your spirit is religion and/or chemical addictions. Rush Limbaugh and Mel Gibson are good example involving religion and chemical substance abuse. You can learn much more about yourself or anyone else by ordering my new book entitled "I Know All About You", "The Power Of The Dragon" or "And God Created The Stars".

2007 — Forecast For Those Born In January

Personal: On June 22nd, 2006, you received the impact of the Dragon's Head in Pisces affecting positively your 3rd house of mental speculations, study and critical thinking. The Dragon's Head will reinforce your mental creativity and may lead you to write a book or a play which will force you to face the world with a more definite attitude for success. This house rules all forms of communication and may induce the learning of foreign languages or the arts; expect lots of mental activity and traveling, however you must avoid any form of stress and take time to relax from hard studies. Matters involving mental creativity and spirituality will become newfound interests. The lucky ones will gain a form of fame based upon mental accomplishments and add a new spiritual way of generating money or spiritual stability in the future. A new way of thinking about security, money, including religion and the arts, will be induced by the Dragon's Head.

Many hard-working Capricorns will get a windfall of creative mental energy, and with it, the opportunity to shine intellectually. Many will also be promoted to higher positions or will be able to publish their work. This will open exciting doors to travel promising new business endeavors; and rewarding financial contacts. Dragon's Tail location in the sign of Virgo in your 9th house (religion/traveling/foreigners) will work hard on your favor to eliminate old archaic mental attitudes and attract a progressive new way of thinking. Some of those unworthy religious doctrines will have to be replaced by a more progressive and spiritual research, including astrology or technology. Avoid stress and even depression during the waning moon periods (see Moon Power publication for dates).

During the New and Full Moons of March and September 2007, serious happenings based upon your personal karma will take place. You are strongly advised to use your will and avoid depressing thoughts when dealing with study or religion or if you are restructuring a new life in a foreign country. Challenging regenerative spiritual endeavors combined with advanced or new spiritual studies and social interaction could prove to be beneficial then. Do not let the nasty pull of the Dragon's Tail get the best of your body and mind with guilt and accept the spiritual imposed changes. The positive Dragon's Head in Pisces will induce a variety of mental exchanges and with them, the option to meet interesting people with new ideas. Within the next few months or so the fruits of many years of spiritual hard work will begin to pay off as you may be forced to face the world with a new mental attitude.

New artistic or religious studies will offer you great opportunities to meet new people, thus the potential to find wisdom and true love. Foreign business associations, contracts, partnerships, traveling, and luck in general will be offered by some of those new friends. Providing you keep busy and avoid nurturing pessimistic thoughts about your past, a very progressive time is ahead of you. As a rule, those born in January strive for spiritual or artistic endeavors. This new Dragon may force you to travel, learn and teach your newfound knowledge away from a non-progressive group or friends. Saturn is solid rational planet when changes may not be easily accepted, but doing so will bring a new restructure of your philosophical and religious outlook that will bring you long lasting peace and stability. Remember to respect the Universal Law (the fish tail of the goat) and Capricorn must move upstream with the tide. In time you reach the pure water of true wisdom, happiness and love. The opportunity to make serious mental progress and travel far is offered to you this year. This celestial process will bring you much luck if you take on the challenge of investing in new ideas, new concepts and metaphysical pursuits through traveling. If you accept the challenges, the Dragon will smile at you and promote true happiness.

In the year 2007, the great Jupiter (luck) will cruise through the sign of Sagittarius in your 12th house regulating your subconscious. Much progress is to be expected in those areas if you take the time to educate yourself on the creative forces of your subconscious and use it at your advantage. Let go of the past, let go of the old teachings avoid guilt and all will be fine.

You may order some DVD or CD on the "Power of the Subconscious" from www.drturi.com. Be ready for new associations and great business deals with those born in August, February, December and October. You may order your taped 90mn Full Life Reading or your Progressive reading to find out more about the upcoming changes in your life. You could also be much more prepared if you had your personal Dragon window dates at hand, allowing you to bet or stay clear on any business or important decisions during those days. Working in good knowledge and respect of your "Personal Lucky Dragon Window Dates" can be a serious investment in itself and may save you time, money, even your life, if you do a lot of traveling You may request this important service anytime. Visit www.drturi.com go to "order" and fill out the form or call our office at 602-265-7667 for more information. Good luck to all of those born in January.

Uranus Governs The Ingenious, Freedom-Oriented Constellation Of Aquarius

Holder of knowledge of the dimensions
The spark of all the inventions
Lover of all things in simplicity
Charged with the power of electricity
I am AQUARIUS, child of Uranus.

Characteristics For Those Born In February

The planet Uranus rules the sign of Aquarius and governs the month of February. You are one of the most original people walking this earth. Aquarius has produced many eccentric people and great inventors. Uranus rules the future and the incredible UFO phenomenon. It commands all celestial knowledge particularly the old science of astrology. You are blessed with curious stars and you are attracted to science, research, electronics, psychology, the food industry, real estate, the police force and Astro-Psychology to name a few. Aquarius rules aeronautics, avionics, television, the Internet and advanced computers. The option to reach fame and fortune is a high probability during the course of your life if you service the world in an advanced and original way. The motion pictures "Back to the Future and The Matrix" are some of the best ways to illustrate Uranus' ingenuity in terms of artistic creativity. Strong and fixed, you have inherited from the stars, accurate intuition, tremendous common sense, ingeniousness, and a powerful will.

Yet, you must learn to listen to others and participate in conversations with equality. Even when the ideas being presented are not of your own making, much knowledge can still be learned. Lend your full ear and do not race ahead with only thoughts of what you need to say. Those born in February must also learn to positively direct Uranus' innovative mental power for the improvement and well being of the world. Acting eccentric and without forethought is a sure downfall for you. Your idealistic views are legendary and your mission is to promote Universal Knowledge and Universal Brotherhood. You will benefit from the opportunity to use the latest technological arsenals to fulfill your unselfish wishes for mankind. You can handle the difficulties of life with a smile and transcend setbacks, by using celestial knowledge to your benefit.

The women of this sign are original, independent, beautiful, intellectual, and make good use of their incredible magnetic sexuality to reach their purposes. As a rule, women born in February produce extraordinarily intelligent children or twins. You are strongly advised not to eat when upset. The medical aspect of Divine Astrology predisposes those born in February to oversensitive stomachs and an overactive mind. A word of caution for those born in February: Many young religious or rational souls will not understand your genius and your advanced message to the world. Many will try hard to stop and hurt you. Remember to respect the Universal Law (see Moon Power), as your awareness and Moon planning will become a major contribution to your happiness and success. The location of your natal Dragons Head or Tail will seriously alter the strength or weakness of Uranus in your chart. (See Nostradamus Dragon Forecast for more information). You can learn much more about yourself or anyone else by ordering my new book entitled "I Know All About You", "The Power Of The Dragon" or "And God Created The Stars".

2007 — Forecast For Those Born In February

Personal: On June 22nd, 2006, you received the impact of the Dragon's Head in Pisces affecting positively your 2nd house of money and self esteem. The Dragon's Head will reinforce your opportunities to make and spend money wisely and may lead you invest with others. The Dragon's Head will reinforce your desire to establish financial security and may force you to face the world with a more definite attitude for success. This house involves possession; thus the Dragon's Head will induce great opportunities to invest or deal with real estate or any business providing food, hotels, traveling and general security. Matters involving family, children, food, or real estate, will become more powerful interests for many souls born in February. The lucky ones will build new homes or add new rooms to their houses.

A new way of making money will be induced by the Dragon's Head and many hard-working Uranus souls will get a windfall of creative energy, and with it, the opportunity to make even more money. Many will also be promoted, especially if they decide to write or use their home base constructively. Many Aquarius will work hard to get better financial help and positions where business partners are concerned, while others will be able to publish their works worldwide. This will open exciting doors to promising new business endeavors and rewarding financial contacts. The Dragon's Tail location in the sign of Virgo will cruise through your 8th house (legacy/spirituality). Sadly enough, some souls close to February' souls will leave this world and through legacy offer them option for serious investments.

Some unworthy business deals or partners will be removed by the Dragon's Tail and may cost you money, too. These experiences could induce legal battles and mental stress, even depression during the waning moon, (see Moon Power publication for dates). During the New and Full Moon (March and September 2007) happenings based upon your personal karma will take place. You are strongly advised to use your will and avoid depressing thoughts when dealing with old partners or dear friends that may be called by God or forced to move away.

Challenging regenerative spiritual endeavors combined with studies and social interaction could prove to be beneficial then. Do not let the nasty pull of the Dragon's Tail get the best of your body and mind. The positive Dragon's Head in Pisces will induce a variety of circumstances to get close or away from the water and exotic places. Within the next two years or so, the fruits of many years of hard work will begin to pay off as you may be forced to face the world with a better business attitude and profound knowledge.

New business partners will also offer great opportunities to meet different people, thus the potential to expand your business: even to find true love. Foreign business association contracts, partnerships, traveling, and luck in general will be offered by some of those business partners. Providing you keep busy and avoid nurturing pessimistic thoughts about your past, a very progressive time is ahead of you. As a rule, those born in February strive for leadership and security. This may lead you to travel, deal, or teach in foreign lands. Uranus is quite unpredictable in his rewards, but when he bestows, it usually lasts for a long time. Some of you may have to spend money for medical purposes, but in all; it is for the best of your health and with good results.

Remember to respect the Universal Law of the Moon fluctuations. Your awareness and respect of the Universal Law will become a major contribution towards establishing emotional, financial and spiritual stability. The opportunity to rebuild and make serious financial progress is offered to you this year. This celestial process will bring you much luck if you take on any challenges of investing in computerized education, metaphysical pursuits, traveling, or if you accept challenges with new partners. The Dragon smiles at you and those shining stars above your head are on your side.

In the year 2007, the great Jupiter (luck) will cruise through the sign of Sagittarius in your 11th house regulating your wishes and your friends. Much progress is to be expected in those areas, especially if you take the time to educate yourself on the creative forces of your subconscious and use it at your advantage. You will be in demand by or for groups where many of your wishes will become a reality. Let go of the past and take chances and all will be fine.

You may order some DVD or CD on the "Power of the Subconscious" from www.drturi.com. Be ready for new associations and great business deals with those born in August, February, December and October. You may order your taped 90mn Full Life Reading or your Progressive reading to find out more about the upcoming changes in your life. You could also be much more prepared if you had your personal Dragon Window Dates at hand allowing you to bet or stay clear on any business or important decisions during those days. Working in good knowledge and respect of your "Personal Lucky Dragon Window Dates" can be a serious investment in itself and may save you time, money, even your life, if you do a lot of traveling. You may request this important service anytime. Visit www.drturi.com go to "order" and fill out the form or call our office at 602-265-7667 for more information. Good luck to all of those born in February.

Neptune Governs the Soft, Dreamy, Intuitive And Artistic Constellation Of Pisces

Mystical and magical
Nebulous and changeable
I work my way up life's rivers and seas
To my place at God's own feet
I am PISCES, child of Neptune.

Characteristics For Those Born In March

The planet Neptune and the sign of Pisces govern the month of March. You are a natural teacher, a philosopher and a perfectionist. You inherited phenomenal intuition and in general, will exercise more perception than logic in dealing with life. You are a gifted artist and you enjoy holistic endeavors. Many advanced Pisces are also involved in the medical profession. The young Pisces soul may also work in the construction fields. However, Pisces must understand the importance of education, if he is to use his full potential and teaching gifts. You are noted for your sensitivity, creativity, and artistic values. Michelangelo, Einstein and George Washington were also Pisces' and used their creativity to the fullest. Your downfall is an over preoccupation with others, guilt feelings, addictions and a blind acceptance of religious dogmas.

Nevertheless, your good heart is not surpassed by any other sign of the zodiac and the advanced ones possess spiritual healing powers. Highly evolved people born in March will lead many lost souls out of the deep clouds of deception towards the true colors of love and cosmic consciousness. Your soul's purpose is to swim upstream towards the ethereal light of oneness to find God. A young March spirit is deceiving, complaining and addicted to religious dogmas, cult endeavors, chemicals, drugs, and alcohol. Pisces is a karmic sign and has within itself the potential to reach immortality, fame and fortune through artistic or spiritual work.

In the medical aspect of Divine Astrology, Pisces rules the feet. It is important for you to walk barefoot on the grass, to regenerate the body through the magnetic fields of the earth itself. Your intuition is remarkable and should be well heeded when confronted with serious decisions. A word of caution for Pisces: Do not swim downstream as your induced faith could take you to Neptune's deepest quicksand with no option for return. David Koresh and the Rev. Jim Jones are good examples of Neptune's deceiving religious captains. Remember to respect the Universal Law (see Moon Power), as your awareness and Moon planning will become a major contribution to happiness and success. The location of your natal Dragons Head or Tail will seriously alter the strengths or weakness of Neptune in your chart. You can learn much more about yourself or anyone else by ordering my new book entitled, " I Know All About You," "The Power Of The Dragon" or "And God Created The Stars".

2007 — Forecast For Those Born In March

Personal: On June 22nd, 2006, you received the impact of the

Dragon's Head in Pisces affecting positively your 1st house of self. Indeed a very important year for you as you must be "reborn" in so many ways. The Dragon's Head will induce a great opportunity to establish a new you and a fresh way of looking at the world. The Dragon may force you to restructure your body, your thoughts, and improve your attitude for success. The Dragon's Head on yourself will also help you to re-create a new image to the world. Right "on yourself" the Dragon will induce serious change and will not accept anything or anybody that might try to limit your progress.

Be ready, and accept the new you and those changes with confidence. Matters involving health, education and partnerships will become powerful driving forces. The lucky ones will enjoy new business or love relationships, while other Pisces will enjoy a child. A new way of dealing with the world and your new self will be induced by the Dragon's Head. Many hard-working Pisces will get the opportunity to improve their health and images, including their knowledge with computers, and initiate good home businesses. Following a study, many Pisces might also be promoted to a new position in servicing the world. This will open exciting doors to pass on your knowledge to others and enjoy new business partnerships. This impact will also bring about rewarding financial contracts. The Dragon's Tail location in the sign of Virgo in your 7th house (others) will impose a total re-structure and attract new worthwhile associations. The Dragon will remove unworthy business or emotional partners that wasted your time or hurt your heart. This turmoil will induce physical and mental stress, even depression during the waning moons, (see Moon Power publication for dates).

During the New and Full moons of March and September 2007 serious happenings based upon your karma with some people will occur, forcing either you or them in or out of business. Be prepared to use your will and avoid disheartening thoughts when dealing with your past. You may not know it just yet, but many of your wishes can only be granted after the painful emotional restructure. Much of the trouble may also come from a new position and your desire to compete adequately and to do so, you must be confident. Challenging regenerative spiritual endeavors, combined with studies and social interaction, could prove to be beneficial then. Do not let the nasty pull of the Dragon's Tail in your marriage area get the best of your body and mind. The positive Dragon's Head on you will induce a variety of circumstances to meet interesting people, especially after the New Moons. Within the next two years or so, the fruits of many years of hard work will begin to pay off, as you might have to relocate by the water (or away from it) and start over again. You must learn to face the world with a new positive attitude and the expectation of a much better partner.

New friends, some born in January and July will also offer you great opportunities to meet new people, thus the potential to find your soul mate and your true purpose in life. Foreign business association contracts, partnerships, traveling, and luck in general will be offered by some of those new friends. Providing you avoid nurturing pessimistic thoughts about a wrong relationship, a very progressive time is ahead of you. As a rule, those born in March strive for security and this year you can do miracles. The Dragon's Tail might induce stress, but it is needed and again, those who do not deserve you will have to go. Neptune, your ruler can be surprising in its rewards to you, especially if you are aware of the Universal Law. Your awareness of this law and planning accordingly will become a major contribution to reach many of your dreams. This celestial process will bring you much luck if you take on the challenges of letting go of the past and investing in computerized education, metaphysical pursuits, traveling, and accepting new interests with foreign partners. The Dragon smiles at you and all of those shining stars right on you are on your side. Be prepared to use your will and avoid destructive thoughts at all costs, when dealing with your past or those losses. This impact will bring about opportunities to deal with the spiritual world and will induce great study and with it spiritual growth. The Tail of the Dragon will still be affecting your 7th house of marriage and will force you to readjust your life in dealing with others.

In the year 2007, the great Jupiter (luck) will cruise through the sign of Sagittarius in your 10th house regulating your career and public standing. Much progress is to be expected in those areas, especially if you take the time to educate yourself on the creative forces of your subconscious and use it at your advantage. You will be in demand and will have to give your best shot to goal and many of your wishes will become a reality. Let go of the past and take chances and all will be fine.

You may order some DVD or CD on the "Power of the Subconscious" from www.drturi.com. Be ready for new associations and great business deals with those born in August, February, December and October. You may order your taped 90mn Full Life Reading or your Progressive reading to find out more about the upcoming changes in your life. You could also be much more prepared, if you had your personal Dragon Window Dates at hand, allowing you to bet or stay clear on any business or important decisions during those days. Working in good knowledge and respect of your "Personal Lucky Dragon Window Dates" can be a serious investment in itself and may save you time, money, even your life, if you do a lot of traveling You may request this important service anytime. Visit www.drturi.com go to "order" and fill out the form or call our office at 602-265-7667 for more information. Good luck to all of those born in March.

Mars Governs the Aggressive - Warlike and Impatient Constellation Of Aries

All will hear my views and voice
Trial and error is my school of choice
Like a dragon, dashing and daring I appear
Fighting for those that I hold dear
I am ARIES, child of Mars.

Characteristics For Those Born In April

Assertive Mars controls the month of April. In Greek Mythology, this planet is called "The Lord of War," and rules the impatient sign of Aries. You were born a leader. However, because of your inborn impatience, you will learn by your mistakes. Your strong and impatient desire to succeed must be controlled and hasty decisions avoided. Others perceive you as a competitive and motivated person. More than any other sign of the zodiac, souls born in April must learn steadiness, organization and most of all, diplomacy. When confronted, grace and charm does not really belong to you. Martian souls possess strong leadership and engineering abilities and April men are attracted to dangerous sports, speed, engineering, and the military. Due to your "turbocharged" personality, you are also accident-prone to the head, and should protect it. Both male and females born in April tend to talk too much and must learn to listen to others and control impatience. You must focus on your needs steadily and finish what you have started. Inadvertently, the "red" uncontrolled Martian personality will hurt sensitive souls; thus damaging the chances for respect and promotion. Your explosive temper is generated by an inborn fear of rejection and an inferiority complex. Do not take rejection or opposition personally. The "childlike" attitude could attract manipulative spirits wishing to structure or use the immense creativity and energy of the Mars competitive spirit. You do love your home and you are responsible with your family. Nevertheless, you prefer to be where the action is, as you get bored easily. If you practice patience, tolerance and diplomacy, there is no limit to where Mars will take you: all the way to the highest level of accomplishment. Your main lesson is to learn all the diplomatic and loving traits of the opposite Venus-ruled sign Libra. Once you find yourself and confidence, the option to become a leader in any chosen field will be given to you. Souls born in the month of April must assume a diplomatic attitude when dealing with others and when dealing with corporate money. The location of your natal Dragon's Head or Tail will seriously alter the strengths or weaknesses of Mars in your chart. See Nostradamus Dragon Forecast for more information. You can learn much more about yourself or anyone else by ordering my new book entitled "I Know All About You", "The Power Of The Dragon" or "And God Created the Stars."

2007— Forecast For Those Born In April

Personal: On June 22nd, 2006, you received the impact of the Dragon's Head in Pisces affecting positively your 12th house regulating all affairs of your subconscious. The Dragon's Head will induce great opportunities to establish a new way of looking at the world of mystery. The Dragon may force you to restructure your own awareness, your inner thoughts and improve your desire to investigate the unknown. The Dragon's Head in Pisces will also help both the studies of metaphysics, dreams and astrology and will sharpen your intuition. This investment will also bring money and spiritual stability to your life. On your subconscious, the Dragon's Head will induce serious fundamental changes and will stimulate your desire for deep mental exploration, but could also bring depression if you use chemicals or nurture negative thoughts. You must keep a positive attitude at all costs, as you will undergo serious psychological changes.

Be ready, and accept those upcoming ethereal changes with confidence. Matters involving the subconscious, your past, mental health, spiritual growth, writing and the arts will become a powerful driving force.

The lucky Aries will enjoy a new and rewarding career, while the older Aries will enjoy watching its children grow. A new way of dealing with your own self worth and creativity will be induced by the Dragon's Head. Many a hard-working souls born in April will get the opportunity to improve their spiritual knowledge and initiate good rewarding careers. Following a spiritual or medical home study, many of you will be promoted to a new position in servicing the world. This will open exciting doors to pass on your knowledge to others and attract very spiritual business partners. In the long run, this impact will also bring about rewarding financial contracts. The Dragon's Tail location in the sign of Virgo in your 6th house (health and work) will impose a total re-structure and may bring serious stress at work and the re-building of your physical appearance. The Dragon will remove unworthy business or emotional partners if needed. This turmoil will induce physical and mental stress, even depression during the waning moons, (see Moon Power publication for dates).

During the New and Full moons of March and September, serious happenings will force you to aim for a different way to service the world. Be prepared to use your will and avoid disheartening thoughts when dealing with all the stress that the Tail of the Dragon may bring. You do not know just yet, but many of your wishes will be granted after the painful restructure. Keep in mind, Aries does well in communication and healing others, thus the Dragon can only help you to further your soul's purpose and help you to run your own show. Much of the trouble may also come from outside forces or too much stress. Challenging regenerative spiritual endeavors, combined with spiritual studies or more social interaction could prove to be beneficial then. Do not let the nasty pull of the Dragon's Tail in your health and work area get the best of your body mind and spirit.

The positive Dragon's Head in Pisces will induce a variety of circumstances to meet new and very spiritual people, especially after the New Moons. Be aware and stay clear from any form of deceiving established religions or guru messages and doctor prescriptions. Within the next two years or so, the spiritual fruits of many years of hard work will begin to pay off. You must learn to face the world with a higher awareness of your self worth. New friends, some born in February and August will also offer you great opportunities to meet different people, thus the potential to find true love and true meaning in life is offered to you. Foreign business association contracts, partnerships, traveling, and luck in general will be offered by some of those new friends. Providing you avoid nurturing pessimistic thoughts about previous failures, a very progressive time is ahead of you. As a rule, those born in April strive for a good position and love, the arts and success can come your way this year. The Dragon's Tail might induce stress at work and on your body but it is needed; those who do not deserve you will have to go. Mars, your ruler, can be surprisingly fast in his rewards to you, especially if you are aware of the Universal Law. When he does, it usually lasts forever. Your awareness of the Moon law and planning accordingly will become a major contribution to reach many of your dreams.

This celestial process will bring you much luck, if you take on the challenge of investing in computerized education, metaphysical pursuits, traveling, and if you accept new challenges with foreign and spiritual partners. The Dragon smiles at you and all of those shining stars will light up your subconscious forces. Serious changes are ahead. Have faith in yourself and the future.

In the year 2007, the great Jupiter (luck) will cruise through the sign of Sagittarius in your 9th house regulating your spiritual learning and teachings. Much progress is to be expected in those areas, especially if you take the time to educate yourself with foreigners and on the creative forces of your subconscious and use it at your advantage. You will need to retire from the world now and then, to recharge your batteries before your wishes can become a reality. Let go of the past and guilt, stay clear for any form of guru or religious deceiving activities and take chances on your own subtle creative power and all will be fine.

You may order some DVD or CD on the "Power of the Subconscious" from www.drturi.com. Be ready for new associations and great business deals with those born in August, February, December and October. You may order your taped 90mn Full Life Reading or your Progressive reading to find out more about the upcoming changes in your life. You could also be much more prepared, if you had your personal Dragon Window Dates at hand, allowing you to bet or stay clear on any business or important decisions during those days. Working in good knowledge and respect of your "Personal Lucky Dragon Window Dates" can be a serious investment in itself and may save you time, money, even your life, if you do a lot of traveling You may request this important service anytime. Visit www.drturi.com go to "order" and fill out the form or call our office at 602-265-7667 for more information. Good luck to all of those born in April.

Venus Governs the Beautiful and Financially Oriented Constellation Of Taurus

> *Luxurious and elegant*
> *I have the memory of an elephant*
> *Loving all of life's finer pleasures*
> *Gifted am I at acquiring more coffers and treasures*
> *I am TAURUS, child of Venus.*

Characteristics For Those Born In May

The month of May is governed by the planet Venus and by the reliable sign of Taurus. Others perceive you as beautiful, somehow stubborn and practical. You are the moneymaking sign of the Zodiac and you have stability and true love to offer to others. You need to control your jealousy, insecurity, and your authoritarian attitudes. You are a gifted artist and strive for organization. You are also attracted to the professions of banking, real estate, the arts, computers, radio, television, Astro-Psychology, aeronautics food, real estate and investigation, to name a few. Many "Bulls" will reach fame and fortune and enjoy the security of a beautiful and big house. Strong and dominant, you have inherited a deep intuition, a tremendous common sense, and a powerful will. Venus rules love and possession; you must avoid destructive thoughts pertaining to jealousy, stubbornness and insecurity. Learn to channel Venus' constructive powers towards creativity, diplomacy and love. If you behave in an insecure stubborn and unattractive manner, you will lose it all in the end. Your down-to-earth approach to life must not interfere with your spiritual growth.

Part of your lesson in this lifetime is to keep an open mind to the world of the spirit and use the metaphysical information to ensure financial growth, by adapting to the moons fluctuations (see Moon Power). Your desire for practicality and riches is legendary, but you will always regenerate with New Age and metaphysical matters. You will courageously handle the difficulties of life with a solid attitude, and you inherited a beautiful nobility of purpose. Girls born in May are beautiful, classic, intellectual, magnetic, and sensitive, and will always combine Venus' beauty and sensual magnetism to attain their goals. You are meticulous and critical about your mate and it is important for you to marry someone well groomed and well respected. With you, love must last forever. Food is often on your mind; do not eat when you are upset. Remember to respect the Universal Law (see Moon

Power), as your awareness and moon planning will become a major contribution towards reaching many of your dreams. The location of your natal Dragons Head or Tail will seriously alter the strengths or weakness of Venus in your chart. You can learn much more about yourself or anyone else by ordering my new book entitled "I Know All About You", "The Power Of The Dragon" or "And God Created The Stars".

2007 — Forecast For Those Born In May

Personal: On June 22nd, 2006, you received the impact of the Dragon's Head in Pisces affecting positively your 11th house regulating all affairs involving your wishes and your friends. The Dragon's Head will induce great opportunities to get involved with new groups and gain new friends, as the old ones must go. The Dragon's Head may force you to restructure many of your wishes and will induce a lot of traveling. Those new friends will stimulate your desire to investigate the unknown or be part of a progressive movement that will benefit your spirit furthering your wishes for great success. The Dragon's Head in Pisces will also induce new study involving computers or a website endeavor and metaphysics. A new desire for mental exploration will become a way to explore your capabilities in servicing the world electronically. Many of you will also consider creating a business (or a child) and you will land on great people or opportunities to do so, because of new acquaintances. On your wish area, the Dragon's Head will induce serious fundamental changes to reach your inner desires and will stimulate traveling both physically and spiritually. Be ready, and accept those upcoming changes with confidence. Matters involving friends, wishes, traveling to Europe/Japan health, education, electronics and the arts, including writing and publishing will become powerful driving forces.

The lucky Taurus soul will enjoy a new home and or a new child, while older Taurus will enjoy their children's children. A new way of dealing with your own self worth and creativity will be induced by the Dragon's Head. Many hard-working May souls will get the opportunity to improve their knowledge with computers and initiate good home businesses. Following home study, many of you will be prone to travel and enjoy a new and stronger position in servicing the world. This will open exciting doors to pass on your knowledge to others, attract very spiritual groups, and make numerous friends. In the end, this impact will also bring about rewarding financial contracts. The Dragon's Tail's location in the sign of Virgo in your 5th house (love and romance) will impose a total re-structure of your love area and may bring serious stress with a strenuous endeavor, a demanding partner, or with a child. The Dragon will remove unworthy business or emotional partners. This turmoil will induce physical and mental stress, even depression, during the waning moons, (see Moon Power publication for dates).

Some Taurus souls will remove or rebirth themselves with an old lover, where all dramatic lessons were painfully learned. Those karmic lovers will undergo a full and total restructure and with it the possibility for an incredible happiness forever after. During the New and Full moons of March and September 2007 serious happenings based upon your karma with some people will take place and force you or them to readjust your views and feelings for them, while others will aim for more personal wishes. Be prepared to use your will and avoid disheartening thoughts when dealing with all the stress that the Tail of the Dragon has or may bring to you. You may not know it just yet, but many of your wishes will be granted after the painful restructure. Keep in mind that Taurus' soul purpose is to further security, feed and protect. Thus the Dragon can only promote your wishes to establish and run your own show if you learn to let go. Challenging regenerative spiritual endeavors, combined with spiritual studies or more social interaction could prove to be beneficial then. Do not let the nasty pull of the Dragon's Tail in your love and speculation area get the best of your body and mind.

Instead, realize the total rebirth-taking place on both sides, and how much both you and your loved one have grown in the process. The potential for true love, respect and long lasting happiness will become a possibility then. The positive Dragon's Head in Pisces will induce a variety of circumstances to meet new and interesting people, especially after the New Moons. The fruits of many months of hard work will begin to pay off, as you might have to relocate to a new house and start fresh again. You must learn to face the world with a higher awareness of your self-worth and work steadily towards your wishes. New friends, some born in July or January will also offer you great opportunities to meet different people, thus the potential to find your true purpose in life. Foreign business association contracts, partnerships, traveling, and luck in general will be offered by some of those new friends.

Providing you avoid nurturing pessimistic thoughts about failure, a very progressive time is ahead of you. As a rule, those born in May strive for security, perfection and health, and this year you can do miracles. The Dragon's Tail might induce trouble, but it is needed. Those who do not deserve you will have to go. Venus your ruler can be surprising in her rewards to you, especially if you are aware of the Universal Law. When she does bestow gifts, they usually last forever. Your awareness of this law and planning accordingly will become a major contribution towards reaching many of your dreams. This celestial process will bring you much luck if you take on the challenge of investing in computerized education, metaphysical pursuits, traveling, and if you accept interests with your new friends. The Dragon smiles at you and all of those shining stars above your head are on your side. Taurus will establish many wishes this year, go for them and let go of your past.

In the year 2007, the great Jupiter (luck) will cruise through the sign of Sagittarius in your 8th house regulating your spiritual learning and corporate endeavors. Much progress is to be expected in those areas, especially if you take the time to educate yourself with foreigners and on the creative forces of your subconscious and use it at your advantage. You may also inherit possessions or money, in a loss that could hurt you at first. Let go of the past and guilt, stay clear for any form of deception or addictions to chemicals and take chances on your own creative power and all will be fine.

You may order some DVD or CD on the "Power of the Subconscious" from www.drturi.com. Be ready for new associations and great business deals with those born in August, February, December and October. You may order your taped 90mn Full Life Reading or your Progressive reading to find out more about the upcoming changes in your life. You could also, be much more prepared, if you had your personal Dragon Window Dates at hand, allowing you to bet or stay clear on any business or important decisions during those days. Working in good knowledge and respect of your "Personal Lucky Dragon Window Dates" can be a serious investment in itself and may save you time, money, even your life, if you do a lot of traveling You may request this important service anytime. Visit www.drturi.com go to "order" and fill out the form or call our office at 602-265-7667 for more information. Good luck to all of those born in May.

Mercury Governs the Nervous and Witty Dual Constellation Of Gemini

Free-Thinking and intelligent
You will not find me under rigorous management
You may think you know me well
Then my other half over you casts a spell
I am GEMINI, child of Mercury.

Characteristics For Those Born In June

The planet Mercury rules the sign of Gemini. You are intellectual, nervous and adaptable. Because of your strong desire to communicate, you are classified in Greek mythology as "The Messengers of the Gods." You inherited a gift of youth, a double personality and a quicksilver mind, enabling you to adapt easily to any situation. On a negative note, Mercury, the "Lord of the Thieves" breeds volatile and unreliable people, due to their dual characteristics. You are a gifted communicator and radio, language, photography, sales, movies, acting, dancing and the medical field and any type of public relations work appeals to you. Your natural speed for life's experiences makes you impatient and nervous. You must learn to focus and crystallize your powerful mind. You have the potential to become an efficient speaker and produce interesting books. Due to your strong desire for security, many of you will be attracted to the real estate and food industries. Your financial potential is unlimited, if you learn and make a good use of the Universal Law in charge of your Second House of income.

A strong Mercury will produce an incredible amount of physical and spiritual energy that must be dissipated. Those children are classified by the unaware psychological fields; as A.D.D. ("Attention Deficit Disorder"). Contrary to what scientists assume and perceive as an indisposition, it is actually a potent gift from God. The soul is simply programmed to naturally reject traditional education, thus opening the rare door to genius and with it the potential for new discovery. Incidentally, President Clinton, Einstein, and I were born with an "ADD affliction." Thus if a teacher is mistaken about some information, the Mercurial soul's inborn sense of curiosity and discovery will bring about potential information leading to the truth. Impatience, nervousness, mental curiosity, and a short attention span are your characteristics. You will never follow long established dogmas. Your Mercurial spirit will open new doors to mental exploration. You are curious by nature and are always questioning. Boredom is your worst enemy and you must associate with intellectual people who can stimulate your incredible mind. Telling jokes is also a part of your mental agility. A word of caution for you: Always be alert when the Moon crosses the deadly sign of Scorpio at work, especially after the Full Moon. Remember to respect the Universal Law (see Moon Power) as your awareness and moon planning will be a major contribution to avoiding dramatic experiences, and will help you reach many of your dreams. The location of your natal Dragon's Head or Tail will seriously alter the strength or weakness of Mercury in your chart. You can learn much more about yourself or anyone else, by ordering my new book entitled "I Know All About You", "The Power Of The Dragon" or "And God Created The Stars".

2007 — Forecast For Those Born In June

Personal: On June 22nd, 2006, you received the impact of the Dragon's Head in Pisces affecting positively your 10th house (career). The Dragon's Head will induce great opportunities to establish a new career or a better option to administer to your world. The Dragon may force you to restructure your education and improve your attitude for success. The Dragon's Head in Pisces will help you to re-create a new image to the world and further your desire to stand high in the eyes of others. Right on your professional life, the Dragon will induce serious change and will not accept anything or anybody trying to stop your progress. Be ready, and accept those changes with confidence. Matters involving medical education, study, the arts, writing languages and publishing will become powerful driving forces.

The lucky Gemini will also enjoy a new home, while older Gemini will enjoy their children's children. A new way of dealing with your home and your family and the real estate will be induced by the Dragon's Tail and may create some stress in your life. Following study, many of those born in June will be promoted to a new position and travel far and fast. This will open exciting doors to pass on your knowledge to others and may bring new business partners. This impact will also bring about rewarding financial contracts. Location of the Dragon's Tail in the sign of Virgo in your 4th house (home) will impose a total re-structure of your base of operation. The Dragon will remove unworthy business deals or wrong emotional partners. This turmoil will induce physical and mental stress, even depression, during the Waning Moons, (see Moon Power publication for dates). During the New and Full moons of March and September 2007 serious happenings, based upon your karma with some people, will take place and force you or them to be in or out of your home and/or business.

Be prepared to use your will and avoid disheartening thoughts when dealing with the failures of your past. You may not know it just yet, but many of your wishes can only be granted after the painful restructure. Much of the trouble may also come from new laws established by your governing superiors or Uncle Sam. Challenging regenerative spiritual endeavors, combined with studies and social interaction, could prove to be beneficial then. Do not let the nasty pull of the Dragon's Tail in your security area get the best of your body and mind. You may be forced to lose a house or experience serious stress with family members. The positive Dragon's Head in Pisces right on your career will induce a variety of circumstances in meeting interesting people and may force a relocation, especially after the New Moons. Within the next two years or so, the fruits of many years of hard work will begin to pay off, as you might have to move and start fresh again. You must learn to face the world with a new positive attitude. New friends, some born in August and February will also offer you great opportunities to meet different people, thus the potential to find love and your true purpose in life. Foreign business association contracts, partnerships, traveling, and luck in general will be offered by some of those new friends.

Provided you avoid nurturing pessimistic thoughts about your past or the family circle, a very progressive time is ahead of you. As a rule, those born in June strive for action, success and mental fame in all aspects of their lives, and this year, you can do miracles. The Dragon's Tail might induce stress, but it is needed. Those who do not deserve you will have to go. Mercury the mental planet is your ruler and can be surprisingly fast in his rewards to you, especially if you are aware of the Universal Laws based upon the moon's fluctuations. Your awareness of this law and planning accordingly will become a major contribution in reaching many of your dreams. This celestial process will bring you much luck if you take on the challenge of investing in any form of education and if you accept new challenges with foreign partners. The Dragon smiles at you and all of those shining stars above your head are supporting your career.

In the year 2007, the great Jupiter (luck) will cruise through the sign of Sagittarius in your 7th house regulating your business or emotional partners. Much progress is to be expected in those areas, especially if you take the time to realize your needs and associate yourself with foreigners. An option to tap the creative forces of your subconscious and use it at your advantage will be offered for you to heal from any emotional stress.

Let go of the past and guilt, stay clear for any form of addictions to chemicals and take chances on your own creative power and all will be fine. You may order some DVD or CD on the "Power of the Subconscious" from www.drturi.com. Be ready for new associations and great business deals with those born in August, February, December and October. You may order your taped 90mn Full Life Reading or your Progressive reading to find out more about the upcoming changes in your life. You could also be much more prepared, if you had your personal Dragon Window Dates at hand, allowing you to bet or stay clear on any business or important decisions during those days. Working in good knowledge and respect of your "Personal Lucky Dragon Window Dates" can be a serious investment in itself and may save you time, money, even your life, if you do a lot of traveling. You may request this important service anytime. Visit www.drturi.com go to "order" and fill out the form or call our office at 602-265-7667 for more information. Good luck to all of those born in June.

The Moon Governs the Nurturing and Caring Constellation Of Cancer

> *I am mother I nurture and provide*
> *In my soul the physical and spiritual collide*
> *I say, "ask and you shall receive."*
> *But also "as you sow, so shall you reap"*
> *I am CANCER, child of the Moon.*

Characteristics For Those Born In July

The moon and the emotional sign of Cancer rule you. You are

a Moonchild and you are strongly affected by the Moon's fluctuations. Family matters will always play an important role in your life. You are classified as the "caretakers" of the Zodiac. Much of your success depends on the awareness and ability to respect and use the moon's passage through the belt of the Zodiac. You are distinctively gifted with real estate and food (cooking or eating it). Lunar children have a solid sense of organization and have inherited strong managerial gifts. You are a perfectionist and are quite critical. Plants, and green appeals to you, and you tend to worry too much about health, to the point of becoming a vegetarian. You will perform very well, in a position of power or management. Financial security is important to you and you will shine through your inner ability to amass riches and possessions. You have a gift with children and you have a natural zest to teach them. You must avoid depressing thoughts of the past and keep control over your powerful imagination. Steadiness, organization, warmth, love, and charm belong to you. Your powerful emotions can be channeled positively with music, singing, and the arts in general (country music is a Cancer/July vibration).

You are attracted to successful people (older or younger mates) and many Cancers marry rich. Your natural tendency to smother family members and friends at all times makes you admired and deeply loved. You must learn to control your overwhelming sensitivity and participate with life outside of your home a little more. As a rule, all Moonchildren are great homemakers unless the soul selected a non-domestic masculine Moon before reincarnating on this dense physical world. Like all other water signs, you regenerate in research, science, and metaphysics. You tend to worry too much about your and others health and you should adopt a more positive spiritual attitude. Learn to let go of the wrong people and move on with life. It is a must, for you to respect the Universal Law (see Moon Power), as your awareness and Moon Planning will become a major contribution toward avoiding dramatic experiences and reaching many of your dreams. The location of your natal Dragon's Head or Tail will seriously alter the strengths or weakness of the Moon in your chart. You can learn much more about yourself or anyone else by ordering my new book entitled "I Know All About You", "The Power Of The Dragon" or "And God Created The Stars".

2007 — Forecast For Those Born in July

On June 22nd, 2006, you received the impact of the Dragon's Head in Pisces affecting positively your 9th house of higher education, philosophy and religion. The Dragon's Head will induce a great opportunity to establish a new mental process of looking positively at the world. After a serious study you may gain serious opportunities to improve your position in life, even recognition, if you decide to crystallize your thoughts, write and publish your work. Dealing with computers is a must, if you have any chance to enjoy this new Dragon's blessing. These studies will help you to structure your thoughts and improve your creativity and prospects for success. The Dragon's Head in Pisces will also seriously sharpen your intuition and improve your desire to travel, physically and mentally. In this new house your potential for a better or improved career will flourish, as long as you are willing to expand and accept the challenges with confidence. Matters involving traveling, education, and foreigners, the arts and publishing, will become a powerful driving force.

The lucky ones will travel far and fast, while others will spend more time shaping up new knowledge. A new way of thinking about your early education and the world at large will be induced by the Dragon's Head. Many hard-working Cancers will also get the opportunity to improve their knowledge of computers, and settle upon a good working position with it. Following study, many souls born in July will also be promoted to a higher position, while others will publish their work worldwide. This restructure will open exciting doors to promising new businesses and careers in foreign lands and dealings with foreigners. This will also bring about rewarding financial contracts. The Dragon's Tail location in the sign of Virgo in your 3rd house (the mind), will impose a total re-vamping of critical thinking, and may induce cosmic consciousness to the advanced soul.

Others more reluctant to accept the Dragon order to seek higher wisdom will solicit peace with dogmatic religious teachings or philosophy and may travel doing so. The Dragon may induce a need to aim for your own higher subconscious creative forces or lead you to guru like study endeavors, where trouble may be awaiting you.

Avoid unworthy or destructive apocalyptic thoughts, as old ideology will have to be removed and replaced by a more spiritually advanced study (astrology etc.) Depression during the waning moons may take place (see Moon Power publication for dates). During the New and Full Moons of September and March 2007 serious happenings based upon your karma will take place, and force you to grow and move away from unworthy partners. Be prepared to use your will to avoid depths of despair when the Dragon's Tail will bother your consciousness. You may not know it just yet, but many of your wishes can only be granted after the painful mental restructure. Stay clear of antidepressants, drugs and alcohol at all costs, as your mental sanity will be challenged to the extreme during this trend.

Much of the trouble may also come from your own self-destructive thoughts. Challenging regenerative spiritual endeavors, combined with new studies and social interaction could prove to be beneficial then. Do not let the nasty pull of the Dragon's Tail in your communication area get the best of your body and mind. Avoid sarcasm at all times, and relax from your creative or spiritual study or work. The positive Dragon's Head in Pisces will induce a variety of circumstances to study, travel and meet interesting foreign people, especially after the New Moons. Within the next two years or so, the fruits of many years of hard work will begin to pay off, as you might have to relocate to a far away place. You must learn to face the world with a new positive attitude. New friends, some born in May, November, March and January will also offer you great opportunities to further your wishes, thus the potential to find love and solid purpose with a good reason to be alive.

Foreign business connections, partnerships, traveling, and luck in general will be offered by some of those new friends. Providing you avoid nurturing pessimistic thoughts about despair or your past, a very progressive time is ahead of you. As a rule, those born in July strive for perfection and a secure love and family life, and this year you can do miracles. The Dragon's Head will induce many opportunities for traveling, speaking, writing and teaching. The Moon your ruler will always reward you while waxing and she can be quite mysterious in rewarding you and when she does it is usually very progressive. Remember to respect the Universal Law (Moon's fluctuations) as your awareness and planning will become a major contribution towards reaching many of your dreams.

In the year 2007, the great Jupiter (luck) will cruise through the sign of Sagittarius in your 6th house regulating your work and health areas, thus don't let unworthy emotional partners drag you down. Much progress is to be expected in those areas, especially if you take the time to realize your needs and associate yourself with foreigners. An option to learn all about the creative forces of your subconscious and use it at your advantage will be offered to you to heal from any emotional stress.

You may order some DVD or CD on the "Power of the Subconscious" from www.drturi.com. Be ready for new associations and great business deals with those born in January, March, May and November. You may order your taped 90mn Full Life Reading or your Progressive reading to find out more about the upcoming changes in your life. You could also be much more prepared, if you had your personal Dragon Window Dates at hand, allowing you to bet or stay clear on any business or important decisions during those days. Working in good knowledge and respect of your "Personal Lucky Dragon Window Dates" can be a serious investment in itself and may save you time, money, even your life, if you do a lot of traveling You may request this important service anytime. Visit www.drturi.com go to "order" and fill out the form or call our office at 602-265-7667 for more information. Good luck to all of those born in July.

The Sun Governs the Flamboyant and Majestic Constellation Of Leo

Powerful and Charming
All things living find me disarming
I step to the center of God's stage
In the books of history I have always a page
I am LEO, child of the Sun.

Characteristics For Those Born In August

The month of August is governed by the all-powerful Sun and by the magnanimous sign of Leo. Your solar sign reflects the dignified Sun's life force energy and classifies you as "The Life Giver". During the day the Sun outshines all the other planets, giving you the option to reach fame, fortune and power during the course of your life. Naturally gifted, you are attracted to professions involving the arts, public life, medicine, research, management, and any endeavors that could offer you a chance to shine. Just as the Sun's rays penetrate the depths of the rainforest, you were born with the potential to bring and promote life to all that you touch. You have a lot to offer others and the world, providing you exercise control over your ego and authoritative nature. The untamed King of the Jungle must positively direct and control the Sun's creative force without burning himself or others in the process. You are fixed and strongly motivated by the will to succeed. Strong and dominant, you nurture a formidable desire to organize and rule others. If you become too overbearing, others will then teach you the lesson of humility, where you will be forced back to start from scratch. Destructive outbursts of emotions and unfettered pride are enemies of success.

Your challenge is to recognize the powerful Sun's energy and diligently work towards a better understanding and respect of others. Acting eccentrically or with pride and without forethought is your weakness. However you will courageously handle all the difficulties of life. The advanced Leo possesses nobility of purpose and great spiritual values. Women born in August are stunning, intellectual, magnetic, and attract others with their enthusiastic solar power. Women born in August are protective and dedicated mothers. The desire for fame could also make them overbearing and try to live through their children's accomplishments. The Sun rules life and you may nurture a subconscious fear of death and decay. But nature gives you a strong mind and a robust body. You love animals, especially horses. You tend to be weak and accident prone in the back, knees and joint areas. (President Clinton was born in August and, busted his knee in Florida!) A word of caution for those born in August: use precaution and moderation when running or jogging. Remember to respect the Universal Law (see Moon Power), as your awareness of Sun/Moon planning will become a major contribution towards reaching love and happiness. The location of your natal Dragon's Head or Tail will seriously alter the strengths or weakness of the Sun in your chart. You can learn much more about yourself or anyone else by ordering my new book entitled "I Know All About You", "The Power Of The Dragon" or "And God Created The Stars".

2007 — Forecast For Those Born in August

Personal: On June 22nd, 2006, you received the impact of the Dragon's Head in Pisces affecting positively your 8th house (corporate money, sex, legacy and spiritual studies). The Dragon's Head will induce great opportunities to gain new partners and their financial support. The Dragon's Head may force you to restructure much of the way you handle corporate endeavors and investments, and could lead you to some new financial real estate endeavors. Some family members or new acquaintances will also stimulate your desire to investigate the unknown and contribute to your advanced intellectual and spiritual gifts. The Dragon's Head in Pisces in your metaphysical area will also help to learn, study, or teach deep matters and sharpen your intuition. In your corporate money house, the Dragon's Head will induce serious financial changes and will stimulate your travel, both physically and spiritually, to improve your options or studies. A new desire for mental exploration will become a way to explore your capabilities in servicing the world. Be ready, and accept those upcoming changes with confidence. Matters involving finances, traveling, health, insurance, legacy, health, metaphysics, education and the arts, including writing and publishing, will become a powerful driving force.

Some lucky souls born in August will enjoy a new spiritual study and gather serious cosmic consciousness, while other older Leo souls will be quite concerned about the affairs of death and lead themselves into a conventional religious upgrade. A new way of dealing with your own self worth and spirituality will be induced by the Dragon's Head. Many hard-working Leos will receive opportunities to improve their knowledge of finance and computers, and initiate good and rewarding businesses. Following an investment in a study, many of you will be traveling and enjoying new positions in servicing the world. This will open exciting doors to pass on your knowledge to others and attract very spiritual friends. In the long run, this impact will also bring about rewarding financial contracts and great self-esteem.

The Dragon's Tail's location in the sign of Virgo in your 2nd house (money/self esteem), will impose a total re-structure of your finances, and this may bring serious stress involving wrong investments. The Dragon will remove unworthy business or emotional partners in the process. This turmoil will induce physical and mental stress, even depression during the Waning Moons (see Moon Power publication for dates). During the New and Full moons of March and September 2007 serious happenings based upon your karma with some people will be forced upon you.

Be prepared to use your will and avoid disheartening thoughts when dealing with all the weight of dealing with death or legacy, including insurance matters brought by the Tail of the Dragon. You may not know it just yet, but many older Leo souls will departs this world and many of your wishes will be granted after the painful restructure. Keep in mind that Leo' soul purpose is to further light, power, love and harmony, in all areas of life. Thus the Dragon can only promote your purpose to establish yourself and run your own show. Much of the trouble may also come from serious losses or new laws established by Uncle Sam. Challenging regenerative spiritual endeavors, combined with spiritual studies or more social interactions, could prove to be beneficial then. Do not let the nasty pull of the Dragon's Tail in your area of finance and spiritual death get the best of your body and mind.

The positive Dragon's Head in Pisces will induce a variety of circumstances to meet new and interesting people, especially after the New Moons. Within the next two years or so, the fruits of many years of hard work will begin to pay off. You must learn to face the world with a higher awareness of your self-worth and work steadily towards your wishes. New friends, some born in February, June, December and April will also offer you great opportunities to meet different people, thus the potential to find love and your true purpose in life. Foreign business connections, partnerships, traveling, and luck in general will be offered by some of those new friends. Providing you avoid nurturing pessimistic thoughts about money or the past, a very progressive time is ahead of you. The Dragon's Tail might induce stress but it is needed. Those who do not deserve your love or your intelligence will have to go. The Sun your ruler can be startling in its rewards to you, especially if you deal with foreigners. And when he does bestow, it usually lasts forever. Your awareness of the Universal Law and planning accordingly will become a major contribution towards reaching many of your dreams. This celestial process will bring you much luck if you take on the challenge and invest in the metaphysical world and spiritual rules. The Dragon will establish many of your financial wishes this year, but you must let go of your past.

In the year 2007, the great Jupiter (luck) will cruise through the sign of Sagittarius in your 5th house regulating your love, children and creativity. So don't let unworthy emotional partners or children drag you down. Much progress is to be expected in those areas, especially if you take the time to realize your need to love and enjoy the children of your own children and associate yourself with foreigners. An option to learn all about the creative forces of your subconscious and use it at your advantage will be offered to you to heal from any emotional stress. Let go of the past and guilt, stay clear for any form of addictions to chemicals and take chances on your own creative power and all will be fine. You may order some DVD or CD on the "Power of the Subconscious" from www.drturi.com. Be ready for new associations and great business deals with those born in August, February, December and October. You may order your taped 90mn Full Life Reading or your Progressive reading to find out more about the upcoming changes in your life.

You could also be much more prepared if you had your personal Dragon Window Dates at hand allowing you to bet or stay clear on any business or important decisions during those days. Working in good knowledge and respect of your "Personal Lucky Dragon Window Dates" can be a serious investment in itself and may save you time, money, even your life, if you do a lot of traveling. You may request this important service anytime. Visit www.drturi.com go to "order" and fill out the form or call our office at 602-265-7667 for more information. Good luck to all of those born in August.

Mercury Governs the Precise and Critical Constellation Of Virgo

Cleansing impurities large and small
Don't think yourself immune, for I see all
Attending to every chore and task
Perfection being all that I ask
I am VIRGO, child of Mercury.

Characteristics For Those Born In September

The month of September is governed by the planet Mercury and by the critical sign of Virgo. You are an intellectual, very critical and picky and you tend to work too hard. You are a master of communication and the option to become a speaker or a great writer is offered to you. You may also misuse this power and become sarcastic to others. You will always combine logic and intuition in dealing with life in general. Astrologically, you have been classified as the "perfectionists". You can do well in the fields of medicine, law, teaching, writing, designing, and office work, and you are in some areas a refined artist. Your downfall is sarcasm and an overly concerned attitude with trivial matters. Some young Mercurial souls are overwhelmed with health matters and turn themselves into health lunatics. Others simply refuse to work and succumb to chemical drug and alcohol abuse. Letting the rational mind scrutinize everything, can hinder your spiritual gifts and neutralize your cosmic consciousness. You have inherited a powerful investigative mind that could lead you to science, chemicals, research, radio, television, newspaper reporting, computer programming and the law.

Advanced souls are great mental leaders and masters in communication. Robert Shapiro and Marcia Clark (O.J. Simpson trial attorneys) are Virgos and indicative of your intellectual potential pertaining to investigation and the law. You may be prone to headaches or head injury, eye and sinus problems. Be aware of your environment in public places. You are prone to poisoning and are strongly advised to keep away from alcohol and narcotics. Also, be aware, diets that are too restrictive may cause just as many problems as over-indulgence. Your body and metabolism are both well equipped to deal with all types of food, including red meat. If your natural desire for perfection prevails and you eliminate this "red" source of food, you must then substitute it with different red foods such as red wine, hot peppers or other thermogenic foods. If you happen to suffer headaches or migraines, you may find relief by walking barefoot on the grass (or close to a body of water) to regenerate from the earth's magnetic field. As a rule all souls born in September are accident prone to head trauma and violent death. Therefore, if you were born in September, do not take chances, especially during or after the Full Moon. Keep in mind to respect the Universal Law (see Moon Power), as your awareness of the Mercury/Moon planning will become a major contribution for happiness. The location of your natal Dragon's Head or Tail will seriously alter the strengths or weakness of Mercury in your chart. You can learn much more about yourself or anyone else by ordering my new book entitled "I Know All About You", "The Power Of The Dragon" or "And God Created The Stars".

2007 — Forecast For Those Born in September

Personal: On June 22nd, 2006, you received the impact of the

Dragon's Head in Pisces affecting positively your 7th house of marriage and business partners. The Dragon's Head will force you to face the world with a different attitude. The Dragon's powerful rays will make you very magnetic to others. Matters involving marriage, contracts and partners will become newfound interests. The lucky souls born in September will find new exotic partners and great financial support, while others may be forced to end long lasting relationships. A new way of thinking about the way you project yourself to the world will be induced by the Dragon, and many hard-working Virgo will get the opportunity to shine with beautiful new partners.

Many Virgo will also be promoted to higher positions or be able to establish new and more powerful personas. This will open exciting doors to promising new business endeavors and rewarding financial contacts. The Dragon's Tail location in your own sign of Virgo in your 1st house (personality) will still force you into a general restructure of your physical and spiritual selves. This could also induce both physical and mental stress including depression, if you let the past or guilt get the best of you. During the New and Full Moons of March and September 2007 serious happenings based upon your personal karma and dealings with others will take place. You are strongly advised to use your will and avoid depressing or destructive thoughts. Challenging regenerative spiritual endeavors, combined with studies and social interaction, could prove to be beneficial then. Do not let the nasty pull of the Dragon's Tail get the best of your body, mind and brilliant spirit. The positive Dragon's Head in Pisces will induce a variety of circumstances to meet interesting, either much younger, or older people in your life.

Within the next few months or so, the fruits of many years of hard work will begin to pay off, as you may be forced to face the world with a new vision or a new partner and a new attitude. Those new partners will offer great opportunities to travel and learn where foreigners will play an important part in your life. The new Dragon's Head in general, will offer foreign business interests, partnerships, traveling, and luck. Providing you keep busy and avoid nurturing pessimistic thoughts about previous unworthy partners or cultivating deep guilt feelings, a very progressive time is ahead of you. As a rule, those born in September strive for power and investigation. Mercury your ruler can be quite fast in his rewards, but when he does offer changes, take them without hesitation. Remember to respect the Universal Law, as your awareness of the moon's fluctuations will become a major contribution for your success. The opportunity to make serious progress with others is available to you. This celestial process will bring you much luck if you take on the challenge of investing and trusting others and if you associate with new advanced or very creative partners, as those shining stars above your head are on your side.

In the year 2007, the great Jupiter (luck) will cruise through the sign of Sagittarius in your 4th house regulating your home security family matters and real estate endeavors. So don't let unworthy emotional partners slow down your progress. Much progress is to be expected in those areas, especially if you take the time to realize your need to be supported by a great partner and solid love and associate yourself with foreigners. An option to learn all about the creative forces of your subconscious and use it at your advantage will also be offered to you to heal from any emotional stress. Let go of the past and guilt, stay clear for any form of addictions to chemicals and take chances on your own creative power and all will be fine. You may order some DVD or CD on the "Power of the Subconscious" from www.drturi.com. Be ready for new associations and great business deals with those born in March, May, January and July. You may order your taped 90mn Full Life Reading or your Progressive reading to find out more about the upcoming changes in your life.

You could also be much more prepared, if you had your personal Dragon Window Dates at hand, allowing you to bet or stay clear on any business or important decisions during those days. Working in good knowledge and respect of your "Personal Lucky Dragon Window Dates" can be a serious investment in itself and may save you time, money, even your life, if you do a lot of traveling. You may request this important service anytime. Visit www.drturi.com go to "order" and fill out the form or call our office at 602-265-7667 for more information. Good luck to all of those born in September.

Venus Governs the Diplomatic and Peaceful Constellation Of Libra

Lover of grace and harmony
Seeking the balance of matrimony
Though there are those that hold to opinions tight
I will see it in all the different lights
I am LIBRA, child of Venus.

Characteristics For Those Born In October

The month of October is ruled by the planet Venus and by the charming sign of Libra. You are strongly motivated by a desire for justice and you must create harmony in all areas of life. You are classified as the "Peacemaker" in Astro-Psychology. You will succeed in your career because of your gentle personality, your sense of diplomacy and your natural "savoir faire." You rarely learn by mistake, but you must avoid prolonged indecision. Those born in October must establish Libra's soul's purpose of achieving balance, emotional, financial, and spiritual stability during the course of their lifetimes. You must stand for yourself and learn decision making by following not only your rational mind but also your accurate intuitions. You possess a strong psychological aptitude and do well in the real estate and the food industries, the stock market, interior design, marriage counseling and the arts in general. You must focus on what you need first by using inner stamina and both your practical and intuitive minds. These gentle personalities will be attracted to competitive people and one can expect many challenges from them. Rough behavior or the abrupt and assertive manner of a business partner easily offends Libras. The same desire for diplomacy is expected from a friend or a lover. You should also avoid taking remarks too personally.

You love a good home and you enjoy the company of business-oriented partners. Your downfall comes from traditional scientific or religious teachings and your refusal to challenge your early tutoring or addictions. Casting aside self-discovery and real spirituality will slow down or eliminate your chances to develop your cosmic consciousness and establish emotional and spiritual stability. This produces mental snobs, librarians, ministers, priests and religious leaders. As indicated by Libra's scale, you must look at both sides of the dilemma. Using both traditional and untraditional means of education will bring about a better awareness of the laws. The limitation of conventional education (psychology or religion) is overridden by a more progressive spiritual attitude (New Age and Astro-Psychology) and will bring about all the answers you seek.

You are a philosopher and a great teacher; likewise, you will travel far in search of the truth. The truth you are aiming for is right above your heads in the stars. A word of caution to you: stay clear of all chemicals, such as pot, drugs, or alcohol, as these destructive habits could lead you to a hospital or worse to jail. Remember to respect the Universal Law (see Moon Power), as your awareness of Moon planning will become a major contribution for your happiness and success. The location of your natal Dragon's Head or Tail will seriously alter the strengths or weaknesses of Venus in your chart. You can learn much more about yourself or anyone else by ordering my new book entitled "I Know All About You", "The Power Of The Dragon" or "And God Created The Stars".

2007 — Forecast For Those Born in October

Personal: On June 22nd, 2006, you received the impact of the Dragon's Head in Pisces affecting positively your 6thth house of work and health. The Dragon's Head will force you to face the world with a different attitude as far as work or your body is concerned and you will be in serious demand by others. Matters involving work, health, and security will become profound interests. The lucky ones will find great real estate deals and will be able to service the world from a new and beautiful base of operation. Other souls born in October may also benefit from a study and improve their service to the world. The Dragon Tail located in your subconscious will induce a new option for you to perceive the spiritual world outside of what you firmly believe to be true. Many Libras will become extraordinarily sensitive, as they will be forced by the Dragon's Tail to undergo deep and serious psychological changes. The unlucky ones will seek help against depressions or panic attacks through religion or traditional psychology or psychiatry. Doing so will make their subconscious even more fragile to the side effects of dangerous medical prescriptions.

The advanced Libra soul will aim for higher learning and gain peace through a rewarding position of responsibility. Those who worked hard the last two years will be able to travel, teach or publish their works. The passage of the Dragon in both the sign of Pisces/Virgo in 2007 will open exciting new doors in both the spiritual and physical worlds. This promises many new business endeavors and rewarding financial contacts. The Dragon's Tail's location in your subconscious 12th house will induce a general restructure of your psyche and your spiritual self. This could induce some depression during the waning moon periods. Invest in celestial spiritual study (astrology) and avoid any form of conventional religious or guru type of endeavors. Stay clear of alcohol, drugs and the use of antidepressants at all costs. Most of all; let go of your past, guilt and the wrong people in your life.

During the New and Full Moons of March and September 2007 (see Moon Power publication for dates) serious happenings based upon your personal karma will take place. Again, you are strongly advised to use your will and avoid depressing or guilty thoughts. Regenerative spiritual endeavors and metaphysical studies, combined with exercise and social interaction, could prove to be beneficial then. Do not let the nasty pull of the Dragon's Tail get the best of your subconscious and your body. The positive Dragon's Head in Pisces will induce a variety of opportunities to improve your spiritual knowledge, your physical body and your working life. Taking care of your body by joining a health club can only prove beneficial in the long run. Within the next few months or so, the fruits of many years of hard work will begin to pay off, as you may be forced to service the world with a more advanced attitude.

The Dragon will also offer great opportunities where foreigners will play an important part of your working life. Foreign business interests, partnerships, traveling, and luck in general will be offered by the new Dragon's Head. Providing you keep busy and avoid nurturing pessimistic thoughts about your physical or mental health, a very progressive time is ahead of you. As a rule, those born in October have tendencies for addictions and many strive for freedom, traveling, and mental exploration. Venus your ruler is fair in her rewards to you and when she does bestow; love and security usually last forever. Remember to respect the Universal Law (see Moon Power), as this is a major contribution to your success in life. The opportunity to make serious progress this year is available to you. This celestial process will bring you much luck if you take on the challenge of investing in astrology, computerized education, metaphysical pursuits, traveling, and if you associate with new partners. Those shining stars above your head are on your side and you can make the most of them.

In the year 2007, the great Jupiter (luck) will cruise through the sign of Sagittarius in your 3rd house regulating your mental process, education, traveling and foreigners, thus don't let unworthy emotional partners slow down your progress. Much progress is to be expected in those areas, especially if you take the time to realize your need to grow spiritually and be supported by a great partner. Associating with foreigners is also a way for you to regenerate your spirit. An option to learn all about the creative forces of your subconscious and use it at your advantage will also be offered to you to heal from any emotional stress. Let go of the past and guilt, stay clear for any form of addictions and take chances on your own creative power and all will be fine. You may order some DVD or CD on the "Power of the Subconscious" from www.drturi.com. Be ready for new associations and great business deals with those born in March May, January and July. You may order your taped 90mn Full Life Reading or your Progressive reading to find out more about the upcoming changes in your life.

You could also be much more prepared, if you had your personal Dragon Window Dates at hand, allowing you to bet or stay clear on any business or important decisions during those days. Working in good knowledge and respect of your "Personal Lucky Dragon Window Dates" can be a serious investment in itself and may save you time, money, even your life, if you do a lot of traveling. You may request this important service anytime. Visit www.drturi.com go to "order" and fill out the form or call our office at 602-265-7667 for more information. Good luck to all of those born in October.

Pluto Governs the Mighty Constellation of Scorpio "The Eagle or Lizard."

Holder of all the secrets deep
Never speaking for they are mine to keep
For those who plunder without care
Tread carefully for I see you there
I am SCORPIO, child of Pluto.

Characteristics For Those Born In November

The planet Pluto and the intense sign of Scorpio govern the month of November. You inherited a powerful will and you are attracted to the unknown; the medical professions, the police force, metaphysics, politics and general investigations. You are classified as the "Eagle" (positive) or the "Lizard" (negative) in Divine Astrology. You are quite private, secretive, even mystic and like all other water signs, you excel in the study of metaphysics. Unless you are aware of your innate powers you are well advised not to sting yourself with your own dart. You carry in your soul the element of life and death, reincarnation and pure sensuality. On a negative note, your magnetic thoughts can reach anyone anywhere for good or for worse, bringing its accompanying karma into your life. The young Scorpio soul will experience drama, despair and imprisonment during the course of its life. However, the destructive energies of Pluto can be channeled positively to accomplish tremendous results. Your sign rules the Mafia, the police force and the absolute power of creation or destruction, including sex. The message is quite clear when representing anyone born in November. No one should take chances under Pluto's command. Realize the Eagle in you is your challenge and your own birthright for creation or destruction. These souls have no known fears in the face of death.

Many advanced Pluto children will "fly" like an eagle above the destructive Lizard emotions and legendary jealousy. You can use your inborn mystical gifts to succeed where others would fail. Strong, private and dominant, you were born with a practical mind and an acute intuition. Your lesson is to control and direct constructively your deep emotions and use Pluto's ultimate power for the well being of society. You regenerate with investigation and spiritual growth, and must uncover your unique mission in life. You are interested and aspire only for the undiluted truth. The women of this sign are seen in Divine Astrology as "la femme fatale." You are sensual, classic, intellectual, reserved, and super magnetic. You tend to use your inner sexual power and physical beauty to reach your goals. However, even as a powerful Scorpio, you are very weak with affairs of the heart and tend to be in love with love. A word of caution for you: Do not use your poisonous stinger against yourself or society. Remember to respect the Universal Law (see Moon Power), as your awareness and Moon planning will become a major contribution to your happiness and success. The location of your natal Dragon's Head or Tail will seriously alter the strength or weakness of Pluto in your chart. (See Nostradamus Dragon Forecast for more information). You can learn much more about yourself or anyone else by ordering my books entitled "I Know All About You", "The Power of the Dragon" or "And God Created The Stars".

2007 — Forecast For Those Born In November

Personal: On June 22nd, 2006, you received the impact of the Dragon's Head in Pisces affecting positively your 5th house of love, romance and speculations. The Dragon's Head will force you to face the world with a different attitude towards love, children and all that you have accepted as true. The Dragon's powerful energy in this house will make you very magnetic to others. Matters involving money, security, love and children may become a powerful new interest. The lucky Scorpio will find new partners and enjoy children and great financial opportunities, while others may be forced to end long lasting relationships with a lover or a child. A new way of thinking about the way you project yourself, your love to others and to the world, will be induced by the Dragon and many hard-working souls born in November will get the opportunity to create a business or a child, and shine in the process. Many will also be promoted to a higher position or be able to publish their light work and endeavors. This will open exciting doors to promising new business endeavors and rewarding financial contacts. The Dragon's Tail's location in Virgo, your 11th house (friends/wishes), will still force you into a general restructure of all affairs ruled by this house. Wrong friends or wrong groups (and their ideals) or impractical wishes will produce physical and mental stress during the waning moon periods of the current year. During the New and Full Moons of March and September 2007, serious happenings based upon your karma with others will take place. You are strongly advised to steer clear of drugs, alcohol and relaxants, and use your will to avoid depressing thoughts.

Challenging regenerative spiritual endeavors, combined with studies and social interaction may prove to be beneficial during those times of depression. Do not let the nasty Dragon's Tail pull at your house of wishes and friends get the best of your body and mind and control gambling. The positive Dragon's Head in Pisces will induce a variety of circumstances to meet either interesting younger or older people, and will promote all the affairs of love and romance. Within the next few months, karma will be burnt and you may be forced to face the world with a new and much better partner, if you learn to let go.

Those new partners will offer great opportunities where foreigners will play an important part of your life. Foreign business association contracts, partnerships, traveling exotic places and luck in general will be offered by the new Dragon's Head in Pisces. Providing you keep busy and avoid nurturing pessimistic thoughts about previous partners, a very progressive time is ahead of you. As a rule, those born in November strive for power and public honorable standing and career position. Pluto is very dramatic in his karmic rewards but when he does bestow, it usually lasts forever. Remember to respect the Universal Law (the moon's fluctuations), as this is a major contribution to your success or failure in life. The opportunity to make serious progress in business and love is available to you this year. This celestial process will bring you much luck, if you take on the challenge of investing in computerized education, metaphysical pursuits, traveling, and if you associate with new partners provided by the Dragon. Those shining stars above your head are on your side.

In the year 2007, the great Jupiter (luck) will cruise through the sign of Sagittarius in your 2nd house regulating your resources and self esteem, thus don't let unworthy emotional partners slow down your progress. Much progress is to be expected in those areas, especially if you take the time to realize your need to let go of the past and grow spiritually. Associating with foreigners is also a way for you to regenerate your spirit. An option to learn all about the creative forces of your subconscious and use it at your advantage will also be offered to you to heal from any emotional stress. Let go of the past and guilt, stay clear for any form of addictions and take chances on your own creative power and all will be fine. You may order some DVD or CD on the "Power of the Subconscious" from www.drturi.com. Be ready for new associations and great business deals with those born in March, May, January and July. You may order your taped 90mn Full Life Reading or your Progressive reading to find out more about the upcoming changes in your life.

You could also be much more prepared if you had your personal Dragon Window Dates at hand, allowing you to bet or stay clear on any business or important decisions during those days. Working in good knowledge and respect of your "Personal Lucky

Dragon Window Dates" can be a serious investment in itself and may save you time money even your life if you do a lot of traveling. You may request this important service anytime. Visit www.drturi.com go to "order" and fill out the form or call our office at 602-265-7667 for more information. Good luck to all of those born in November.

Jupiter Governs the Philosophical and Educated Constellation of Sagittarius

I have traveled the worldwide
With naught but the law on my side
Yearning for the higher knowledge
All of God's creation as my college
I am SAGITTARIUS, child of Jupiter.

- Characteristics For Those Born In December

The planet Jupiter and the sign of Sagittarius govern the month of December. You are a philosopher, a natural teacher and classified in Divine Astrology as "Truth Seeker." You would do well in learning or teaching computers, aeronautics, law, religion, communications, radio, and language. You are also attracted to holistic healing, animals, Indians, and the world of sports. Your desire to travel to foreign lands is quite strong. Doing so will take you far away, giving you the option to return with incredible knowledge to teach to the rest of us. You were born with the gift of teaching and you will always promote a form of purity and organization in life. You can do quite well in office work and you can be extremely organized. You inherited a quick mind from the stars and you can keep up with anyone willing to discuss knowledge and philosophy. You need to realize the importance of education and you must focus on your chosen goals. Jupiter, "The Lord of Luck," will throw you many blessings in your life. With discipline and determination, you have the potential to produce interesting books, even novels. The young Sagittarius soul is too concerned with finances and must learn to give so that he may receive help from the accumulated good karma.

You must adapt to the saying, "to be a millionaire, you must act and think like one." Your sign rules the wilderness, the desert, and the Indians. This also represents some of your past lives with the Incas, the Sumerians and Atlantis, where you had a position of spiritual power. A word of caution: Souls born with an overbearing Jupiter energy must guard against the codification of thoughts (books) and biblical materials; your lesson is to realize that God cannot be confined to any man-made buildings, deities or archaic doctrines. The advanced ones (truth seekers) will lead the rest of us towards the reality of God's manifestation through the stars. Remember to respect the Universal Law (see Moon Power), as your awareness of Moon planning will become a major contribution to your happiness and success. The location of your natal Dragon's Head or Tail will seriously alter the strength or weakness of Jupiter in your chart. You can learn much more about yourself or anyone else by ordering my books entitled "I Know All About You", "The Power Of The Dragon" or "And God Created The Stars".

2007 — Forecast For Those Born In December

Personal: On June 22nd, 2006, you received the impact of the Dragon's Head in Pisces affecting positively your 4th house of home, real estate and family matters. The Dragon's Head will force you to face the world with a different attitude as far as general security is concerned. Matters involving moving, family, purchasing a new home or improving the old one will be of profound interest. The lucky ones will find great real estate deals and will be able to service the world from a new and beautiful base of operation. A new way of thinking about the way you perceive your security and your old days will be induced by the Dragon's Head. Many souls born in December operating in the food industry or teachings will also be promoted to a higher place and gain a position of responsibility. The passage of the Dragon in Pisces and Virgo will open exciting new doors in both the 4th (home) and 10th houses (career) and all affairs related to those houses have to change for the better. This promises many new business endeavors and rewarding financial contacts especially with foreigners. The Dragon's Tail location in your house of career will induce a general restructure of your occupation where much work will be accomplished from the home and then travels to far away places. This could induce quite a lot of activity and social interaction during the Waxing Moon periods. Some lucky Sagittarius will expand the family circle with new arrivals.

During the New and Full Moons of March and September 2007 (see Moon Power publication for dates), serious positive or difficult happenings based upon your personal karma will take place. Again, you are strongly advised to use your will and avoid depressing thoughts. Regenerative spiritual endeavors, combined with studies, exercise and social interaction, could prove to be beneficial at those moments. Do not let the nasty pull of the Dragon's Tail affecting your career get the best of your body and mind. The positive Dragon's Head in Pisces has much to offer and will induce a variety of opportunities to improve your working life, right from your base of operation. Building and promoting a group or some kind of club from home can only prove beneficial in the long run. Within the next few months or so, the fruits of many years of hard work will begin to pay off as you may be forced to service the world on a much higher level.

The Dragon will also offer great opportunities where security and family matters will play an important part of your working life. Foreign business associations, contracts, partnerships and traveling are also ahead. The new Dragon's Head in Pisces, the sign of the cinematography industry and the spirit will offer you with luck. Provided you keep busy and avoid nurturing pessimistic thoughts about your new career, a very progressive time is ahead of you. As a rule, those born in December strive for freedom, traveling and mental exploration. Jupiter is a lucky planet and will reward you in time. Remember to respect the Universal Law (see Moon Power), as this is a major contribution to your success or failure in life. The opportunity to make serious progress this year is available to you. This celestial process will bring you much luck if you take on the new challenge and invest in education, metaphysical pursuits, traveling, and if you associate with new partners. Those shining stars above your head are on your side and you can make the most of them.

In the year 2007, the great Jupiter (luck) will cruise through the sign of Sagittarius in your 1st house regulating yourself and the way the world sees you. Thus don't let unworthy emotional partners slow down your progress. Much progress is to be expected in your health and business, if you discipline yourself with food intake and regular exercises. Associating with foreigners is also a way for you to regenerate your spirit. An option to learn all about the creative forces of your subconscious and use it at your health advantage will also be offered to you to heal from any emotional stress. Let go of the past and guilt, stay clear for any form of addictions and take chances on your own creative power and all will be fine. You may order some DVD or CD on the "Power of the Subconscious" from www.drturi.com. Be ready for new associations and great business deals with those born in June, August, February and April. You may order your taped 90mn Full Life Reading or your Progressive reading to find out more about the upcoming changes in your life.

You could also be much more prepared, if you had your personal Dragon Window Dates at hand, allowing you to bet or stay clear on any business or important decisions during those days. Working in good knowledge and respect of your "Personal Lucky Dragon Window Dates" can be a serious investment in itself and may save you time, money, even your life, if you do a lot of traveling. You may request this important service anytime. Visit www.drturi.com go to "order" and fill out the form or call our office at 602-265-7667 for more information. Good luck to all of those born in December.

He is wise who understands that the stars are luminaries, created as signs. He who conquers the stars will hold the golden keys to God's mysterious universe
— Nostradamus

⁕ 2007 Moon Power Starguide ⁕

Welcome to Your Day - to - Day Guidance
For January 2007

January 3rd, 2007 – Full Moon in Cancer: The Full Moon will mature in the loving, family-oriented sign of Cancer. Expect some serious career or personal developments to take place. Some will be starting new jobs and others will drop them; this may also include a business relationship. Promotion or deception, whichever happens to you (or others) will mark an important part of your life. Just be ready to accept the upcoming changes with faith in your new future. Be ready to provide a supportive shoulder to the victims. Nature may also decide to do some nasty tricks in some states, promoting bad weather or earthquakes. The government will have to take serious steps to keep peace in some parts of the world. The Moon rules this sign. Expect the beginning or ending of important phases of your life. This lunation could represent a very important part your destiny. You may be forced to let go of your past, accept your new future with confidence. Many will be affected and forced to move on around you. The US will be touched directly and the dramatic impact will affect many families in the long run. Keep a positive attitude and have faith in the government decisions for the future. Do something for someone you care about and offer my book to them, remember Moon Power is a limited edition and many people get really frustrated, when they cannot get their copy of Moon Power. Think of it as a present and realize how much help you are offering the people you care for most, with my guidance.

Lunation impact on all signs

Aries - Relocation ahead of you and changes in your career soon. Accept those changes.

Taurus - An important letter or disturbing news is ahead of you, have faith.

Gemini - You will be forced to spend money for home or your family.

Cancer - Serious business or emotional stress is ahead of you. Changes are needed in your life.

Leo - Let go of your past, move on. Time to look for the future and avoid guilt, be ready.

Virgo - You need to go out with your friends. New ones will bring you love and wishes soon.

Libra - Great career changes are ahead of you. You might have to go or look somewhere else.

Scorpio - A trip or someone far away will need you. Big business must be done.

Sagittarius - A legacy or a present is in store for you. Be strong, you will need it.

Capricorn - You will have to work on yourself and your partner soon. Endings are ahead.

Aquarius - A great new opportunity to serve the world will be offered to you. Move on.

Pisces - A chance to find new love is offered to you. A friend will need your help.

January 4, 2007 — Venus enters Aquarius: With the planet of love in the independent sign of Aquarius, an opportunity to fall for an original, even powerful person, will be given to you. This trend will allow many freedom-oriented souls to find intellectual, new age partners, and to enjoy their magnetism and the respect they worked so hard to establish. Some lucky souls will be given the opportunities to enjoy electrifying love experiences; they may end up with memorable moments to cherish for the rest of their lives. If your natal Venus is in a hard aspect to Uranus, your desire for freedom and experience will take over the real feeling and need for true love. If she is well aspected, then an incredible and solid marriage will take place and surprise many people. Souls born now will be given the opportunity to experience love on an intellectual level and will have to learn to show more emotion and compassion. Again, If Venus is badly aspected then the soul will suffer many disturbing and short relationships with abusive partners, who will behave badly especially on a sexual level. Intellectual exchanges, honesty and freedom are needed with this position. Blessed with such a universal love, Venus in Aquarius will offer the soul an opportunity to attract an incredible, loyal, creative, intellectual, even original partner. This position makes for one of the most original and magnetic partners. Usually artistic talent in writing, talking, photography, acting, and mental medicine is present with this position. This is a top position for those involved in the artistic, medical or scientific and research fields. Souls born now will travel the world in their lifetimes. They will be attracted to beautiful, intellectually stimulating partners and will be inclined to marry foreigners. I was born with this Mercury position.

※

MON., TUE., WED., THU. — JANUARY 1, 2, 3, 4:
RULERS —Mercury (Rational power / traveling) and the Moon (Ending parts of life):

Work, Career and Business: The Moon is nearly Full (difficult) and the universe won't further new opportunities for much longer. This may force you into a change with your business endeavors. Use Mercury's mental power to promote yourself or clarify a difficult situation with others. For those involved in sales, this lunation will not bring worthwhile arrangements and some of us will have to deal with important legal documents. During the upcoming waning moon, you may be forced to sign important paper work, if you decide to get rid of a situation (or a person!).

Partnerships: Nothing is made to last forever, not even relationships and you may be able to see what's ahead of you. This process will impose many changes, prodding you towards new experiences and valuable knowledge. Do not hold tightly to your past; you only make yourself miserable until you can't take

Day-to-Day Guidance ❖ January

it any more. Only when the changes are accepted will the stars shine upon you and your new destiny. Keep a positive attitude no matter what.

Family and Friends: Many will enjoy good food and the family circle these days. If you decide to dine out it would be wise to make reservations, as the local restaurants will be busy. Don't expect good service or good food. It is a good time to enjoy wide-open spaces with children and pets. Expect news from mom, brothers or sisters, soon.

Love Affairs: Do some listening; avoid talking too much about you or your past. Nurture positive thoughts about life in general. A trip close to nature or the water would be great for both of you. Candlelight, good wine, great food, and soft music are there for you to enjoy with your partner. Take some pictures and have fun. If single, go out with friends you know and do not be too trusting of a stranger's words. Participate with life wisely. Those born in January will be attracted to older or younger people born in September, July or May.

Travel and Communication: Do not expect much good news to arrive via mail or telephone close to a Full Moon. A person you know who is going in a direction that you disapprove of, could benefit from your advice. This individual might need more emotional support to deal with past experiences; don't let this affect your own psyche and learn to say no. Soon depressed friends may need more support from you; don't expect much reward from them. Avoid being critical with old friends, as your remarks could be misinterpreted and could haunt you for a while. Be aware, if you're invited to a party this weekend, don't believe in all that you hear. Be nice and happy; impress everyone with your attitude. With a bit of luck, one of your wishes can be granted before the Full Moon, if you mean business with your subconscious. A trip to your past could bring you joy. Keep in mind to service the car before leaving your city, and drive safely.

Environment: Thousands of people will be forced to relocate during this type of celestial configuration soon. Nature may decide to throw a nasty message to man; quakes, volcanoes, tornadoes, explosions, floods are very high on the list. Let's hope for the sake of many, that this lunation won't be too difficult. Take NO chances after or during this lunation and check my website for my quatrains and heed my warnings.

Famous Personalities: Many prominent people will come in or out of a situation, business or a bad marriage. The beginning or ending of important phases of life is active for all of us. Famous or not, they are under the same stars and will suffer the reality of life.

Events: Be ready for the government (foreign or the U.S.) to make important decisions. Some elected officials might be forced to depart from office. The United States, France and Japan could be touched directly.

Shopping: Avoid spending too much money on anything. If you need a new answering machine or a new telephone, wait for the next New Moon. Purchase books now that could teach you something spiritual. Its not too late to offer Moon Power, if it works for you, it will work for someone you know in need.

※

FRI., SAT., SUN ., MON., TUE. — JANUARY 5, 6, 7, 8, 9:
RULERS — The Moon (Endings) Sun (Love/children) and Mercury (Travel/words):

Work, Career and Business: With the Waning Moon upon you, do not expect much luck these days. A new job or a better position may be what you need and could be attained in the near future. Renew your confidence and support to your worldly ambitions and don't let the waning moon affect you negatively. Keep a low profile for now.

Partnerships: Come clean with what you mean with a partner; miscommunication does happen and usually leads to trouble. Go easy in expressing your feelings; don't let the sad Moon blur your vision or your words. Re-schedule an important meeting.

Family and Friends: Don't expect much with family members or friends either. Expect disturbing news from children or some friends and help them to get on with their lives. Avoid stressing and let them know when they abuse your time on the phone. Children will also be a bit unmanageable and nervous. Use lots of patience with them and remember their sensitivity, if they are teenagers. They could be hurt with your attitude and this could damage your relationship later in life. Discipline them carefully, assist their young wills, and help build their self-esteem.

Love Affairs: With the Waning Moon above your head, any reliable love relationship won't be available for a while. An unexpected invitation to a gathering could bring an interesting person into your life. Use your head, not your heart, and you'll be fine. The Sun's revitalizing power should be used to rekindle your feelings for some of the friends or lovers you really trust. A good romantic movie will help you release some feelings you may have for someone you care about. If you are single, and born in February, spend valuable time with those born under the sign of Leo, Gemini or Libra.

Travel and Communication: As always, with Mercury in charge, take good care of your car and drive cautiously. Be ready for bad surprises coming your way. You may be unexpectedly asked to drive somewhere soon; wherever you want to be, drive slow and be aware of the Waning Moon and don't take any chances with the cops. Avoid gossiping about someone close to you. Words travel fast; be aware as you may lose that person's friendship.

Environment: With the Waning Moon in progress, Mother Nature might respond to our closest satellite's disturbing the earths magnetic field. Some lives may be swept away with flooding. Some surprising developments will make the news on CNN. Explosions and volcanic eruptions are on the way. Some naturalist groups will be concerned and active in making the rest of us aware of nature's wonderful blessings.

Famous Personalities: A famous person will see the surprising end of his/her life and many will miss the great soul. Under the same type of energy on February 19, 1997, Beijing China formally declared six days of mourning for Deng Xiaoping, as the nation began to come to terms with the death of its leader of two decades.

Events: This is the type of occurrence with these energies at play: December 17, 1997- More than 100 dead after typhoon lashes Vietnam. On February 24, 1997, in New York -- A man opened fire on an observation deck of the Empire State Building, killing one person and wounding six before shooting himself in the head. The gunman, Ali Abu Kamal a 69-year-old Palestinian, was taken to a hospital where he died more than five hours later. The children will be in danger keep an eye on them on the road.

Shopping: If you are an investor, hold on to your gold assets or you may be stuck in a bad transaction and lose. Presents will be offered to those deserving loving souls. Do not invest right now in a specific interest or creative study. A garage sale is where great bargains are available now.

※

Note: Attention Pluto is back with us — With Mars now in the sign of Sagittarius and during a waning moon expect dramatic happenings from foreign lands; control is a must. The Lord of Hades doesn't forget and doesn't forgive; don't be a victim. Be aware of Pluto's destructive power and terrorist offspring.

WED., THU., FRI., SAT., SUN. — JANUARY 10, 11, 12, 13, 14:
RULERS — Venus (Hot love/lust) Pluto (Drama/secrets/sex):

Work, Career and Business: Don't let Pluto tempt you to take any form of unlawful shortcut, consider the dramatic impact and the potential for disaster, even death. These days will bring about wake-up calls for many unaware people. Do not expect anything to go your way, as people will show the worse traits of their personality. Be easy with your words, avoid meetings with strangers, and don't take any phone calls or threats lightly. Don't let Pluto and Mars sting everyone and everything to death. Use your intuition in all you do and be ready for concealed financial or sexual business to surface. Early plans have to be suddenly abandoned and this means business and career momentum could be lost.

Partnerships: Spend time reorganizing the home and the office, throw old things away and look busy at all times. The boss or co-workers are also affected by those negative stars and could make your life misery. Someone may try to show you the error of your ways on your dietary habits, perhaps a co-worker or a critical friend. The stars want you to consider, re-think and be cautious. You may have to slow down now and put on your thinking and rational judgment caps concerning key partnerships. Be diplomatic, as your weakness or errors won't go unnoticed. You may want to listen carefully to what is said for or against you; those comments deserve your attention. Pluto will damage your partnership if you do not consider, re-think or be cautious. You may have to use your rational judgment concerning key partnerships. Some changes are imminent.

Family and Friends: Some of your friends will experience dramatic endings to some portions of their lives and your supportive shoulder will be requested. At home or at work expect arguments, making these days miserable. Aggravations that could continue into the evening hours could have serious repercussions and may bring police into the neighborhood. Keep your head cool; stay calm and patient.

Love Affairs: Be ready for secrets to surface; however, bits and pieces of information may be wrong or missing. Do not make important decisions about a situation or a person just now. Concealed love trysts will be taking place all over, and will keep a bunch of insidious investigators active. Don't trust strangers; Pluto always induces drugs, alcohol and rapes. Protect yourself at all cost if you're sexually active now; the signature of Pluto is death and AIDS! If you were born under the sign of Pisces, those born in September, November or July will be strongly attracted to you. Use your head, not your heart!

Travel and Communication: Avoid long trips by air, plane or ship, the stars and terrorists are not positive and do not care about anyone — they just do the work they were intended to do by God's higher order.

Environment: Be ready for nasty surprises, especially the ones with nature's forces at work. Expect events such as -- A powerful 7.3 earthquake shook southwest Pakistan killing at least 40 people in an impoverished area dotted with flimsy homes made of sun-baked mud. During this Plutonic time another quake killed 100, injures 250 in northern Iran. See the power of Pluto by investigating my site and how this disruptive planet affects the world on the quatrains and results that will soon be posted on my site.

Famous Personalities: Pluto likes to take away famous personalities when in charge. Expect a well-know figure to pass away soon. In energies similar to what is at play now, the following events happened: 2/7/99 - King Hussein died - In February 1998 under the same celestial energy, author of 13 novels, War correspondent

Martha Gellhorn died in London- A lot of secret activity will come to the light and the unaware wealthy and famous souls will have to pay heavy prices for involving themselves with the wrong elements.

Mimi Fahenstock   June Carter dies   Robert Stack dies

Memo from 2004 Moon Power: for MAY 15 -18: RULERS - Pluto (drama/death). Famous Personalities: Many financial or sexual secrets about a famous person will reach the media. Some unlucky souls will get wake-up calls from the dramatic planet. A public figure will make dramatic news or may be called to God. Mimi Fahnestock had an affair with JFK.

Events: Awful news involving tragic accidents, mass murderers, suicide and drama will plague the media. Everything you say or do now will have serious repercussions later on.

Shopping: Invest in anything that will help you to destroy any form of life; this should be efficiently used. Insecticides and other things to get rid of insects and household nuisances should be high on your list now. If you need to purchase a firearm, you are strongly advised to wait until after the New Moon, if not, it could be used against you or kill a family member. As for the sexually active: Preservatives will stop any chance of sexually transmitted diseases.

※

January 16th, 2007 — Mercury enters Aquarius: If you inherited this Mercury position you are a free thinker. You also regenerate in investigations, health, metaphysics, and anything related to electronic, electricity UFO and New Age matters. Work on your inventiveness and don't be afraid to use computers. You will gain fame because of your originality and your ability to communicate. Invest or design some software and investigate astrology. The near future promises to divulge surprising news pertaining to Japan, France, electronics, aeronautics, NASA, inventions and UFO's. This Mercurial position creates geniuses or people born with an original mental gratification, they are the thinkers of the future. I was also born with this Mercury position.

MON., TUE., WED., THU., FRI. — 15, 16, 17, 18, 19:
RULERS — Jupiter (Cheerfulness/Latino) and Saturn (Adjustment/Uncle Sam):

Work, Career and Business: We are still on a Waning Moon period; caution is advised in all you do. With the guardianship of Jupiter, the finances, resources and expertise of others could spell a profitable opportunity, especially after the upcoming New Moon. Real estate deals, trades, and credit approval will be among workable developments then. However, with the Waning Moon still with us, better keep a low profile and avoid asking too many favors. Be ready for the beginning or ending of an important portion of your business life. Surprising, even destructive news is ahead of you; be ready to welcome any changes. Life is a constant process of change and your existence on this dense physical world has specific purposes. Be patient and promote your business life only after the next New Moon.

Partnerships: Saturn may make you feel depressed, especially during the very last days of the Waning Moon. Do not put any strain on your relationships, and don't put stress on your significant other. Be ready to provide spiritual support to those close to you, and learn to say "NO" if needed. Work toward your heart's desire and don't let Saturn drag you down. Don't make too many demands on your partner and don't be too concerned with little details. No one will do things right just now. Errors are parts of your business life; don't hate yourself if you make some. Get involved with computers or learn a different program to make your business life easier.

Family and Friends: As usual in a Waning Moon period, assign your spiritual help but do not involve your personal feelings about a difficult situation with a family member or a trusted friend. Give practical directions and don't be too pessimistic about the end. With freedom-oriented Jupiter above these days, an out-of-doors trip for the family will be rewarding. A trip to your local church on Sunday could also give you a sense of faith in the creator and in your future. Hope and believe and a wish will come true.

Love Affairs: That Waning Moon will induce stress in your psyche; caution in your speech is advised. Expect surprising news soon, related to a legal situation, a marriage or a divorce. If you happen to be the victim, be patient and sooner or later you will find peace of mind and true love with the right partner. If you were born in April, a Leo, a Sagittarius or a Libra will be strongly attracted to you. An Aquarius or Leo friend could make one of your wishes a reality soon.

Travel and Communication: Be careful on the road as the waning moon brings bad tempers to some "lunatic" drivers. No one attracts bees with vinegar; use honey instead! Avoid arguments at all costs and use diplomacy to save situations, which could turn dangerous on the road. Be careful driving; don't trust anyone and keep your eyes on your speed. The Cops will be watching you with their electronic eye.

Environment: Gloomy news may come from Mexico, Japan and some faraway continents. Nature may decide to stretch herself and do harm to people in different places. She will produce a bad quake or a volcanic eruption within the next few days.

Famous Personalities: Some well-known entertainment figures may make dramatic news or lose their life. Expect secrets to come to light.

Events: A prominent political person either from the US, France or Japan will make an important announcement. Important meetings will take place to bring calm to certain parts of the world. The government may come up with important news or decisions that could affect many families in the future.

Shopping: Use this trend to find great Indian or foreign bargains in a garage sale or enjoy shopping your local antique shop with a Capricorn, Taurus or Cancer friend. Do not invest in anything new or any plants now; the ones that you will pick won't stay alive for long.

※

January 19, 2007 – New Moon in Capricorn: Expect the beginning or ending of important phases of your life. Watch for friends and family members too, the stars will force them into new sections of their lives. Count on the government to make important political decisions during this trend. The Waxing Moon (positive) is a sure sign of progress within the next two weeks. Push now; be confident and swim with the tide. Remember Shakespeare saying "There is a tide in the affairs of men, when taken at its crest, leads on to fortune!" Now is the tide. Expect serious restructuring to take place in your personal and business lives due to numerous and vital decisions issued from the Government. Have faith and never forget that the future is nothing other than the reincarnation of our common thoughts. Promote faith, love, peace and respect for all.

Lunation impact on all signs:

Aries - A promotion or a new business proposition is ahead, have faith and go for it now.

Taurus - News and deals from foreign lands and foreigners, an important study is ahead.

Gemini - News about legacy, investment or a new job or of spiritual work is ahead of you.

Cancer - Wrong people must be eliminated and better partnerships are on the horizon.
Leo - Don't worry about your health; a new job endeavor and a good deal is ahead, relax.

Virgo - A lover or idea gives you great options. Time to makes some emotional choices.

Libra - Your mind is on career changes. You may consider moving or improving your home.

Scorpio - Control your emotions and make plans for the future, listen to your intuition.

Sagittarius - Money is on your mind; a good deal will be offered to you soon.

Capricorn - Well-deserved promotions and deals are ahead, be happy you can't lose.

Aquarius - A secret deal, a person or a situation will come to light. Intuition is high.

Pisces - An older or younger person will bring one of your wishes if you swim upstream.

※

SAT., SUN., MON., TUE. — JANUARY 20, 21, 22, 23:
RULERS — Uranus (Surprises/explosions) Neptune (Religion/water):

Work, Career and Business: With the New Moon upon us you will encounter interesting people and incredible situations. Neptune may induce a trip for business close to the water. Many of us will be forced into new circumstances involving career moves or jobs. Get out now! Many Saturnine people will be standing next to you and could further your wishes; don't be afraid to start a conversation with an older person. Don't take anything personally if some of their comments seem harsh; they might know better than you. Use this progressive trend and invest some thought into new business opportunities. A change in schedules or rules could affect you; take chances now. Keep busy and be courteous to the Boss and pleasant to everyone, you're being noticed for your gentle nature. Be easy on yourself, don't be too critical of anyone in the office; nobody is perfect.

Partnerships: Be ready for a wave of surprising news coming your way. Karmic Neptunian souls will not benefit from that unexpected news, and some will be forced to accept the realities of life. Listen to an older person, he may play an important part in helping your emotional life and will give you good advice. Uranus, "the Lord of surprises" and Neptune "Poseidon" could also bring about boating misadventures; be aware if you happen to get close to the river or the ocean this weekend. Avoid drinking heavily and watch your possessions.

Family and Friends: Trust the Waxing Moon and the upcoming changes; be confident in the new situation, as it will affect your security and your finances positively. Keep an eye on the children; Uranus will make them behave irrationally, they will be overactive and you do not want anything bad to happen. An adolescent or a younger friend may need your support and may ask for direction. Do not turn down invitations, and you may also invite a long-standing friend to spend valuable time in your company. Some of those friends will bring your wishes home; be active on the social front. Wishes can only take place if you participate with life fully.

Love Affairs: Neptune may grasp the spirit of a person close to you and induce emotional stress and confusion. Be considerate or you may lose that person in the future if you do nothing. Expect some people to fall for Uranus' erratic personality and to surprise you in public places. Love is in the air for many while for others Neptune may lead them into a secret love affair. Be aware of weird souls hanging around, but you can still enjoy their original company. Again, don't fall for Neptune's deceiving powers, avoid drinking during the late hours, as your emotions will run unusually high and could alter your driving or behavior. If you were born in July, Capricorn, and Scorpio will be strongly attracted to you. A Pisces friend will provide a wish.

Travel and Communication: With Uranus' eccentricity, be aware of crazy drivers while driving to trips or work during this trend. Take plenty of time to reach your destinations and be ready for some driver's unexpected behavior on the road. Neptune may make you feel sleepy, rest or walk a bit along the way.

Famous Personalities: Expect startling developments with some well-known people trying to get more publicity. This energy doesn't stop with famous people; regular souls may act oddly, too. News of love, marriage, and children will make many famous people happy and ready to throw expensive social gatherings.

Events: New Moon or not, Uranus will surprise many of us with nature's destructive forces. Be ready for earthquakes, tornadoes, volcanic eruptions or incredible weather developments soon. Uranus might also disturb sophisticated electronic equipment and produce aeronautic disasters. Under his power Israel invaded Lebanon and the UK thwarted terrorist attacks to bomb UK and US airliners. The worse oil spill in Indonesia took place after a devastative typhoon hit the region. Also, a U.S. military cargo plane crashed and caught fire on a street in Tegucigalpa in April 1997 while trying to land at the airport, narrowly missing two gas stations. Three soldiers were killed in this U.S. military plane crash in Honduras.

Shopping: This is a good time to visit your favorite spiritual person for his divine guidance. Spend on anything electronic now; this will prove to be beneficial for your business life in the long run. Invest in my course by mail and enjoy the 16 - CD's and 4 - DVD and become an Astro-Psychologist.

※

WED., THU., FRI., SAT. — JANUARY 24, 25, 26, 27:
RULERS — Mars (Hostility/war) and Venus (Highly valued/ love):

Work, Career and Business: The New Moon will exert a revitalizing pull that will be felt in your business affairs. You may use this lunation to perhaps resolve conflicts in a difficult situation with a person of authority or a co-worker. Control Mars' opposing tendencies; don't let him affect your words, your attitude or your emotions. Practice patience during this Martian trend and use diplomacy; if you do so, you'll make serious progress. You may also use the tough energy of Mars to do some needed tasks around the office such as removing furniture; in any case, don't get hurt.

Partnerships: Even with the Waxing Moon, learn to keep Mars' impatience under control and use Venus' diplomatic gifts to save difficult situations. Everyone is so intent on having his or her own way and there could be little cooperation around you. It's time to practice tact with the same dedication as a diplomat. Impatience could be detrimental to you and others, so use the knowledge found in this publication accordingly.

Family and Friends: With Venus' blessings upon us, you should try your creativity at home. Your fruitful Venusians imagination will lead you to creations of perfect interior designs. Realize your limits with troubled friends, and don't allow them to rely too heavily on you. As always, give spiritual support but avoid getting emotionally involved with their personal problems. You and your mate or family member can gain through financial endeavors, but discuss all possibilities before making any commitments. You might have an idea yourself that could be used; talk about it. Use what's left of the Waxing Moon to plan and enjoy a gathering this weekend.

Love Affairs: Don't let your relationship becoming shaky because you sense that the person in question may be deceiving in some way. Do not fall for your own insecurity, false information or a wild imagination. Avoid guilt in any of your decisions, and if you feel a change is unavoidable, trust your future. Expect much from a night out on Friday or Saturday if you take a chance on someone. Enjoy social life, but don't drink and drive. Mars (action) and Neptune (deception) don't cohabit too well. When alcohol and speed are mixed, it can produce serious accidents. If you are a Gemini, then Aquarius, Sagittarius and Libra will be strongly attracted to you. A friend born in April has a surprise for you.

Travel and Communication: Be vigilant if you must drive, and don't take chances on the road, as Mars' energy could make you careless. Don't let his aggressive nature make you complain about a person, and use your words cautiously. Venus has much more to offer, and it's your choice, so use your will and your knowledge. Someone from your past may call.

Environment: Some people will learn about fire the hard way. However, many thoughtful people will use Mars' power to further environmental knowledge on preventing fires in nature. As usual, Mars, the red and violent planet, doesn't seem to care much for the Waxing Moon. He may decide to pull a nasty trick with nature's devastating forces, where all the elements could be invited for a destructive dance. Explosions and fires are common during his reign, be aware.

Famous Personalities: The oblivious rich and famous may be Mar's victims or make sad news involving accidents, drugs or alcohol. On a positive note, Venus will shine and induce love to those often-lonely famous souls.

Events: The Martian energy is tough and has in the past produced explosions and accidents of all sorts; be prudent. Venus will put up a serious fight against her destructive brother and may save many souls. Violent and dangerous sports will attract many people challenging their respective sides. Some unsuspecting souls may fall victim to Mars and suffer head injuries.

Shopping: Invest in anything involving love, creativity or the arts. Show someone for whom you care, the depth of your love. Under Mar's power, dangerous tools and machinery bought now will bring financial opportunities.

※

January 28, 2007 — Venus enters Pisces: This is the ideal celestial position to invest in an artistic or spiritual study. Empower yourself with spirituality and display your creativity to the world. Souls born now will inherit natural gifts in music and the arts. This is a great astrological position and the option is given to the soul to become a leader in the artistic fields. A weak or badly asserted Venus in this sign will induce deception in love, abuse of alcohol and drugs, leading to secret love affairs and deception in the long run. If you're born with Venus in Pisces, you are strongly advised to learn to love with your head, not your heart, to avoid the awful guilt. When well assisted by other celestial bodies, this is a perfect position for total commitment and endless love. Many souls will choose to serve "Poseidon, Lord or the sea" and will work and serve marine life.

※

SUN., MON., TUE., WED. — JANUARY 28, 29, 30, 31:
RULERS — Mercury (News/transportation) and the Moon (Important Changes):

Work, Career and Business: The blessings of a waxing moon are with us for a few more days; you should fight lethargy and depressions. Be confident, as much needed change is ahead for you and those you care. You may also consider using Mercury's mental agility to pass on new ideas to improve your business or communicate with the family. You could use these waning days to re-write or plan new advertisements or publicity. The telephone will be particularly busy, but the news could be depressive. Don't leave the office upset; you do not need to bring stress at home. Stay active and be mentally alert.

Partnerships: Dealing with others has and will always be a challenge for us all. Some of you have learnt hard lessons and the scars take time to heal; don't re-open them again. Move on to better ground, the future has always better to offer. Keep a positive attitude in your conversations and promote only the great times of your past. Some karmic souls will have to experience a rebirth of their relationships. Whatever unfolds, accept the changes with confidence; the truth is that, life is a constant process of change and it always seems to be for the better.

Family and Friends: Mercury is fast and rules communication, so expect family members to get in touch with you via mail or telephone. Some will be invited to enjoy great cooking at their friend's homes. "The messenger of the Gods" loves to talk and throw jokes all over. Control Mercury's desire to exaggerate and do not fall for the negative things you may hear now. Keep in mind that your friends have the potential to fulfill all your wishes; get active in the social arena after the New Moon. As always, you might have a karmic debt with a long-standing friend; if so, you may have to experience annoyance. Try to clear it all up and you'll win the person back.

Love Affairs: Be ready for the beginning or ending of important phases of your love life. Keep your eyes and ears open on the people you know, as the Moon affects everybody. If you were born in July, someone much older or younger than you born in March, November or January will be attracted to you. A friend may bring you sad news soon.

Travel and Communication: Use Mercury's mental powers accordingly. Time to write those letters, as Mercury improves your mental faculties. He will reward you favorably if you decide to invest in your education or start a book after the upcoming New Moon. Control his strong desire to be a "chatterbox," and save money on your telephone bill. Mercury rules transportation and general motion; he also makes people restless on the road. Under his command you should be a defensive driver. It's time to plan for your future travels, or visit parts of the world via great books. Wait for the next New Moon to launch the trip. You'll be glad to know and respect God's Universal Laws.

Environment: We are coming into a Full Moon period soon and some states will experience severe weather systems. If you are into videotaping lightning, storms, volcanic eruptions, earthquakes, etc., be ready for those soon. Some will see the beginning or ending of dramatic times. This may force thousands of people to relocate. Be ready for disturbing news soon that will force thousands of people to flee nature's destructive forces. Check my website regularly for additional predictions and to read my quatrains. This book works in conjunction with my home page as to teach you how to read Moon Power accurately.

Famous Personalities: Much too close to the next Full Moon for comfort next week end, thus some famous artist or important political figure will experience shame with love, and their children will be directly affected.

Events: Prominent political personalities either from the Russia, US, France or Japan will make an important announcement. The government may come up with drastic news or decisions that could affect many families in the future. Let's hope for the best.

Shopping: Invest faithfully in anything to clean the house or the office. Equipment purchased now will bring trouble to its owner. This is a perfect time to take care of your car. Mercury also rules literature and great deals on old books will be available under its influence.

Welcome to
Your Day - to - Day Guidance
For February 2007

Full Moon - February 2, 2007 in Leo: Be gentle with affairs of love and watch over the children. Keep Mrs. Pride and Mr. Ego in control if you intend to sustain your loving partner's relationship! Disturbing and surprising news with children are ahead be ready for agonizing happenings but learn not to dwell on them. Life is a constant process of change; the future has better to offer. Expect earthquakes above 6.0, and avoid flying. Be patient, take chances and as a rule promote your life only after the next New Moon. Kings, Queens, famous birth, France, Italy and Japan will make the news soon.

Lunation impact on all signs:

Aries - A rebirth of your love life or stress with children is ahead. Accept the changes.

Taurus - An important decision about home or family matters is ahead. Use your stamina.

Gemini - Your mind is on love, children, and your family. Don't get too stressed.

Cancer - Serious financial or emotional stress is ahead. Changes are needed in your life.

Leo - Let go of your past, move on. It's time to look for that position or a new love, be ready.

Virgo - A secret love affair can only bring you more trouble. Clean it all and start fresh soon.

Libra - Some friends will put stress in your life. You might have to go or look somewhere else.

Scorpio - A decision about your career and love must be made. Use your intuition.

Sagittarius - A study or a trip or sad news could bring depression to you. Be patient.

Capricorn - News of legacy or death is ahead. Hopefully it is just a contract for business.

Aquarius - An opportunity to look for a new business or emotional partners is ahead.

Pisces - A chance to improve your health and stress at work. Challenged by the stars.

※

THU., FRI., SAT., SUN., MON. — FEBRUARY 1, 2, 3, 4, 5:
RULERS —The Sun (Love/surprises/children) and Mercury (Mental power/sad news):

Work, Career and Business: Some surprising developments are on the way, but with the Full Moon upon us don't expect them to make you happy. Progress will still be made in the few weeks ahead of you, but be ready for a bumpy ride. Take on new technical studies, or improve your knowledge of computers, as this endeavor will give you better opportunities later.

Partnerships: Don't take any chances these days, keep a low profile; use Mercury's creative power to clean up a business situation. Important legal papers might come your way; sign them only if it is to get rid of an unhealthy situation. Whomever you come in contact with, don't misbehave in public.

Family and Friends: Keep busy with close friends and family; watch the children, as they will be accident-prone. In the past, many of them got in trouble or had accidents during this type of lunation. It's a great time to enjoy the people you know well, but because of the Waning Moon, avoid overcrowded public places. Don't expect new people met under this lunar cycle to bring many of your wishes. Some friends have surprising, even disturbing news for you and could affect you emotionally. Again, watch the children. They are accident-prone, especially on the road with fire, weapons and explosives. Under this lunation (April 8, 1998) the news reported that in CHAPPELL HILL, Texas -- A loaded school bus was hit from behind by a tractor-trailer truck on a Texas highway; injuring at least 22 children, some of them seriously.

Love Affairs: Expect an aggravating surprise coming your way and learn to let go of deceitful people. Do not invite interlopers into your home, and socialize only with the friends you know well. Make good use of the Waning Moon; learn to relax, enjoy nature and the sea, and look for inner peace. If you're single, a chance to find the "right one" will be given to you at a later date. What you may perceive as love, may enter your life but without much to expect. Use your head on Friday night, not your heart. If you were born under the sign of Leo, an Aries, an Aquarius or a foreigner born in December could be a source of trouble in your life. Wait for better auspices.

Travel and Communication: Not a time to take chances at flying; many karmic souls will pay the ultimate price. Expect all sorts of little problems arising, which could turn lethal for some unlearned souls. Anticipate disturbing telephone calls from friends in trouble; as usual, provide spiritual help, but know your limits and stay clear of depression.

Environment: Earth activists will feel this puritanical lunation and will do all to protect nature and its wild life; some may fall victim to ill-advised conflicts with unscrupulous large organizations. Expect unusual oceanic or earth activity soon that could prove disastrous for the environment. Not good times to play with fire, as explosions are very high on my list of trouble for this specific trend. The news may bring about startling explosive developments.

Famous Personalities: Certain famous people will find themselves in difficult situations. Some will try anything to get the attention they need. Eccentricity is in the air and could lead to the use of force or involvement with the law. Under this lunation Pop star George Michael was arrested for lewd conduct on April 8 1998, in Beverly Hills California: On that day the news reported that pop star George Michael, the British-born heartthrob whose hit songs include the too-hot-for-radio "I Want Your Sex," was arrested on suspicion of committing a lewd act in a park restroom.

Events: Expect massive power outages without readily known causes. NASA could make some bad news soon due to poor weather conditions or electronic malfunctions. On the positive side, some high-tech scientific news as well as great medical breakthroughs is on the way. On December 17, 1997 under this type of celestial energy a typhoon-blasted Guam: Paka; top wind gusts of 236 mph - Electricity out, no water and many people ran for their lives'

Shopping: Do not invest on anything electronic; you will not get a good deal. Do not invest in toys for your children now; they could prove to be fatal at a later date. Some will plan to travel to Europe.

February 2, 2007 — Mercury enters Pisces: Souls born with this celestial position will be gifted in the arts while some will pursue artistic, medical, spiritual or religious endeavors and will use their incredible imagination in exotic places. Their sensitive natures combined with strong religious intonations could lead many young March souls swimming downstream towards the ministry pulpit. The advanced ones will swim upstream and turn into great light workers, while other less advanced types will develop into (religious or cult leaders, terrorists or ministers). On a negative note, this Mercurial position produces mental ailments such as phobias, fears, drug and alcohol addictions, confinement, depressions and religious fanaticism. This planetary position will lead the soul towards creative imagination; true spiritual values, the performing arts and great success can be achieved if the intellectual energy of Mercury in Pisces is applied positively. In a negative chart, this position produces the entire reveille to breed a "born" terrorist and the world's secret services would make such a great use of Astro-Psychology instead of using common facial expressions (traditional psychology) in International airport to detect the physiology and deadly potential of individuals.

2007 First Supernova Window

February / March: First SUPERNOVA window - From Saturday February 10th 2007, through Monday March 12th, 2007.

EXPLANATION OF A SUPERNOVA WINDOW

Concentration of negative celestial energy approaching; Be extremely prudent in driving, and expect chain-reaction accidents. Be prepared for delays, strikes, and nature producing awful weather, including hurricanes and tornadoes. The same energy that produced the Titanic disaster, the Asia tsunami, the Northridge Los Angeles and Kobe Japan earthquakes and major other calamities is approaching again. Remember the thwarted terrorist attack of August 2006 in the UK where the BA canceled thousands of flights, because the BAA ordered all passengers not to take or check ALL handbags before boarding their planes? Those people did not have a copy of Moon Power and paid the price of ignorance. Double-check all your appointments, and if you can, postpone traveling and flying during this Supernova "window". If you must fly like I do very often, simply make sure to purchase your ticket and make your reservation during a Waxing Moon and the stars will not bother you. Remember the Universal Laws do not care for birthday or religious holidays or else, simply think of crossing the street while the light is red or ignore a stop sign, and then see what will happen to you. Those laws are impartial and written by God not men and messing them up will bring about serious penalty. Note that; I flew only a few days before the Full Moon in August 2006 to Thailand during a "Supernova Window" to write this book and I traveled safely and avoided all trouble. Remember, knowledge is power ignorance is evil!

Communication and electricity will be cut off, and a general loss of power is to be expected. Appliances, computers, telephones, planes, trains, cars, all of these "tools" will be affected by this energy. They will be stopped in one way or another. The people of the past will make the news and will reenter your life. Expect trouble with the post office, education, students, strikes, prisoner's escape, newspapers, broadcasting industries and computer viruses may bother us again.

Many a failed mission and expensive electronic equipment (Mars probe etc.) and our tax dollars have been wasted because of the scientist's lack of knowledge of the stars. As usual NASA, which is not aware of the science of astrology, will waste our tax money with failed missions, due to bad weather and electronic malfunctions. In the name of ignorance a few years ago, in the Challenger explosion seven astronauts lost their lives when NASA launched the shuttle under a "Supernova Window".
Marine life sharks, whales etc may also beach themselves due to Mercury retrograde affecting their natural inborn navigational systems. All these malevolent predictions and waste of lives and equipment do not have to occur. Those predictions do not have to affect you directly as they unfold. Instead, they are printed to prepare you for setbacks and frustrations, thus advising you to be patient and prudent during this trend. There is no room for ignorance, and those who are not aware of the celestial order, including the NASA space-program management team, will continue to pay a heavy price. In all mankind's' affairs, ignorance is true evil. Why any scientists who are against my research do not honor the word science, which is based upon solid investigation, is solid proof of mental snobbery. By omitting any physical or spiritual laws can only bring penalty; for science's purpose is to explore all possibilities, even those laws written in light via the stars.

Attention: Pluto will become very destructive in this waning Moon period; he is back with us — You can expect dramatic happenings with nature all over; control is a must. He has produced much sensational news including the California Rancho Santa Fe mass-suicide. Mass murderers are again on the lookout for innocent victims as Pluto always stimulates the criminal element, the insane and the police force fighting all ill purposes. Don't be victims; be aware of Pluto's destructive power. Secrets from the past will return to your life. The police will be touched directly and terrorists will be actively planning destruction.

TUE., WED., THU., FRI., SAT. — FEBRUARY 6, 7, 8, 9, 10:

RULERS — Venus (Sexuality/secret love) and Pluto (Passion/drama/death):

Work, Career and Business: Chances are that your boss may not be aware of the power of Pluto and could make your life miserable. Odds are also, that many countries' leaders are totally ignorant of the power of Pluto and may decide to make hasty decisions that will bring death to many people. Do not take anything too personally and forgive anyone's sharp sarcasm and destructive tempers. A wake-up call for some karmic souls where reality must be accepted is around the corner.

Partnerships: On a Waning Moon period, never take a Pluto trend lightly as his impact is usually dramatic and could produce serious stress in your partnership and its future. Use all the diplomacy you know, as anything you say or do will have serious repercussions. Not a time to play with anyone's emotions; stay cool in all you do. Changes must take place, as life is a constant process of change itself.

Family and Friends: Secrets will pop out from a person close to you; be sure to keep silent if you intend to keep this relationship. If you decide to speak up and force the truth on this person, keep cool and do the clean up gently. Don't expect anyone to be sensitive or respond to your needs. Instead, be ready for bitterness and harsh comments. Don't let Pluto's sarcastic nature destroy the serenity of your home life. Many ignorant souls will pay the heavy price of ignorance and lose much in the process.

Love Affairs: A surely stressful time is ahead for some, with Pluto's desire to demolish it all. Beautiful Venus will make you quite magnetic these days. You could become a prime target for some Plutonic soul's thirst for sex. If you become active on the dating scene, don't take chances on strangers; protect yourself and avoid heavy drinking. Pluto knows how vulnerable you are to his power when under the influence, and he will teach you one of the hardest lessons in your life. Relationships started now could be of a destructive nature, filled with jealousy and drama, and could lead you to harm or even death. This dramatic relationship could also be of a karmic nature, but hopefully short lived. Be very aware out there and avoid negative group situations. Your intuition will be very accurate and should be followed with full trust. For those born under the sign of Pisces, a Scorpio or a Taurus will be strongly attracted to you. A Cancer friend has disturbing news for you.

Travel and Communication: Be smart and patient on the road we are under a dangerous "Super Nova Window". Avoid the sarcastic remarks of others, and be aware of Pluto's desire for drama. Some people may call you for advice or share their secrets. Better keep it a secret for now, as Pluto does not like to talk. Pluto may decide to take many human lives in dramatic accidents or terrorists act.

Famous Personalities: You will most likely hear more about the infamous than the famous under Pluto's command. Venus will try everything she can to subdue her violent brother and smooth things out. The great loss of an old and eminent political, religious or entertainment figure will vex the media.

Events: Expect dramatic headlines like the following: Botched L.A. bank heist turns into bloody shoot-out — February 1997 — Manhunt on for suspects. "It was like the OK Corral." Or, New York -- The crash of China Airlines Flight 676 on Taiwan, killing 205 people. The same energy was active when flight 800 was blown out of the sky, killing all people on board. Pluto rules death and secrets involving death. On May 15th, 2003 Moon Power said: Attention: Pluto is back with us - Expect secrets to surface and news from the police force.

Iraq grave holds 11,000

Hundreds of grieving relatives gathered today at a mass grave that was discovered about 55 miles from Baghdad, Iraq. A forensic team working at the site says up to 11,000 bodies may be buried there. The dead are thought to be mostly Iraqis -- killed during an uprising against Saddam Hussein, in the wake of the 1991 Gulf War.

Shopping: Buy now anything related to sex, spying, metaphysics, and especially healing products. Do not purchase guns, knives or anything that could kill humans under Pluto's power. They may be used against you or your loved ones. Invest in dangerous pesticides to use in and around the house, they will work perfectly.

※

SUN., MON., TUE., WED., THU. — FEBRUARY 11, 12, 13, 14, 15:
RULERS — Jupiter (Middle East) Saturn (Politics) and Uranus (Shocking news):

Work, Career and Business: Pluto's legacy is dramatic experiences, and the acceptance of the transformation will open new doors to you. With Jupiter's touch, you should be confident in all your transactions. Expect this transformation to become a new beginning for your career life. Great Jupiter may induce foreigners to play an important part of this trend. Listen to your intuition and keep a positive attitude until the worst is gone.

Partnerships: New partners are on the horizon for some, while others must learn from previous errors. Money and general security will also be on your mind, serious decisions will have to be made soon. Be patient and wait for the upcoming New Moon, nothing comes easily in this life and one must strive and plan if one is to succeed. Letting go and rebuilding is a must.

Family and Friends: Jupiter's optimistic spirit will replenish you with hopes and a new approach to life. Spend some time with family members or dear friends, and be ready to listen to a wise soul. Enjoy the family and the good food offered to you, fight depression, and invite a friend over. Because of the Waning Moon, a night out will not bring you much pleasure; better stay home, relax and read. An old friend may stimulate your life; this will make you happy and further an important wish later on.

Love Affairs: Someone much older or much younger may enter your life soon. Don't look for love these days; there is plenty to gain in yourself, and the stars want you to be in isolation for a while. You will feel spiritual and some of the questions of life will trigger your imagination. Indians affairs will strive. If you were born in October an Aries, a Gemini or an Aquarius will need you. A friend born in June may be interested in you.

Travel and Communication: Expect your telephone to be busy, but do not hope for super-positive mail to reach you just yet. If you have to drive, be cautious and take extra time to get there; don't rush as the police could spoil your day. Don't be depressed about anything that may come your way; the stars have better for you on a later date.

Environment: During the last breath of the waning moon, Mother Nature may become capricious and surprise us with bad weather soon. Environmental groups will become active and will find support from the media, in saving the earth from uncaring corporations. Sad news may come from foreign grounds or the Middle East soon.

Famous Personalities: A well-known foreign personality involved in communication, television or writing will gain international attention where sorrow, tears and memory will make many followers cry.

Events: Some militant groups from a faraway continent will disturb the peace and become dangerous. Surprising destructive explosions are on the way. Also expect sad news such as; November 4, 1997 when a dual typhoon lashed the Pacific islands and destroyed all on his passage. Moon Power memo; Prediction -
WED., THU. - MAY 21st, 22nd 2003: RULERS - Uranus (shocking news). Environment: Stay clear of thunder and lightning; *Uranus takes many lives without warning. Expect him to throw a quake,* a tornado or volcano to erupt soon.

Shopping: Not a good time for the gamblers; however, if you happen to be in Las Vegas, keep the spending in control. The Moon is still Waning (negative); be patient and make major moves only after the fast approaching New Moon.

New Moon — February 17, 2007 in Aquarius: The New Moon will mature in the futuristic sign of Aquarius. Expect surprising developments everywhere. The Waxing "positive" Moon means it is a progressive time to launch any new project. The next two weeks are going to be full of surprises, and a good chance to move forward will be offered to those asking for progress. Try anything now, aim as high as you are capable; coincidence be will magical. Don't waste this great lunation; be original, ask and you will receive! Expect incredible news involving explosions, natures destructive forces at work, electronics, UFOs, celestial bodies, (yes Pluto is a planet and belong to our solar system!). Airport news such as the August 2006 London impeded terrorist attack on UK airliners, etc. A perfect time to start a spiritual Astro-Psychology, Kabalistic
Healing or Astro-Tarot course (Get the course by mail - see www.drturi.com or call me the office for more info at 602-265-7667 don't put if off any longer, get a new career and help the children of the future with true wisdom.

Lunation impact on all signs:

Aries - A good friend will bring a great opportunity to grow and travel. You're lucky.

Taurus - A new career opportunity is ahead of you, master computers, TV soon.

Gemini - More opportunities to travel and study will be offered to you.

Cancer - A wealthy partner will offer financial support and will promote your business.

Leo - Big changes in your business and emotional life is ahead of you.

Virgo - You are due for some significant changes at work, be ready.

Libra - Your love life will turn surprisingly positive, opportunities are ahead for you.

Scorpio - You may be forced to move and your home life will undergo positive changes.

Sagittarius - Be ready to travel physically and spiritually. Learn and use computers.

Capricorn - Positive financial changes are ahead, electronic knowledge is a must.

Aquarius - A new door is about to open to you, be ready, you can't lose.

Pisces - Your perception of the future will be right, be positive. Swim upstream.

✹

FRI., SAT., SUN., MON., TUE. — FEBRUARY 16, 17, 18, 19, 20: RULERS — Uranus (Explosions/shocking news) Neptune (Deception/religion):

Work, Career and Business: The New Moon in upon you and she will bring a high level of good surprises into your business affairs. Set up a difficult situation now to avoid a conflict later. Don't let Neptune's deceiving powers affect your attitude with life in general; be positive and listen to your intuition. Beware of get-rich-quick schemes, clean up your act and invest in new equipment that may let you down soon. Use the ingenuousness of Uranus to do some investigation around the office and let him provide you with great ideas with computers to promote your career. Progress is to be made now.

Partnerships: Keep Neptune's complaining attitude in check and control your thought processes. Think positive and your wishes will come true. Expect much from co-workers but Neptune may induce daydreams. Supervise yourself closely; you might forget something important, errands or returning vital telephone calls. Everyone will feel the "dreamy" side of Neptune, so be patient in your dealings with others. It's time to build others' confidence and practice tact with the same dedication as a diplomat. Be aware of Neptune sensitivity and be tolerant.

Family and Friends: As always, with Neptune in charge, you may dwell on your intuition, but you must control your imagination. With Uranus driving next to him, your psychic abilities are enhanced; just tune in and you will receive the wisdom of the stars. A friend may become difficult; do not let this person rely on you too much and avoid getting too emotionally involved. Both Uranus and Neptune strive in new-age endeavors; you may decide to share your own psychic knowledge with a friend. You could gain through new-age financial endeavors if you educate yourself in metaphysics. Do not allow Neptune's deceiving tendency to make your life misery. Clean your thoughts; you have a choice, be happy.

Love Affairs: A romantic relationship may fall short of your expectations, mainly because your intuition tells you differently. Did you meet that person on the Waxing Moon? If your Neptune is badly aspected by Venus (love) you will sense that perhaps the person may be deceiving in certain ways. Someone may try to lead you into a secret love affair, do not fall for it. Don't be deceived, especially if the person in question happens to be married. Avoid any form of guilt in your decision and stay miles away from alcohol during the night hours. With this New Moon, expect much from weekend dating and social plans. If you were born in May, Pisces and Virgo will be strongly attracted to you. A Cancer friend has a good advice for you.

Travel and Communication: Neptune and Uranus may decide to strand you somewhere with the police. Wherever you go, keep an eye on your possessions; the crooks will be active. Enjoy life in many ways this weekend; go after your wishes, but don't drink and drive. Uranus and Neptune are not great co-habitants and when alcohol and speed are mixed, it produces serious accidents. Be cautious if you must drive a long way; take plenty of rest as

Neptune's energy could make you sleepy. Chew gum, it will keep you more alert. Don't let Neptune grasp your spirit and complain; use positive words and keep busy to avoid depression or guilty feelings from your past.

Environment: Uranus (explosions) will be strong and with the Head of the Dragon in watery Pisces expect bad surprises with nature's devastating forces. Crazy people and all the elements will be invited for a mad dance. This energy will be quite strong and will disturb electronics and could produce aeronautic disasters. Memo from Moon Power 2003/4/5/6/7 - will be the worst year for death and suicide attacks, dam terrorist acts and natural disasters (volcanoes/eruptions/earthquakes and water damages since 1948).

Famous Personalities: Some rich and famous people may make sad news and be involved with drugs or alcohol.

Events: Uranus, the Lord of Surprises could also bring about explosions and misadventures, especially if you happen to get close to the river or the ocean this weekend. Under the same celestial energy on October 1996 — BLUE ISLAND, Illinois — An explosion rocked an oil refinery south of Chicago, jolting neighborhood homes for miles around and sending clouds of black smoke into the air.

Shopping: Invest in anything related to the arts, fishing, metaphysics and electronics. Put a big smile on your face and use your will and your knowledge; the New Moon will sharpen your spiritual values. Visit an old friend and spend time by the water.

✵

February 21, 2007 — Venus enters Aries: Time to use your head, not your heart in dealing with love. Aries is much too impulsive and impatient to look thoughtfully into others people's values or motives and some young people will get hurt in the process. On a more positive note, souls born with this celestial signature will be quite artistic and extremely magnetic. The aggressive and rough attitude of the Lord of War, Mars (ruler of Aries) will be toned down by his diplomatic sister Venus (planet of love). All fire signs (Leo/Sagittarius/ Aries) will see an improvement or changes in the love area. For all other signs, wherever Venus is cruising through by sign or house, expect to find love or happiness. Souls born with this Venus position won't wait for you to make a move to find love. Aries needs to be first in any area that he is to be found in your chart.

※

WED., THU., FRI., SAT. — FEBRUARY 21, 22, 23, 24:
RULERS — Mars (Danger) Mercury (Traveling) and Venus (Dedication):

Work, Career and Business: Control Mars' fighting spirit or he may slow down some of your projects. With the New Moon around, you may also use his power constructively to improve your business endeavors. This fortuitous timing will strengthen your chances for success in the near future. Trust your ability to communicate with Mercury and follow your intuition. The next few days will be vital to launch yourself and Venus' lucky touch will bring additional developments. With the Waxing Moon at work, the next few days should be used to the maximum to promote your business life.

Partnerships: Be ready for some people of your past to re-enter your life, with all the activities around they can only further your wishes. Remember Mars is also around and you should use his strength and concentrate your efforts to get things done. The future promises to bring about good results from interviews, employment applications, promotions and other job opportunities. A pivotal turning point is to be expected this week in a key relationship. As always, consider the long-term implications and respectability of the offer, before making up your mind.

Family and Friends: With Mercury the "Lord" of communication in charge these days you can expect your telephone to be busy. Everybody will have something to share with you. Use Venus' loving touch in your verbal exchanges and avoid Mars' invective remarks about an unlucky friend. Don't be shy; pass on your message, be confident and direct in your approach, and your impact on others will surprise you. Do all this with "savoir faire." Take the family out and enjoy the wilderness with the children. As always keep an eye on them, as Mars will make them restless and accident-prone.

Love Affairs: Use the kind-hearted touch of Venus to your advantage; you may decide to treat someone you truly love with your best intentions. You're apt to make significant progress with love this weekend (especially close to the water) and you should really make the most out of this trend. Social life and romance is up; a trip is on the way for some. If you were born in June, a Sagittarius, a Libra or an Aquarius may fall for you.

Travel and Communication: This week promises to be worthwhile for the more creative souls and your writing skills will improve dramatically. Under Mercury and Venus' auspices, especially in time of a New Moon, a new book could be started or finished. A trip to your past will pay off for some. Don't let Mars make you impatient or accident-prone on the road; be patient and don't trust other drivers.

Environment: Mars' destructive temper may produce tornadoes, explosions, high winds or flooding. Be aware and don't take any chances. Moon Power memo: CNN: Saturday, May 31, 2003 -- *A wave of tornadoes swept through central and northern Illinois Friday evening, damaging homes, businesses, power lines and trees in several communities*

Famous Personalities: Listen for news to come to light about great projects from the old or forgotten famous.

Events: Remember Mars is around; don't take any chances with confrontations or the police. A positive attitude and diplomacy will keep you out of trouble. Impending breakthroughs with religion, the Pope, medicine or science are to be expected soon.

Shopping: It's a great time to buy interesting books and telephone appliances for your business. As Mercury rules transportation, it would be a good idea for you to take care of your wheels or invest in a new car.

February 26, 2007 — Mars enters Aquarius: The Lord of war is now entering the explosive sign of Aquarius, until April. On the negative side, we can only expect this mixture to shake the world with real nuclear threats from foreign powers. Mother Earth will stretch and restructure her insides with quakes and volcanic activities. Aeronautic accidents are high on the list too. Incredible out-of-this-world events will take place with comets, meteorites, UFOs, etc. We are living in incredible times, and we are lucky to be participants in the action. Expect New York and other US City airports to make some surprising news soon. The incredible is around the corner and will touch many of us. Have faith in governments, as mankind will have to make life and death decisions soon. A new consciousness for the entire world is slowly but surely taking place where ignorance, fear and dogma will be replaced by a higher knowledge based upon the study and understanding of God's celestial tools.

February 26th, 2007: Today is your astrologer's birthday and because it's the New Moon, I am going to enjoy a great birthday with good friends and the people I love. Again thank you for all your good wishes and support. Each year I am getting more and more birthday cards and emails from all of you. It is an honor to receive so many blessings from all around the world. Please forgive me if I do not personally answer you, but it is from the depth of my heart that I sincerely thank you. God bless you all.

"The greatness of the Universe is unknown, but the magnetic forces that direct and move all the planets in our galaxy are known: this Divine source of power can be used to guide and bring man a life filled with happiness, peace, and harmony."
-Dr. Turi

SUN., MON., TUE., WED. — FEBRUARY 25, 26, 27, 28:
RULERS — Venus (Love) Mercury (Traveling) Moon (Changing cycles):

Work, Career and Business: The last few days of February will be progressive and may force you into many great changes for the best in the long run. Thus, be ready for a variety of new starts concerning some areas of your career and your life. Some dutiful souls will land on a great opportunity for a new career. This energy will affect the "executives," so meeting one of them can seriously promote your career. Make the most of those days and have faith in all you do. Venus may send you an opportunity for a party or some flowers.

Partnerships: Venus' gentle touch will improve your magnetism and make you desirable to many. Expect the beginning or ending of important phases of your emotional life. Keep your eyes and ears open and listen to your friends, this New Moon (changes) combined with Mercury (communication) and Venus (love) will affect them too. Many will be forced into new partnerships or marriage where a commitment will be asked. This is a great lunation for many lucky people. Spend those days in the outdoors, close to the water or in the high mountains. The wilderness will do great healing on your spirit and recharge your soul for future challenges. Be aware of Mercury's tendencies to talk too much and listen to your partner a little more.

Family and Friends: You will be in demand from your active friends, calling you to join them in a social gathering. Don't turn down any invitation from friends; many of your wishes may come true through them. Some close friends or children will have to move away but not without tears, and carry on with their independent lives. Expect the family circle to be emotional, busy, with Mom and the kids to be the center of attraction. Enjoy the warm family circle, the food and all the children around you. They would love you forever if you decided to take them to the zoo soon. Happiness will rule these days and you should make more plans for the near future.

Love Affairs: Many mercurial spirits will be out there enjoying what life has to offer. Do not be afraid to take chances on anything or anybody now; these stars are extremely lucky and your competitiveness will pay off. Do not stay home this weekend; you may have to wait a long time to get this type of positive energy around again. Go out, ask and you may even find true love. If you were born in December, foreigners will play an important part of your life. An Aries or a Leo will want to know you and a Gemini will be strongly attracted to you.

Travel and Communication: Mercury will make you curious and will help you to communicate adequately with others. Your telephone will be busy, as this rare beautiful trio energy will boost everybody around you. Enjoy your life and if you have to be at work, be ready for an interesting meeting with some beautiful people after work.

Environment: Expect the weather to be decent or windy and Venus to show off her finest garments. Control speedy Mercury to avoid freak accidents.

Famous Personalities: Good news pertaining to children and love is to be expected from famous people.

Events: Let's hope this trio and the new moon will stop any dramatic happenings but it could also mean that thousands of people may be fleeing nature, forced to relocate to start a new and better life.

Shopping: Invest in anything and everything for your children. Tools used for the home or the arts will also bring luck to future projects. (Purchase your plane ticket now if you need to fly far away this summer.

Welcome to Your Day - to - Day Guidance
For March 2007

Full Moon — March 3rd, 2007 in Virgo: Be ready for the ending of a portion of your working life. Disturbing news is ahead of you, be ready to accept these changes, as you might have to service this world in a different manner. Life is never stagnant so learning to embrace change is part of the whole lesson. Don't be too critical with your or other people performances. Naturally health oriented Virgo, Taurus, and Capricorn will be touched directly: this Full Moon will affect your mental processes and could make you prone to worry about your health. If you were born with a Moon in an earth sign or a Dragon's Tail in this sign this applies to you too. Instead of anxiety or hurting your self-esteem, use this lunation to join a club and rebuild your physical figure. On a negative note you can expect oil spills and aeronautic accidents, so avoid flying if you can. Not times to take chances; forestall signing important contracts. To travel or start new projects, wait until the next New Moon. This lunation will take place on the Dragon's Tail and will mark serious negative times ahead of us. If you feel too depressed consider a Full Life reading or invest in one of my DVD or CD to learn and use your subconscious creative forces positively.

Lunation impact on all signs:

Aries - Don't worry too much about your health; expect some changes at work soon.

Taurus - Don't be too critical about a lover and don't worry about the children too much.

Gemini - Planning on a move? Don't let your family put too much stress on you.

Cancer - Keep your imagination in control, no one is perfect.

Paper work must be done.

Leo - Be ready to positively spend money on your health or your image. Look good.

Virgo - Love or business may bring stress, don't be sarcastic and you'll be fine.

Libra - Some affairs of your past may surface, don't nurture any guilt and move on.

Scorpio - A friend may deceive you; wait a while for one of your wishes to come true.

Sagittarius -Career and travel plans must be changed; the next New Moon will bring joy.

Capricorn - Difficult news from foreign lands, don't stress in any of your studies.

Aquarius - Money spent against your will, difficult news if your stars are afflicted.

Pisces - A business or emotional partner makes your life misery, clean up time.

THU., FRI., SAT., SUN. — MARCH 1, 2, 3, 4:
RULERS — The Moon (Changing cycles/Growth of soul) and the Sun (Higher self):

Work, Career and Business: Some people will see the end and the beginning of a business situation. New people will move in to replace others. The Moon is still Waxing (positive); make the most out of these couple days ahead and have faith in your ability to deal with any changes. Hope and faith will take you places.

Partnerships: This lunation means a great new start, relocation, and a promotion, even the start of a brand new life. Those changing stars do not care about your sadness, guilt or anything else; don't turn back, move on to your future. Your situation or feelings do not match your wishes; changes must take place. You'll be glad you did it. Remember life is a constant process of change, so go for it.

Family and Friends: Mom may get in touch with you, and your past is calling you back. The moon will make the children quite emotional; they will need your attention and will be demanding. With the Sun's vitality invest some time with them and do something special; they will cherish these days in their heart forever. A surprising new involvement with a child or love is ahead of you. A friend surprises you with an invitation; restaurants will be busy, so you'd better make a reservation if you do not want to stand in line for a table.

Love Affairs: Control your feelings about the past and let them lead you towards your future. Some relationships might end with sorrow, but the stars are on your side. Promote your next section of life without delay. Expect some surprises too and go full speed after your desires; anything incredible can happen especially during the weekend and you shouldn't stay home. These surprises should be positive and unexpected and there is much to gain if you interact with others. Visit friends, socialize or throw a party to celebrate this great solar and lunar energy. It's time to do your cabalistic candles ritual, white for the purification of the spirit, green for the purification of the physical, and blue to pray and ask favors of your guardian Angel. Don't forget to burn some sage and the use of the circle of salt. This lunation has the potential to bring about one of your greatest wishes. Again, don't waste it, go out there now, push and have faith. If you were born in July, a younger or older person born in January, November or March won't be able to resist your magnetism.

Travel and Communication: Expect news from brothers and sisters; be part of the action and communicate with those you love. Use plenty words of love and care for others; somehow you'll be rewarded. Bring your camera; great things and great surprises are imminent.

Environment: Many people are forced to relocate during this celestial energy, sometimes due to nature's destructive forces. Typhoons and other water disasters are to be expected.

Memo: Bangaladesh flood kills 45

Events: Foreign governments will have to make important decisions soon. This type of energy was present on October 20, 1997 - Typhoon Winnie killed 140 people in east China and forced relocation for many. Under the same star pattern, in June 1995, worried about its capital's growing population, the North Korean government reportedly began moving hundreds of thousands of people out of the city of Pyongyang. DHAKA, Bangladesh (AP) – June 2003 - Monsoon floods battering parts of Bangladesh have claimed 45 lives in the past four days, washed away many houses and displaced thousands of villagers. Thus, as predicted in Moon Power for these dates, thousands have and will have to be forced into a new part of their lives due to forced relocation.

Famous Personalities: Famous and powerful personalities will be ending or starting a very important part of their love lives. Some will have finished their work on this physical plane, and will work as guides for whom they cared on earth.

Memo: Katherine Hepburn dies

Shopping: Only real estate endeavors from your past are protected; a new house bought now could bring much trouble to the new owners. If you do so, make sure to do a candle ritual. Burn white, green and blue candles, and mix them with incense to clean up some psychic residues left behind by disturbed souls. Some of your local stores may also be affected and may rebuild or close down completely.

※

MON., TUE., WED., THU — MARCH 5, 6, 7, 8:
RULERS — Mercury (Gift of gab/siblings) and Venus (Good taste/sweetheart):

Work, Career and Business: The Moon is now Waning (negative), and opportunities to further your position in life will depend on your interaction with others. Social contacts will pay off at a later date if you use Venus' gentle touch in all you do. Remember the power of your own thoughts; don't be crippled by your own fears and anxieties, or you may attract setbacks to your life. Go after what you really want and don't be afraid to communicate your feelings. Expect some deceiving developments soon. Contracts will be signed and will bring great financial rewards if you decide clean up and start again.

Partnerships: Do not assume the worst without first finding all the facts, nor break your spirit by suppressing all faith in your abilities. Mercury could make you talkative; listen to your partner a little more. Keep an open mind and be receptive when direction is being offered, especially if the person in question is older than you. Being patient and working harder to attain your goals is the key. If you are inquisitive enough, secrets of a financial nature may be revealed to you. Important legal paper work to clean up your past may be on the way for you to sign; be confident in doing so as the future has better to offer.

Family and Friends: Use your exceptional insight into the secret motives of a friend close to you and avoid all unnecessary gossip. Be patient and practice diplomacy with loved ones. During a Waning Moon, Mercury may promote intellectual challenges, even confrontations. Use plenty of words of love to those for whom you care, and keep your eyes on the children. Friends may ask for financial favors; provide help, but watch your own security.

Love Affairs: Those stars above your head are tough, but your knowledge is well placed; use your will in all occasions. The kindhearted touch of Venus can only alter those nasty stars if you have faith in the right people and yourself. Avoid being too critical about someone you value; no one is perfect, not even you. Learn to love yourself and concentrate on the qualities you and others possess. If you were born in August, an Aries will help you but a Scorpio could be giving you trouble.

Travel and Communication: Venus' diplomatic powers will be felt in your words and will further many of your requests. Just remember that no one attracts bees with vinegar. Invest in your own thought power and do not expect too much from others. Many souls will be forced to deal with the past and some will have take a long and difficult journey. You will learn about people getting in trouble with the law or getting a divorce soon.

Environment: As usual with the Waning Moon expect dramatic news soon with Mother Nature. Let's hope that with the gentle touch of Venus, nature will be quiet. Many environmentalist groups will be active; some may get out of hand while trying to get their message out.

Famous Personalities: A prominent person will promote a new diet or a specific product. It will use only natural goods and be very eastern in conception. Some will announce health problems.

Events: Some disturbing, even shocking news will arrive soon, pertaining to unhappy people willing to start trouble. College students or the post office may make the news.

Shopping: Now is the perfect time to invest in a diet or a health program to lose those unwanted pounds. You may also find great deals with children's second hand products.

※

FRI., SAT., SUN., MON., TUE. — MARCH 9, 10, 11, 12, 13:
RULERS — Pluto (Death/trauma) Venus (Heartbroken) Jupiter (Foreigners):

Note: Attention Pluto is back with us and we can only expect dramatic happenings; control is a must. Do not be one of his victims; be aware of Pluto's destructive power. Anything you say or do under his power will follow you for the rest of your life. Time to use extreme caution in all you do.

He who reigns himself and rules his passion, desire and fears is more than a king.
— Goethe

Work, Career and Business: Don't take chances, be cool, be smart, pull in a safe place and be quiet for a while; that is the best advice I can give you now. You are at the time of the month when you must wait for the green light; keep a low profile and all will be fine. Watch the dramatic news during this trend and realize the importance of having your Moon Power close by. As always, if Starguide works for you, it also works for others, so don't be afraid to tell others to "cool" down. We are all under the incredible will of the cosmos, and Pluto will punish some unlucky souls for their ignorance of God's universal rules.

Partnerships: Be courteous with everyone as your true motives feelings and desires are sure to be heard and felt. This is the time to use your will and apply your knowledge of the stars. Avoid outbursts of emotion, even if your partner gets completely out of hand with jealousy or bad temper. With Jupiter and Venus' protective presence these days, some of the upcoming dramatic news and predictions might pass by without harming your relationships.

Family and Friends: After a Full Moon, Pluto will enjoy himself and will become destructive; use Moon Power's wisdom or you may be very sorry you didn't. Many of us will undergo some form of metamorphosis, as Pluto gives serious wake-up calls. If friends and family members need help or guidance, share your knowledge for the common good. Not a time to plan a visit or get away from home; wait for better stars. Many disturbances are reported during this trend, especially the ones with domestic violence, and the police will have their hands full. Keep a low profile with all; you have the right to be scared and Pluto means business and will hurt you if he has to.

Love Affairs: These days could bring an element of drama, and you are advised to stay clear of other people's problems. Be ready for some secrets to surface. Some people for whom you care may become very uncooperative or decide to fight with you, and could lead you to depression. Better enjoy your own home and cooking on the weekend nights. Social life can only bring unwanted situations as Pluto may send one of his awful children to teach you a lesson. Don't take chances with sex and stay clear of strangers. In the game of love, protect yourself. If you were born in September, a Taurus or a Capricorn could be difficult to deal with. If you are having trouble with a person whom is a water sign having problems with alcohol, move on and look for a better soul.

Travel and Communication: Do not travel unless you absolutely have to. Your car may decide to let you down, so take care of the wheels before taking a risky journey. Double-check all plans and arrangements to avoid further hazards. Now is the time to speak clearly and concisely, as you're prone to miscommunication. Do not broach subjects that are controversial these days, with emotions running high and logic out the window. For those who find themselves in a difficult spot communicating, it may be better to save the subject for later and excuse yourself before it's too late. You will usually find that the argument occurred as a result of what might happen, rather than what will. Lots of secrets will come to light and money will be a disturbing topic for some.

Environment: Remember Pluto. Under this planet's immense destructive power, chemical plants explode, airliners crash, nature goes crazy, products are tampered with, and potentially dangerous technology is sold to hostile powers. It's now time to get close to God in your local church and pray for the unaware victims of deadly Pluto. Be particularly aware of terrorist activity.

Famous Personalities: The world will lose a famous personality under Pluto's command. He may also decide to do it dramatically (assassination). Pluto will not stop with famous people, so watch yourself and choose your environment carefully.

Events: This disreputable planet has always promoted dramatic news involving the police, sex, drama and death. Be ready for a bumpy ride. Pluto is also a factor that stimulates and dramatizes ethics issues and makes them even more complex. On the window posted for April 23rd 1997, I also mentioned on the Internet to watch for surprises with the police and explosions. April 23, 1997 — MOSCOW — A bomb ripped through a railway station in southern Russia on the night of Wednesday April 23rd, killing two people and wounding some 20 others. All these dramatic news happened under the destructive power of Pluto, the Lord of death and drama; so be aware and do not be one of its victims.

Shopping: Buy now anything related to the unknown, magic, candles, and incense. Some old souls will be busy writing their wills. Visit your favorite psychic or astrologer and deal with the unknown. Invest in anything that will bring death to pests, but stay clear of weaponry, it could be used against you or a family member.

※

WED., THU., FRI., SAT., SUN., MON. — MARCH 14, 15, 16, 17, 18, 19:
RULERS — Saturn (Dominion) Uranus (Detonation) Neptune (Trickery):

Work, Career and Business: We are on the Waning time (negative) and faith could be quite low for many. Hold on a little longer for the upcoming New Moon and life will improve for us all. Use patience with everyone around, and wait before launching important business or signing documents. Don't trust any business propositions now and don't take any chances with your finances. The worse is now over, just be patient.

Partnerships: Don't let Saturn's gloomy nature affect your psyche and try smiling if you can. Moon Power mentioned a concentration of negative influences with this last Pluto impact and some of us had to experience a rebirth in partnerships. Again, do not to fall prey to depression or self-destruction. Use all your abilities to deal with your new life and help the ones you care about. Enjoy a good movie and a good bottle of wine at home in the evening hours.

Family and Friends: You may not like it, but a friend or a family member's surprising visit has you scrambling to make your home presentable in advance of the arrival. This person may bring a lot of excitement, but also some unhealthy news. If you decide to socialize, keep an eye on your possessions and lock your car. During a Waning Moon and under Uranus' grip expect bad surprises, as crooks become active. Get rid of unwanted things: have a garage sale or give it away to the Salvation Army, to the unfortunate. Now is a good time to clean, take care of your gardens or even your houseplants. Don't fall for guilt; avoid depressing thoughts of your past. Look for happy people and try to enjoy what life has to offer for now. Keep an eye on the kids especially if there is water around, as Neptune may play tricks on them. An introduction to harmful drugs is always a possibility with them now.

Love Affairs: Stay clear of strangers, especially if alcohol is offered. Not a good time get involved sexually; take precautions. Bad aspects to Neptune in your horoscope will promote, even induce sexually transmitted diseases and narcotic abuse. Secret love affairs may start now, but if you are in one, make sure you are not taken for a ride, as all those promises may be too good to be true! Be practical and review any promises with common sense. If you were born in October, an Aries or an Aquarius will find you quite attractive and may bring more trouble than love into your life.

Travel and Communication: Traveling now may be too risky for comfort; be sure you're prepared for any road emergency or difficult weather. If you must take longs journey be very careful on the road and if possible avoid flying. With the Waning Moon your energy level won't be that high and if you must drive, take plenty of rest before hitting the road. Keep to the speed limit, as the police will be out there ready to penalize you. Avoid drinking at all costs during the evening hours and keep a positive attitude in all you say. Your imagination will be high and must be kept in control.

Environment: Uranus (surprising disruptions) Neptune and Saturn (karma) are not a good combination under a Waning Moon and will upset the poor unaware human on earth below. Many eruptions have taken place under this energy and the weather won't cooperate. April 29, 1997 Mexico City — The Popocatepetl volcano erupts near Mexico City and — April 30, 1997 — Explosion at Albanian weapons depot kills 20 — TIRANA, Albania — At least 20 people were killed when a weapons depot exploded in a central Albanian town. Be aware don't take chances.

Famous Personalities: Sad news will be coming from famous people and their involvement with deceiving activities. Some will exit this world and others could be incarcerated or receive emergency care.

Events: On a large scale disturbing news is to be expected and may disturb the population. The government may be forced to make very important decisions that could affect us. Be ready to hear about disasters such as the following memo of a quatrain posted on my website.
SURPRISES AND EXPLOSIONS! "Mars, the Lord of War" will show his power while none suspect, the surprise of lightning will strike" and the results of my prediction are quite obvious.

- Feb. 24th - Central Florida -- At least 35 people were killed when severe storms hit in and around Orlando, Florida spawning tornadoes that damaged or destroyed scores of buildings and knocked out power.
- Feb.23rd- Portadown, Northern Ireland-- Police suspect a group of anti-British extremists is responsible for a car bomb that devastated the center of the fiercely pro-British Northern Ireland town of Portadown.
- Feb.24th- 3 injured as blast rips through Rome apartment- Three people were injured Tuesday when an explosion, possibly caused by a gas stove, ripped through an apartment in a historic district of Rome.
- Feb. 24th- Algeria train bombing kills 18- a bomb exploded Monday under a passing train, killing 18 people and injuring 25.

Shopping: Difficult energy coming from the Universe will manifest itself, thus not a time to deal with metaphysics or trust psychics. Neptune may blur their vision of the future. Avoid investing in Uranus' tools (computers/electronics).

※

New Moon — March 19, 2007 in Pisces: With the Head of the Dragon in Pisces and Uranus in Pisces expect surprising terrorist activities on the US and Allied interests. Disturbing news about water damage, poisoning, religious fanatics, abortion, the Pope and the Middle East. Many diplomats will be active on the political front, trying to avoid religious wars in different parts of the world. With Mars in Aquarius acts of destruction and nuclear devices is the aim of terrorist. Prominent politicians of the Middle East run the risk of assassination and some unlucky souls will not survive this dangerous trend. With Mercury in Pisces souls born now will further for good or for worse their respective country's religious belief systems. Expect progressive news involving science, chemical research, religion and the abortion dilemma. Meanwhile, it is a sure sign that drastic change is still in store for parts of the Middle East and Asia. Nature and the weather could also turn out particularly difficult and may sink ships, produce devastating oil spills and flooding. However, with the Waxing Moon (positive) we can only hope for less damage than anticipated. Push now, be confident and like the fish, swim with the upward tide.

Lunation impact on all signs:

Aries - A secret about your past will be divulged to you, your intuition is accurate.

Taurus - A new friend will enter your life and further one of your important wishes.

Gemini - Be alert, an opportunity to further your career is ahead of you.

Cancer - A trip close to the water will be bring you joy and a foreigner will please you.

Leo - A great opportunity to make more money or a legacy is ahead of you.

Virgo - A new business or emotional partner will be close by; don't miss this option.

Libra - A new job opportunity or a promotion is around the corner, simply ask for it.

Scorpio - A new business offer, a new love or a child will make you happy.

Sagittarius -Thinking about buying a house or moving, the family needs you.

Capricorn - A new study and a trip is on the agenda. Make the most of it.

Aquarius - A deal will bring you money, but be practical in your spending.

Pisces - A new start in many areas of your life will further your position. Move on.

✹

March 18, 2007 — Venus enters Taurus: Souls born with this celestial gift will need emotional security at all times. Unless the partner is solid and strong, insecurity will bring about a swift break. Great ability is often found in moneymaking schemes, the arts, poetry, writing, photography and drawing. A natural zest for diplomacy is often found with this position. The soul could also marry wealthy and operate in an artistic environment during the course of this reincarnation. Expect presents, love and general uplifting news where your Venus transits your housing system. Perfect time to concentrate on improving your wardrobe and shape the body for the new you. Invest in your desire for beauty and perfection. Souls born now will be possessive in matters related to love, and lucky with money. As the Bull is stubborn, many of them will have to detect wrong relationships and learn to let go and trust again. This is the ideal celestial position to invest in an artistic study. Empower yourself with spirituality and display your creativity to the world.

Souls born now will inherit natural gifts in music and the arts. This is a top position to become a leader in the artistic fields for some. When well assisted by other celestial bodies, this is a perfect position for total commitment and endless love. This position makes for one of the most beautiful woman of the Zodiac. A sincere gift in loving, creating and a distinguished magnetism will lead her to a successful career. These souls were born to reach emotional, financial and spiritual security, teach genuine love and be loved back. A top position involving financial security, communication, writing, and success in any artistic fields is offered to these lucky souls.

✹

TUE., WED. — MARCH 20, 21:
RULERS — Neptune (Magical hopes/ Water) and Mars (War/

action):

Work, Career and Business: The New Moon will make you lucky but Mars could upset your plans. Be nice with others at work; use your knowledge and don't expect your boss to be aware of Mars' impatience and irritability. The Waxing Moon will provide you many opportunities soon. Neptune may make it difficult for you to concentrate these days. Try to be more practical in your endeavors, important matters related to finances will be on your mind, and all will be fine soon.

Partnerships: As always communicate my work to others and make good use of Starguide. You may also suggest it to your partner, as two souls aware of the stars are better than one. Using Neptune's intuitive power may save a situation, but avoid complaining and do something about it. Control Mars' impatience and understand the needs of your partner, too.

Family and Friends: In time of a New or Full Moon, people have some problems sleeping. Use tons of diplomacy with the children; Mars will want to keep them up late. A great time is to be expected soon as the New Moon is now shining on us all. Enjoy the love and good food provided by those who really care for you. Spend some time with the children; teach them love and harmony as Mars may make them play rough. Remember dangerous Mars is with us and with Neptune nearby, be aware around water.

Love Affairs: Avoid any intense Martian situation with your partner; support, love and respect will take you miles. Use Neptune's soft values to apologize to someone you deeply care for and control your imagination. Offer a present or some flowers; this always works. If you were born in November, a Pisces or a Cancer will want to know you. A trip close to the water or a movie will make you feel good.

Travel and Communication: Mars' speedy nature may affect your driving and response to others. Be courteous, psychotics and lunatics share the same road with you and one of those dangerous drivers may get you in trouble. As always, under Neptune's power, stay clear of alcohol if you take a long trip, and rest if you feel tired. Anticipate this New Moon to be great and put a big smile on your face.

Environment: Combined with Mars' accident prone nature and Neptune's absent-mindedness, expect sad news from water, oil or the Middle East. Once more, Mars' destructive instinct is unpredictable, so avoid dangerous situations, especially if you spend time close to the water this weekend.

Famous Personalities: Life is a constant process of change, and like all of us, famous figures must also accept the sad reality of demise. Light will be brought up to some famous people's hidden problems with alcohol or unlawful endeavors. Soon, the end of a notable person's life will reach the media.

Events: With Mars, even on a Waxing positive Moon, fires, destruction, violence, war and nature's devastating forces at work are on the agenda. Difficult weather including explosions, tornadoes or flooding may affect some of the states and surprise a number of people. Much of the difficult news may be coming from Japan, Germany, the Middle East and the US.

Shopping: Now is the perfect time to purchase sharp tools, a camera or get a good deal on any form of chemicals or paint. A new car can also be bought now, but with its Martian nature, controlling speed will be difficult. With Neptune on those wheels, you may be asking for trouble later, if you drink and drive fast.

THU., FRI., SAT., SUN., MON., TUE. — MARCH 22, 23, 24, 25, 26, 27:
RULERS — Venus (Affection) Mercury (Conversation) Moon (Changing life):

Work, Career and Business: The blessings of a Waxing Moon is with us, make the most of her white and protective blanket. This long trend lunation will be progressive and may force you into many changes; no matter how painful they may seem to be, those changes are for the best in the long run. Be confident, as much needed change is ahead. You may also consider using Mercury's mental agility to pass on new ideas to improve your business. You still have time to write or invest in advertisements or publicity. The telephone will be particularly busy. Don't leave the office without your answering machine on, or you could miss a great opportunity. Stay active and be mentally alert.

Partnerships: Dealing with others has and will always be a challenge for us all. Some of you have learnt hard lessons and the scars takes time to heal; don't re-open them again. Move on to better ground, the future has always better to offer. Keep a positive attitude in your conversations and promote only the great times of your past. Some karmic souls will have to experience a rebirth of their relationships. Whatever unfolds, accept the changes with confidence; the truth is that, life is a constant process of change and it always seems to be for the better.

Family and Friends: Mercury is fast and rules communication, so expect family members to get in touch with you via mail or telephone. With Venus around, some will be invited to enjoy great cooking at their friend's homes. "The messenger of the Gods" loves to talk and throw jokes all over. Control Mercury's desire to exaggerate or make things up, and do not fall for the negative things you may hear now. Keep in mind that your friends have the potential to fulfill all your wishes; get active in the social arena and make good use of what is left of this positive Moon. As always, you might have a karmic debt with a long-standing friend; if so, you may have to experience annoyance. Try to clear it all up and you'll win. Brothers and sister could experience rivalry.

Love Affairs: Venus may want you to experience the beginning or ending of important love phases in your life. Keep your eyes and ears open on the people you know, as the Moon affects everybody, especially family members. If you were born in July, someone much older or younger than you born in March, November or January will be attracted to you. A Pisces friend may bring you good news soon.

Travel and Communication: Use Mercury's mental powers accordingly. Time to write those letters, as Mercury improves your mental faculties. He will reward you favorably if you decide to invest in your education or start a book. Control his strong desire to be a "chatterbox," and save money on your telephone bill. Mercury rules transportation and general motion; he also makes people restless on the road. Under his command, be a defensive driver. It's time to plan for your future travels, or visit parts of the world via great books. Wait for the next New Moon to launch the trip. You'll be glad to know and respect God's Universal Laws.

Environment: We still are a few days away from a Full Moon period and you must be ready for nature's power to show off soon. If you are into wild weather be ready for those soon. Some will see the beginning or ending of dramatic times. Be ready for this type of news soon, where thousands of people will be forced to flee nature's destructive forces.

Famous Personalities: Some famous artist or important political figure will experience changes with their children and you will be directly affected too.

※

WED., THU., FRI., SAT. — MARCH 28, 29, 30, 31:
RULERS — The Moon (Readjustment/new) and the Sun (Children/fame/surprises).

Work, Career and Business: Those days will start on a note of faith with many new financial breaks ahead of you. You can expect serious beginnings or endings of important phases of your and others' lives. Be ready for anything coming your way, adjust to life demands. Life is a constant process of change and the stars are always working for you even if you don't realize it just yet.

Partnerships: You will be forced into a new relationship or to let go of the wrong people and their problems; take a chance on yourself and have faith. Many will hear about friends ending something or with someone. The lucky souls will enjoy new beginnings. Many of your wishes may see the light soon, be confident.

Family and Friends: The Sun rules love, romance and children and with what is left of the Waxing Moon, surprising news are ahead of you. If something wrong happens to a child under a good moon, maybe you should check out when you had bought the toy that was used. The Sun gives life to anything that he touches but for some mystical reasons, fatalistic experiences involving children can still happen. As usual, watch over them, especially close to the water. On a more positive note, he will put his undiscriminating light on the incredible UFO manifestation. You may hear about someone's heart problem or surgery.

Love Affairs: Be ready for new starts in love matters and provide spiritual help for the victims suffering painful broken hearts. The right partner might not be the one you want to be with. You should use your newfound freedom to look for someone who deserves your love. With the Waxing Moon, keep looking for that special person and by miracle it will happen. Some teenagers may find their first love or suffer the heartbreak of it. If you are born in January, a much older or younger person born in September or July may want to let you know how much you mean to them.

Travel and Communication: If you decide to take the children with you, be aware on the road; you are responsible for their young lives. Order them to put their seat belts on and be ready for anything. Enjoy all that nature has to offer and be prepared for surprises; enjoy — a great time is ahead of you.

Environment: What was once built by man (cities/homes) or nature (forests), somehow with time, will have to be destroyed. What was once born must eventually die; this is the great cycle of life. Be ready for surprising explosions and fires, so be aware and be prudent if you happen to go into the wilderness.

Famous Personalities: Expect interesting, even weird surprises with children and the rich and famous. Be ready for the unexpected with their words and actions. You may take some calculated chances with the Sun in charge, but understand your limits.

Events: Terrible tragedies such as the Kobe, Japan earthquake and many volcanic eruptions are around the corner, even in a Waxing Moon. Nature will force thousands of people out of their homes because of nature's destructive forces. Let's hope that the powerful life giving Sun will slow or stop bad news.

Shopping: Buy anything for children as long as it is new. Invest in gold or expensive items; you may also invest in computers or anything involving creativity and the arts.

Welcome to Your Day - to - Day Guidance
For April 2004

Full Moon — April 2, 2007 in Libra: The next two weeks are going to be a trying time for many of us. Keep a cool head, as changes in business and partnerships are due for changes with this lunation. Be ready for the beginning or ending of a portion of your business or emotional life. Disturbing and surprising news is ahead of you from the government. Be ready to accept those dramatic upcoming changes. The world is getting ready for serious drama where many young lives will be wasted and death for some innocent souls is inescapable. Keep in mind that, life is a constant process of change, and the future usually has better to offer. Take chances, sign contracts, travel and promote your life only after the next New Moon. Be ready for a bumpy couple of weeks ahead of you. Be strong, you'll need to be, for when all is said and done, you and the world will be in better positions. Some foreign governments will work hard to avoid wars.

Lunation impact on all signs:

Aries - A full restructure of your business and emotional life is ahead. Be patient.

Taurus - Don't be concerned or too worried, your work and your health are connected.

Gemini - Stress and changes with love, business and children are a part of life.

Cancer - Problems at home, and your security should not keep you depressed for long.

Leo - Control your speech, important contracts are ahead, so use diplomacy.

Virgo - Money and commitment is thought, important paper work and your signature is ahead.

Libra - Your emotions and imagination runs high, a new relationship for you?

Scorpio - Let go of wrong associations, a secret love affair could bring trouble; move on.

Sagittarius - A wish can not come true with the person you are with now, change ahead.

Capricorn - Career commitments, contracts and changes are best for you.

Aquarius - A trip must be canceled, a partner gives you trouble, you'll see through it.

Pisces - A friend will let you down soon, you deserve better association in all you do.

SUN., MON., TUE. — APRIL 1, 2, 3, 4:
RULERS — Mercury (Travel news/telephone) and Venus (Love/lust).

Work, Career and Business: Just days away from the Full Moon, make the most of Venus' new fresh breath of life and be aware. With Mercury's vital intellectual genius, push your business now. Advertisements, important calls, traveling, and meetings will pay off before the upcoming Full Moon. Respect the Universal Law, use Moon Power and your knowledge and have faith in your abilities.

Partnerships: Mercury rules the mail, telephone and communication in general; expect drama and secrets coming your way soon. Venus may decide to offer you a get-together after work, but Mercury will have everyone "gossiping." Promote only faith and love, and pass on your message to the world around you.

Family and Friends: Provide a generous shoulder to those who suffered karmic experiences the last few months. However, let no one exhaust your spirit, and avoid being frustrated with loved ones. Some of those friends really need spiritual regeneration or a helping hand. Do so, but realize your limits, especially where money is concerned.

Love Affairs: Your sense of perfection will expand with Venus in charge until the Full Moon. Don't be too picky or demanding with your loved ones; no one is perfect. You may feel like starting a diet; but don't get too concerned with your appearance or your health. Work first on yourself, and the results will stimulate those close to you. Venus hates cigarette smoke, so with her help, apply your will and try to give up smoking. By doing so, the opportunity to find real and healthy love will be given to you. If you were born in February, someone born in August or June may fall in love with you.

Travel and Communication: Use Venus' touch of love to show your affection to those you care for, and offer them flowers. Mercury will get your telephone ringing. Further happiness and love, and you will benefit from your own positive attitude.

Environment: You need to recharge your batteries; a trip in the wilderness is strongly recommended if you have been under stress lately. Venus' energy will make you appreciate the beauty of Mother Nature and the people around you. Many animal rights activists and environmentalists will make serious progress and gain the attention they deserve when passing on their important message.

Famous Personalities: A new diet is on your mind; a famous person will promote a new health product.

Events: With the Full Moon upon, Mother Nature may still decide to relax a bit and keep the approaching Pluto's destructive power under control. Some large financial corporations may decide to merge to secure themselves against competition.

Shopping: Great bargains will be offered if you want to invest in products to improve your life and body. Some may decide to join the local gym or enroll in a weight loss program.

April 6, 2007 — Mars enters Pisces: Mars (the warrior) into the sign of religious Pisces will continue bringing trouble where religion, oil and acts of terrorism from the Middle East are concerned. Expect this trend to be loaded with dramatic news. Many diplomats will be active on the political front to save serious trouble, even war. Many thoughts will be geared towards restructuring or enforcing laws to stop terrorism and secret relationships with certain countries. Prominent politicians either traveling to or coming from the Middle East, run the real risk of assassination. Some unlucky souls will not survive this awful upcoming trend. Some young souls born now may meet with their explosive deaths as martyrs. They will be unafraid of death, extremely destructive with the affairs of religion and will have to learn to control their powerful destructive emotions.

What is really bothering me is that; none of the secret Agency has yet invested in my methodology or Astro-Psychology and this science is well ahead of both conventional psychology and psychiatry. There are obvious traits in one's natal UCI (Unique Celestial Identity) that produces an indisputable terrorist. Especially, when it comes to the Head and Tail of the Dragon or any significant planet in the pious sign of Pisces. This predisposition produces the entire reveille and breed a natural "born" terrorist. The world's secret services would make such a great use of Astro-Psychology instead of using common facial expressions (traditional psychology) in International Airports to detect the physiology and deadly potential of individuals.

All Governmental Secret Agency Administrations nowadays are enslaved to uncover anything about terrorism and I have the Golden Key. Omitting or ignoring any physical or spiritual laws can only bring penalty; for science's purpose is to explore all possibilities, even those laws written in light via the stars. There is art in the imaginativeness don't get me wrong, but there is a big difference between imagination and divination and my writings are designed to raise my readers' (or the FBI) spiritual vibrations and guide them into a more productive endeavor to save lives.

On a more positive note, many of them will be gifted in the arts and will regenerate doing metaphysical work. This Mars' position will lead them towards fame and fortune if they swim upstream or violent death if they chose going downstream. This Mars' position makes for one of the most creative or destructive signs of the Zodiac. As Mars in Scorpio, this hot-tempered energy will lead the soul towards danger, competition and great success if Mars is applied positively. Karmic souls will meet with an early death or imprisonment. Be aware around water and as Pisces rules the feet don't hurt your foot.

※

Attention: Pluto is back with us — As always with the Lord of Hell in charge of this trend, better think twice before saying or acting on impulse. With Pluto in action, expect many affairs of the past and secrets to be divulged. Affairs and foreign leaders will soon make the news again while man and nature's destroying forces will be felt all over the world. The police and blackguards will make the news. More than ever, use diplomacy, as whatever you do now will have very serious repercussions in your future.

THU., FRI., SAT., SUN. — APRIL 5, 6, 7, 8:
RULERS — Pluto (Demise/secrets) and Jupiter (Foreigners/religion):

Work, Career and Business: You are now walking on fire! You'd better use all the "savoir faire" you know if you are to go through this lunation without trouble. A serious wake-up call will come to many abusers, as the heavy hand of karma will fall on the victims. The possibility to lose and rebuild it all will be a serious matter for some karmic souls. Not a time to deal with money matters; you better keep a low profile for a while.

Partnerships: The offensive secret life of a person may surface; you may learn something valuable about a partner. Whatever it is you find out, do not divulge the secret. Stinky moneymaking schemes will play an important part of this trend; you should listen to your intuition in all you do. Stay clear of dark alleys; your life hangs upon your awareness. Many people will learn the hard way these days.

Family and Friends: Do not expect anyone you care about to be diplomatic with you during this trend. Do not fall for Pluto's destructive or sarcastic remarks; words of love and support will pay off in the long run. Be ready for some dramatic news from someone close to you. Whatever happens, be strong; life must go on as Pluto has important work to do and he is part of the celestial design devised by God. Time to further my work and offer knowledge to those for whom you care by letting them read

Moon Power. Remember to go now and then to my website and check my quatrains, as this book will work better for you if you do so.

Love Affairs: Secret affairs of sex and passionate love may be divulged to the public, forcing people to take a stand in destroying and rebuilding relationships. This might happen to you, too. In any case, use tons of diplomacy to save unwanted trouble in your love life. If you are water sign or have any planet in Scorpio, be ready for a wake-up call of some form. Stay clear of any new relationship, stick with the old one or refrain from social interaction.

Travel and Communication: Expect news pertaining to secrets, sex, the police force, and medical discovery. Be careful of what you do or say during this trend. Drive carefully; stay clear of strangers and strange places. Be ready for dramatic news to plague the media.

Environment: Pluto will have fun destroying it all, but remember he belongs to the divine family and has a specific work to do. His dramatic impact on this earth (and people) is needed. As Pluto demolishes, he also gives opportunities to rebuild stronger and better bridges and buildings. Be ready for dramatic news with the police and nature's forces soon.

Famous Personalities: Some famous people will be called back to God. Sometimes famous spoiled children get involved with the wrong crowd, and some are found shot to death alongside a road. Pluto couldn't care less about famous people.

Events: Hopefully, knowledgeable Jupiter will slow down Pluto's rampage and thirst for blood. Under his power, a plane plowed into crowd at an air show. Under Pluto jurisdiction planes crash, avoid flying and be ready for a repetition of the past soon. A Bell 212 helicopter belonging to the Mexican Attorney General's Office crashed upon landing in rural Mexico killing the navigator and injuring five people.

Shopping: All water and earth signs will see an important part of their business or financial life taking a specific direction within this lunation. With Jupiter here too, the worst might be avoided by some miraculous development. A visit to your local church to pray for Pluto's victims will be of benefit to you. Do not invest in weapons, if you do so you might have to use them against crooks later. Anything bought now that can be used for metaphysics will bring unusual power to you.

※

April 11, 2007 — Mercury enter Aries: With the planet of communication cruising through the aggressive sign of Aries, be aware of your speech and your speed. On a more positive side, your intellectual potential will regenerate with new studies. This is a perfect time to launch a magazine or any form of study involving the mind or new topics. Souls born with this celestial signature will be extremely competitive, intelligent, curious and great communicators. They will need to discipline their minds and learn to listen to others. An opportunity to make an impact in the world of speed and communication is offered to the soul. Dr. Turi needs your help to pass on his very important star message to the world. See www.drturi.com or call 602-999-3010 to help us to set a crash course in your area.

※

April 12, 2007 — Venus enters Gemini: The planet of love in the sign of dual Gemini needs a lot of variety and spiritual gymnastics. Souls born with this celestial gift will need mental stimulation at all times. Unless the partner is physically and intellectually animated, boredom will bring about a swift break. Great ability is often found in poetry, writing, photography and drawing. A natural zest for diplomacy and learning foreign languages is often found with this position. The soul could also marry and reside in a foreign land during the course of this reincarnation. Expect lots of great news, and to spend money on anything that writes, reads, rolls and speaks.

※

**MON., TUE., WED., THU., FRI. — APRIL 9, 10, 11, 12, 13:
RULERS — Saturn (Uncle Sam decisions) and Uranus (Shocking news/explosions):**

Work, Career and Business: Expect a forced ending passed to your service to the world or your career. Something must be done, something must change; be ready. The undertaking that you are doing leaves you unsatisfied and is a source of stress; you might be forced to modify your direction. Resolve to find a new way of handling your career soon and for the lucky ones expect a well-deserved promotion. The unlucky ones will be forced to realize their limits.

Partnerships: Don't let anyone pressure you into using their ideas, instead of your own. You came across this plan to stimulate you and your entrepreneurial spirit to become more independent. Meditate to understand where this partnership is going in your life. Did you make the right choices and can you live with them? If not, there will be a better time to deal with those questions; these days will help you to change it all. Some surprising news is ahead of you.

Family and Friends: Your friends will be requesting your presence and may invite you to a gathering. Enjoy this opportunity, but you will be amazed with what you are about to hear. Uranus also makes the children very active and accident-prone; watch them closely. They will lean heavy on you; be patient with their young demanding spirits. Let them enjoy Uranus' world of miracles, maybe by going to a place you went before like Disneyland or the Zoo. Keep your eyes on everything they do and everywhere they go and you will have a smashing time.

Love Affairs: Expect spicy consternation during these days, as many people will surprise you. With Uranus' disturbing touch these days, avoid going places or doing things you never did before. Stay with what you do or know best. Karmic love is around the corner for some, especially if you were born under an air sign. Someone from your past will be attracted to you. If you are an Aquarius, a Leo or a Gemini may bring someone much younger or older in your life.

Travel and Communication: Here are some ideas for a small trip not far from town. Uranus rules electronics, the future, astrology, psychic phenomena, and UFOs. If you want to see something unusual, talk about it and do it now. However, be aware of the negative Moon as you may attract wrong experiences. If you're lucky, Uranus may decide to grant one of your wishes. Stay clear of storms; sudden blackouts and danger coming from lightning is very real.

Environment: On a sad note, keep in mind that Uranus rules explosions, earthquakes and volcanoes. He may also decide to throw a tornado or produce violent explosions. Let's hope he won't. Similar energies were in force on February 23rd 1998, the police suspected a group of anti-British extremists to be responsible for a car bomb that devastated the center of the fiercely pro-British Northern Ireland town of Portadown. The weather will turn really nasty and will induce serious chain reaction accident.

Famous Personalities: Be ready as expected, for unusual types of news coming from extroverted celebrities. Much will be done for children during this trend, but the negative tendency could touch some of them. Let's hope I am wrong, I hate to say anything drastic about the children. Sadly enough, Uranus or Pluto couldn't care a bit about my personal feelings and will do whatever pleases them. A famous person will provide and help to make important decisions pertaining to the younger generation, computers and education.

Events: Under Uranus' surprising explosive power, large earthquakes and incredible news tends to take place.

Shopping: You may feel like spending time and money on your appearance; it's a great time to shop for second hand wardrobe items, or consult a beautician if you experience any skin problems. Not a good time to pay a visit to your local psychic unless you know him/her well; stay practical and use your own intuition.

※

New Moon – April 17, 2007 in Aries: The New Moon will mature in the sign of Aries. Explosive and destructive news about fires, wars, and explosions is to be expected soon. Mother Earth is alive and may stretch her self vigorously, producing powerful volcanic or earthquake activity. Souls born with this celestial identity will be competitive, aggressive and will use their inner leadership abilities to gain positions of power during their lifetimes. Discipline and patience must be induced at an early age to avoid serious head injury. Many endeavors will be launched successfully within the next two waxing weeks and you should be confident of the outcome.

Lunation impact on all signs:

Aries - This lunation is on you, a new start of a section of your life is imminent.

Taurus - A secret will come to light soon and relieve some guilt of your past.

Gemini - A new friend will bring you an important wish, you're lucky this month.

Cancer - Your career will see some great developments, use this new moon accordingly.

Leo - A trip or a study will help you to deal with business or foreign affairs.

Virgo - A partner will help you to make money, a legal action or a contract is ahead.

Libra - A new business deal or a new emotional partner is on the horizon.

Scorpio - Changes at work, don't stress and your health will improve for sure.

Sagittarius - A new hobby or a child will make you happy; love is in the air!

Capricorn - You will have to re-structure your home or move, be aware of fire.

Aquarius - Great news by mail or telephone is ahead of you, a sibling needs you.

Pisces - A new way to make money or invest in your education is on the way.

SAT., SUN., MON., TUE. — APRIL 14, 15, 16, 17:

RULERS – Neptune (Middle East/oceans) and Mars (War/trouble).

Work, Career and Business: Make good use of the information printed in Starguide; this work translates the energies ahead of us. With the Waning Moon upon us it is time to slow down and do some clean up around the office. Avoid signing important contracts, and postpone every important meeting until the approaching New Moon. Slow down, be patient; there won't be much that you can do, apart from finishing up or preparing your next move. Anything else could be a waste of your time and money.

Partnerships: Do not let anything bad to happen to your psyche; avoid Neptune's deceiving nature. With Mars around, you'd better use a diplomatic attitude in all your endeavors and avoid any confrontation with co-workers or your supervisor. Time to rescue some depressed spirits without letting your self be affected by their personal problems. A good movie or a great video will do for tonight.

Family and Friends: Friends and family in trouble will call you. They might be experiencing anxiety in their relationships; provide them with your support. Talk about the Moon's impact upon their lives and psyches and mention my book. Expect a difficult time where you should be prudent and patient with others. The depressing power of Neptune also affects your friends; sadly enough some of them will abuse alcohol and may pay a heavy price. DO NOT DRINK and drive and if you do drink, designate a safe driver or have a cab take you back home. Neptune could seriously blind your vision and with Mars' impatience you could visit the emergency room (or the cemetery!). Don't take a chance on your life; stay clear of chemicals and use tons of patience on your family members.

Love Affairs: A secret love affair may be a temptation to some but it will bring deception to the unaware initiator. Time to give strong support to your mate especially if they are water signs, as the Waning Moon will make them "moody." If you are a Pisces, Cancer or Scorpio do not expect much with love, romance or with your children. Just be patient, control your imagination and do not nurture guilt from past endeavors. A long walk to the mall or the sea will keep your mind away from Neptune's depressing cries.

Travel and Communication: The majority of people is not yet aware of the power of Mars and Neptune upon their psyches and will become depressed or behave like aggressive robots. Drive slowly, be alert and most of all stay calm in any situation. Be very forthright and patient in your speech, as miscommunications now could have disastrous results. Further love and understanding and all will be fine.

Environment: This celestial duo has in the past produced oil spills, chemical plant explosions and will produce extremely high tides. Avoid the sea if you can to be safe, as many vessels will go down to Poseidon's world. Stressing news about chemicals and flooding is to be expected soon.

Famous Personalities: An interesting but deceiving news about some actors. Elizabeth Taylor, Mohammed Ali and Michael Jackson could make sad news. The Pope and the church could give us sad news as abortion and religious groups will insist on their personal wars. Neptune rules news about the Navy, deception, jails, hospitals, the Middle East, oil, and all religions combined together. Under his illusive power on May 3 1997, the Pope made an important announcement. VATICAN CITY — When Pope John Paul II makes a choice for sainthood; it's often to make a point. On Sunday, he draws attention to a long neglected and often despised group in Europe, beatifying a Gypsy for the first time in the history of the Roman Catholic Church. Beatification is the last step before possible canonization or sainthood. With Uranus (shocking) in pious Pisces (religion/Middle East) expect anything weird again soon to take place. The church authorities will find another way to probe into society to grasp more sinners (Gays/Gypsies) to pay for their enormous legal battle and failing abusive financial infrastructure. The age of ignorance, manipulation and religion is giving place to the more advanced universal and brilliant sign of Aquarius.

Events: Mars (the warrior) rules Germany and parts of Europe; disturbing news may come from there. The weather could turn real nasty again and water and slides could be a serious threat to some regions of the US.

Shopping: Sad news about gas price is on the way but good deals could be found in a garage sale or your local flea market. But anything related to chemicals to rid the house of pests or the garden of unwanted weeds. Avoid buying any hard medicines and stay clear of heavy prescriptions. With Uranus (New Age matters) in Pisces (your subconscious, invest in some of my DVD's or CD's and learn how to use the creative forces of your subconscious at your advantage.

※

WED., THU., FRI., SAT. — APRIL 18, 19, 20, 21:
RULERS — Mars (Fight/hazard) Venus (Love/cherished) and Mercury (Traveling).

Work, Career and Business: Mars is still active, so emotional reactions in the office should be avoided. Use patience and diplomacy with who ever is around, and good progress will be made. Make plans for the future and act upon them while the Moon is New. Money and communication will play an important part of this trend.

Partnerships: Some interesting news may come your way. You have free will, so don't allow Mars to let anyone force his opinion on you. With Mercury's sense of exaggeration, do not fall for all you hear, and don't be afraid to challenge people's information. You need to use your intuition, and sensitive Venus can help you in doing so. Use words of love and be patient with everyone; the New Moon will induce a new energy in them. Time to proceed forward, you are protected.

Family and Friends: In the anticipation of the upcoming weekend, Venus will bring an element of love and joy. Mercury will make us very communicative, and Mars will further a desire for action. This trend will be an interesting one where friends and family members will try to get in touch with you all at the same time. Make the most of those beautiful stars and enjoy life. Listen to a young person's needs.

Love Affairs: If you use Venus' "savoir faire" in any situation, you will win over Mars' argumentative temperament. A great time to show love and affection to those you care for. Avoid depressing conversations of your past, stay in the future, and look to the bright side of life. If you were born under the fiery sign of

Leo, keep a cool head with someone born in April or November. An Aquarius may fall in love with you. Get going and reach your wishes now.

Travel and Communication: Don't let this trio drive you crazy, as you will have a million things to do at the same time. The strength of Mars combined with the speed of Mercury may bring trouble in your driving, so slow down. Use precautions and take your time if you have to travel far; don't let accident-prone Mars create obstacles. Be alert and slow down and nothing wrong will happen. Make your future plans to travel now.

Environment: Keep in mind that impatient Mars is also with us and he doesn't care for any of your plans; he may decide to create an earthquake or produce disturbing weather. If Mars wins over Venus and Mercury, his destructive power will be felt with explosions. "Mars, the Lord of War will show his power, while none suspect, the surprise of lightning will strike"-- Note: Algeria train bombing kills 18- A bomb exploded under a passing train, killing 18 people and injuring 25, state radio reported. It was the latest in a new wave of attacks the government blamed on Muslim militants.

Famous Personalities: This powerful threesome may take the life of an important political person. Someone famous may also meet a sad fate in the water or on the road. Be aware and be prudent.

Events: Pluto (ultimate power/ life and death) is still in the sign of Sagittarius (religion). He will keep enforcing a slow but sure decay of dogmatic religious doctrines. Religions as they are known at present will be completely transformed. The rebirth will result in one Universal Religion based on man's direct cosmic consciousness with God. This celestial configuration will bring real spiritual leaders to the fore passing on their inborn gift of teaching the fundamental laws governing all life in the universe. Disturbing news from the Pope or the Middle East is ahead.

Shopping: Invest in tools or anything brand new, as great deals await you. Be confident in spending large amounts of money on clothes or jewelry now, they will bring you luck or the magnetism you're looking for.

SUN., MON., TUE., WED. — APRIL 22, 23, 24, 25:
RULERS — The Moon (New life/home) and the Sun (Children/spirit of love).

Work, Career and Business: Do not try to hold on to your past; accept the upcoming changes with faith. The stars' pattern and changes are imposed by God to continually promote experiences and a better life. This will be an interesting Universal trend full of changes and surprises for us all. With the Waxing Moon, try anything new and take chances on new opportunities. Someone's advice regarding an investment may be worthwhile. Examine all business propositions carefully and sign the paperwork now. With the Sun around, expect some surprising progress in the near future.

Partnerships: Be ready for the beginning or ending of an important part of your life. It is a strong possibility to find a new business partner. You may feel comfortable with the person involved and sense that you can succeed with his inborn talent. Make a full commitment to succeed and work harder to get there. If the people you are with do not fit your wishes, the New Moon will induce new ones, so go out now.

Family and Friends: The Sun will give tons of radiant energy to the children. If you don't take them out to the park, your hands will be full for a couple of days! Let them get rid of their surplus solar energy, and be sure to keep your eyes on them. Many kids get hurt under this energy. You may be requested to enjoy Mom's great food at home in the security and safety of your own family. The family circle will be active these days and mother would be happy to hear about your progress. Expect an element of surprise coming your way by a friends surprising arrival. You may want to plan a special gathering for a person to whom you are close. Great food, love and joy are on the agenda. Make the most of these rare and beautiful stars.

Love Affairs: Use this New Moon fully. Romance is on your mind more than ever, and a meeting with some friends could lead to an exciting love affair with an interesting stranger. Visit or call your friends; they need to share interesting news pertaining to love, romance and children. During the night hours, enjoy the artistic intonations of the Sun with a great show. If you are a Capricorn,

Virgo, or a Taurus, a much younger or older person needs to know you.

Travel and Communication: Again, this is the time where anything you really want could happen if you ask hard enough. The Moon is Waxing and your trips are protected if you take precautions on the road. Flying is also under good auspices and planning for trips now will add more protection.

Environment: Some dramatic happenings related to nature will force the government to make decisions about a situation. Many will be forced to relocate and start a new life due to natural catastrophes. Let's hope the New Moon will slow down any structural damages. Food and clothing could also be needed and sent to some parts of the world.

Famous Personalities: Many famous people will take part in charity events and many will donate money to alleviate the suffering of the world. Great news pertaining to new arrivals will make the family happy.

Events: The Sun's expansive power may affect a number of organizations. Expect some conservative groups to make the news about the earth, abortion or religion. Children could also be affected, so watch over them.

Shopping: Invest in gold; the stock market will take some by surprise. Anything charming and beautiful bought now will further fame or love. Use the light of the Sun to further your creativity and invest in any form of healing art now. Dr. Turi needs your help to pass on his very important star message to the world, please sign on to his free Dragon Newsletter from his home page and pass it on to all the people you care and always think of offering Moon Power to a friend in need.

※

April 28, 2007 — Mercury enter Taurus: This is the ideal time to review new financial endeavors or investigate possibilities for future investments. Empower yourself to structure your future financial security, and remember to sign the legal forms after the New Moon only. Souls born now will be naturally artistic, while others will display gifts in handling corporate money.

Many souls born with this celestial intonation are born financial planners, and much of their patience will pay off in the long run. A top position to lead in any financial organizations, the arts and beauty will prevail. The quality of stubbornness is often present in these souls, and needs to be controlled and or eliminated. A gift or appreciation for music, gemology, geology or even massage is usually present.

※

THU., FRI., SAT., SUN., MON. — APRIL 26, 27, 28, 29, 30:
RULERS — The Sun (Children) Mercury (Sibling) and Venus (Love):

Work, Career and Business: This trio will make these days quite interesting in terms of action and news. You will be occupied trying to cope with all the demands made upon you. Local errands will keep you busy and bring you in contact with interesting people. Don't rush if you feel you won't make progress or if things don't go your way; all will change soon. Use the Waxing Moon to your advantage and be patient.

Partnerships: Expect new partners to show you their talents, and be patient with them if they cannot follow your pace. The deserving hard-working souls will benefit soon with well-deserved promotions or new opportunities for growth. Your wishes could be granted if you mean business and become active on the social scenery.

Family and Friends: A family member or a friend in need may request your advice. Be willing to consider the issues from their point of view, but try to avoid emotional outbursts and do not force your opinion on them. You may receive an invitation to be part of a gathering; use this opportunity to get some of your wishes. You miss some people you know well who have moved away. You may decide to relocate soon yourself.

Love Affairs: Don't be insecure or shy; go after the person you are attracted to. Propose to dine out or offer flowers. With the great Sun in charge your romanticism will be accepted. Use positive words and further your life now. With Mercury in the air, get on the phone; you will use a convincing approach to stimulate someone you care about. Your words can make a difference with a person who has lost some of the feelings they had for you. If you were born in July, a curious foreigner born in March or November may be looking for your love. Keep busy on the social scenery.

Travel and Communication: Some lucky people will decide to take a trip to Las Vegas and enjoy the nightlife. The Waxing Moon (positive) may bring you luck. If you plan to travel, always make all your plans within the New Moon to protect yourself and further your wishes. Enjoy the wilderness and enjoy the best of what life has to offer. Use the growing New Moon's energy to your advantage.

Environment: Wind could be a problem and speedy Mercury could produce sudden tornadoes in some parts of the US. Expect activity from environmentalists fighting for the survival of wildlife and the earth.

Famous Personalities: Much talk and gossip will be available from celebrity magazines. A brother, a sister or a pair of twins may make the news.

Events: Hopefully, Venus will stop any damage from explosions. News from France or Japan or the Middle East could be troublesome. Interesting new developments in biology, science and research are to be expected soon.

Shopping: Gifts offered to those for whom you care will bring much luck to their happy owners. You can find a good deal on a big-ticket item by comparison shopping. Offer Starguide as a birthday gift, and bring the light of true predictions and guidance into someone's life.

Welcome to Your Day - to - Day Guidance
For May 2007

Full Moon — May 2, 2007 in Scorpio: Use extreme caution. The next two weeks are going to be trying and dramatic for some. Be ready for a rough journey. Disturbing news from foreign lands is to be expected. Pluto (suicide/drama/death) will bring a dance of destruction to this world where fanatic religious young souls will impose their deadly, righteous, dogmatic views on others. Powerful transformations in the world of faith and the church are ahead. The previous wake-up call provided by Pluto's impact on the WTC on 9/11 will induce a form of awareness, but also a death and rebirth for some people. Pluto will bring to light the shameful manipulation, sexual and financial secrets of organized religions and some of their religious leaders. As always with the Lord of Hell in charge of this trend, better think twice before saying or acting on impulse. Expect nature's devastating forces to be active, and secrets, affairs of sex, and finances to be divulged. The police and blackguards will make the news. More than ever use diplomacy, as whatever you do now will have serious repercussions in your future. Time to keep a cool head and be aware in all you do or say. Pray for the souls of the poor victims and let's hope my message gets out to the world at large this time.

Lunation impact on all signs:

Aries - News of life and death and trouble with corporate money is ahead. Be patient.

Taurus - Partnerships in business or marriage will become serious problems; clean up.

Gemini - Stress and change with your health or your work, use your will and win.

Cancer - Problems with love, romance and children; don't respond to the negative moon.

Leo - Important change at home or with the family is ahead, use diplomacy, you'll win.

Virgo - Be aware of your words and your speech, or a sexual encounter could bring trouble.

Libra - Finances will cause worry, don't hurt your self-esteem, be positive.

Scorpio - Time to use all your will to avoid drama in all areas of your life, be the Eagle.

Sagittarius - Let go of your past, a secret will come to light and good change is ahead.

Capricorn - Sad news and secrets from friends will bother you, be strong.

Aquarius - A setback to your career but so much more for you. See through it.

Pisces - A study or a trip will become stressful and wake up calls from a foreigner.

※

Note: Attention: Pluto is back with us — Be ready for dramatic happenings all over; control is a must. Don't be Pluto's victims; be aware of its destructive power. Anything you say or do under his power will follow you for the rest of your life. Time to use extreme caution in all you do. Killers, rapists, psychotics, and the worst of society will be active. While Pluto reigns, you'd better stay home and let the ignorant get killed. Make good use of my work and pass on this site www.drturi.com to those you care for solid guidance. Expect secrets to surface and news from the police force and terrorist acts soon.

TUE., WED., THU., FRI., SAT., SUN. — MAY 1, 2, 3, 4, 5, 6:
RULERS — Pluto (Death/police) Venus (Secret love) and Jupiter

(Foreigners).

Work, Career and Business: In time of a Full Moon, don't let Pluto make you too direct or radical until you really know what you're talking about. Be cautious in all you say and do. Pluto stimulates the animal nature in man and will make us behave accordingly. Be aware that whatever you say or do now will have serious repercussions in your life. Stay on the side of the law and make a good use of Venus' diplomacy or you could end up sorry. Money will play an important part of this trend; use your intuition and turn down a hazardous business proposition.

Partnerships: Pluto is very choleric, and nothing will stop him from inducing trouble in your life. Death, secrets, power, manipulation, sex and extra-marital affairs are his favorites. Venus is no match for her powerful brother Pluto and this duo will change you into a walking sexual magnet to others. Be aware and stay close to the one you trust.

Family and Friends: Be aware of everything and everybody around you. Keep an eye on the children; Pluto takes their young lives swiftly. Be patient with family and friends, avoid gossiping, and help by cooling things down. This is the perfect time to mention my work before this celestial trend; the skeptics will receive a full wake-up call pertaining to the stars' impact in their lives.

Love Affairs: With Jupiter around, a foreigner you know will play an important part in the next dilemma of your life. Pluto will also make you highly sensual and magnetic; you should take all the precautions needed to avoid sexually transmitted disease. A love affair started now will have a profound, even dramatic impact on your life. All water and earth signs, especially Scorpio and Taurus, will be affected by this plutonic impact; be aware, be prudent. Better stay home and watch TV.

Travel and Communication: Not a time at all to plan a long-distance trip or even to travel to faraway places. Use diplomacy in all your conversation and listen carefully; you will hear about secrets. Understand the limits to your investigations, and let neither sarcasm nor the Scorpio's stinger affect your self-esteem. Stay clear of psychotic leaders and crowded places loaded with maniacs suggesting castration, suicide or drugs.

Environment: Nothing will stop Pluto from his tragic assaults to the earth. Be ready for some serious messes from the worst of our society who will shock the media.

Famous Personalities: Many financial or sexual secrets about a famous person will reach the media. Some unlucky souls will get wake-up calls from the dramatic planet. A public figure will make dramatic news or may be called to God.

Events: As usual, be aware of the power of Pluto, as dramatic news will plague the media. Expect news pertaining to the police force, sex, scandals, earthquakes, secrets, abortion and AIDS. The police will be busy trying to catch the villains. Hopefully none of the brave public servants will die doing so. The police force will make the news as they always do when their Plutonic ruler is in charge. In the past, I have sent certified letters to many prominent governmental figures and ex- police chiefs of Los Angeles and San Diego Daryl Gate and Burgreen) well before and after the dramatic happenings unfolded. Copies were sent of both pages 87 and 36 of Starguide 1996/1997 where I predicted (over a year before) the "Rancho Santa Fe mass suicide" of March 26th 1997 and "Bill Cosby's loss." Including the Rodney King and Torrey Pines (San Diego) police officer rapists killer. No reply ever came.

None of those governmental officials had the decency to answer my mail. Even with the plain facts in their face, none of those public executives ever acknowledged my work in predictive astrology. Fear of ridicule kills your children and our police officers. I hope and pray that someday they will train our valiant and courageous policemen on the incredible dangers they face when Pluto is in charge. My research is unarguable and too many police officers have died in the name of their superiors' ignorance and fear of ridicule. In ignorance of Pluto's laws, too many lives have been wasted; not only with the police, but also by the "Death Wish Generation", where children kill teachers and classmates (see my book, "The Power of the Dragon" and learn more about it).

Shopping: Avoid investing in dangerous tools, weapons or ammunition. Pluto's awful signature of death should not be stored in your home. Doing so could kill your own children or family members. Beware of what cannot be seen or understood, yet in terms of metaphysics could greatly cost you or your loved ones. You may invest in anything that can be used to kill nuisances.

If you buy dangerous substances, keep them well away from children. Share my valuable forecast from www.drturi.com or accurate guidance for someone's birthday or offer a comparison chart for a newly wed couple.

※

May 8, 2007 — Venus enters Cancer: Wait until after the New Moon to launch any financial or real estate endeavors. Home improvement and buying or selling a beautiful house is on the agenda for some. Souls born now will be soft and emotional in matters related to love and family. They will make money with hotels and restaurant business endeavors. Many of them will strive to find a partner willing to exchange deep emotions and spiritual research. Some will have to learn to let go of wrong relationships. This position makes for one of the most sensitive signs of the Zodiac. Usually a gift in cooking is present with this position. Those souls are born to feed the world with food and love. This position of Venus is a top position for financial security, communication and success in real estate.

※

MON., TUE., WED., THU. — MAY 7, 8, 9, 10:
RULERS — Saturn (Power for changes/karma) and Uranus (Explosion/shocking).

Work, Career and Business: With a Waning Moon (negative) many of your wishes won't be granted just yet. Don't invest in your future; you may regret it. Do not turn down an invitation offered by friends that you know well; they may require your presence at a gathering. Chatter from those you meet now should not be taken seriously. Those of a certain age will offer valuable intellectual guidance. Be patient until the next New Moon.

Partnerships: Expect the beginning or ending of important parts of your life and be ready for surprising developments. Your life at work may be unstable now but those changes will give you the opportunity to focus on plans for a better future. Support your partner with words of courage. Don't let Saturn's depressing thoughts get to you.

Family and Friends: The weekend could be spent with family members, good friends and Mom's good food. Some will prefer to dine out with lovers or business partners, but the experience could be troublesome. This is the time to practice patience with everyone around, and avoid doing anything original. Help a younger spirit in need.

Love Affairs: Absolutely anything great can happen if you are lucky enough to be involved with the right partner who really loves you. Don't gamble on anything or try to reach for your dreams just yet. Throw a party, but avoid new faces; old friends have the best to offer. Participate with life to avoid depression. If you are a Capricorn, then a Cancer or a Virgo may fall for you. If the person is new in your life then don't dream, use your head.

Travel and Communication: Make the best of Saturn and "Moon Power" in your life by planning future trips and by being prudent on the road. Curiosity is the pathway to fulfillment and happiness and Saturn will reward you for your celestial planning. Take care of the children and let them participate in all the great activities. Be aware of eccentric Uranus affecting them; have a good time and enjoy it all. Some may have to relocate to different residences; make sure you do your Astro-Carto-Graphy before then, as these "new" stars may affect you positively or negatively. Read the section on Astro-Carto-Graphy at the end of this book and if you need more information don't be afraid to call the office at 602-265-7667. Being at the right place at the right time has a lot to do with your progress in terms of opportunities. The knowledge found in Astro-Carto-Graphy would be a major contribution to your success (or your failure) in one of these new locations. Keep this opportunity in mind and give it a try — it works!

Environment: Stay clear of thunder and lightning; Uranus takes many lives without warning. Expect him to throw a quake, a tornado or blow up a volcano soon. Let's just hope you won't be in his way! Explosions in Japan, France or the US are to be expected soon. Under Uranus power - TOKYO -- A bomb damaged the home of an official at Tokyo's international airport, police suspected leftists, who have long opposed the airport.

Famous Personalities: Crazy behavior by some famous people in public is high on the list. Some will become engaged, or married in very large gatherings, and others will expose their strong desires for freedom.

Events: Under Uranus' power in CONROE, Texas — A fire ignited a small oil tank causing several explosions outside an Exxon oil refinery and forcing the evacuation of 40 refinery workers and nearby residents. Disco death Philippines — 150 people died in a discotheque fire. Alaska fire burns 'out of control'. HOUSTON, Alaska — Fueled by gusty winds, a wildfire has swept "out of control" in south-central Alaska, where it has engulfed 7,000 acres and destroyed as many as 100 homes. Expect earthquake and volcanic activity soon.

Shopping: Invest in Uranus now: visit your astrologer or favorite psychic only if you know him/her well. Don't bring a new spiritualist into your life at this time, especially if you have never dealt with him before. Unless you feel strongly or know otherwise about him, don't do it. Any of those light workers are karmically attracted to you and the reading could be one of your best or your worst psychic experiences. Stay with the professionals, some of those psychics need more help than you do! Uranus rules astrology and if you are attracted to the stars there won't be a better time for you to realize what the old science has to offer you.

※

May 11, 2007 — Mercury enters Gemini: Speedy Mercury enters his own sign of Gemini. You will feel like talking about traveling or furthering your business and emotional relationships. Be prudent on the road as Mercury rules cars and speed. Many people driving with you are not aware of this celestial activity and could pay the price of their cosmic ignorance. Make good use of "Moon Power" and keep reminding yourself of this fact and your real knowledge. Your telephone will be red hot and action will be everywhere. Mercury rules all the motion parts, your arms, fingers, shoulders, etc. Don't let him crack some of your bones because of impatience. Be prudent and be patient in all you do and you will be protected. Investing in a car after the New Moon may protect you from violent death.

※

FRI., SAT., SUN., MON., TUE. — MAY 11, 12, 13, 14, 15:
RULERS — Neptune (Oil/ocean) and Mars (Assault/war).

Work, Career and Business: As usual with Mars' aggressive personality, expect all sorts of trouble with business partnerships. You are strongly advised to use diplomacy to avoid serious complications, especially during a Waning Moon. If you are experiencing some trouble in your career, a serious change may be ahead of you. Neptune will make you absent-minded; try to concentrate. A little walk by the water would do your spirit good. Be patient, we are getting closer to the next New Moon.

Partnerships: The Lord of dreams may make your spiritual life busy and some of your dreams may come true in the near future. Learn to translate your subconscious impressions and write down your dreams first thing in the morning. You or your partner may be responding to Neptune's power, so you may want to reach your inner self asking for God's help in your prayers. Some may feel tuned into the universe and miraculously guided out of a bad situation. Provide spiritual support to those in need.

Family and Friends: As usual with Neptune's sad touch and combined with the Waning Moon, sensitive friends may get depressed. Be there to help, but don't let their problems get to you. The lonely old ones will feel the impact of Neptune and its accompanying deception upon their lives. Give a thought and pay them a visit or send them a little card. This gesture will make them feel less lonely and will make their own world more exciting. Be ready to offer a strong shoulder and realize the impact of Neptune upon your world. If you are a Pisces or a Gemini a positive friend could help you.

Love Affairs: Keep your eyes on your possessions as things may "disappear" now. Don't let yourself into a deceiving business deal or worthless situation; learn to love with your head, first and give your heart later. Your intuition will be sharp; use it to your advantage. A secret love affair may start for some earth signs and might last a while.

Travel and Communication: Remember, Neptune is also part of this trend and if you have to drive, you MUST stay clear of any alcohol. Neptune leads many unaware people to jail, left with a DUI to deal with. If you were born under a water sign stay clear of trouble if you feel depressed, don't drink tonight.

Environment: Venus will try to stop her violent brother from stirring the earth's innards, as Mars loves earthquakes, explosions, volcanoes and mass disasters. Sad news may come from the ocean, the Middle East and oil spills. Mother earth is alive, resourceful, and must heal.

Famous Personalities: Some prominent people may be caught in secret sexual or love affairs. Their dependency on chemicals, drugs or alcohol will be made public. The lucky ones will promote new movies. Under Neptune's power — WEST HOLLYWOOD, California — Sheriff's deputies pulled over Eddie Murphy early Friday and arrested a transsexual prostitute who was riding in his car, authorities said. A spokesman for the actor maintained Murphy was just being a "good Samaritan" by offering the transsexual a ride.

Events: Under Neptune and Mars' powers, CAIRO, Egypt — A powerful sandstorm tore through southern Egypt Saturday, killing at least four people. The storm comes a day after the worst sandstorm in 30 years blasted across the country. With Mars' aggressive nature, expect this type of news again. Villains will be active during this trend; do not trust strangers and do not put yourself in any situation that could make you a potential victim. Avoid dark streets and keep your personal alarm (intuition) on all the time.

Shopping: Try to participate in volunteer work to provide love and help to the needy. Shop in places promoting good causes; they need your financial support. Not a good time to invest in prescription drugs or decide to visit your spiritual advisor, unless you know him/her very well.

※

May 16, 2007 — Mars enters Aries: With the planet of war in its own sign Aries (dignified), expect news of war and explosions soon. Mars (Lord of war) rules Germany and destructive news may come from there or Japan too. You need to use critical diplomacy when Mars cruises through a house in your chart. Many people will become especially affected by fire or accidents, and to their heads; Aries rules the head, in the medical aspect of my work. You may also use this planet to tackle difficult projects. Children born with this configuration are born leaders and will be attracted to dangerous sports (daredevils) and to the Army or Navy. Discipline must be enforced at an early age without hurting the fragile ego of the child.

※

New Moon — May 16, 2007 in Taurus: The peaceful planet Venus rules this sign. However, combined with the magnetic pull of Mars for the next few days, we may experience explosions, accidents and damaging earthquakes. Hopefully, gracious Venus will stop her turbulent brother Mars from disturbing the earth's entrails. Use this lunation to further your finances and utilize Venus' diplomatic power to deal with others. If you play your cards right, she might also reward you with love. Money will play an important part of this lunation.

Lunation impact on all signs:

Aries - An opportunity to improve your finances is ahead, don't miss it.

Taurus - This lunation is right on top of you, you cannot miss the new start.

Gemini - A secret will be revealed and a close person needs you.

Cancer - An important wish will be granted by a friend, be active.

Leo - Positive changes in your career will make you happy, stay on top.

Virgo - A new study or a far away trip is in store for you, be confident.

Libra - A legacy or a legal affair will turn in your favor; travel soon.

Scorpio - A new relationship or a new business venture is ahead for you.

Sagittarius - Your health and work will improve and you'll be lucky these days.

Capricorn - Good news from love, business ventures or children, invest now.

Aquarius - Buy or do something important for your home or family these days.

Pisces - Interesting surprises by mail or telephone. Be ready, a trip is ahead.

※

WED., THU., FRI., SAT. — MAY 16, 17, 18, 19:
RULERS — Venus (Old love/friends) and Mercury (Transportation/sad news).

Work, Career and Business: The Moon is now positive for a few days, so be confident to make progress. This is a time where you should make new plans. Try your best while you can and take on all challenges. Keep your head out of the swarm of stress and put a big smile on your face. People tend to react positively to a smiling face and a happy heart. Better times are on the way; the New Moon is on your side.

Partnerships: Someone close to you is upset. Time to apologize with a romantic dinner; don't expect it to be perfect but it would help your situation. Mercury will pass on all sorts of news including some financial or sexual secrets. Improve your cosmic consciousness and do some inside soul-searching. See what makes you so different and what can be done to make your lives better. Don't believe all you hear about a person.

Family and Friends: Save a difficult relationship with a friend or a family member while the moon is up. Its time to use diplomacy and understanding. Expect news with brothers or sisters and take the time to reply to them. Mercury rules communication and will help you pass on your thoughts deeply and correctly. Don't let the last few day of the Waning Moon sap your faith; stand strong, tomorrow is always better. Life is changing around you and you know it.

Love Affairs: This trend may induce luck and may require both of you to let go of the past and dismiss destructive emotions such as jealousy and suspicion. Love Affairs started now could be real good in the long run; use your head, use Moon power's knowledge. This energy will also force many unsuited couples to get out of their unhealthy relationships. The best of both of these planets is to be expected and great changes will come your way.

If you are a Libra, don't be too critical about an older or younger person born in February, April or June who may be attracted to you.

Travel and Communication: Many police officers will meet with trouble in speedy chases and dangerous confrontations, while trying hard to stop lunatics. Venus will help those who are willing to use her gentle touch of love in all they do. If you were born with a passionate Venus in a water sign, you will be helped by this celestial trend. A very high level of hope and great energy will be imposed upon many souls these days. Stay clear of chemicals, drugs and alcohol if you decide to take a trip.

Environment: The police will be needed in some situation where nature will get out of hand. Let's hope Venus will slow down Mercury's windy nature and stop him from producing hard weather or tornadoes.

Famous Personalities: Good Will comes from this lunation pertaining to the rich and famous. Scandals, sex, drugs and all the tools used by the "devil" could also be made public. A very famous but unlucky person may have some secrets to share.

Events: Use Moon Power Starguide wisely and if you know someone involved in Law Enforcement, let them read this book. With Pluto (death) still cruising through the sign of Sagittarius and a nasty happening fuelled buy destructive passions will be avoided. The diplomats will work hard to form a common agreement to stop the religious madness and territory.

Shopping: You may purchase anything dealing with cleaning the environment. With Venus' desire for peace and love, buy flowers and give fresh love. Take serious precautions if you happen to be in the dating game with a stranger met in a Waning Moon. Invest and wear the protective sex item if you are not sure. Think of Starguide as a solid gift to help someone you care.

SUN., MON., TUE., WED. — MAY 20, 21, 22, 23:
RULERS — The Moon (Changing life) and the Sun (Light of love).

Work, Career and Business: Let go of your past and take chances, you have two great weeks ahead of you. Examine all business propositions carefully and if they fit your rational mind, then go for it. The Moon is now Waxing and progress is to be expected soon. Some may be forced to relocate, start or finish a business. Many of the stars are on your side and you should be confident in the outcome. Invest in your business now.

Partnerships: Either the beginning or ending of an important part of your life, or a business partnership is a strong possibility within the next few days. As you know, nothing is made to last forever and somehow a wrong business partnership must end. Again this is a time where anything you really need could happen if you trust in yourself. Be patient with someone responding to the Sun's desire for power. It's a good time to meditate by the ocean or the river about the high purpose of your joined fate, your relationship and how it fits in your life. The Sun will make these days particularly romantic and beautiful for some.

Family and Friends: The Sun rules the children and love. Take the kids out to the park, but keep your eyes on them as, sadly enough, combined with other negative stars, some have disappeared under this energy. Unspecified vampires out there regenerate only by dealing with children and they will do all it takes to satisfy their unhealthy hunger. Accept the upcoming transformation with faith, as the changes will promote a better life. You may want to plan a special gathering with someone you are close to. A friend will have to move away soon and this could bring tears. The family circle will also be active these days and Mother will be requesting your presence. Enjoy Mom's food at home in the security and safety of your own family if you are in a new area and do not know many people. Expect an element of surprise from friends.

Love Affairs: Romance is on your mind more than ever and a meeting with some playmate can lead to an exciting love affair. You may feel comfortable with the person involved and sense that you can succeed; with the New Moon on your side you may end up with a form of commitment. If you are a Pisces, someone born in July or November may give you the opportunity to experience real love. The stars are on your side, look for it now.

Travel and Communication: Surely an interesting trend full of changes and surprises. Still, be careful in all you do and don't take chances. Visit or call your friends; they need to share interesting news. This is a great time to plan for future trips to Europe; you may also use the creativity of the Sun to start or finish a book. With the Sun (life) in charge, much of the destructive news will be seriously altered. Flying is also under his protective power, unless the doomed pilot was born with an Aquarius Dragon's Tail and was introduced to flying for the first time in his life after the Full Moon. Use a positive approach in all your words and you will attract more luck.

Environment: Much work will be done to further life and security these days and nature will be radiant with life. If you are out in the wilderness and you plan to cook, beware. Some accidental explosions could still occur, as some of the propane gas containers might have been purchased under a vicious energy or under the bad Moon. Mother Nature is still very much alive and may decide to show her power, forcing thousands of people to relocate.

Famous Personalities: On the negative side expect weird news and dramatic ending of relationships. Be ready for good news of births and marriages. Much will be done for the children these days.

Events: This will be an important time for your company or your local government to make decisions about a situation that needs to be dealt with. Thousands of people may be forced to relocate and start life anew, due to new construction plans or previous natural catastrophes. Expect some stubborn conservative groups to make the news about abortion and religion. The light is green thus many will succeed.

Shopping: This is a perfect time to invest in real estate and expensive items will bring great joy to some people. Great opportunities are to be found also at the swap meets and antique shops. Shop for anything that will further life and happiness. If you need to invest in something dangerous such as gas propane, cookers or sharp and dangerous items to take out to the wilderness, you can do it now. Share my valuable forecast on www.drturi.com with others. For someone's birthday, obtain accurate guidance in the form of a full life reading, or offer my book or a comparison chart for a newly wed couple.

THU., FRI., SAT., SUN., MON. — MAY 24, 25, 26, 27, 28:

RULERS — Mercury (Traveling/talks) Venus (love) Pluto (Drama/secrets).

Work, Career and Business: Be very careful towards the last days of this month. Pluto will punish the ignorant of induce serious dramatic wake up call for the unlucky. Time to reorganize your approach and a few things around you. Use the New Moon to look for a better way to develop your business. The New Moon will make everyone happy and very communicative. Your boss or your employees are going through some changes and you must be patient with them. With the New Moon on us, all will be fine again. Make the most of these days. Secrets of all sorts will come to light; you heard mine about John Gray and Art Bell!

Partnerships: Important people are watching you; present an attitude of brightness and courage in front of difficulties. Some of your partners can only admire your inner strengths and will follow your example. Don't let anyone create negative energy with uncontrolled disturbing thoughts. Show others the power of positive thinking.

Family and Friends: Keep busy with the children, as speedy Mercury will give them tons of energy. Let them spend time outside the house. Watch them closely and see yourself as a child doing exactly what kids do best, playing! Use that opportunity to burn some calories if you can keep up with them. Take the time to listen, as one of them may need specific attention.

Love Affairs: Expect an interesting surprise coming your way. With Venus around, love may enter your life without much notice; however, this world is a physical one and you must participate in the activities if you have any chance to succeed in finding what you're looking for. Do not stay home now as anything great could happen to you. Use that magnificent New Moon to enjoy nature and the sea. Keep in mind that Venus rules love and romance, and if you are single this is your chance. If you are a Sagittarius, a Leo or an Aries will find you irresistible.

Travel and Communication: We are still in the positive Moon, and a strong desire for change will be felt everywhere. Go on the road and make the most of this lunation. Also with Venus, some may drive to or find the love they are looking for.

Environment: Expect progressive news pertaining to concerned groups warring for the environment. They are after those wealthy executives who make money destroying the earth. Great news is in store for the earth workers.

Famous Personalities: Positive news is ahead with some famous personalities endorsing and supporting great community acts. New and beautiful love partners are in the air for some. A new birth will make many people happy. Moon Power 2003 LOS ANGELES, California -- Buddy Ebsen, the loose-limbed Broadway dancer who achieved stardom and riches in the television series "The Beverly Hillbillies" and "Barnaby Jones," died. He was 95.

Events: Nature should be quiet during this great trend where love, romance and communication will reign. The only trouble I expect is with Mercury's winds; he may decide to announce himself and create tornadoes in parts of the US. Interesting news from France and England could surprise some scientists.

Shopping: Satisfy Venus' desire for beauty. Invest in a fitness program or a diet; the results will amaze you. If you need a checkup now, the stars are in your favor as your physician will be accurate in his prognostication. Surgery is also fine and you can add anything to your body; cutting is permissible with those stars. Control your imagination as Mercury could get your mind going wild with all sorts of silly fears about your health.

Note: Attention: Pluto is back with us — Expect dramatic happenings all over; control is a must. Do not be one of Pluto's many victims; be aware of Pluto's destructive power. Anything you say or do under his power will follow you for the rest of your life. This is time to use extreme caution so close to a Waning (negative) Moon.

TUE., WED., THU. — MAY 29, 30, 31:
RULERS — Venus (Sexual temptation) and Pluto (Fatal attraction).

Work, Career and Business: You may be forced to realize the end of an era and the beginning of a new portion of your financial life. Your wishes for better business may not match your situation; Pluto will see to it and force a rebirth. It is all to your benefit in the long run; be at peace with yourself.

Partnerships: Time to enjoy good food, red wine and real safe sex! If you are in the wrong relationship, Pluto will free you soon. The opportunity to find real love will finally be given to you then. Better use diplomacy in all you say, or do; you may end up sorry if you don't. Some secrets may come your way; keep them for yourself and respect Pluto's desire for privacy.

Family and Friends: Expect dramatic news from all over within the next few days; be ready to take care of some friends in trouble, but realize your limits. Everyone will have a short temper; don't let Pluto affect your psyche. Use beautiful Venus' diplomatic power with everyone around you.

Love Affairs: The great planet of love will make you feel good about yourself and will give tons of charm and beauty. Be aware of mysterious Pluto and his sensual magnetism. Accompanying Venus he could transform you into an irresistible sex magnet. Trouble may come your way if you fall for passion in unprotected sex activity. Fight insecurity and jealousy avoid stressing. A love relationship started under this trend will become passionate and will stay (for good or for worse) with you forever. If you were born in January, a Virgo or a Taurus will get your heart. A friend born in November could prove difficult around you.

Travel and Communication: Pluto tends to choose the weakest or the strongest members of our society and play with their emotions. Whatever you say or do now will have incredible consequences; be diplomatic, stay clear of trouble. Do not stop for anyone on the road and let the police deal with Pluto. If you are with the children, it's time to watch them closely; this celestial mixture is totally against the children and many will fall victims to abusers. Anything you hear about school or drama should be taken with consideration, remember the growing children of the "Death Wish generation, see my book the power of the Dragon". Terrorist's plots and planning for death and destruction are taking place behind a curtain of deception.

Environment: As always, keep in mind that Pluto is very

dangerous and could do some serious damage with nature's devastating forces, just to remind us of his power. The police could make drastic news too.

Famous Personalities: Famous people will meet with their death. Under Pluto's power,
CNN anchor Don Harrison died after a long battle with cancer. He was 61 years old. Avoid large crowds where emotion and passion reign. Be aware of the destructive power of Pluto; do not take chances. Be patient.

Events: Do not trust strangers and avoid unfamiliar places. Pluto stirs man's animal tendencies. Pluto rules the crooks and the cops, and has the infinite forces of good and evil constantly teasing each other. The crooks will become more active and the police will try hard to cope. Under Pluto's power CARMEL, Indiana -- A man apparently upset that his loan application had been denied, opened fire on four bank employees and killed a woman who was going to offer him an umbrella to ward off the rain. The shooting was followed less than an hour later by a bank holdup a few miles away in Indianapolis. A suspect in that robbery was critically injured after police shot him. A third bank robbery was reported in Richmond, Indiana, about 65 miles east of Indianapolis, an hour after the second. Two men wearing ski masks, one armed with a pistol, escaped with an undetermined amount of money. If you are a police officer or a security guard on duty now, don't take chances, as the worst could happen to you. Offer Moon Power and true guidance to anyone involved in the law agency, you may save their life. Some children will make dramatic news.

Shopping: Invest in your soul and your reason to be on earth. Not the right time to visit your psychic or ask for direction unless you know him/her well. If you are into kinky stuff be careful as Pluto children kill with sex. Weird sexual behaviors are often produced by a mixture of Pluto (power/leather/sex) and Venus (sensuality/enticement/beauty) and combined with Uranus (weird/freedom/original), this could lead to unusual sexual escapades even death. Religious Neptune's vibration (deception/guilt/hidden/drugs) in your chart mixing with these energies will enhance deadly sexual encounters.

Welcome to Your Day - to - Day Guidance
For June 2007

Full Moon — June 1, 2007 in Sagittarius: Disturbing news from foreign lands is to be expected. Jupiter, the Lord of law and religion, will impose his righteous, dogmatic views on some lost souls. Dramatic transformations in the world of faith and the church are ahead. The previous wake-up call provided by Pluto's impact will induce a form of financial death for the Vatican and a rebirth for some peoples psyche where exploitation, fear, religious poisoning and ignorance won't prevail for long. Pluto will bring to light the shameful manipulation, sexual and financial secrets deals of organized religions and some of their religious leaders. Pluto is still interacting with Uranus to further the truth and the new Age of Aquarius against the dying Piscean Age. There is still a war in heaven while the Middle East and Asia are rebirthing through death, diseases and wars.

Lunation impact on all signs:

Aries - Difficult news from a foreign land, a study or a trip gets you worried.

Taurus - Trouble with a contract or corporation don't sign anything now.

Gemini - Stress coming from a business or emotional partner is heavy.

Cancer - Don't worry about your health, stress at work is expected soon.

Leo - Love, romance and children or a new endeavor will start you worrying.

Virgo - A change of residency or a problem with the family is ahead, be patient.

Libra - The mail or telephone may bring you sad news soon, be strong.

Scorpio - Expect a restructure of your self-esteem and finances soon.

Sagittarius - Don't take any chances within the next two weeks, be patient.

Capricorn - Let go of your past, eliminate all guilt to be happy, and no drinking.

Aquarius - Some of your wishes won't be granted for a while, just be cool.

Pisces - Your career may not go as expected, wait for the next New Moon.

FRI., SAT., SUN., MON. — JUNE 1, 2, 3, 4:
RULERS — Jupiter (Rescue/religion) and Saturn (Karma/obligations):

Work, Career and Business: With Pluto's dramatic experiences behind, many will keep low profiles and accept the intense transformation. With benevolent Jupiter, the future has much better to offer, and now you should be more confident in all your dealings. Jupiter, "the Lord of Luck," will make this transition easy and may even decide to throw you some luck; listen to your intuition and keep a positive attitude. A new career or a new beginning is on the horizon. Have faith and pray.

Partnerships: With Saturn's touch you can expect to work harder to organize or rebuild. For the hard-working souls, a promotion of some sort is coming your way. Your career will also be on your mind, and serious decisions will have to be made soon. Nothing comes easily; one must strive and plan if he is to succeed. With the Full Moon upon us, you might have to let go of someone or a portion of your business life soon. Let go.

Family and Friends: You may receive or give presents to the deserving family member or dear friend. Take the time to enjoy the week and the good food offered to you and if you decide to socialize during the night, you should be aware of the Waning Moon. A foreigner could make you happy and further an important wish. An older person has something to share with you, listen to the advice.

Love Affairs: Someone you have known for a while, much older or much younger, could surprise you — Don't be shy with life; take a chance with someone you care for; there is plenty to gain in the long run if this person came into your life in a Waxing Moon. This endeavor may lead to an opportunity to further your career. If you were born under any of the earth signs, avoid the Full Moon's depressing power. If you are a Gemini, a Libra or an Aquarius will be getting closer to you. Listen to a friend born in April.

Travel and Communication: Expect your telephone to be busy, but the messages won't be too good. Don't try to be in so many places at the same time. If you have to drive, take extra time to get there; don't rush, as the police could spoil your day. A brother or a sister needs to talk to you. Keep a positive attitude; positive people attract positive experiences. Remember a magnet won't attract a piece of wood.

Environment: In a Full Moon time, Mother Nature may decide to stretch herself and surprise some. Environmental groups will become active and will receive support from the media to save the earth from uncaring corporations. The earth will be active soon; stay clear of bridges as much as you can. Don't take any chances for a while.

Famous Personalities: The great loss of an old and eminent political, religious or entertainment figure will trouble the media soon. A group of people will work hard to help those starving in an area affected negatively by nature. Life goes on.

Events: Under this energy 80 people were killed in a fire that gutted a shopping center in the West Java town of Bogor and in South-Central Alaska a fire engulfed 7,000 acres and destroyed as many as 100 homes. Some terrorists groups could also get really ugly, and surprising destructive explosions are on the way.

Shopping: You may spend money on your pet or invest in anything to be used in nature of for your pet. It is surely a good time to spend with those you know well, as Jupiter will replenish you with fresh air and a new approach to life.

※

TUE., WED., THU., FRI. — JUNE 5, 6, 7, 8:
RULERS — Uranus (Explosions/surprises) and Neptune (Oil/Middle East):

Work, Career and Business: Combined with the Full Moon, Uranus may make you feel erratic and Neptune may make you feel depressed and overemotional at work; this could lead you to think about a new job. Keep your eyes and ears open; with Neptune's "dreamy" nature, you are prone to making serious errors or forgetting something important. Do not sign any contracts now; in the long run, you will be sorry if you do. Be patient and wait until the next New Moon.

Partnerships: Crazy things may happen now; do not make a fool of yourself in public. Things done or words said without forethought might bring trouble later. Use your will; be positive in all you say. Expect disturbing news by mail or telephone but avoid fears, as insecurity could take over your common sense; all will be fine, there is a Divine plan for you. This timing is ideal for meditation and renewing your faith in each other and the universe. You must control negative thoughts, even if many things around you do not seem positive. Have faith in yourself and those you care for during these days.

Family and Friends: Spend some valuable time with your family. Do not expect the affairs of the heart to progress or get better for a while, and teenagers may get themselves in trouble. Watch for the use of drugs, as Neptune will lead them towards wrong friends. Give them solid direction and be ready for some friction. Depressed friends may call you asking for spiritual support or direction. With Neptune, confusion and deception is in the air. If you socialize during the night hours, keep your eyes on your possessions as they may disappear. Don't misplace your keys. Avoid complaining about life's problems to those who care about you.

Love Affairs: Love and romance may suffer as during a Waning Moon, Uranus' erratic emotions may preside and disturb your relationship. Be patient with the partner and use diplomacy to save trouble. However don't let someone else's problem get to you and affect your feelings. If you were born in August expect a Gemini friend to give you disturbing news soon. A friend from a foreign land may bring better but surprising news soon. All fire signs will suffer this lunation emotionally, so try not to let it happen to you, use you will. If you are a Leo, Sagittarius or Aries remember the Waning Moon and be patient.

Travel and Communication: If you can, avoid flying during this trend unless you made your reservations before the Waning Moon. Protect yourself against aeronautic accidents; use "Moon Power" and your knowledge take no chances. This is the perfect time to pass on the light and talk about Starguide's guidance. Avoid drinking and driving at all costs; many accidents happen under Neptune and Uranus' iniquitous energy. If you have to play or travel be aware of the ocean or the river these days.

Environment: Expect bad news about quakes and the possibilities of sea/air accidents. Many naturalists will be upset and some groups will make dramatic decisions followed by dangerous actions. Nature will start to go berserk and may throw a cluster of negative weather patterns such as tornadoes or earthquakes in the near future. Remember the series of tornadoes outside of the regular season and in Florida in 1998? Uranus was in charge then.

Famous Personalities: Under Uranus power the British Artist John Michael made weird news in Los Angeles in a public bathroom, again surprising Uranus (weird) and Neptune (kinky sex) was in charge. Remember another British singer O'Connor? She cut up a picture Pope's face on national TV in one of her performances, right in front of the entire audience. Again Uranus (freedom) and Neptune (religion) were in charge. Many unaware famous daredevils will lose their lives because they have no knowledge of the stars' impact on human affairs. Do not take chances after the Full Moon, ever, and all will be fine.

Events: Under Uranus' powers expect anything weird and explosive to take place. New from Japan or earthquakes are high on he list. Stay clear of strangers and any suspicious packages, especially in airports or dams. Let's hope for the best!

Shopping: Provide spiritual guidance and support to all in need. Many will fall victim to Neptune's deceiving and Uranus' eccentric wills. Do not start any medical prescription now; you would further a disaster on your health later on. Some people out there are not aware of the stars' impact on their lives and may decide to jump from a bridge or a plane and take chances; good luck to them. You may invest in my work for them, mention or offer them Moon Power as this can and will save them trouble. Avoid investing in any form of electronics; a nasty virus may get to your computer.

June 6, 2007 - Venus enter Leo: Perfect time to contemplate launching any artistic endeavor. Giving and receiving expensive items is on the agenda for some. You may also think of traveling or investing in a car or expensive items. Souls born now will be very magnetic and dramatic in matters related to love. They will make good livings, and will attract money in artistic endeavors. Many of them will strive to find beautiful, rich and famous partners willing to experience the best of life. Some will have to learn to control Mr. Pride and Mrs. Ego to save true love. This position makes for one of the most dramatic but lucky signs of the Zodiac. Usually a gift in acting or other great talents is present with this position. Those souls are born to experience a flamboyant and busy love life. This is a good position of Venus promoting fame and fortune. Countries and people from France, Italy and Japan will be beneficial for the soul.

2007 Second Supernova Window

June / July: Second SUPERNOVA window
From Monday June 11th through Friday July 13th 2007

EXPLANATION OF A SUPERNOVA WINDOW

Concentration of negative celestial energy approaching Be extremely prudent in driving, and expect chain-reaction accidents. Be prepared for delays, strikes, and nature producing awful weather, including hurricanes and tornadoes. The same energy that produced the Titanic disaster, the Asia tsunami the Northridge Los Angeles and Kobe Japan earthquakes and major other calamities is approaching again. Remember the thwarted terrorist attack of August 2006 in the UK where the BA canceled thousands of flights because the BAA ordered all passengers not to take or check ALL handbags before boarding their planes? Those people did not have a copy of Moon Power and paid the price of ignorance. Double-check all your appointments, and if you can postpone traveling and flying during this Supernova "window". If you must fly like I do very often simply make sure to purchase your ticket and make your reservation during a Waxing Moon and the stars will not bother you. Remember the Universal Laws do not care for birthday or religious holidays or else, simply think of crossing the street while the light is red or ignore a stop sign, and then see what will happen to you. Those laws are impartial and written by God not men and messing them up will bring about serious penalty. Note that; I flew only a few days before the Full Moon in August 2006 to Thailand during a "Supernova Window" to write this book and I traveled safely and avoided all trouble. Remember knowledge is power ignorance is evil!

Communication and electricity will be cut off, and a general loss of power is to be expected. Appliances, computers, telephones, planes, trains, cars, all of these "tools" will be affected by this energy. They will be stopped in one way or another. The people of the past will make the news and will reenter your life. Expect trouble with the post office, education, students, strikes, prisoner's escape, newspapers, broadcasting industries and computer viruses may bother us again.

Many a failed mission and expensive electronic equipment (Mars probe etc.) and our tax dollars have been wasted because of the scientist's lack of knowledge of the stars. As usual NASA, which is not aware of the science of astrology, will waste our tax money with failed missions due to bad weather and electronic malfunctions. In the name of ignorance a few years ago, in the Challenger explosion seven astronauts lost their lives when NASA launched the shuttle under a "Supernova Window".

Marine life sharks, whales etc may also beach themselves due to Mercury Retrograde affecting their natural inborn navigational systems. All these malevolent predictions and waste of lives and equipment do not have to occur. Those predictions do not have to affect you directly as they unfold. Instead, they are printed to prepare you for setbacks and frustrations, thus advising you to be patient and prudent during this trend. There is no room for ignorance, and those who are not aware of the celestial order, including the NASA space-program management team, will continue to pay a heavy price. In all mankind's' affairs, ignorance is true evil. Why any scientists who are against my research do not honor the word science, which is based upon solid investigation, is solid proof of mental snobbery. By omitting any physical or spiritual laws can only bring penalty; for science's purpose is to explore all possibilities, even those laws written in light via the stars.

※

SAT., SUN., MON., TUE., WED. — JUNE 9, 10, 11, 12, 13:
RULERS — Mars (Danger/men) and Venus (Docile/women):

Work, Career and Business: The Moon is still Waning (negative) so think twice before committing to an investment program. A powerful hunch might save you trouble if you are unsure about a person or a business scheme. Don't let Mars affect your judgment; be patient with everyone around. Expect upsetting financial news;

don't let it get to you, you can only do so much. The future will offer better opportunities. Wait patiently for the next New Moon; right now just clean up and reorganize.

Partnerships: As usual with Mars' aggressive personality, expect all sorts of trouble with partnerships. As always with the Lord of war around these days, you are seriously advised to use discretion in all you do or mention to avoid serious complications. Keep in mind that the Moon is Waning (negative) so don't expect progress in any of your endeavors for now. Finish up a project or re-evaluate a situation, but most of all, be patient.

Family and Friends: A difficult trend is taking place; do not let it get to you. Use your will and look for happy people. Starguide is preparing you for this type of celestial affliction; take a passive attitude and all will go your way. Use Venus' loving touches with practical advice to provide spiritual help to those you care for, but realize your limits. You need your own spiritual strength to face those tough stars and you can do it.

Love Affairs: Expect some secrets to be divulged, especially the ones related to sex or financial scandals. Venus' gentle nature will reward you if you use her diplomatic, loving powers to smooth things out. Better stay home and enjoy good food during the late hours. A great movie with the one you care about this weekend is your best shot. Many will fall prey to con artists and weird sexual endeavors. If you are a Virgo someone born in March, a Taurus or a Capricorn could be looking for you. A Cancer friend will give you good advice, but do not complain too much if you want to save your friendship. Stay clear of alcohol consumption.

Travel and Communication: The people of your past will soon show up. After the Full Moon always stay clear of suspicious deals. Deal with the people you know and avoid dangerous dark alleys. Keep your eyes open and your personal alarm (intuition) on all the time. Mars rules man's animal instincts and he could stimulate one of his aggressive children (Mars in bad aspect) to hurt you, given the occasion. With any trouble on the highway, stay inside your car with the doors secured. Many violent crimes have been reported during this type of energy, especially when drugs or alcohol are involved; take no chances.

Environment: Soft Venus will try to stop her violent brother

Mars and his friend Pluto from stirring the earth's entrails and producing earthquakes, explosions, volcanoes and disasters. In time of a Waning Moon and with a Supernova Window in action, she might not have much influence. Be ready for destruction from both Pluto and the red planet, Mars, "The Lord of War."

Famous Personalities: This same type of energy has taken the lives of many famous people, sometimes dramatically. Drama, sex, and scandals of all sorts will go public and may induce suicidal tendencies in some prominent people. Stay clear of any chemicals and be aware around the water.

Events: Mars is like Pluto in some ways and will stimulate the villains; expect them to be nasty and active during this trend. Again, do not trust strangers and do not put yourself in any situation that could make you a potential victim. The police will make disturbing news and many officers will be dispatched to cool off situations, especially those of domestic violence. If you are in law enforcement, beware; Mars or Pluto could hurt you; don't take any chances.

Shopping: Do not deal with finances these days. Avoid investing in tools or sharp instruments. Some will get bad news from their creditors and bank accounts or credit cards will be a source of trouble. Do not open a bank account now; the negative energy will induce unneeded financial stress in your life.

※

New Moon — June 15, 2007 in Gemini: Now is the perfect time to start any intellectual pursuit, begin or finish a book, learn photography, a foreign language, find a publisher and communicate your feelings to all. With the New Moon upon us soon, you may plan to invest in a new car or anything related to communication. Traveling and foreigners will play important parts of this lunation. Plans made to travel under this New Moon will bring excitement and many wishes. On a larger scale, combined with the New Moon, witty Mercury will help in promoting better relations with other countries around the world.

Lunation impact on all signs:

Aries - A letter or a telephone call will make you happy soon.

Your sibling needs you.

Taurus - Great news involving money or a business endeavor is on the way.

Gemini - The Moon shines on you, make the most of it, you're lucky for a while.

Cancer - A secret will come your way but don't talk too much about it later.

Leo - One of your wishes will come true because of a friend, good news ahead.

Virgo - Your career gets you very busy, lots of opportunity in communication. Write.

Libra - Good news from far away and a gambling trip will bring luck.

Scorpio - Corporate money, a contract, legacy, and a deep spiritual study is coming.

Sagittarius - A new business or emotional relationship is about to start.

Capricorn - Your health and your work will improve and good opportunities are ahead.

Aquarius - Love and creativity are on the way, good news from the children.

Pisces - A change of residency or a new set of wheels will make you happy.

※

THU., FRI., SAT., SUN. — JUNE 14, 15, 16, 17:
RULERS — Mercury (Good News/travel) and the Moon (New beginning/Moving).

Work, Career and Business: Great news is to be expected soon in the work and career scenes, and progressive changes are on the way. Make the most of Mercury's intellectual powers to review your business life and do some financial planning. Concentrate on everything important, and then go for it with faith. Lots of progress is ahead, make the most of this positive trend. As always drive with caution, don't let speedy Mercury ruin your day with the police.

Partnerships: The Moon is up and happy for the next few days; do all you can to further your partnerships and if you have to, let go of your past and look for someone else. There are plenty of great souls walking this earth; just ask for your happiness and let go of the past. Use Mercury's strength to take a trip with your partner.

Family and Friends: Your maternal instinct will show itself to your children. Share your knowledge with friends; help them to understand some of the secrets of life and make them understand their emotions, which are regulated by the Moon's passage through each and every sign of the zodiac. The subconscious response to the moon's fluctuations upon humans is referred as "lunatic behavior or moodiness" and right now she will make you and others feeling happy. Expect the beginning or ending of important parts of your or others' life. Expect some surprising news from the children. A close friend needs your attention to deal with an emotional situation. Give help.

Love Affairs: Realize your limits with the wrong people, be honest with your feelings and make the needed changes. Your own future, positive or negative, is mostly based upon your decisions, and is the reincarnation of your thoughts. An old friend who lives far away may need to communicate with you, use Mercury and write those letters. The mail could bring you great news and everyone will want to talk to you. If you are a Virgo a Capricorn or a Pisces will want you. Someone born in July needs to spend some time with you very soon.

Travel and Communication: If you have to travel for business purposes, do it now and always use the two weeks following a New Moon to do so. Don't let insecurity stop your progress, and promote important business now. Expect the mail and your telephone to bring you interesting news. Many will be going back home while others will have to go away.

Environment: The Moon's Waxing energy could induce stress on the faults, so that many people will be forced to relocate soon following natural disasters. It's time for her to stretch herself and restructure her inside. Mars is still in Scorpio; be aware of fires and destructive emotional behaviors.

Famous Personalities: The rich and famous will be investing or planning reunions to feed the children of the world. Their artistic gifts will benefit many generous organizations. Some other crazy famous people may make surprising news trying to use Mercury's (the press) power to gain free publicity.

Events: Expect the military to make the news or perform deeds that will aid the general public and provide relief from disasters or war areas. Nature will begin to feel agitated and under this celestial manifestation — Wildfires that had burned nearly a quarter-million acres in the Western United States remained out of control Thursday in at least six states. The same energy was active in SIDON, Lebanon — Five people died and 15 were wounded when explosions sparked by an electrical fire ripped through a house used as an arms depot, Lebanese security sources said. Seven other houses were also destroyed.

Shopping: Buy anything that your home or garden needs. You are under the protection of the New Moon, thus signing anything related to real estate, hotels or restaurants is OK. Share my valuable forecast on www.drturi.com or offer my Starguide and its accurate guidance for someone's birthday, or offer a comparison chart for a newly wed couple.

※

MON., TUE., WED., THU. — JUNE 18, 19, 20, 21:
RULERS — The Sun (Children/Light and life) and Mercury (On the road):

Work, Career and Business: Don't let the egotistic power of the Sun take over your management skills. Keep in mind that we are still human and have egos that sometimes get out of hand. Make the most of the Sun and Mercury's revitalizing energy to further your business life. Interesting progress and surprises are on the way. You've been waiting for this New Moon long enough; push now.

Partnerships: We are under the white power of the Moon and you can also feel the valiant Sun's strength light up your life and your relationships. This is the time to offer presents or flowers to those for whom you care. You should nurture happiness and feel rejuvenated; your spirit is free and happy. Use this long-awaited New Moon to your advantage; get active with life. You may hear about a birth soon.

Family and Friends: Remembrance of the past will activate for many, and great time is ahead. Let the golden protective Sun's rays further everything related to children, love and creativity these days. A trip to the wild or the zoo would be rejuvenating for the entire family; get your camera as those laughs and sincere smiles are priceless. With Mercury's speed affecting the kids, and dangerous Mars in Scorpio watch over them carefully around the water. If you feel confused about a situation, Mercury will help you find the perfect words to fix the situation. Expect interesting surprises coming your way via telephone, mail or social activities. Use this powerful lunation to your advantage; get yourself in shape and do something different this weekend.

Love Affairs: Time to get active as love can be found practically anywhere, especially if you set your mind to it and participate in all events. Throwing a party will pay off for some people and love may just enter your own home. Again, don't stay home if you are invited to a gathering; the Sun may reward your heart's desire. One of your important wishes is in the hands of a friend; don't miss the party. If you were born in May, a Scorpio or a Virgo will be strongly attracted to you. A friend born in March or January may need your help.

Travel and Communication: Use all the beautiful words you can come up with. Everyone will sparkle with the Sun's power. Make plans now for a trip close to the water. Let your loved ones know that you miss them and that you'll be there soon. Travel is under the protection of the Sun but please remember the Supernova Window.

Environment: The Moon will make hard aspect to other planets these days and this will remind us of our vulnerability to the shocking destructive forces of nature. With the New Moon upon us, let's hope no earthquakes will come to remind us that the earth is still very much alive. Trouble may be coming from an accident involving children. Again, keep your eyes open, especially close to the water.

Famous Personalities: Many new figures will show up on the entertainment field and much work will be done to produce the finest in the arts. Great movies are being made and expected to appear in the fall. Some famous actors will get in or out of business and love relationships. A famous personality will make weird news.

Events: Are you into the extraordinary? If so, go to the desert now; bring your camera, as this energy activates UFOs sightings. The Sun's light brings the undiluted truth to whoever wants to see or experience the incredible power of the divine. Nature may do things of her own and disturb power and electronics in some areas. Be aware of Mars and children producing accidents including explosions, earthquakes, tornadoes and volcanic eruptions are high on the list.

Shopping: Buy anything expensive: gold, cars, electronics for the children. Presents bought now will bring luck to both of you. Invest in all that shows true love and you will win the heart of that person later. Now is the perfect time to invest in the light and my Astro-Psychology course and learn all about the stars.

June 25, 2007 — Mars enters Taurus: Wherever your Mars is located in your chart dictates the best man for a woman or how a man "goes hunting" for a woman. Mars regulates your desire principle and a strong Mars produces sportsmen. Mars will always promote the soul towards dangerous and competitive career endeavors. Famous author John Gray (a Libra) uses a catching title for his book "Men are from Mars, women from Venus". A few years ago we met in San Francisco, I gave him a reading and he bought all my books and became a student of mine by investing in my Astro-Psychology course (Divine Astrology). Like many other famous and competitive people John (and Art Bell) will never endorse my work or my name publicly. Be cautious with Mars going through a specific house and sign in your chart. Danger and aggression is its signature. It may be a good idea for you to know where "The Lord of War" in Greek Mythology is located in your chart at birth, or where it is now, so that you can use his energy constructively. Souls born now will be extremely artistic with a strong desire to establish security. Taurus rules Switzerland (banking capital of the world) and many financial corporations subconsciously use the symbol of the bull to represent security and solidity.

Note: Attention: Pluto is back with us for a few days — Expect dramatic happenings all over; control is a must. Don't be one of his victim; be aware of Pluto's destructive power. Anything you say or do under his power will follow you for the rest of your life. This is the time to use extreme caution, even in the time of a Waxing (positive) Moon. Make sure to check my quatrains posted on my home page www.drturi.com regularly as this will help your understanding and the use of Moon Power.

FRI., SAT., SUN., MON., TUE., WED. — JUNE 22, 23, 24, 25, 26, 27:
RULERS — Venus (Passion/love) and Pluto (Death/drama/sex):

Work, Career and Business: The Moon is Waxing (positive) and much can happen as long as you understand how to use Pluto and Venus' energies positively. Promote your business life now: advertise and reach the people, travel. Do that and soon your telephone will be busy and the mail will bring awakening news. You will be soon being forced to realize what is wrong in your career, and the needed changes are on the way.

Partnerships: A new plan is needed to succeed in your endeavor; use this trend to get rid of whatever or whoever is bothering you. Expect some secret to resurface soon. Nothing can really go wrong if you use Venus' diplomatic gifts to deal with others and aim high. Diplomacy with others will pay off.

Family and Friends: Expect shocking news from people around you; you might get in touch with some of your friends for a good chat. Do not fall for gossip; you may end up sandwiched between two friends. Use the positive Moon and Venus kind-hearted natures to promote your life. Surely a good time to appreciate your loved ones or plan a dinner at home, or maybe just see a great movie. Avoid Pluto's sarcastic remarks or you might be sorry later. Many will experience drama in their own homes, keep the police away.

Love Affairs: Combined with Venus' sensuality, Pluto will give you the power to "stimulate" your partner in many ways. Candlelight, soft music and words of love will pay off considerably if you are in a solid relationship. This is a trend loaded with powerful emotions and good energy, where nothing can go wrong if you play your cards right. A foreigner could play an important part in this trend and later in your future. If you were born under a water sign you are advised to keep your emotions in control. If you are a Gemini, a person born under the sign of Libra or Sagittarius will be strongly attracted to you.

Travel and Communication: The call of nature will be strong for many. Enjoy the wild and water and make plans for fishing trips. The river and the sea have lots of fish to give away and for some magical reason they will all bite the bait. Drive slowly; don't spoil your day with a speeding ticket. Watch over Pluto's destructive communication and use Venus' diplomatic manner instead.

Environment: Many mother earth supporters will march to be heard by government officials and they will succeed in their requests to save the environment. Pluto is about to show mankind the awful power of destruction. Dramatic news for some unlucky souls is to be expected.

Famous Personalities: Legal action in the news from a famous entertainer. Another famous figure may have to leave this world. News from similar past energies produced the story of "Arab world's longest-serving monarch dead at 70." Large corporations will find strength in their new associations. Moon Power 2003– DENVER (AP) -- Kobe Bryant, one of basketball's brightest stars, was arrested after a woman accused the Los Angeles Lakers' guard of sexual misconduct at a hotel near Vail.

Events: This energy will touch the police force, so don't take any chances now. The police will make disturbing news, as Pluto will induce drama and death. Expect nature to get out of hand, and accidents to plague the media. Under Pluto's power a mother's hysterical reaction after a gunman brings a lesson in terror to a buffalo school. Police arrest an Erie county sheriff's deputy accused of gunning down his estranged wife... and wounding a bystander right inside school. 18 were terrified after a man, opened fire inside the elementary school right after the morning bell. Police say, 37-year-old Juan Roman, an Erie county sheriff's deputy, chased his estranged wife into the school in a domestic dispute.

Shopping: Cameras bought now will take dramatic pictures or will be used against criminals. Invest in anything that will be used to clean up your environment. Good metaphysical books can also be bought and used for your own mental progression. Spruce yourself up by brightening your wardrobe. Purchase or wear black or red garments; they will bring magic to you. Your favorite astrologer or psychic will have great insights for you; visit them now.

Full Moon — June 30, 2007 in Capricorn: Expect some serious career or personal developments to take place. Some will be starting a new job, and others dropping one, this could include a business relationship. Promotion or deception, whichever happens, will mark an important part of your life. Just be ready to accept the upcoming changes with faith in your new future. Be ready to provide a supportive shoulder to the victims. Nature can also decide to do nasty tricks in some states, promoting destructive weather or earthquakes in the very near future. The government will have to take serious, crucial steps, to avoid trouble and promote peace in the world. Expect news coming from important political figures, and England and India.

Lunation impact on all signs:

Aries - Your career and home life will undergo important but needed changes. Have faith.

Taurus - A study, a sibling or stressful news from foreign lands will start you worrying.

Gemini - Sad news from low self-esteem, corporate money, a legacy could reach you soon.

Cancer - Problems with a lover, a partner or a business associate are to be expected.

Leo - Don't put stress on your health because your work is tiring. No guilt is needed.

Virgo - Doubt about a lover, person or a job situation will upset you, just let go.

Libra - You might need to relocate or deal with a stressful situation at home and your career.

Scorpio - Control your imagination; don't believe in what others say, take a trip to forget.

Sagittarius - Money setbacks will let down your self-esteem, be patient all will be fine.

Capricorn - Big changes are needed in your all areas of your life, have faith in your abilities.

Aquarius - Let go of your past, you belong to the future. Career and home changes ahead.

Pisces - A friend or a lover will become too burdensome; you need your spirit and freedom.

THU., FRI., SAT. – JUNE 28, 29, 30:
RULERS: Pluto (Rehabilitation) Jupiter (From abroad) and Saturn (Bureaucracy):

Work, Career and Business: Jupiter's positive energy will help restore faith and new opportunities in your life. You could use this trend to gather your thoughts and get close to God in your local church or in nature and enjoy the wildness. Keep your notion of life clean; avoid poisoning your future with negative attitudes. Pray for the world, for the children of the future. Many of those restorative thoughts are needed, then slowly but surely a healing process will take place. With the New Moon upon us you may begin to see the light. Signing important documents is OK while the Moon is still Waxing, and valuable opportunities are on the way. Be ready for the beginning or ending of important parts of your life.

Partnerships: A new business partner wants to share a great plan with you; it probably is! Don't rush. Listen to your intuition before and add your own creative force in the process. A foreigner could also enter the scenery and the meeting could positively affect your future. Avoid tensions this weekend about a specific project or trip. Nothing can really stop you if you mean business. Keep a positive attitude.

Family and Friends: Friends will be active and many will be requesting your presence. Do not refuse invitations. The Waxing Moon through your great friends can still grant many of your wishes. You may plan to throw your own party with some good friends this weekend. Keep your eyes open for an older person with good deals or kind words to offer. Kids sense that they are the center of attention, be patient with their demands. If Mom is far away, she may call you; don't dwell on the past and avoid gossip. Be happy. Don't let other people's trouble upset you, and all will be fine.

Love Affairs: Socialize with friends and have faith in the stars. You will feel positive away from home with the people around you. They will enjoy your company and one of your wishes may come true. Avoid impulsive actions where romance is concerned and drive carefully on your way back home during the late hours. Do not fall victim to Saturn's gloomy power; forget about your responsibility, go out, meet new people and expect a lot. If you're born in January or September, your magnetism will be high and you could find love. The future has better to offer, so put a big smile on your face and be confident. Progressive changes are ahead; be patient and participate in life. If you were born in August, someone born in April, or an Aquarius or Gemini could be strongly attracted to you.

Travel and Communication: Saturn rules old people and parts of your past. Take care of the old people you love. Make these days' good ones, as those folks might not be around for the next cycle. Some will plan to travel far this weekend, and some just around town to meet their pasts. Be aware of early celebrations as people could drink too much and drive dangerously. Stay safe and watch the roads. Many will find themselves with car problems or stuck in airports. City workers may also decide to cut off traffic making you late for work.

Events: Jupiter may decide to entertain us with some news from foreign powers. Under Saturn's power, people challenge governmental structure. For instance a few years ago the news reported that many Taliban fighters asserted authority in northern Afghanistan. Warlord Dostum flees to Turkey. Taliban fighters moved swiftly Sunday to assert their authority over this northern stronghold, whose capture nearly completed a three-year campaign to unite Afghanistan under the white flag of the radical Islamic army.

Famous Personalities: The rich and famous will busy themselves to alleviate pain in the world.

Events: A political person may make surprising news. Be ready for startling news from a foreign land soon. The Middle East, Mexico or a Spanish-speaking country needs help.

Shopping: Invest in traveling or learning a foreign language, and you will have a rewarding time ahead of you. Use Jupiter's philosophical values to improve your consciousness, or plan to start an important study. Invest in anything for your pet.

Welcome to Your Day - to - Day Guidance
For July 2007

Happy 4th of July to all readers. Just be aware that this holiday falls after a Full Moon and could be quite memorable, even negative for some. Remember last year, it was just a day before the Full Moon! Regardless how much I tried to get close to the action, the police, the madness, and the people walking all over, made the situation unsafe and caused me to turn back a few minutes before the fireworks show. Please make a good use of my work, watch the children with fireworks and if you spend some time by the water, be aware of Neptune's tricks. Share the knowledge with others, recommend my book and help them to understand the will of God throughout the cosmos. Have a great time but be careful with children around the water and with fireworks please.

SUN., MON., TUE., WED. — JULY 1, 2, 3, 4:
RULERS — Saturn (Control of state) Uranus (Explosions) Neptune (Deceiving):

Work, Career and Business: Do not expect to make much progress for a while; many of your plans will fall apart. Listen to other people's stories; the stars affect everybody and they may come up with interesting, even surprising news. Be ready to invest in some appliances or equipment. Saturn will help you make some great adjustments after careful planning. Wait for the next New Moon for more progress.

Partnerships: With Uranus in charge, anything and everything unusual can happen and with a Waning Moon (negative) upon us, do not expect great news. Restaurants will be busy; better make reservations if you don't want to be turned down. However, any changes should be accepted with faith in yourself and the new future. Be patient with everyone, as Uranus may make them eccentric and Saturn depressed. Avoid drinking at night.

Family and Friends: An opportunity to meet with some family members you have not seen for a while will be given to you by this lunation. The past will come alive again and an old friend will reappear soon. A person who owes you money sincerely wants to repay, but may be in such a difficult set of circumstances that he can't. Be patient as he may repay you in a different way. A friend who has invited himself and who has been a house guest for a while may need a little push to get him out of your domicile. Providing help is great, but let people know your limits.

Love Affairs: Be ready for the incredible to happen; if you are in a karmic relationship, changes are needed. Friends may fall in love with other friends or mistake love for friendship. An old love or an old friend long gone will reappear in your life soon. If you were born under any of the water signs expect needed changes. If you are a Libra, a Leo friend needs to talk to you and someone born in April or February needs to understand you. A friend born in June might fall for you.

Travel and Communication: A business trip or an invitation may lead you to many good contacts from the past. However, you might have problems getting to the given address and may get lost a few times. Be patient, as you will still have plenty of time to play and enjoy yourself with various unusual people. For paranormal investigators, now is the time to look for UFOs in secluded places. Don't forget your video camera; you may be sorry if you are not ready when Uranus is willing to display the secret of extraterrestrial intelligence. Stay clear from tall trees and posts to avoid lightning; many people met with their deaths in stormy Uranus trends.

Environment: General electronic failures or viruses could produce aeronautic disasters soon. Expect this type of news to happen: Australian wildlife officials made repeated attempts to prevent up to 300 long-finned pilot whales from beaching themselves on a remote part of Australia's west coast. Mammals' birds and man's navigational systems are confused when Uranus is in charge and many get lost. Tornadoes are high on the list. See my quatrains and additional information on my site at www.drturi.com all year round. Your questions and comments are welcome on the newsgroup, too.

Famous Personalities: Very surprising behavior or news will come from the rich and famous. Disturbing and sad news about a famous child could reach the media. Fire and electrocution are also high on the list; be aware. On July 4th 2003 Velvet-voiced R&B crooner Barry White, renowned for his lush baritone and lyrics that oozed sex appeal on songs such as "Can't Get Enough of Your Love, Babe," died. White, who had suffered kidney failure from years of high blood pressure, died at Cedars-Sinai Medical Center around 9:30 a.m., said manager Ned Shankman. He was 58. Note for my student. *Mr. White was born in September, under the sign of Virgo. His 3rd house of communication, singing is located in the sexy, mystical, hypnotic sign of Scorpio and gave him that deep sensual voice that brought him fame in his stimulating singing career.*

Events: Uranus loves accidents and explosions; under his power expect surprising and original pieces of news such as: QUETTA, Pakistan (CNN) 07/04/03 -- Three attackers set off explosives at a Shiite mosque killing at least 44 people and wounding 65 others. Four people died when a Marine Corps electronic warfare plane went down in the desert. Also on July 5th, 2003 - Two female suicide bombers killed at least 14 people today outside a rock concert in Moscow. Expect more shocking news, like two teen-agers were killed when a butane pipeline broke and exploded in northeast Texas. Lastly, I gave the date of August 18th and asked the readers to be prepared for "electronic failures". On the exact date (printed months earlier) NASA shuttle lost his main computer in space and made international news. The costly loss of the Mars probe and the loss of astronauts' lives also took place under this disturbing Supernova Window and Uranian energy.

Shopping: This is not a time to purchase new electronic equipment or plan a long voyage by air to a foreign land. As always, Uranus rules the future, and his psychic powers can be used through your trusted local psychic or astrologer. Second-hand shopping of Hi-tech will pay off for some.

※

THU., FRI., SAT., SUN. — JULY 5, 6, 7, 8:
RULERS — Neptune (Doctrine/drinking) and Mars (Disagreement/war).

Work, Career and Business: Use Neptune's intuition and meditation, as great tools to face setbacks and difficulties. Don't let the Waning Moon bring you down; reevaluate your business ventures. You may need to take more time to focus clearly on your future and create a vision that will become a blueprint or a pathway. New goals require hard work, but you have all the needed tools to make them happen. Be confident of your abilities and steady in your efforts. Do not give up on your dreams and be practical.

Partnerships: Gloomy Saturn in the sign of Cancer may induce insecurity or financial worries. He may force many of us to find practical ways of restructuring our finances and experience forms of rebirth. A word of caution about Saturn's depressing nature: be patient and use his structural power to your advantage. You must get rid of feelings of insecurity, as they could seriously affect your partnerships. A good investment would be in financial planning, to promote your business sense. Under his command you could also improve your planning abilities. With Jupiter (learning) in Virgo (health) you may be able to regenerate your body by starting a good and productive diet. Complete or start a spiritual study and you will experience the realization of an important wish.

Family and Friends: Take care of your health without being overly concerned with it; Neptune may produce melancholy and vivid imagination that could affect the "Temple of God," your body. You and your loved ones will feel a lot better after the New Moon, just be patient. Eat right and get plenty of exercise. A better attitude will help you through this negative lunation. Keep away from alcohol and Neptune's depressing effects. Use words of support for the victims of Neptune's gloomy mode.

Love Affairs: You may have an attraction for an interesting happy person, or you may be asked to take a trip soon. Some will start a secret love affair that will bring deception in the long run. Love can be found close to the water this weekend, but don't count on the promises you may hear. If you were born in October, an Aries or an Aquarius will be strongly attracted to you. A movie at home is your best shot for now, be patient with life.

Travel and Communication: Stay clear of alcohol consumption if you have to take the road. You might have to go back in your past and enjoy some old friends soon. Take plenty of rest if you decide to take a long trip; Neptune may sap your energy and make you feel sleepy on the highway. Chew gum if this happens to you, Neptune hates it! You may not arrive on time, but you will reach your destination in one piece. Be patient and courteous to others as the Waning Moon may make them aggressive and impatient. Check your wheels before leaving on a trip.

Environment: The Titanic sank when Neptune, "Lord of the seas," got angry. Especially after the Full Moon, he likes creating huge waves and sinking ships. That phrase was printed in the 1993 Starguide "Moon Power." I gave the date to watch as January 6th, 1993. The New York Times reported the following disaster on Thursday January 7th, 1993: "The Liberian oil tanker Braer sank yesterday off the Shetland Islands. Rough waters prevented the containment of what officials said, "Could be an environmental disaster." Many devastating oil spills have happened under Supernova windows. Let's hope I am wrong this time. The weather will turn out really nasty and may stop you. You might have to reschedule some of your plans. Be patient.

Famous Personalities: Prominent religious figures will make sad news, some involving drugs, sex and alcohol. Some water sport individuals are in serious danger now. Bad news for the Pope or religions in general as experienced on May 5th, 1998. The Pontiff expressed sadness over a Swiss Guard slaying- VATICAN CITY -- Pope John Paul II expressed his profound sadness over Monday's killing of Alois Estermann, the newly appointed head of the Swiss Guard. The pontiff's message of condolence came as Vatican officials said the shooting, apparently carried out by a lower-ranking Swiss Guard member, may have been motivated by disgruntlement.

Events: Towards the end of the week Mars is growing stronger and may decide to create serious trouble with nature's forces.

Expect devastating news of explosions, earthquakes, tornadoes and very uncooperative weather. Better stay home these days or be extremely prudent in your words and actions.

Shopping: It's a great time to conclude artistic projects, but avoid starting new classes involving the arts now. Don't invest in your future yet, and stay away from psychics. Their caring spirits will suffer Neptune's illusion and deception. Much depends on your awareness of Mars' dangerous temper to save children from trouble. On a more positive note, Mars will deepen your creativity and may lead you to invest in new metaphysical studies. Buy candles and do the cabalistic candles ritual. Burn white, blue and green candles and use incense to purify the environment and your spirit.

※

MON., TUE., WED., THU. — JULY 9, 10, 11, 12:
RULERS — Venus (Connection/caring) and Mercury (Meaningless gibberish).

Work, Career and Business: The most harmful of both of these planets' energy is to be expected mainly due to the Waning Moon (negative) and the pessimistic trend of the Dragon's Tail. Do not fall for depression or self-defeating attitudes. You may communicate your feelings but avoid uncontrolled imagination. The stars have a specific role to play in your life and you are the actor. Go with the trend, do not force issues, be patient and further your business life after the next New Moon. At work keep a low profile, your co-workers or your boss may not be aware of the work of the Moon on their psyches, and may become "lunatic" towards you. Keep busy and rearrange your desk or your paper work.

Partnerships: If you want to save a difficult business relationship, now is the time to use full diplomacy and understanding. With affairs of the heart, use Venus' loving touch; you could apologize with some flowers or a romantic dinner. Take serious precautions if you happen to be in the road as Mercury could mean impatience and speed.

Family and Friends: Expect disturbing news involving friends, brothers or sisters and take the time to reply to the mail. If you get caught on the telephone, steer the discussion towards a positive tone. Mercury rules communication and will help you pass on your thoughts deeply and correctly. Again, provide a helping hand, but do not let abusive or depressing friends take the best of your own spirit.

Love Affairs: Many will feel the disheartening energy of the Waning Moon. Secret love affairs may be started. However, do not expect this undercover relationship to stay a secret for long. A love affair started now could have a dramatic impact in your life. Many unsuited couples will also be forced out of their unhealthy relationships and realize the end of a section of their lives. With the tail in Virgo danger may come from the home, and the emphasis these days will be on destructive behavior and violence. If you were born in November, a Cancer or a Pisces could be difficult just now. Listen to a Virgo friend for good advice.

Travel and Communication: Mercury will pass on all sorts of news including some of a secret nature. Improve your cosmic consciousness and do some "deep" reading concerning life and death or metaphysics. Finish your book if you are into writing. Drive slowly and be ready for obstacles on the road.

Environment: Tornadoes, hurricanes, earthquakes, and chain-reaction accidents due to bad weather are high on the list. Stay safe and be aware of Mother Nature's destructive forces. She is alive and she needs to stretch herself now and then.

Famous personalities: A famous individual from a foreign country will see the end of his life. Many will miss his message and his great spirit.

Events: With the Tail of the Dragon affecting unstable parts of the world acts of terrorism could produce devastating explosions soon. Stay clear of crowds, and listen to your intuition at all times. Avoid crowded places and beware of suspicious foreigners.

Shopping: Electronic equipment, cars, telephones, computers, etc., may decide to give you trouble. The purpose behind this disturbing energy is to re-evaluate your existence and life's mission and restructure your opportunities to make progress. Fix it or rent it but do not buy anything new now. Take care of your car as the machine may decide to let you down at the wrong time and in the wrong place. Be cautious and be patient.

✳

New Moon — July 14, 2007 in Cancer: With the Moon so close to the earth, this specific lunation will have an important effect on many of us especially France's "La Bastille" day festivities. Expect the beginning or ending of important phases of your and other people's lives (especially if you were born on that day☺). This lunation could represent a very significant part of your destiny, even the United States of America, a Cancer nation (July 4th 1776). You may be forced by the universe to let go of your past and forge into your new future. Whatever the changes are, go with confidence. Many will be affected and forced to move on due to war and/or natural catastrophes or simply to further specific wishes. Dr. Turi needs your help to pass on his very important star message to the world. See www.drturi.com or call 602-265-7667 to help us to set a week course in your area on Astro-Psychology, Kabalistic Healing or the Astro-Tarot).

Lunation impact on all signs:

Aries - New home and good news from the family are ahead of you. Be happy.

Taurus - A trip or a study will pay off, great news by mail or the telephone soon.

Gemini - Opportunity to invest in a home and a great financial deal is on the way.

Cancer - This New Moon is on you, be ready for super progressive changes.

Leo - The past is about to show itself, you can fix some financial situations.

Virgo - A friend may bring your past alive and with it good wishes.

Libra - Great news about your career, changes are needed.

Scorpio - A far away trip and a study will pay off in the long run.

Sagittarius - A legacy or business will bring a partner with the money you need.

Capricorn - A great business or emotional partner is ahead if you go out more.

Aquarius - Your health and your work will undergo very progressive changes.

Pisces - Good news about love, romance and children is due to you.

July 15, 2007 — Venus enters Virgo: A perfect time to concentrate on your health and launch an exercise program or a diet. Giving and receiving plants or flowers are on the agenda for some. You may also decide to invest in some good deals with clothing. Souls born now will be quite critical in matters related to love. They will concentrate and achieve perfection in many of their artistic endeavors. Many of them will strive to find a "perfect" and hard working partner willing to exchange a love/career relationship in their lives. Some will have to learn to be less critical of the world around them in order to avoid loneliness. This position makes for one of the most practical and enjoyable business or emotional partners. Usually a gift in dealing with details and an interest in health matters are present with this position. These souls are born to experience love on a practical level. This is a great Venus position, producing success in the medical or clothing fields. Plants or gardens are needed around these souls.

FRI., SAT., SUN., MON., TUE., WED. — JULY 13, 14, 15, 16, 17, 18.
RULERS — Mercury (Information) the Sun (Children) the Moon (New beginnings).

Work, Career and Business: We are on New Moon timing, but you may find it difficult to concentrate on your duties as your mind will wander over everything you must accomplish. The deserving hard-working souls will benefit from bonuses or new opportunities to promote their careers. Some may face the ultimate end of a portion of their business lives. Whatever happens, you must accept the changes with faith. Your desires or dreams may not fit your present situation and the stars may decide to shut you down. It's for your best interest.

Partnerships: Some of the people you know will have to move away from you, or you yourself may decide to relocate. Expect the beginning or ending of an important phase of your life. Watch the drama of life taking place, as the old must be replaced in many aspects of the human experience.

Family and Friends: You may receive an invitation to socialize with some faraway dear friends or family members; use this opportunity to get closer to them. This New Moon trend may prove to be both sad and great for many. You and some friends get together to socialize; you may be the one doing the entertaining. A family member or a child needs your advice. Be willing to consider the issue from their point of view; avoid emotional involvement or forcing your opinion on others. Most of all, provide spiritual support.

Love Affairs: With a Waxing Moon upon us, expect much progress in the area of love. But some people from the past may become heavy in your heart and could produce stress in your life. If they bring good memories, have fun, but don't get too caught up in the nostalgia. If they were negative in the first place, stay far away from their charms the second time around, unless the hard lesson has been learnt from both sides. If you were born on one of these days, happy birthday to you and count on some really good times ahead. If you were born in December, a Leo or an Aries may find you too depressing lately. Listen to a friend born in October; you may learn something. Don't let guilt drag you down; life must go on. Many will enjoy a trip to Europe, France and Italy.

Travel and Communication: Local errands keep you busy and bring you in contact with interesting people. This trend will bring surprising news and reminds us of our responsibility. Mostly, be cautious and prudent in driving, as people may not see you. Drive slowly and enjoy the trip.

Environment: Nature may also go berserk and news could be significantly large and destructive. TEHRAN, Iran — A powerful earthquake jolted Iran's rugged Khorasan province, killing nearly 2,400 people and injuring an estimated 6,000. The U.S. Geological Survey told CNN the quake had a magnitude of 7.3. Nature may also show her power with shocking weather. Thousands of people may be forced to relocate. Many unaware daredevils or unlucky souls will lose their lives because they have no knowledge of the stars' impact on human affairs. You may suggest or offer them a copy of *Starguide;* a little information is better than none, and that is the purpose of this publication. They will probably love you forever because of this practical, thoughtful gesture.

Famous Personalities: A famous person or his child could make dramatic news. Expect interesting news about many famous people. The church could also make sad news such as in FAISALABAD, Pakistan. A 67-year-old Pakistani Roman Catholic bishop shot himself to death outside a court, to protest against a death sentence on a fellow Christian for blasphemy. Some will work hard providing housing or clothing to the world at large.

Events: Under the same celestial energy in LIMA, Peru -- Twelve people survived and 75 were killed when a Peruvian air force Boeing 737, chartered by the Occidental Petroleum Corp., crashed in a northern Amazon jungle. Blackout, tornadoes, volcanic eruptions, including rough weather is high on the list.

Shopping: Don't overspend, no matter how glittery the gift in question is. You can find a good deal on a big-ticket item by comparison shopping. Some will want to use the Waxing Moon and visit Las Vegas' casinos and may strike luck. Better make all your plans now and go with the New Moon. Don't stress; understand and use the stars; they are there to be used and make life easier. Share my valuable forecast from www.drturi.com with accurate guidance or offer a reading for someone's birthday or offer a comparison chart for a newly wed couple.

THU., FRI., SAT. — JULY 19, 20, 21:
RULERS — Mercury (Intercommunication/cars) and Venus (Tenderness/love).

Work, Career and Business: The Moon is still Waxing (positive) and much can happen as long as you understand how to use her energy constructively. Promote your business life now, advertise, reach the people, travel and participate in universal growth. If you do, soon your telephone will be busy and the mail will bring promising news. Get going in all your communications; use Mercury's wit to find a solution to your problems.

Partnerships: A plan is needed to succeed in your endeavor; use this trend to acquire new equipment for your office and reorganize your environment. Nothing can go wrong if you aim high and do something about it. Use Venus' "tact" to get what you need from others. Enjoy the evening with a romantic dinner talking about a potential business venture.

Family and Friends: Expect news from your brother or sister; you might get in touch with some of your friends for a good chat. Don't let Mercury get out of hand; avoid gossip; you may end up sandwiched between two friends. Use the positive Moon to promote your life and try to excel in all your wishes. Appreciate your loved ones; plan a dinner at home, or maybe rent a great movie. Kids need attention; give them some time especially if they ask for help.

Love Affairs: With Venus in the air these days, candlelight, soft music and words of love are pretty much on your mind. This is a trend loaded with good energy, where nothing wrong can happen if you know how to play your cards right. A foreign person will play a considerable part in your future. If you were born in January, a Virgo or a Taurus wants to know you. Listen to a Scorpio friend's advice.

Travel and Communication: Driving away from the city would be a good idea. The call of nature will be strong and the fresh smell of the out-of-doors or seascape will regenerate your soul. Enjoy the water and make plans for fishing trips, the river or sea, but keep an eye on the young ones. Drive slowly; don't spoil your day with trouble.

Environment: Many Mother Earth supporters will march to be heard by government officials and they will succeed in their request to save the environment. Nature may surprise some of us with a volcanic eruption.

Famous Personalities: A famous entertainer will take an

important legal action. Large corporations will find strength in their new associations. Concerned groups will do much work for the welfare of children.

Events: Parts of the US, France or Japan may make interesting, even surprising news soon. The government will make important decisions to change or establish laws that will benefit children or the arts.

Shopping: You may invest in anything that will further your education or the arts. Cameras bought now will last long and take incredible pictures. Good books can also be bought and used positively for your own progression and mental exploration. Spruce yourself up by brightening your wardrobe or, if you can afford to, invest in expensive jewelry.

※

Note: Attention: Pluto doesn't care much for the Waxing Moon, he is back with us — Expect dramatic happenings all over; control is a must. Don't be on e of his ignorant victims: be aware of Pluto's destructive power.

SUN., MON., TUE., WED., THU. — JULY 22, 23, 24, 25, 26:
RULERS — Pluto (Terror/dramatic news) and Jupiter (Religion/foreigners):

Work, Career and Business: Hopefully the New Moon energy will make all of those changes positive in the long run. Push forward for the next few days; make the most of this lunation. At last the negative Supernova trend that has plagued many of us is over. You may also find out why you had to go through so much stress. Be ready for a form of rebirth and accept your limits. A new business proposition may further your entire business life. This is the time to review all your accomplishments and the reasons for your failures. Meditate on improving your future and if you feel you need to educate yourself in some area, do it now; there is no time like the present!

Partnerships: Money will play an important part in your life now, and you are advised to keep a close eye on your bank account. You may inherit a few expensive items, and this will help relieve a form of stress you had to experience. Commitments made now could become very fruitful in the long run. You may also make a commitment on paper as we are still under the blessing of the New Moon. You may decide to spend some time in nature or to visit an old Church in response to Jupiter's religious nature. Some may decide to go to the desert and "see" the creator display his face of lightening to the universe. We will all receive God's full support from the stars.

Family and Friends: Many will be enjoying foreign places and the different cultures of these people. Expect news from brothers and sisters from afar and let yourself be immersed in this great summer season. The circle of friends will be extremely busy as we are all enjoying the best of what life has to offer. Children are very excited and will be enjoying the festivities. Uranus may make them restless, and a trip out of the house is in order. Watch over them, especially close to the water. Use diplomacy at all costs; Pluto will make everyone around very susceptible to your comments. Control emotions and watch what's going on in the house, especially if there are children around. A great time is ahead of you, if you listen to your intuition. A friend may bring a stranger into your house; watch the young ones closely. Be aware of Pluto and don't let him upset your life. Enjoy it all.

Love Affairs: Expect secrets of a sexual nature to surface to light and new secret affairs to be born. The planet of passion will make you feel good about yourself and will give tons of charm. Be aware of mysterious Pluto and his sensual magnetism. Do not drink too much during the evenings. Accompanying Jupiter could transform you into an irresistible sex magnet with a passionate foreigner. The Moon is still Waxing, but trouble may come your way if you let your passion express itself with unprotected sex. If you're born in August be aware at home and avoid drama, an Aquarius or a Sagittarius could mean love to you.

Travel and Communication: Pluto rules ultimate power, the Mafia and the police force. News pertaining to the police force will always appear during his ruling days. I can hear Police Executives of the future, in the training Academy warning their officers of the impact of the power of Pluto and how vulnerable they all are under his destructive jurisdiction. Once the system catches up with my advanced perception of the human psyche outside of the limited field of mental research, I can foresee the use of Astrology in the police force. They so desperately need this knowledge to pinpoint suspects by using the natal profiles. The impact of Pluto to a sensitive house may predispose the suspect for murder. Most of all, in the name of ignorance, many brave public servants won't have to waste their precious lives. Time will tell.

Environment: Keep in mind that Pluto does not care much about the New Moon and could disturb the earth's belly, producing a bad earthquake. On my newsgroup weeks before the following events, I had posted this note and quatrain. "Please make a note and save this post and explore my predictions on the given dates: May 11th, 18th, 24th, and 30th, 1998. *'The tenth day and when the moon will shine in her fullest, in the month of the Bull. A digit of one's hand of destruction will rule upon the human race. Water, wind and dirt will blind many with the smell of death. Rage and destruction is the legacy, nature will speak to the mortals.'* Result: - May 8, 1998- Tornadoes, windstorms sock U.S. South again- EDGEFIELD, South Carolina -- In four Southern states, thousands of people began a task Friday, that has become somewhat routine during this year's severe storm season. As usual with Pluto in charge, be ready for many interesting secrets to surface and remember to use these secrets to your own advantage.

Famous Personalities: A famous personality will be called to God and many will miss the soul. It will be a reminder of our own mortality and the real power of Pluto's impact upon the earth and humans below.

Events: October 7th, 1970 - Pluto will take many people away; expect this type of news again. Gene Marshall's sports information director and play-by-play broadcaster was among the 43 players and coaches and 32 administrators, fans and crew who died in a plane crash 25 years ago. To survive their Plutonic awful deal, the victims had to eat raw human flesh and walk through the mountains in a pure cold hell. Pluto rules death, drama and does not usually spare anyone's life. In this case the sheer will for life did the horrible trick. The Moon was New when the plane crashed and is the only reason why a few "lucky" people survived Pluto's deadly will. Do **NOT TRUST** any strangers now, as Pluto stirs man's animal tendencies. Pluto rules the crooks and the cops, or the infinite forces of good and evil constantly teasing each other. Thus, the villains will become more active and the police will be busy trying to stop them. Of course if you are a Police officer and on duty now, don't take chances and let your fellow officers know about Pluto's jurisdiction of the police force. Make good use of my knowledge and realize that your "bosses", regardless of their high position and accomplishments, are NOT aware of this fact. Many lives have been wasted in the name of ignorance; you can make a difference and even save your life, by being aware of my work.

Shopping: Invest in anything that can kill pests. Use Jupiter to find a great traveling bargain or start a spiritual course in metaphysical.

Full Moon — July 30, 2007 in the explosive sign of Aquarius: Expect some serious surprising or shocking developments to take place in the near future. NASA could make shocking news again soon, especially if they avoid using the value of the stars. This is the same energy that produced many mishaps with expense electronic equipments and the death of many courageous astronauts. Also under Uranus power the Middle East suffered the "US surprise bomb attacks" on Saddam Hussein's forces in Iraq and under the same energy, Israel invaded Lebanon. This energy can affect sophisticated electronic equipment and could produce bad aeronautic accidents. Unlucky children could suffer this disturbing dramatic lunation; keep an eye on all of them. They are accident-prone for a while. Just be ready to accept the upcoming changes with faith in God's desire to restructure the earth's crust. Be ready for nature's devastating forces, producing destructive weather, tornadoes, earthquakes and volcanic eruptions. Expect anything surprising, even incredible including out space manifestation to take place soon. Be ready to see the real power of Uranus, the planet of sudden releases of energy, in action. Explosions are also expected and the US, UK, Asia and Japan or France may make disturbing news soon. News of nuclear deals or planning/endeavors is in the secret agenda.

Lunation impact on all signs:

Aries - One of your wishes may take time to manifest. Simply, be patient.

Taurus - Your career will see needed changes soon, be strong.

Gemini - Difficult news from far away is expected; a trip is ahead.

Cancer - Stress from your investments, a metaphysical study is needed.

Leo - Change with a partner is ahead, sign important papers.

Virgo - Change at work is ahead, concentrate on communication and hi-tech.

Libra - God created the heavens and the stars, not man-made books to study.

Scorpio - You might have to review a move or a deal about your home soon.

Sagittarius - Learn about your relationship with nature, the stars and the Indians.

Capricorn - Difficult news with money, just improve your computer skills.

Aquarius - Stress with friends, and be patient with some of your wishes.

Pisces - Move on to the future, let go of apocalyptic material, astrology liberates from fears.

※

FRI., SAT., SUN., MON., TUE. — JULY 27, 28, 29, 30, 31:
RULERS — Saturn (Government order/creditability) and Uranus (Extraordinary news)

Work, Career and Business: Expect this trend to promote surprising changes pertaining to your career. The lucky ones will benefit all the way with this ending New Moon. Make the most of the last days of the Waxing Moon, while you can and go after your wishes. Saturn may force you to realize what needs to be done to further your career.

Partnerships: Time to socialize this weekend as Saturn's children

(CEOs) will be out in public places and many of them can further your career wishes. This trend will induce serious changes and interesting surprises in your partnerships. A business trip or an invitation may lead you to many good contacts that could prove to be rewarding in the long run. You must take the time to play and enjoy yourself with unusual people.

Family and Friends: A friend may request some money from you or another one who owes you money sincerely wants to repay, but may be in a difficult set of circumstances. Be patient; they may repay you in a better way. A friend may surprise you and may decide to get closer. Providing help is great, but let some of your friends understand their limits. Keep in mind that Uranus rules friends and wishes; do not turn down an invitation during a New Moon. With Uranus, anything great can happen and you have until the Full Moon to do so. After the Full Moon the surprises will be negative.

Love Affairs: As usual with Uranus, be ready for nice surprises brought by friends bringing new people into your life. The Moon is still up for a short while, so those surprises should be of a positive nature. Many lucky souls will find love, and this new relationship may lead you to a rewarding future. Remember that serious Saturn is also part of the festivities and you must not overindulge. If you were born under the sign of Pisces, a Virgo, a Cancer, even a Scorpio will find you irresistible.

Travel and Communication: Your telephone and your mail will bring you all sorts of news and invitations. The lucky ones will enjoy or plan faraway trips close to those they love. Expect news from many people around and get in touch with some of your friends for a good chat. However, do not fall for gossip about other friends, as sooner or later you will have some explaining to do. Use what's left of the positive Moon to promote your life and excel in your mental capacity.

Environment: As always when Uranus is with us, a volcano could erupt soon, be ready for surprising news about the weather. Stay clear of lightning. If you're into UFOs, anything extraordinary from the heavens could happen now.

Famous Personalities: Famous people will behave in a weird way, while others will offer the best of their performance and the money will be presented to organizations supporting the very old or the very young.

Events: Saturn (structure) still resides in the sign of Cancer (security) and could induce some worries about your finances. Don't let him get the best of your spirit, have faith. Financial affairs will be a concern for many, as the government will make very important decisions about other countries and wars in the world. With this very last day of the New Moon trend be careful in all you do. Uranus rules the incredible. Paranormal investigators; now is the time to carry your camera and look for UFOs in secluded places. Blackouts, explosions or bad weather could plague some parts of the US. Expect news about nuclear endeavors and electronic devices soon.

Shopping: Purchase electronic equipment or plan a long voyage in foreign lands before the Full Moon. As always, Uranus rules the future, and his psychic powers can be used. Don't waste these days; do something original as your wishes depend on your interaction with others. Visit your favorite astrologer or psychic now. Share my valuable forecast from www.drturi.com with accurate guidance for someone's birthday, or offer a comparison chart for a newly wed couple.

Welcome to Your Day - to - Day Guidance
For August 2007

WED., THU., FRI., SAT. — AUGUST 1, 2, 3, 4:
RULERS — Uranus (Bombardment) Neptune (Religion) and Mars (War):

Work, Career and Business: We are now into the Full Moon. Listen to intangible impulses from a different plane than the physical, before making important decisions. Avoid insecurity and imagination blurring your vision or your faith during this trend. Neurotic tendencies and depression come from a heavy Neptune in anyone's chart; use your will and see the bright side of your business life. You may find it hard to concentrate at work, but everything will be clear again in a couple of days. Keep emotions in control; use plenty of patience and diplomacy with co-workers or the boss at work. Try to concentrate on the future.

Partnerships: Mars is called the "Lord of War" for good reasons. Do not let him aggravate a situation, as this could hurt a friend or a loved one. The purpose of Moon Power Starguide is to teach you firm control over the stars and to manage positively the outcome of any situation. If you know someone who needs help, offer this book as a birthday present. Mars also rules cars and machinery, and with deceiving Neptune around you should avoid drinking and driving (you should never do this but right now, even a little could hurt you). Danger could enter the lives of those ignorant of the celestial rules just now; beware. You will be given energy from the red planet; make good use of it by channeling the power constructively. Still, Mars' energy can help you start a new project, new business, even a new relationship. Keep a positive attitude.

Family and Friends: Help some family members see through the veil of self-deceit. Some of your friends may need spiritual support; work with them without getting emotionally involved in their problems. Again, keep away from alcohol after dark if you decide to meet them. A trip close to the water or Sea World will be rewarding. Keep a vigilant eye on the kids and your pet, as impatient drivers could hurt them. Be prudent; be patient, but firm and confident. Spend some time with the children, teach them love and harmony as Mars may make them play rough. Be aware around water. Remember my prediction about children playing rough with Mars. (Moon Power 1997 page 116) Memo: Water slide collapses kills one, injures 32 — An amusement park water slide collapsed Monday June 2nd, 1997 after a group of high school seniors on a graduation outing, ignored a lifeguard's warning and went down together. One student was killed and 32 were injured, six critically. Be aware; watch the kids around water.

Love Affairs: Come right out with what you feel and don't be vague in love matters. Secret love affairs will start under Neptune's deceiving power and many will end up deceived; beware whom you tell! Avoid drinking heavily and enjoy a great walk by the sea or any watery area. If you were born in April, a Leo or a Sagittarius will be strongly attracted to you. At any rate do not expect much with love now; you'd better wait for better auspices.

Travel and Communication: Some of us may experience strange things in unfamiliar places or find themselves with weird people. Keep an eye on your personal belongings and learn to rely on your gut feelings. Nevertheless, you can expect heavenly intervention in a dangerous situation. For those at sea, take all precautions as the weather could turn nasty without much notice.

Environment: Disturbing news from the sea, oil and flooding is a possibility. News about medicine and chemical explosions and broken dams can also be expected.

Famous Personalities: Sad news regarding alcoholism, drugs and incarceration will come about the rich and famous. Some famous souls might have to learn the law and may find themselves in trouble. The release of a new movie will make some of them very happy. Certain famous people will suffer incarceration or hospitalization.

Events: Depressing and explosive news will come from the Middle East. — Oil prices may rise due to another oil spill. Expect water, tornadoes, typhoons, hurricanes and earthquakes such as; August 31, 1999 - ISTANBUL, Turkey -- A strong earthquake and an aftershock shook northwestern Turkey, just two weeks after a deadly 7.4 magnitude quake left more than 14,000 dead. About oil spills, look to September 8, 1999 - EUREKA, California (AP) -- Coast Guard officials have managed to clean up only a small portion of about 2,000 gallons of oil that has leaked into Humboldt Bay from a dredging vessel. The oil leak from the ruptured fuel tank of The Stuyvesant occurred Monday night, after rough seas apparently tossed part of the dredging apparatus against the vessel. Part of the equipment sliced through the hull, cutting a 6-inch to 8-inch-wide hole in the tank.

Shopping: This is not a great time to invest in anything related to the spiritual arts. As a rule, musical instruments, painting and spiritual materials should be bought before the Full Moon. Invest in cleansing tools, only.

✷

August 5, 2007 — Mercury enters Leo: This next trend's promise is a rich mixture of love, romance, creativity and children. Many thoughts will be geared towards immense feelings of both hope and true love. Souls born with Mercury in Leo will be gifted with natural managerial dispositions. Many of them will be shrewd in business, and attracted to professions offering fame and fortune. Artistic talents involving music, dancing, and painting will lead these souls toward the great fame and security they seek. This position makes for one of the most mentally domineering signs of the Zodiac, where the soul will be forced to learn humility and service to others. This Mercury position will lead the soul toward success in many artistic endeavors. An opportunity to experience mental fame is also offered to the soul. The parent educated in Astro-Psychology, will realize the child's gift and promote the new soul towards communication, acting or writing. Dr. Turi can help you; if you have a problem child, call 602-265-7667 and trust him to guide you and your child towards love and success.

✷

August 7, 2007 — Mars enters Gemini: The Lord of war in the sign of communication will instigate a sharp tongue. Be concerned with others feelings and be diplomatic at all time. If not, someone might give you a kick in the mouth, and you would have to learn the hard way to control Mars' aggressive verbal power. On a more productive note, use this powerful planet to start a book, take a long trip, or use your mental power for any spiritual task. Winds are forecasted; producing devastative tornadoes, soon. Drive slowly and beware of crazy blind souls that will fall victim to Mars' speedy nature. Souls born with this celestial gift will be geared into sales, mental exploration, writing, broadcasting, general communication and speed. This Mars position breeds dares devils, racing drivers, and boxers who break bones. Note: Pluto will become very destructive in this period; — You can expect dramatic happenings with nature all over; control is a must. He has produced much sensational news, including the California Rancho Santa Fe mass-suicide. Mass murderers are again on the lookout for innocent victims, as Pluto always stimulates the criminal element, the insane and the police force fighting all ill purposes. Don't be victims; be aware of Pluto's destructive power. Secrets and people from the past will return to your life.

SUN., MON., TUE., WED. — AUGUST 5, 6, 7, 8:
RULERS — Venus (Artfulness/Diplomacy) and Mercury (Words exchanged):

Work, Career and Business: Fight the depressing mood you may find yourself in; you need to reach out to new people and expand the various social networks in your life. The Moon might be against you, but you can still make significant progress; reorganize it all. Business started now won't bring much financial security to all parties involved. Not a time to ask for a loan from your bank or a financial favor from a friend or family member. Money and security will play an important part of this trend and you might find yourself investing in a good deal from the past that you missed earlier. You should be confident no matter what, as your will (the part of God in you) is still stronger than the Moon.

Partnerships: Candlelight, soft music, courtship and social gatherings for the upcoming weekend are on the agenda for some. The soft Venus energy will tone down the aggressiveness of many people around you. The time is upon you to make peace and apologize for your mistakes. You need to reach out to the people you know, but avoid expanding the various social networks in your life. Use finesse in all you do, you can't miss. Under Venus' blessings, you must keep in mind that whatever is offered with true love will bring luck to the giver. Abusing her kindness, will bring back heavy karma and will be paid in full (fool). Let your partner know about your deep feelings and see the good side of life.

Family and Friends: Do not turn down an invitation or a chance to socialize with old friends; weird new people will also be there waiting for you. Communication is on the fore; don't hesitate to participate in it; everybody will listen to your comments. However, avoid falling into useless gossip over the telephone — only "Ma Bell" will benefit from that! You may hear distressing news about brothers or sisters. Use Mercury's power of expression to write those long overdue letters.

Love Affairs: Some will happily give; some will gladly receive presents that will last forever in their hearts. Promote words of love and be aware of the feelings of others; lovely Venus will change uneasiness into love, attention and respect. You and a long-standing friend may discover that your relationship is growing towards romance and both are surprised. A dual situation may force some to make a decision, use your intuition, and keep a cool head. The lessons of the past should be remembered. If you were born in February, a Leo or a Gemini may make your life a misery. Be patient with all the people around you.

Travel and Communication: Do not expect interesting news, as your telephone might be full of distressing messages. Not a time for traveling, however, avoid the impulsive Mercurial need for speed. You might have to deal with high winds or water. It's time to express your self, write letters and start (or finish) a book.

Environment: With the Waning Moon upon us, nature may get out of hand with a bad earthquake. A monetary scandal could also make the news. A famous personality may pay a heavy price for a stupid and selfish act.

Events: A financial scandal or some secrets may reach you. Foreign affairs could be distressing for many governments, forcing some dramatic interaction soon.

Shopping: Take care of your wheels and shop around for things for the office. If you decide to purchase a second-hand car, you could strike a good bargain; don't be afraid to barter aggressively. Mercury loves mental stimulation and your wit will help you to save money. Be happy and alert — don't be afraid to use your powers of communication.

※

THU., FRI., SAT., SUN., MON.— AUGUST 9, 10, 11, 12, 13:
RULERS — The Moon (Ending of life/new start) and the Sun (Love/children matters):

Work, Career and Business: You may find yourself discussing goals for the future with someone close to you. Some will even sell their homes or move to better locations. Life is a process of constant change and this lunation will touch you or someone close to you. Make the most out of this change and trust the upcoming future. Not exactly a time to promote any endeavors, sign contracts or travel; wait for the upcoming New Moon to move or deal with important matters.

Partnerships: Time to promote only faith and have confidence in all you do. This type of energy will be difficult for some as they might be forced in or out important situations. Accept those changes you may not be able to control. You might be going through a hard time now, but the Universe will pay you back in spades, if you learn from your experiences and keep faith in yourself.

Family and Friends: Listen to your friends' stories and be ready for the beginning or ending of an important part of their lives. Keep in mind that the Moon is Waning (negative) and those unexpected changes must be faced with courage, no matter what. Give special attention to the children these days and provide them guidance, if needed. Their young and fragile spirits need constant reassurance and appreciation. Also, with the Sun in charge, you might stimulate their creativity and enjoy their youth and boundless energy. This energy could also work against them, and some may be accident-prone, so watch them carefully.

Love Affairs: Some people might surprise you; however, don't dream or hope for finding a lost love now. Be ready for the beginning or ending of an important part of your life. If you are stuck in the wrong relationship, this lunation will force you out of this stressful situation very soon. Accept the upcoming changes with grace and have faith in the future. Those changes will bring someone worthy of your feelings. Wait for the next upcoming New Moon to get active in your social circle again. Your friends possess all your wishes and you should spend more time with them, especially if you are single and looking for love. For those born in May, a Pisces or a Virgo will be strongly attracted to you. Enjoy a great show when possible; you need to forget a few things in your own life.

Travel and Communication: With the Waning Moon affecting our psyches, tears and depression might be a problem. Keep busy, avoid negative thoughts of the past and look for positive endeavors. Free yourself from pessimistic people or stressful situations; use your will and surprise others with a formidable optimistic attitude. Be a defensive driver, ever ready to give way to the crazies of the freeway. Plans to travel far may be imposed upon your life by Uncle Sam.

Environment: The weather will turn very nasty in some states, and many will lose their lives and possessions. Thousands may be forced to relocate due to dramatic experiences with nature. A loss of power is part of this trend; don't take any chances, stay safe. April 9, 1998 -- 39 die in Southeast storms - At least 39 people were killed in tornadoes and thunderstorms that raked the Southeast overnight. Most of the deaths were in Alabama.

Famous Personalities: An important figure could suffer a heart attack or surgery! A naughty love affair may dramatically end. Some unlucky children could be involved in awful accidents.

Events: On a large scale, many governments may also make news that will affect all of us. Disturbing news may be coming from The US, France or Japan. Read the headlines of the past under similar stars; in NAHA, Japan -- A powerful undersea earthquake rumbled through Okinawa, Taiwan and the Philippines Monday, setting off a tidal wave. The earthquake struck at 8:30 a.m. Japan time (7:30 p.m. Sunday EDT/2330 GMT Sunday) and had a preliminary magnitude of 7.7, according to Japan's Central Meteorological Agency. ATHENS -- At least 27 people were killed Tuesday when a powerful earthquake struck just north of Athens, trapping dozens beneath the rubble of collapsed buildings.

Shopping: It's the perfect time to give old toys or clothes to unlucky children. Avoid spending money on expensive items for your own children. Now is not the time to find good deals in your local flea market. Spend time doing something creative; it doesn't have to be a masterpiece, just something to ease your spirit. We are getting closer to the New Moon and all will be much better soon.

New Moon — August 12, 2007 in Leo: This sign is ruled by the Sun, thus affairs of love and romance will be on the rise. Expect some surprises this month; the stars are giving you the possibility to reach one of your important wishes, if you try hard within the next two weeks. This lunation could play an important part in your love life, with your children, your wishes, and will surely improve your relationships. You may also be forced to let go of a deteriorating love involvement and experience a new one. This month promises to be very interesting for many of us. Make the most of this incredible time; don't waste it.

Lunation impact on all signs:

Aries - Love is on the rise and a project with a friend will turn out great. Take chances now.

Taurus - Plan to move or improve your surroundings, throw a party and help find love.

Gemini - Great news from foreign lands and siblings take a trip or a study on photography.

Cancer - Great news about money; you may invest in an expensive item; invest.

Leo - A new door for love, light, children and success will open to you, changes with partners.

Virgo - A possibility to do something with love or children is ahead for you.

Libra - A friend will bring you good wishes, socialize to get it, enjoy gambling and love.

Scorpio - Your career will see important and constructive changes soon.

Sagittarius - Traveling, speaking and publishing is on the agenda for you, talk to a sibling.

Capricorn - Others fortune will touch you financially, study deep matters, talk to others more.

Aquarius - You will be in demand for love and for fame, travel now and enjoy the light.

Pisces - A great opportunity to improve your health and your work is given to you.

※

TUE., WED., THU., FRI., SAT. — AUGUST 14, 15, 16, 17, 18: RULERS — Mercury (Travel/telephone) and Venus (Marriage/children/promise):

Work, Career and Business: You may find yourself in an awkward or difficult situation with a co-worker, and something must be done soon. Don't let this stressful situation in your working life become a major problem for you and others; handle your affairs with discretion and dignity. Meditate for insight; use your intuition and be patient; the right opportunity is on the way. Use the New Moon to push forward.

Partnerships: With the New Moon upon you, much transformation will take place soon. However, avoid getting into a heated argument with a friend or an acquaintance that will challenge you about politics at work or your personal philosophy of life. Be patient and tolerant.

Family and Friends: Expect interesting news from close friends or family members and provide some spiritual support. Avoid gossip, and make sure that what you say is actually what you mean, as others could interpret it the wrong way. Nothing really can happen to you now; have faith in the stars and your new future.

Love Affairs: Romance is on your mind and therefore you may consider a trip with your special someone. An important person close to you may be a challenge to understand; just realize that none of us is perfect. A desire for a permanent commitment from a lover or the chance to find love this weekend has a good possibility of working out. You may find yourself focusing on personal relationships; you feel better with others' approval. Don't be tempted to let sadness or depression or the ending of a situation get the best of you. This emotional approach to decision-making can be the source of strife; use diplomacy and coordinate your efforts with your mate's. If you were born in June, a Libra or an Aquarius could denote love to you. Make the most of this New Moon; with Venus' touch, you can't go wrong.

Travel and Communication: Take extra time in explaining yourself, as the possibility of miscommunication is high and ill will could ensue. Venus will see to it that there is harmony these days. Also, emotions may run high and could affect your words; make sure they are well thought out and supportive. Remember that Mercury rules transportation, and impatient drivers could promote accidents. Time to take care of your car's brakes, oil or anything else it may need, as you might have to take a journey soon.

Environment: Expect difficult news about the ocean or a chemical accident. News of medicine and hospitals may also come your way. The weather will not be too cooperative and many thousands of people might have to relocate due to nature's devastating forces.

Famous Personalities: News of hospitalization, drugs or alcohol may plague the media as the rich and famous won't be able to hide their dependency.

Events: Leaders of the Middle East may surprise some of their neighbors. Religion and many difficult topics, such as abortion or chemical warfare will trouble the world.

Shopping: This is surely a great time to invest in anything you need to make your home a better or safer place to live. You may also invest money in shopping for clothes, plants, food and little surprises for your loved ones.

August 20, 2007 — Mercury enters Virgo: A trend loaded with communication related to work, health and service to the world. Many thoughts will be geared toward finding a better job or working on improving health. Souls born now, will be gifted with a natural ability for details and the opportunity to learn everything they can about health. Many of them will be born with an aptitude for investigation and literary powers. Some will be attracted to the professions offering mental work; rewards of fame and fortune will come to the writers. The artistic talents of editing, dancing, writing, photography, painting and general health will lead these souls towards the body and mind security they seek. This position makes for one of the most critical signs of the Zodiac. Souls born with this Mercury position will have to learn to avoid criticism, as the soul is looking for a perfect mate, with a perfect attitude and a perfect job. The problem is that no one is perfect and the soul may suffer long periods of time alone. However, an opportunity to experience mental fame is offered to the advanced soul. This is a great position of Mercury for writers and editors.

Note: We may be in a New Moon period, but be alert of Pluto's power upon us for a few days. As always with the Lord of Hades, expect dramatic happenings all over; control is a must. Anything you say or do now, will have serious repercussions in your and other's future. Be aware of Pluto's emotional and dramatic nature.

SUN., MON., TUE., WED., THU. — AUGUST 19, 20, 21, 22, 23: RULERS — Pluto (Tragedy/sex secrets) and Jupiter (Foreigners/law enforcement):

Work, Career and Business: Don't be a Pluto victim - avoid all confrontations. Emotion, destruction, hate and crime are all part of Pluto's signature. You are aware of Pluto; many others are not! Compromise in the office and don't let the stinger of the beast get to you. Sarcasm is the last thing you need to use just now. You will be forced to recognize many of your errors and your limits. A wake-up call for some dreamers is ahead.

Partnerships: The crooks and the police are going to be busy; avoid the unsafe or unknown. Pluto's power is not for unity, but discord and will affect the masses, including your very own relationships. Do not participate in large gatherings, as death may strike anytime, anywhere, against the unaware. Secrets like Whitewater, RTC's allegations, sex scandals, police, CIA, and FBI's wrong doings will be divulged to the public. Expect news pertaining to AIDS, abortion and religious groups to make the news once more. I fully predicted the Rodney King dilemma the WA sniper attacks and the awful Rancho Santa Fe mass suicide in my Moon Power and this type of dilemma will always take place under a Plutonic trend. Both Chiefs of police Burgreen (San Diego) and Daryl Gate (Los Angeles) received my mail and predictions, but never took notice of my guidance. When will the police authorities wake up to true knowledge and save lives?

Family and Friends: The influence of benevolent Jupiter should tone down Pluto's desire for drama. Participate in promoting cosmic consciousness among friends and family, and share your knowledge about Pluto's destructive energy. Build up good karma for yourself and let them know about the energies that control them — share your knowledge. The good thing about Pluto is that you, your friends and family members will all be forced to realize their limits and do something about any and all aggravated situations. Stay alert! Be patient and practice super diplomacy during this trend. Use the secrets you hear, to your advantage and don't repeat them to others!

Love Affairs: The real you, the raw you, and the plain truth around you and its impact in your life, will force you to mutate or transform with your newly acquired knowledge. Expect secrets pertaining to sex and money, but most of all, stay calm in your dealings. Take smart precautions, if you are going to be sexually active. If you were born under water or an earth sign, a Cancer, a Scorpio or a Pisces can either go crazy for you or against you.

Travel and Communication: You had better stay and enjoy your home, read a good book or watch a movie! Observe and listen to your intuition. The less you talk the less chance of being hurt. Control your own thoughts; don't fall for jealousy or depression. If you must take to the road, be extremely prudent and don't trust any strangers. Watch the children; the vampires are out. Mention my work to depressed friends by suggesting www.drturi.com

and let them learn about real astrology. You may also offer him a copy of the current Starguide Moon Power for his birthday.

Environment: We are still in a Waxing Moon period, but let's hope that Pluto won't stir a tragedy with nature's devastating forces, like an earthquake or a series of floods. Anything dramatic can happen now; let's pray for the victims of the planet of death. If you are a law enforcement officer or a security guard, be extremely cautious, as violent and dangerous karmic souls will roam the streets. Remember the Rodney King beating also took place under Pluto, and those who lost control over their emotions will have forever to pay the ultimate price. The legacy of this action that took place on that night transformed later on into the Los Angeles riots, where disorder and fires ruled the nights. Be ready for news such as Sept.14, 1999 - Hurricane Floyd smashes through low-lying Bahamas - Hurricane Floyd tore through the Bahamas on Tuesday, uprooting trees, shearing off roofs and hurling debris into buildings, as frightened tourists and residents hunkered down in shelters or barricaded houses to wait out the monstrous storm.

Famous Personalities: Lots of people die under Pluto's rule and those who had a significant life, will also have a significant departure from this world. The same energy may also remove a famous public figure in a secret way where drugs, sex, and rock and roll are never far away. Eldridge Cleaver, the 1960s Black Panther activist and fugitive who later swung to the other side of the political spectrum to become a Republican, died at the age of 62 under a Plutonic trend. Pluto rules the police force and brings the hidden facts to life. There can be a form of rebirth, a new part of life for the parties involved and for some, million-dollar lawsuits!

Events: This is a particularly destructive time, even in a good Moon, and I want you to be aware of everything around you and your loved ones. Under Pluto's power, May 1997, a brutal slaying follows beer drinking in Central Park, New York. Two teenagers stabbed a real estate agent at least 30 times and tried to chop off his hands, so police couldn't use fingerprints to identify him before dumping him in a lake in Central Park. The perpetrators, Daphne Abdela, 15, and her boyfriend, 15-year-old Christopher Vasquez, "gutted the body, so it would sink." Both of those young souls were born in the dramatic Pluto "Death Wish Generation."

See Pluto's impact upon generations or order any of my two new books "And God Created the Stars" and "The Power of the Dragon" to learn more about this phenomenon. Some unlucky souls will have to undergo sorrow and loss, such as those kids mentioned above. Be ready to help those in need, as the favor may hit close to home. Expect the weather to be harsh and crime to be high. Expect news such as 'Calm' gunman walks into a church and kills 7 before committing suicide on September 16, 1999.

Shopping: A great time to purchase anything related to metaphysics or to look for a good attorney. Anything related to checkups, investigations, or cleansing, are under good stars. Do not invest in dangerous tools or weapons just now.

Full Moon – August 28, 2007 in the religious sign of Pisces:

Important Note: Expect sad news from the Pope, the Middle East, oil and the elements. The same Neptunian energy produced the terrorist WTC destruction of September 11 in New York. Two years prior to the attack, read what I wrote in Moon Power. This exact portion of Moon Power and its deadly message was posted on my site www.drturi.com two weeks prior to the destruction of both towers and printed in Moon Power, well before the deadly terrorist attacks in New York.

Pisces rules the *Middle East, religion,* drugs, alcohol, deception, the difficult abortion dilemma, the Pope, the church, oil, etc. This could also mean bad news for denominations where religious figures will "pass over." Deception, illusion **and** *secret affairs are on the agenda. This lunation marks a significant point involving the US and the Middle East conflict* and will negatively affect the young generation. *Many souls will suffer this disturbing lunation. Just be ready to provide as much help as needed and do not lose faith in the future.* More devastating forces producing destructive weather and floods will make themselves known in the very near future. *Expect a general feeling of hopelessness to plague the media and church authorities. Deceiving news will take place and affect many of us; some desperate souls will fall for Neptune's suicidal tendencies, and some will end up in jail or mental institutions. This trend will be very difficult for* *some, but do not lose faith in yourself and trust the Universe; get all the help you can to fight Neptune's depressing tendencies.* Amuse yourself, keep busy and let go of the past. Life must go on. Anticipate shocking news about volcanoes, earthquakes, tornadoes, etc. *Expect anything surprising, even incredible to happen soon; see in action the real power of both Uranus ruling sudden releases of energy, and Saturn forcing the government to take drastic action.*

Lunation impact on all signs:

Aries - Forget the past and build new confidence, changes at work keep positive.

Taurus - A friend could become a problem; stay clear of deceiving people or groups.

Gemini - More challenges involving your position in the world and at home, be patient.

Cancer - Some foreigners could prove to be burdensome, learn about metaphysics, no religion.

Leo - Don't get sued; do the right thing, no guilt, financial drama is ahead but you'll do fine.

Virgo - Use your head, let go of your heart, wrong people are around you, move on.

Libra - Don't put stress on your health because of your work and no religion or drugs.

Scorpio - Love, romance and children need serious attention, a deal won't go too well.

Sagittarius - Stress coming from home, family, career or real estate is ahead.

Capricorn - Avoid depression and stay clear of Prozac or religious material, sad mail is ahead.

Aquarius - You'll experience financial worries or stress, be more practical with money.

Pisces - The stars are against you for a while; swim upstream and have faith. Don't drink.

※

FRI., SAT., SUN., MON., TUE. — AUGUST 24, 25, 26, 27, 28:
RULERS — Saturn (Politics) and Uranus (Explosive news):

Work, Career and Business: You better keep a good attitude or eccentric Uranus could jeopardize your job or image. With the Waxing Moon, some of your wishes may take place. Keep in mind that sometimes a full breakdown is needed, if you hope for restoration. Be ready for anything to happen these days and accept the challenges with a sunny disposition. A beginning and ending of an important phase of your life is about to take place. Many ingenious ideas of rebuilding or investing will come to fruition during this trend.

Partnerships: Like Pluto, Uranus is a rebel and he likes to destroy relationships, so caution is also advised in all you do or say to others. Be patient or suffer the consequences of impetuosity. The light is green for friendship and hope, and so much can happen if you participate in life. Try something different this weekend; you'll be surprised by the payoff. Throw a party; you may bring a wish to you or a dear friend.

Family and Friends: Help a friend in trouble and meditate on the world around you. The more positive people think, the more definite things will happen in this world. Don't turn down any opportunity to socialize, but be responsible with children. Some of them need to burn off some energy and will be begging for a boisterous outdoor romp. A trip close to nature or to the nearest electronic attraction will do wonders for the entire family. Make the most of what is left of this New Moon trend.

Love Affairs: Absolutely anything can happen this weekend; stay alert and participate with the best of your social life. A chance to find love or reach a dream will be given to you if you try hard enough. You may encounter funny people or be involved in strange situations; make the most of it. If you were born in June, a Libra or a Sagittarius will want to know you.

Travel and Communication: Your desire to travel will become intense. Some will plan a very long trip by airplane. As always, make your plans and try to travel after the New Moon. Be gentle with words and realize your inner mental power; promote your future. Remember, the future is the reincarnation of all your thoughts and you may use the universal mind to influence your fate. Knowledge is power.

Environment: I have noticed also, that the sudden release of Uranus' energy has in the past produced serious explosions and terrible accidents, such as the US shuttle explosion, so be aware of his discharging power. Both US attacks on Iraq happened under his command and I wonder if our Presidents were just lucky or if they follow the advice of wise astrologers! Remember, Uranus rules the future; computers, avionics, atomic and aeronautics, and both wars were very much "electronics-oriented, with the introduction of the Patriot missiles." Keep in mind that Uranus also rules earthquakes and volcanoes; many surprising things take place on these particular days. Be ready for the ending of important phases of your life and expect the government to make serious decisions pertaining to other countries. Japan, France and China will be on the news soon. Expect news such as September 20, 1999 - 6:01 p.m. ET when a powerful earthquake rocketed Taiwan, toppling buildings and knocking out power across the island. The U.S. Geological Survey measured this quake at a preliminary magnitude of 7.6. A series of aftershocks added to the chaos.

Famous Personalities: Many "crazy" souls will fall for Uranus' desire for originality and some will do all they can to make weird news. Famous people will be caught doing silly things, such as a movie star slapping a police officer, or a well-known actor caught having sex in a car with a prostitute, not to mention a famed British singer caught doing weird things in a public restroom. Japanese and French personalities may also make the news. Some scientists will gain fame for their accomplishments.

Events: During a Saturn (traditions) and Uranus (changes) trend, Iranian voters stunned the experts and their country's conservative rulers by choosing as president, a man who is considered open-minded, intellectual and tolerant. If you are into UFOs, now is the time to look for them. Uranus rules the incredible and extraterrestrial may need this sophisticated energy to manifest in our dense physical world. Don't forget your video camera! Uranus also helps produce explosions, volcanoes, tornadoes etc., so be prepared to hear about these kinds of situations.

Shopping: The futuristic spirit of Uranus rejects anything religious or traditional and promotes the New Age. Uranus hates dogma and needs to deal with the future only. Use his advanced energy to tap into your own subconscious or visit your local psychic or astrologer. Remember that you get what you pay for, so not to give your psyche to unprofessional that may need more help than you. Others may just decide to update their stereo equipment or buy some of those flashy trendy fashions, as seen on those famous Paris runways.

※

WED., THU., FRI. — AUGUST 29, 30, 31:
RULERS — Neptune (Oil/ Middle East/religion/deception) and Mars (War):

Work, Career and Business: Be practical at work and clean around the office and don't challenge authority. Don't initiate actions these days and slow down. With Neptune in charge, many of your wishes to further your career may just be a deceiving dream and you should be practical in your expectations of all the promises made.

Partnerships: The Full Moon's energy will induce depression to some sensitive souls. Hope and activity will once again show the way to a better future after the New Moon, just be patient. Neptune will sharpen your intuition and your creativity; many will ask you for direction in their personal lives. Support your partner and build self-confidence. Peace of mind can be found close to the water.

Family and Friends: Give spiritual support to those you care for, but don't get emotionally involved in their personal problems. Don't let them waste too much of your time talking or complaining over the telephone. If you feel blue yourself, know that it is Neptune's deceiving power and use your will to fight him. At home, stimulate love and attention to the ones around you and be careful of fire (Mars) or water (Neptune). As always, don't overindulge in alcohol, as it will only make things worse. Narcotics will only further those gloomy thoughts of your past and promote accidents. A trip to the local playhouse or a Movie Theater may be just what your soul needs for inspiration. For those with a laid-back attitude, some good tunes and a walk by the ocean will do the trick. Get close to God and meditate about your life in general; Neptune may reward you magically.

Love Affairs: Under Neptune's auspices, secret love affairs flourish. Whatever you choose to do, make a solid decision about your own relationship and be aware of deception. Aggressive Mars may stimulate your desire for action; dancing and music would be a good outlet. Mars is far from being diplomatic; use gentleness if you intend to have a smooth evening. If you were born under the sign of Virgo, a Pisces or a Taurus needs your help.

Travel and Communication: Use Neptune's dreamy nature, and consider spending time by the water, away from the city's stressful activities. If you have to drive a long way, remember to take plenty of rest beforehand, because dreamy Neptune could make you sleepy. Some will have to take a trip to the hospital, to visit a person. Others may hear deceiving news about a legal decision pertaining to arrest and imprisonment. Come clear with what you mean these days and control your imagination. Watch your possessions.

Environment: Mars is an aggressive planet. Like Pluto he could put stress on some of the earth's faults, producing tremors and terrifying the inhabitants above. This negative trend of calamities will be with us for a while, and caution is advised in all you do. Let's hope that Mars will be tolerant for the people living on this earth and play somewhere else in those worlds above and below us.

Famous Personalities: The cinematography industry will prepare many great movies, and numerous actors and actresses will parade all over. Some will be caught doing the wrong thing at the wrong time and others will pay a visit to an "alcoholics anonymous" organization. The unlucky ones will be caught doing something nasty and will pay a heavy price for it.

Events: With this powerful duo, Neptune (oceans) and Mars (explosions) the worse that could happen is another devastating oil spill or chemical explosion. Mars is a warrior and favors accident on the road. Be extremely careful when driving. Boating is something you should forget about, especially after the Full Moon. Bad news from the Middle East and terrorist activities will trouble the media.

Shopping: Use Neptune's sensitivity to further artistic talents and become more creative. Finishing a metaphysical study will favor this lunation. Visit your spiritual friend but avoid a trip into your future; Neptune will blur his intuition. Neptune will offer bargains on alcohol and paint, and by Mars's sharp tools, but invest in those items before the Full Moon. Do NOT invest in any chemicals or dangerous tools during this lunation.

Welcome to Your Day - to - Day Guidance
For September 2007

September 3, 2007 — Saturn enters Virgo: The karmic planet will oblige many wealthy corporations until July 22nd, 2010 to clean up the mess they produced and to become more aware of natural resources. A trend loaded with actions related to better working conditions, retirement plans (Social Security), health and general service and health to the world. Many thoughts will be geared toward doing a better job or working on improving medications and saving Mother Earth. Souls born now will be gifted with a natural ability for details and the opportunity to learn everything they can about health. Many of them will be born with an aptitude for investigation and literary powers and a natural drive for political position, where their impact will change the world for the better. Some will be attracted to the medical professions offering mental work; rewards of fame and fortune will come to the doctor and hardest worker of the zodiac and serious non-fiction writers. The stresses coming from their high position will be felt in their digestive system, if they do not take time off their responsibilities. Artistic talents of editing, dancing, writing, photography, painting and general health will lead these souls towards the body and mind security they seek. This position makes for one of the most critical but dedicated signs of the Zodiac. Souls born with this Saturn position will have to learn to avoid criticism, as the soul is looking for perfection in all areas of their life. The problem is that no one is perfect and the soul may suffer long periods of time alone. However, an opportunity to experience mental fame is offered to the advanced soul. This is a great position for Saturn producing phenomenal physicians, great microbiology research writers and editors.

SAT., SUN., MON., TUE., WED. — SEPTEMBER: 1, 2, 3, 4, 5:
RULERS — Mars (Bloodthirsty/fires) Venus (Peace) and Mercury (Disagreements).

Work, Career and Business: The worst of all these planets is to be expected, due to the pessimistic trend of the Full Moon. Do not fall for depression and self-defeating attitudes. The stars have a specific role to play and you are an actor on the big stage of life. Go with the trend; do not force issues, be patient for a few days. At work keep a low profile; your co-workers and your boss may not be aware of the work of the Moon on their own psyches, and could become "lunatic." Keep busy on Wednesday and rearrange your desk or your paperwork. Use patience.

Partnerships: If you want to save trouble in your relationship, now is the time to use full diplomacy and understanding. Don't let the Waning Moon make you feel down or "moody." If you experienced trouble with the one you care about, you could make up with a romantic dinner at home. With Pluto in Sagittarius, much of your thoughts will be spiritually oriented. Use Venus as much as you can, to uplift any difficult situation.

Family and friends: Disturbing situations involving friends or family members will come to the fore. Take the time to review all the reasons and find a way to make peace with the party involved. Mercury rules communication and will help you pass on your thoughts deeply and correctly. Provide a helping hand, but do not let disrespectful friends take the best of your spirit. Emotions will run high these days; keep a cool head.

Love Affairs: Many will feel the desire to further romance at home. However, new love affairs started now, will need much work to survive. Many unsuited couples will also be forced out of their unhealthy relationships. Mars (the desire principle) may induce attractive foreigners into your life. Because of the Waning Moon, the general feeling will be geared towards destructive behavior, even violence. Many young souls will find themselves fighting with someone about an ideal love. They will be forced to realize the limits of their actions and Mars will destroy the old degrading relationship. You cannot build a new house on weak or unsuitable foundations, so the stars may decide to free you soon. If you were born in October, a Gemini or a Sagittarius will drive you nuts.

Travel and Communication: Mercury will pass on all sorts of news. Use his power to convey your ideas to those willing to listen. Work on improving your cosmic consciousness and do some "deep" reading, concerning life and death or metaphysics. You should finish or a start a book, if you are into writing. Be aware on the road and take care of your wheels.

Environment: Following the Full Moon, tornadoes, high winds, earthquakes, and aeronautical accidents due to bad weather are very high on the list. The earth is alive and she needs to stretch herself, now and then. Stay safe and be prudent on the road.

Famous Personalities: A famous personality will see the end of his life. Many will miss the Great Spirit. Rumors from a powerful politician in the Middle East could vex the media soon.

Events: As usual after the Full Moon, stay clear of the crazy crowd and listen to your intuition at all times.

Shopping: Rent anything; do not buy anything new now. Take care of your car as she may decide to let you down at the wrong time and in the wrong place. Be cautious and be patient.

September 6, 2007 — Mercury enters Libra: A trend loaded with communication related to peace, treaties, justice, partners, contracts, legal activity, marriage and divorce. Many thoughts will be geared towards finding a better working environment or a new business partner. Souls born now will be gifted with a natural ability for diplomacy and "savoir faire." The opportunity to learn everything under the sun is offered to the soul. Many of them will be born with aptitudes for judicial investigation and psychology. Some will be attracted to the professions that offer artistic skills, such as interior designing. Fame and fortune will come to the writers and teachers. Artistic talents in harmony and mental health will lead these souls toward the balance they seek. This position makes for one of the most well balanced signs of the Zodiac. The soul must avoid being too diplomatic with others and may be suffering a lack of expression and direction. However, an opportunity to experience justice, real love and harmony is offered to the advanced souls.

THU., FRI., SAT., SUN., MON. — SEPTEMBER 6, 7, 8, 9, 10:
RULERS: The Moon (End of life/moving) and the Sun (Hope/children).

Work, Career and Business: The general mood will be depressing. You can expect a serious beginning or ending of important parts of your (and others') life. Be ready for those upcoming progressive variations. Keep in mind that life is a constant process of change and even if you don't realize it, the stars are working for your benefit. With Mercury (communication) in Scorpio (directness), avoid sarcasm with others. Be patient with everyone around the office.

Partnerships: You will be forced to let go of negative people in your life and disturbing situations. You must take a chance on the new future with faith. Many will experience the closing of a destructive relationship and others may see the new beginning. Under these stars any new relationship is doomed to fail in the long run. Further the positive only and don't fall for the Waning Moon.

Family and Friends: The Sun rules love, romance and children, but we are still under a difficult trend, so this energy won't bring you good news. The Sun gives life to children, but watch over them, especially close to the water. On a more positive note, he will put his undiscriminating light on many secrets. Friends will need spiritual support; give love and attention and build good karma for yourself.

Love Affairs: Be ready for new starts in love matters and provide a solid shoulder for the victims suffering a broken heart. The right partner might not be the one you were with; use the newfound freedom to look (after the New Moon) for someone who really deserves your love. Under the Sun's command, the lucky ones will find great happiness with true love relationships. A new arrival is to be expected by a young couple. If you are a Scorpio, a Cancer or a Taurus, this lunation could induce serious stress in your life. A Virgo friend has a good discernment for you; you must listen.

Travel and Communication: You may be asked to go home and see Mom. Be aware on the road; Do not trust any driver and be ready for sudden action. Under the same destructive stars in LIMA, Peru -- A Peruvian air force plane carrying civilians fleeing El Niño-driven floods crashed into a canal that cuts through a shantytown in the northern city of Piura Sunday morning, killing at least 28 people. Surprises are on the way and the people from your past will come into the picture soon. Expect this type of news again and again - Death toll jumps in London commuter train crash - A shattering train collision near Paddington Station during rush hour Tuesday morning killed at least 26 people and injured scores. Police said more bodies were still trapped in the tangled wreckage of the crash, which happened in Ladbroke Grove in west London, about a mile (1.2 km) from the Notting Hill neighborhood.

Environment: What was once built by man (cities/homes) or nature must be destroyed; what was once born must eventually die, and this is the grand cycle of life. Recycling is the key word in nature and not anything is really wasted. There is nothing one can do other than accept the ultimate changes imposed by God, and usually the future offers better.

Famous personalities: Expect interesting but not necessarily positive surprises with the rich and famous. Be ready for the unexpected in their words and actions. Don't take chances unless you know what you're in for and be prudent.

Events: Large quakes and nature forces may force thousands of victims to relocate to rebuild a new life. Terrible tragedies such the Kobe, Japan earthquake and many volcanic eruptions have happened under this configuration and thousands of people were forced out of their homes because of nature's destructive forces. Expect news such as -VILLAHERMOSA, Mexico. The Mexican government declared a state of emergency Tuesday in four states where rampant flooding has caused seven rivers to overflow, killing at least 15 people and forcing the evacuation of more than 100,000. VILLAHERMOSA, Mexico. Swollen rivers and mudslides have killed at least 83 people throughout Mexico, officials said Thursday. - The rains that flooded 10 states in eastern and southern Mexico have driven more than 157,000 people from their home and several people got hurt as a quake rattled southwest Turkey.

Shopping: Buy anything for children as long as it is not new. This is a great time to get rid of the extra stuff clogging the house or the garage, and a garage sale would not be a bad idea. Do not invest in silver, gold or expensive items. Anything to clean the house will do you well.

New Moon — September 11, 2007 in the practical, health-oriented sign of Virgo: Much progress is ahead of you in terms of employment and foreign affairs. Mercury rules this critical sign, so the affairs of work and health will be on the rise. Expect an overwhelming feeling of perfection and an unusual worry about health and working on foreign grounds; do not let this lunation pressure you. This trend will play an important part in your health and working life and in some ways will affect your environment. You may be forced to let go of a deteriorating work situation and forced into a new one. The emphasis is on the body (perfect health) and the mind (education) to perform efficiently in serving the world at large. All the changes you may be forced to experience are positive in nature, and will in the long run, further your deep desire for a better state of affairs.

Lunation impact on all signs:

Aries - A great opportunity will be offered for your health or your work.

Taurus - Your love life will improve, you may hear about a birth soon.

Gemini - You may have to consider doing something from home or relocate soon.

Cancer - A great study or a new health program will appeal to you, talk to your siblings.

Leo - Great news involving your finances and your self-esteem is ahead.

Virgo - The stars shine on you, you can't loose, make the most of them.

Libra - A secret will bring light to your world. Let go of the past.

Scorpio - A friend has a wish for you, socialize more these days.

Sagittarius - Your career is moving on the right direction, if not study computers.

Capricorn - News from far away or a trip will make you happy, study and rewards.

Aquarius - Some unexpected financial help will bring joy to your life.

Pisces - A chance to face the world with a new emotional or business partner is ahead.

※

September 11, 2007: The anniversary of 9/11 and the memory of what took place on these days, will affect many people all over the world. All the memorable activities will take place on the day of the New Moon at the lowest time of the month and many unaware people will travel within the Waning Moon to be present, while many other souls will suffer this depressive new lunation. Just be ready to provide as much help as needed and do not lose faith in the future.

TUE., WED., THU., FRI. — SEPTEMBER 11, 12, 13, 14:
RULERS — The Sun (Teens) Mercury (Travel) and Venus (Feelings)

Work, Career and Business: This New Moon will make your life much easier, embrace her upcoming white light blessings, and then take your opportunities. Do not try to push your business until she lights up. Advertisements, important calls, traveling, and meetings will pay off, if you learn to wait for the green light. Use "Moon Power" wisely and respect the Universal Laws. Knowledge is power; have faith in your abilities.

Partnerships: Mercury rules the mail, telephone and communications in general; expect disturbing calls before the new moon to reach you. Deal with it now and clean up the situation before the New Moon. A get-together after work could also be a great idea; Mercury will have everyone "gossiping."

Family and Friends: The very last days of the Waning Moon did sap your spiritual and physical energy. Help those in need to clean up their mess generated by karmic experiences. Let no one exhaust your spirit, and show no frustration to loved ones. Some of your friends need spiritual regeneration, even a helping hand; as usual do so, but realize your limits. Use Venus' generosity and show your love to everyone. Avoid spending too much time on the telephone with a depressing person and mention the good Moon.

Love Affairs: Don't be too picky or demanding with those for whom you care; no one is perfect. However, use your head not your heart with someone who drinks too much, and realize your limits if you are in a deceiving relationship. With Venus around, the opportunity to find love will be given to you after the New Moon. If you were born in September, you may decide to work harder on your diet or your looks. A friend born in July has a few thoughts for you. You may also use Uranus in Aquarius to learn all about your partner with a comparison chart for the two of you. Now is the perfect time to apply your will and start a spiritual Astro-Psychology, Kabalistic Healing or Astro-Tarot course (see www.drturi.com or call 602-957-1617 to help us to set a crash course in your area.

Travel and Communication: You may feel like traveling either physically or spiritually, make the most of an upcoming opportunity. Get your wheels in action; prepare for traveling under the protection of the New Moon.

Environment: Recharge your batteries; a trip to the mountains is strongly recommended. Both Mercury and Venus will make you appreciate the beauty of Mother Nature. Many environmentalists will make serious progress and get the attention they deserve. Sad news from the ocean or the Middle East may reach the media soon.

Famous Personalities: A famous person will promote a new product pertaining to health. News of water management is also on the horizon. A notorious religious person could make depressing news soon.

Events: Mother Nature may decide to disturb us with bad weather.

Negative news may come from the ocean or the water. Be aware of abductors; this type of energy has swiftly taken many children and also a plane away from its initial course.

Shopping: Do not poison your mind with imagination and fears of the apocalyptic end times. Use your own positive thinking, to avoid negativity entering your life or your body. Some may decide to join spiritual groups or invest in far away trips. Anything to clean can only be a good thing to buy now.

※

Note: Even though it is a New Moon, Pluto is back and caution is a necessity. As always with the Lord of Hell in charge of this trend, better think twice before saying or acting on impulse. Expect secrets to be divulged, affairs of sex, and nature's devastating forces to be at work. The police and blackguards will make the news. **More than ever, use diplomacy, as whatever you do now will have very serious repercussions in your life.**

SAT., SUN., MON., TUE., WED. — SEPTEMBER 15, 16, 17, 18, 19:
RULERS — Pluto (Climax/Secrets) Venus (Love), and Jupiter (Doctrines)

Work, Career and Business: You are now walking on a fine razor blade and it's windy. You know what I mean! You'd better use all the "savoir faire" you know. A serious wake-up call will come to many unaware skeptics of predictive Divine Astrology's powers. The possibility to lose it all (and rebuild it) will be a serious matter for some karmic souls. You will be able to see exactly what's wrong in your business life soon. The New Moon will help you make all the changes needed. Have faith in yourself.

Partnerships: Many ugly secrets may surface now. You could learn something sexual or financial about a partner. Keep his trust; do not divulge the secret. Money will play an important part of this trend; listen to your intuition in all you do. Venus will help tone down the stress induced by Pluto.

Family and Friends: Be patient with all. Do not expect anyone you care about to be diplomatic to you during this trend, if Venus (diplomacy) is weak in his or her chart. Again, do not fall for Pluto's destructive or sarcastic remarks; words of love will pay off in the long run. Be ready for some dramatic news from someone close to you. Whatever happens, be strong; life must go on. Pluto will work to your benefit.

Love Affairs: Passion is in the air. Secret affairs involving sex and passion may be publicly divulged, forcing people to take stands to destroy and rebuild relationships. This might happen to you, too. In any case, use tons of diplomacy to save unwanted trouble in your love life. If you are a water sign such as Scorpio, Pisces or Cancer, this lunation will touch you directly. Leos must take it easy at home and avoid traumatic experiences involving the police force.

Travel and Communication: Expect news pertaining to the police force and crooks. Nature's destructive forces will be obvious in some parts of the world. Be careful of what you do or say during this trend. Drive carefully, and stay clear of weird strangers and strange places. Again, if you learn about someone else's secret, do not tell, you may be asking for trouble. Your intuition will be accurate; listen to the little voice within.

Environment: Pluto belongs to the Divine family and has specific regenerative work to accomplish, and his impact on earth and its people is needed. As Pluto destroys it all, he also gives the opportunity to rebuild stronger and better. Be ready for all sorts of dramatic news everywhere. Stay safe; don't try the devil. Many people will lose their precious lives. Expect such news COLLEGE STATION, Texas -- Had Brandon Kallmeyer dozed off and let his truck slide onto the shoulder almost anywhere else, he might have simply awakened and steered back onto the highway. But police said Kallmeyer tragically veered off a straight, flat four-lane road at precisely the place where a group of college students had gathered en route to a fraternity party, leaving six dead. GABORONE, Botswana (AP) -- A disgruntled airline pilot today commandeered an Air Botswana plane at the country's main airport, circled above and crashed it into two planes on the ground, in a suicide mission. More ACALAMA, Mexico -- The danger of new erosion forced rescuers to abandon their search for victims of another landslide in southeastern Mexico that has left as many as 170 dead.

Famous Personalities: Some famous people will be called back to God. A famous person's secrets will be made available to the media. Expect news such as Death of a legend: NBA great Wilt Chamberlain found dead at his home in LOS ANGELES -- Wilt Chamberlain, a center so big, agile and dominant that he forced basketball to change its rules and the only player to score 100 points in an NBA game, died Tuesday at 63. Secrets comes to light under Pluto jurisdiction, such as October 12, 1999 - MIAMI- - O.J. Simpson called 911, saying he was trying to get help for a woman he said had been on a two-day cocaine binge with a former baseball player. Simpson, 52, placed the call Sunday night from the townhouse of his 26-year-old girlfriend, Christie Prody, in southwest Miami-Dade County.

Events: Hopefully with the New Moon, lovely Venus and knowledgeable Jupiter, we can only hope they will stop Pluto from damaging us by way of dramatic happenings. With the Lord of Hades in Sagittarius (religion/foreigners) we can only expect drama in these areas. If you are a Police officer or a security guard, be very careful during this trend. The wildest crooks may be facing you soon. Don't take any chances and stay alert. Often the police make dramatic news and kill people. Union Nigerian police kill 10. AJUBA, Nigeria (CNN) -- Ten protesting strikers have been shot dead by police in Lagos, a top union official said. If you know someone involved with the police or dealing with death on a daily basis, offer him a copy of my book. He may well avoid serious trouble and perhaps save his life.

Shopping: As Jupiter is with us; a visit to your local church for God's guidance or your favorite psychic/astrologer will do you well. Anything bought now that can be used for metaphysics will bring unusual power to you. Alarms bought now will stop the crooks.

✷

THU., FRI., SAT., SUN. SEPTEMBER 20, 21, 22, 23:
RULERS — Saturn (Politicians) Uranus (Explosions) and Neptune (Suicide/religion).

Work, Career and Business: This busy trio will be with us for the next few days and a few surprises will bring about progressive changes. Do not turn down an invitation, as a professional contact could bring people who will positively influence your career. Expect a new beginning concerning your service to the world or your career. Work that you are doing leaves you unsatisfied and is a source of stress; you might be forced to change direction. Many souls are late starters in life and no one should feel depressed about it. Resolve to find a new career that fits your natural talent. The lucky ones can expect a well-deserved promotion. Use Neptune's intuitive power to find your way through the clouds.

Partnerships: Stand strong against opposition; don't let others pressure you into pursuing their opinion instead of your own. Meditate on the possibility of improving and understanding where your partnership is going. Did you make the right choices and can you live with them? If not, there won't be a better time to deal with those questions; Uranus' desire for change and freedom will help you to transform it all. With the Waxing Moon upon the world, nothing can really go wrong if you act scrupulously.

Family and Friends: Make the most of this great trend. Some friends may invite you to a gathering or a party soon. Enjoy this opportunity and be ready for lovely surprises. Uranus also makes the children very active and accident-prone. They will lean heavy on you; so be patient with their young demanding spirits. No one but yourself can bring about joy in your life; just participate with an open heart. Let the children enjoy Uranus' world of miracles, maybe by going to Disneyland or the zoo. Keep your eyes on everything they do and everywhere they go. Saturn will make it hard to forget your responsibilities. You should enjoy your life while you can, as tomorrow is another day.

Love Affairs: Expect interesting surprises during these days, many friends will bring some of your dearest wishes. With Uranus' touch (surprises) try doing things you would usually not do and go to places you have never been. Love is around the corner for some willing to go out and get it. If you are a Taurus, a Capricorn or a Virgo may enter your life. Leo, Sagittarius and Aries, your magnetism will be very high and you will also be in demand for love.

Travel and Communication: Some lucky souls will travel far and fast or make great plans to visit the past soon. Uranus rules electronics, the future, astrology, psychic phenomena, and UFOs. If you want to see something unusual, talk about it and do it now! Who knows, Uranus may decide to grant one of your important wishes. Keep an eye on your possessions and avoid drinking too much in public places.

Environment: On a sad note, keep in mind that Uranus rules earthquakes and volcanoes. He may also decide to disturb the weather or produce a violent explosion. Let's hope the positive Moon will stop him from getting close to you and those you care about. A magnitude 7.0 earthquake rumbled under the Mojave Desert east of Los Angeles before dawn, derailing an Amtrak train passing nearby the epicenter. Irene heads for Carolinas after soaking Florida. North Carolina Gov. Jim Hunt, declared a state of emergency Saturday as Hurricane Irene threatened to let loose a new round of serious flooding in the already flood weary state. With Uranus around expect this type of news soon - Evacuations ordered as Ecuadorian volcano threatens. Clouds of gas and ashes rise from the Tungurahua volcano 120 kilometers (75 miles) south of Quito, Ecuador, on Sunday-- The Ecuadorian government has ordered the evacuation of some 25,000 people from a popular tourist town as a nearby volcano continues to spew ash and appears on the verge of a major eruption. NUEVO LAREDO, Mexico (AP) -- In what was Mexico's second fatal fireworks accident in a month, an explosion in a candy store illegally selling fireworks, killed at least five people in the border city of Nuevo Laredo.

Famous Personalities: Be ready as usual for strange types of news coming from some extroverted celebrities. Much will be done for children during this trend, but this type of energy can also be surprisingly dramatic. Uranus took the life of British singer Eric Clapton's baby son in New York a few years ago. The unattended child fell to his death from a high building. Be aware, be prudent and watch the children closely.

Events: Under Uranus' surprising power anything weird could happen. The news will be somehow original. Avoid playing in the rain; many people have lost their lives under Uranus' lightning power. The government will make important decisions pertaining to the younger generation, computers, and education.

Shopping: For this occasion, you may feel like spending time and money on your appearance; it's a great time to shop for new wardrobe items or consult a beautician. This is the time to pay a visit to your future and your favorite "spiritual guide." A sense of freedom and brotherhood will be felt all over.

Full Moon in Aries — September 26, 2007: Ruled by Mars, this trend will be tough for many as Mars is very strong these days and will bring about serious confrontations, explosions, fires and the possibility of war. Be ready for serious, even fatalistic news in the near future. With Neptune's religious and deceiving tendency accompanying him in his dance, expect more disturbing developments with the Middle East. These will be negative, pertaining to oil spills, explosions and more terrorist activities in the near future. Be ready for devastating forces producing destructive weather and flooding in different parts of the world. Do not lose faith in the future, as we all must go on. The stars are a reflection of God and his divine plan for all of us and we must go through it.

Lunation impact on all signs:

Aries – The Full Moon in your sign means lots of pain and restructures for you.

Taurus – Do not let this Full Moon distress you. Let go of the past.

Gemini – A friend will deceive you and a wish will not come true.

Cancer – Career setbacks are ahead. Just be patient and then, all will be fine.

Leo – Stress from foreign affairs or a difficult study; perseverance is the key.

Virgo – A legacy won't go well and someone close to you may have to go.

Libra – A secret will light your world. Let go of the past.

Scorpio – Problems at work might affect your health so take it easy.

Sagittarius – Stress with love, gambling and children is on your agenda.

Capricorn – Be aware of fire and avoid fighting in the home. Stress from real estate.

Aquarius – Slow down your brain if you can and better learn to listen to others.

Pisces – Money matters won't go well for a while, so embrace patience.

※

MON., TUE., WED.,THU. — SEPTEMBER 24, 25, 26, 27: RULERS — Neptune (Belief/dreams), and Mars (War/aggression).

Work, Career and Business: You still have a few days in front of you to push forward, but then be ready for the impact of the Full Moon. An important decision involving a business situation will have to be made. Wait patiently for the next New Moon (positive) to restructure or sign important documents. Don't let Mars show his aggressive face to those close to you. Try to be nice to others.

Partnerships: Just before the Full Moon, expect interesting news coming your way via your telephone or mailbox. It's time to realize the truth about yourself, a situation or a person whom you trusted. Make the most of what is left of the Waxing Moon, get out of the gloom and do something interesting this weekend. The Dragon's Tail will bring consternation and needed changes to you soon.

Family and Friends: The family circle could be quite the dramatic place for a while. Again, do not let aggressive Mars and the Full Moon take over your words or your attitude. Keep emotions in control and be ready for secrets to surface. You can still have a good time, enjoy life and friends, but be aware of what you say or do. Do not lend money to anyone.

Love Affairs: Mars and Neptune's captivating personalities will stimulate sexual activity; your magnetism will improve dramatically. As always with Neptune, take precautions if you are sexually active. If you're married, plan a romantic dinner with a great French wine and soft music. You have a few more days to enjoy what's left of the good celestial energy; make the most of it. If you are an air sign such as Aquarius, Libra or Gemini, you may feel a strong sense of independence and freedom enveloping you. If you're a Cancer, expect some stress in your relationships soon. You may be in for a long over-due change where you could experience real love.

Travel and Communication: You may uncover a clandestine relationship or a secret about someone who travels a lot. You may be forced to look inside yourself and see your own strengths or weaknesses. Don't take any chances on the road and avoid flying after the Full Moon. You'd better stay away from anything that moves, as this lunation will take many lives. Always plan your trips before the Full Moon and you will save yourself much unwanted trouble. Use the power of Starguide and help those in trouble with life.

Environment: In time of a Full Moon and with ruinous Mars around we can only expect nature's destructive forces. Drama and demise are around the corner; protect your self at all times. Do a candle ritual if you feel down or if you want to protect someone you care for. Email me from www.drturi.com and order a Cabalistic Candle Ritual for $15.00 and learn how to burn white, green, and blue candles for full protection the use your Guardian Angel protection.

Famous Personalities: A serious wake-up call is in for some. More secrets, more drama, more doom is on the way for famous people. This upcoming Full Moon will be nasty for some well-known people. Germany will make some stressing news and a famous Army figure will be called close to God, having terminated his work on earth.

Events: The powerful Dragon will steer the religious fanatics and many of them will get out of hand. Pray for the safety of your loved ones, as this lunation will be extremely difficult. Stay home and watch a good movie is my best advice; let the drama reach the unaware souls. You will see and appreciate the power of Starguide and the importance of letting others know about my work. Expect news such as preliminary radar data shows that an Egypt Air 767 jet made a rapid plunge before crashing into the Atlantic Ocean about 60 miles (96 kilometers) off the coast of Nantucket early Sunday morning. Also, in MEXICO CITY (CNN) -- All 18 people aboard a Mexican DC-9 jetliner were killed Tuesday, when it crashed shortly after takeoff in a mountainous region of central Mexico.

Shopping: Now is the time to buy pesticides and things of this nature. If you want to get rid of something, now is definitely the time. Make absolutely no investment in weapons, sharp tools, or anything that could explode. Let this nasty energy dissipate; stay safe.

※

September 28, 2007 — Mercury enters Scorpio: A trend loaded with communication related to finance, sex, legacy, death and metaphysics for the advanced souls. Much thought will be geared towards finding the meaning of life for some, and for others finding the weakest part and reviving an unproductive business. Children born now will be gifted with incredible staying power, and natural abilities for investigation. The opportunity to learn anything hidden is offered to the soul. Many will be born with an aptitude for deep medical investigations or financial endeavors. Some will be attracted to the professions of danger such as the police force, or emergency service where quick thinking and courage can make a difference between life and death. Fame and fortune will come to the ones involved in writing and teaching, or to those deeply involved in science, research, and the medical or metaphysical fields. This position makes for one of the most intense researchers of the Zodiac. The soul must learn to use diplomacy in times of confrontation and may suffer a lack of communication skills. However, an opportunity to experience cosmic consciousness and spiritual peace is offered to the advanced soul. This celestial position makes the thoughts deadly and attracted to drama and natural bred terrorists.

※

September 29, 2007 — Mars enters Cancer: Wait for the upcoming New Moon to launch any financial or real estate endeavors. Home improvement, buying or selling a beautiful house is on the agenda for some. Souls born now will be geared by Mars to be involved with matters related to construction, the Government, and general country and family securities. They will invest time and money in hotels and restaurants and real estate endeavors.

Many of them will strive to find total security and a husband or wife with protective qualities. Some will have to learn to let go of wrong relationships without drama and tantrums. This Mars position makes the soul very sensitive to home and family. Usually a gift in building and cooking is to be found in this position. Those souls are born to feed the world with food and love. Under stress, this Mars position produces overwhelming stomach acidity and ulcers.

FRI., SAT., SUN. — SEPTEMBER 28, 29, 30:
RULERS — Venus (Friends) Mercury (Division) Moon (Endings) and Mars (Danger):

Work, Career and Business: This powerful trend will be quite dramatic, emotionally stressful, and depression and difficulties are ahead for many of us. Work and career matters won't please you much. Serious changes are on the way. Make the most of Mercury's revitalizing energy to plan a form of rebirth in your working life. Be patient; anything weak or insincere must give way.

Partnerships: A long-standing partnership could be coming to an end, possibly because you sense that you may do better by yourself, or maybe your partner lost his enterprising spirit. Avoid nurturing depressing thoughts and provide spiritual help for those who have been touched by these difficult changes. Mercury will help you to pass on the right words to those in need. Avoid complaining and hold back your negative words and thoughts.

Family and Friends: Your maternal instincts will show and will be needed for your children. Share your knowledge with them. A friend needs help, reflecting the full impact of this difficult Full Moon. The subconscious response to the moon's fluctuations upon humans is referred as "lunatic behavior or moodiness," and right now, you may realize this yourself. Expect the beginning or ending of important parts of your life. Anticipate some surprising news from children; some people close to you need serious attention and plenty of love. Help a close friend deal with a departure.

Love Affairs: Ask yourself about your deep feelings for a person who seems to be moving away from you. An old lover from your past may surprise you soon. An old friend who lives far away may need to communicate with you. Don't expect great news, and provide the help required, as long as you are not being used. Another person from your past will bring you relief, but could also mean more trouble for you than anything else. If you were born under a fire sign, such as Leo, Sagittarius or Aries, don't let the Full Moon depress you. If you are a Scorpio, you will be forced to deal with some drama at work.

Travel and Communication: A business deal that would have required you to travel may be postponed or canceled without much notice. Don't let it get to you and avoid promoting important business just yet. Expect the mail and your telephone to bring you difficult news. Keep a strong spirit and face life's difficulties with faith and courage. Remember, if there is a Hell, its right here on this dense physical world. Have faith in your abilities and face all that comes your way with courage.

Environment: The Moon's energy could also make the human race aware of its vulnerability against the shocking destructive forces of nature. It's time for her to stretch herself and restructure her insides.

Famous Personalities: The rich and famous will be planning an event for the well being of many children of the world. Their artistic gifts will benefit numerous organizations. Some others may make surprising news trying to use Mercury for free publicity. An accident on the road could take a prominent person.

Events: You will hear about the military performing deeds that will aid the general community and save lives from a disaster area. Thousands of people will be forced to relocate to start new lives. War and destruction is a part of this lunation.

Shopping: Anything that needs to be replaced in the home or the garden may be bought now. Avoid signing anything related to real estate endeavors. Do not invest in appliances or a car just yet.

Welcome to Your Day - to - Day Guidance
For October 2007

MON., TUE., WED., THU. — OCTOBER 1, 2, 3, 4:
RULERS — The Moon (ending of life) and the Sun (love/life matters/Explosive news):

Work, Career and Business: You may find yourself discussing goals for the future with someone close to you. Some will even sell their homes or move to better locations. Life is a process of constant change and this lunation will touch you or someone close to you. Make the most out of this change and trust the upcoming future. Not exactly a time to promote any endeavors, sign contracts or travel; wait for the upcoming New Moon to move or deal with important matters.

Partnerships: Time to promote only faith and have confidence in all you do. This type of energy will be difficult for some, as they might be forced in or out important situations. Accept those changes you may not be able to control. You might be going through a hard time now, but the Universe will pay you back in spades; if you learn from your experiences and keep faith in yourself.

Family and Friends: Listen to your friends' stories and be ready for the beginning or ending of an important part of their lives. Keep in mind that the Moon is Waning (negative) and those unexpected changes must be faced with courage, no matter what. Give special attention to the children these days and provide them guidance, if needed. Their young and fragile spirits need constant reassurance and appreciation. Also, with the Sun in charge, you might stimulate their creativity and enjoy their youth and boundless energy. This energy could also work against them, and some may be accident-prone, so watch them carefully.

Love Affairs: Some people might surprise you; however, don't dream or hope for finding a lost love now. Be ready for the beginning or ending of an important part of your life. If you are stuck in the wrong relationship, this lunation will force you out of this stressful situation very soon. Accept the upcoming changes with grace and have faith in the future. Those changes will bring someone worthy of your feelings. Wait for the next upcoming New Moon to get active in your social circle again. Your friends possess all your wishes and you should spend more time with them, especially if you are single and looking for love. For those born in May, a Pisces or a Virgo will be strongly attracted to you. Enjoy a great show when possible; you need to forget a few things in your own life.

Travel and Communication: With the Waning Moon affecting our psyches, tears and depression might be a problem. Keep busy, avoid negative thoughts of the past and look for positive endeavors. Free yourself from pessimistic people or stressful situations; use your will and surprise others with a formidable optimistic attitude. Be a defensive driver ever ready to give way to the crazies of the freeway. Plans to travel far may be imposed upon your life by Uncle Sam and go back to your past.

Environment: The weather will turn very nasty in some states, and many will lose their lives and possessions. Thousands may be forced to relocate, due to dramatic experiences with nature. A loss of power is part of this trend; don't take any chances, stay safe. April 9, 1998 -- 39 die in Southeast storms - At least 39 people were killed in tornadoes and thunderstorms that raked the Southeast overnight. Most of the deaths were in Alabama.

Famous Personalities: An important figure could suffer a heart attack or surgery! A naughty love affair may dramatically end. Some unlucky children could be involved in awful accidents.

Events: On a large scale, many governments may also make news that will affect all of us. Disturbing news may be coming from The US, France or Japan. Read the headlines of the past under similar stars; in NAHA, Japan -- A powerful undersea earthquake rumbled through Okinawa, Taiwan and the Philippines Monday, setting off a tidal wave. The earthquake struck at 8:30 a.m. Japan time (7:30 p.m. Sunday EDT/2330 GMT Sunday) and had a preliminary magnitude of 7.7, according to Japan's Central

Meteorological Agency. ATHENS -- At least 27 people were killed Tuesday when a powerful earthquake struck just north of Athens, trapping dozens beneath the rubble of collapsed buildings.

Shopping: It's the perfect time to give old toys or clothes to unlucky children. Avoid spending money on expensive items for your own children. Now is not the time to find good deals in your local flea market. Spend time doing something creative; it doesn't have to be a masterpiece, just something to ease your spirit. We are getting closer to the New Moon and all will be much better soon.

2007 Third Supernova Window

October / November: Third SUPERNOVA window
From Sunday October 7th through Friday November 2nd 2007

EXPLANATION OF A SUPERNOVA WINDOW

Concentration of negative celestial energy approaching; Be extremely prudent in driving, and expect chain-reaction accidents. Be prepared for delays, strikes, and nature producing awful weather, including hurricanes and tornadoes. The same energy that produced the Titanic disaster, the Asia tsunami the Northridge Los Angeles and Kobe Japan earthquakes and major other calamities is approaching again. Remember the thwarted terrorist attack of August 2006 in the UK where the BA canceled thousands of flights because the BAA ordered all passengers not to take or check ALL handbags before boarding their planes? Those people did not have a copy of Moon Power and paid the price of ignorance. Double-check all your appointments, and if you can postpone traveling and flying during this Supernova "Window". If you must fly like I do very often, simply make sure to purchase your ticket and make your reservation during a Waxing Moon and the stars will not bother you. Remember the Universal Laws do not care for birthday or religious holidays or else, simply think of crossing the street while the light is red or ignore a stop sign, then, see what will happen to you. Those laws are impartial and written by God, not men and messing them up will bring about serious penalty. Note that; I flew only a few days before the Full Moon in August 2006 to Thailand during a "Supernova Window" to write this book and I traveled safely and avoided all trouble. Remember knowledge is power ignorance is evil!

Communication and electricity will be cut off, and a general loss of power is to be expected. Appliances, computers, telephones, planes, trains, cars, all of these "tools" will be affected by this energy. They will be stopped in one way or another. The people of the past will make the news and will reenter your life. Expect trouble with the post office, education, students, strikes, prisoner's escape, newspapers, broadcasting industries and computer viruses may bother us again.

Many a failed mission and expensive electronic equipment (Mars probe etc.) and our tax dollars have been wasted, because of the scientist's lack of knowledge of the stars. As usual NASA, which is not aware of the science of astrology, will waste our tax money with failed missions due to bad weather and electronic malfunctions. In the name of ignorance a few years ago, in the Challenger explosion seven astronauts lost their lives when NASA launched the shuttle under a "Supernova Window".

Marine life sharks, whales etc may also beach themselves due to Mercury Retrograde affecting their natural inborn navigational systems. All these malevolent predictions and waste of lives and equipment do not have to occur. Those predictions do not have to affect you directly as they unfold. Instead, they are printed to prepare you for setbacks and frustrations, thus advising you to be patient and prudent during this trend. There is no room for ignorance, and those who are not aware of the celestial order, including the NASA space-program management team, will continue to pay a heavy price. In all mankind's' affairs, ignorance is true evil. Why any scientists who are against my research do not honor the word science, which is based upon solid investigation, is solid proof of mental snobbery. By omitting any physical or spiritual laws can only bring penalty; for science's purpose is to explore all possibilities, even those laws written in light via the stars.

October 8, 2007 — Venus enters Virgo: A perfect time to concentrate on your health and launch an exercise program or a diet. Giving and receiving plants or flowers are on the agenda for some. You may also decide to invest in some good deals with clothing. Souls born now will be quite critical in matters related to love. They will concentrate and achieve perfection in many of their artistic endeavors. Many of them will strive to find a "perfect" and hard working partner willing to exchange a love/career relationship in their lives. Some will have to learn to be less critical of the world around them, in order to avoid loneliness. This position makes for one of the most practical and enjoyable business or emotional partners. Usually a gift in dealing with details and an interest in health matters are present with this position. These souls are born to experience love on a practical level. This is a great Venus position, producing success in the medical or clothing fields. Plants or gardens are needed around these souls.

FRI., SAT., SUN., MON.,TUE — OCTOBER 5, 6, 7, 8, 9:
RULERS — The Sun (Love/surprises) and Mercury (Mental power/Siblings):

Work, Career and Business: Some surprising developments are on the way, but with the Full Moon upon us don't expect them to make you happy. Progress will still be made in the few weeks ahead of you, but be ready for a bumpy ride. Take on new technical studies, or improve your knowledge of computers, as this endeavor will give you better opportunities later.

Partnerships: Don't take any chances these days, keep a low profile; use Mercury's creative power to clean up a business situation. Important legal papers might come your way; sign them only if it is to get rid of an unhealthy situation. Whomever you come in contact with, don't misbehave in public.

Family and Friends: Keep busy with close friends and family; watch the children, as they will be accident-prone. In the past, many of them got in trouble or had accidents during this type of lunation. It's a great time to enjoy the people you know well, but because of the Waning Moon, avoid overcrowded public places. Don't expect new people met under this lunar cycle to bring many of your wishes. Some friends have surprising, even disturbing news for you and could affect you emotionally. Again, watch the children. They are accident-prone, especially on the road with fire, weapons and explosives. Under this lunation (April 8, 1998) the news reported that in CHAPPELL HILL, Texas -- A loaded school bus, was hit from behind by a tractor-trailer truck on a Texas highway injuring at least 22 children, some of them seriously.

Love Affairs: Expect aggravating surprises coming your way and learn to let go of deceitful people. Do not invite interlopers into your home, and socialize only with the friends you know well. Make good use of the Waning Moon; learn to relax, enjoy nature and the sea, and look for inner peace. If you're single, a chance to find the "right one" will be given to you at a later date. What you may perceive as love, may enter your life, but without much to expect. Use your head on Friday night, not your heart. If you were born under the sign of Leo, an Aries, an Aquarius or a foreigner born in December could be a source of trouble in your life. Wait for better auspices.

Travel and Communication: Not a time to take chances at flying unless your purchase your ticket in a good Moon auspice; many karmic souls will pay the ultimate price. Expect all sorts of little problems arising, which could turn lethal for some unlearned souls. Anticipate disturbing telephone calls from friends in trouble; as usual, provide spiritual help, but know your limits and stay clear of depression.

Environment: Earth activists will feel this puritanical lunation and will do all they can to protect nature and wild life; some may fall victim to ill-advised conflicts with unscrupulous large organizations. Expect unusual oceanic or earth activity soon that could prove disastrous for the environment. Not a good time to play with fire, as explosions is very high on my list of trouble for this specific trend. The news may bring about startling explosive developments.

Famous Personalities: Certain famous people will find themselves in difficult situations. Some will try anything to get the attention they need. Eccentricity is in the air and could lead to the use of force or involvement with the law. Under this lunation Pop star George Michael was arrested for lewd conduct on April 8 1998, in Beverly Hills California: On that day, the news reported that Pop star George Michael, the British-born heartthrob whose hit songs include the too-hot-for-radio "I Want Your Sex," was arrested on suspicion of committing a lewd act in a park restroom.

Events: Expect massive power outages without readily known causes. NASA could make some bad news soon, due to poor weather conditions or electronic malfunctions. On the positive side, some high-tech scientific news as well as great medical breakthroughs; are on the way. On December 17, 1997 under this type of celestial energy a typhoon-blasted Guam: Paka; top wind gusts of 236 mph - Electricity out, no water 'People ran for their lives'

Shopping: Do not invest on anything electronic; you will not get a good deal. Do not invest in toys for your children now; they could prove to be fatal at a later date. Some will plan to travel to

Europe.

※

New Moon — October 11, 2007 in the diplomatic oriented sign of Libra: The planet Venus rules this sign, thus affairs of love, the law and politics will be on the rise. Expect an overwhelming feeling for peace and diplomacy instead of war, to take over the world and your psyche. Many famous politicians will work hard to avoid dangerous conflicts during this trend. Stand firm on your decision and do not let this lunation stress you, as balance and harmony must prevail. This trend will play an important part in the equilibrium of your physical and spiritual lives. This trend will affect some of your business and emotional relationships. The upcoming changes must be accepted, as the New Moon (positive) has a great plan that you may not understand just yet. Some will be involved in the signing of very important documents, contracts or the legal system. You may be forced to realize the importance of evaluating a serious situation and making painful decisions. The emphasis is on balance and harmony in all, if we are to perform efficiently and live in peace with the rest of the world. Diplomats will be requested and busy in many parts of this crazy world, to prevent future wars.

Lunation impact on all signs:

Aries - The New Moon will fall in your partnership area and changes are needed.

Taurus - Important changes at work are eminent, and legal matters are on the way.

Gemini - Love and romance will improve; a new deal is ahead of you.

Cancer - Important decisions about home, real estate and the family soon.

Leo - A new trip or a study is ahead of you, good news soon.

Virgo - Great opportunities to improve your finances and your self-esteem is ahead.

Libra - Try anything and everything. The stars shine on you, a new start.

Scorpio - A secret relationship will start or finish, a secret will come to light.

Sagittarius - A friend will bring about a good wish, a marriage or a contract.

Capricorn - A great opportunity to further your career and make a new commitment.

Aquarius - A far away trip or a publishing promotion is a blessing for you.

Pisces - People in power will want to help you in your affairs, go out more.

※

WED., THU., FRI., SAT., SUN., MON. — OCTOBER 10, 11, 12, 13, 14, 15:
RULERS — Venus (Sexy) Pluto (Drama) and Jupiter (Faith).

Work, Career and Business: Even in this good Moon phase, Pluto's deadly touch is upon us, so keep a low profile and be aware of all you do or say. Some won't be able to stop the upcoming changes and drama. Your intuition about situations will be quite accurate. The future has much better to offer and you should be confident in your dealings. Jupiter, "the Lord of Luck," will make the transition easy and may decide to throw you some luck; listen to your intuition. There will be a serious wake-up call for some people who did not respect others. Avoid dealing with money now.

Partnerships: Money will also be on your mind and serious decisions will have to be made soon. Wait for the upcoming New Moon to share new ideas with others. You may take calculated chances now, but you'd better know your limits. As always with Pluto around you can only expect to dig into other people's financial or sexual secrets. Become involved with the world of investigation, metaphysics or astrology and promote your own cosmic consciousness. The Lord of mysteries may reward you with ultimate light if you take a chance to find answers in the "forbidden" world. Use diplomacy in all your deals and stay on the right side of the law.

Family and Friends: Emotions and passion are running high these days and Pluto may induce sexual encounters with magnetic strangers. Keep an eye on strangers that may be brought into your home and watch over your children.

Love Affairs: Do not take chances and listen to your intuition wherever you happen to be. If you are in a relationship, this is a great trend to stimulate your spouse or lover for some good lovemaking. Good wine, candlelight, soft music and your imagination are all you need with sexual Pluto involved. Jupiter may decide to send you news from a faraway friend. Any new relationship started now will be full of sex and passion. Better take precautions if you are a single person and be ready for that "new" relationship to be full of drama. Spend some time in the wild; Jupiter will replenish you with fresh air, fresh spirits and a new approach to life. All the water signs will feel Pluto's allure and will become walking magnets.

Travel and Communication: You may receive news from far away or give presents to a deserving family member or dear friend. You can also expect your telephone to be busy and interesting mail to come your way. Don't try to be in too many places at the same time and if you have to drive, take a little take extra time to get there; don't rush as the police could spoil your day. People from the past will get in touch with you. Be aware on the road with Pluto in charge these days as absolutely anything nasty can happen to you now.

Environment: Pluto will surely trigger the earth's entrails somewhere in the world and produce dramatic news with the weather. Many human and animal lives have been lost during his dramatic reign. As usual, be ready for negative news such as Air Botswana pilot crashes his plane in suicide mission at airport - Quake rocks Colombia, some damage seen - November 8, 1999 BOGOTA, Colombia (Reuters) -- A powerful earthquake rocked much of Colombia and destroyed a number of homes in a northeastern mountain town while residents slept early Monday, authorities said. November 11, 1999 ISTANBUL, Turkey (AP) -- A strong aftershock Thursday shook a region of western Turkey that is still struggling to recover from a massive earthquake that killed thousands this summer. At least 91 people were injured Thursday, most after jumping out of buildings in panic.

Famous Personalities: Pluto will reward those who will take chances but prudent too. Many lives will undergo metamorphosis and Jupiter will extend their minds and horizons. Many secrets will come to light. A very famous public person may go to the other side.

Events: If you are a police officer or a security guard beware of Pluto. The crooks will be active and deadly. Passion may ensnare a lost spirit, and Pluto will lead the unwise young spirit to kill innocent people. The worst of Pluto's choleric thunders and lightning are about to strike the earth. Under his power, April 30, 1998 in CARMEL, Indiana -- - Two people died and four were wounded in three Indiana bank robberies, while a third bank robbery was reported in Richmond, Indiana, about 65 miles east of Indianapolis, an hour after the second. Two men wearing ski masks, one armed with a pistol, escaped with an undetermined amount of money. Also, in April 1998, Pluto took the lives of 28 people who died in a Peru plane crash. Don't take chances now.

Shopping: Invest in anything that can clean or kill pests. Do not invest in anything that could bring danger to those for whom you care.

※

MON., TUE., WED., THU. — OCTOBER 15, 16, 17, 18:
RULERS — Saturn (Politicians/Rules) and Uranus (Explosions/sovereignty).

Work, Career and Business: Following the last few days of destructive Pluto in our lives, Saturn's restructuring power will be a blessing for some organizations and your own business. Expect a new beginning offered to you. Uranus might also throw great surprising developments your way. With the New Moon, get active and get what you need; the timing is now right. If the work that you are doing is inappropriate or stressful, with Uranus in charge, you can only happily look for the needed changes. Resolve to find a new career soon, and for the lucky ones expect a well-deserved promotion.

Partnerships: Be original; don't let others pressure you into following them, instead of your own heart. You will not build anything until you break new ground. Stressful situations stimulate you to become more independent. Meditate on where you are going in your life and don't be afraid of tomorrow. There is no better time for new and progressive change. Be nice to others and get active on the social scenery.

Family and Friends: Expect interesting surprises during these days as many will be back with the people of their past. Uranus also makes the children very active and they will drive you a little crazy. Don't be afraid of computers; a study in this area will open many new opportunities. Watch the children carefully this weekend, especially close to bodies of water.

Love Affairs: Friends will call you and with Uranus' touch (surprises) try-doing things you would not usually do and go to unusual places on a whim. Visit your future and invest in astrology or the psychic phenomena. Time for catching UFOs on film, and see them materializing in this dense physical world. If you want to see something astonishing go for it now! Uranus may decide to grant one of your important wishes. Love can be found now; get active, do not turn down any invitations. If you are an Aries, a Libra or a Leo may fall for you. An Aquarius friend will surprise you.

Travel and Communication: You may be thinking to visit your past. Do not turn down an invitation, as a professional contact could bring people who will positively influence your career. For this occasion, you may feel like spending some money on your car. Some may get stuck in airports as Uranus may disturb electronic equipment. If some of your plans get canceled; don't be mad, be patient.

Environment: On a sad note, keep in mind that Uranus rules earthquakes. Thus volcanoes, earthquakes, explosions, are high on the list. Let's hope that he won't do anything silly now, but he usually does. Flying is fine but the weather will make the trip bumpy. A blackout or trouble with electronics is high on the list too.

Famous Personalities: Many famous people will be really active in helping those less fortunate. Beautiful music, great movies and great actors of the past will come alive.

Events: Saturn rules politics, so expect surprising announcements from foreign governments. Under his power in 1997 in Africa, many armed men staged a coup attempt in Sierra Leone. President reportedly flees to Guinea. Armed men launched a coup attempt and said they had taken power in this West African nation. A spokesman, who identified himself as Cpl. Gborie, went on national radio and said that junior army ranks had ousted President Ahmed Tejan Kabbah.

Shopping: Electronic components will fail; you may be forced to invest in new equipment. You may want to pay a visit to your future and meet with your favorite "spiritual guide." Any electronic tools bought now will bring you luck in your business.

※

FRI., SAT., SUN., MON., TUE. — OCTOBER 19, 20, 21, 22, 23: RULERS — Uranus (Surprises) Neptune (Faith) and Mars (Desires)

Work, Career and Business: This trio's long impact will make life quite interesting for the next few days. Neptune's blurring nature may affect your judgment. Uranus will certainly bring some spice and surprise to your life soon. Be practical in all your expectations. If a business is not going well, you might be going in the wrong direction. Use all those above-mentioned planets to look for the right one. With the good Moon around, the opportunity might be in your local newspaper; take the time to cruise through it. Communicate your desires to whoever can help.

Partnerships: Come clear with what you mean. Some people could be deceiving; ask pertinent questions and watch their reaction. Be ready to support depressed partners, but don't let their problems affect your judgment and feelings. A trip related to your business life could prove beneficial. A contract or a deal may be offered to you; sign it before the Full Moon.

Family and Friends: Expect tons of action around you, and with Mars cruising above use patience and diplomacy with others. Uranus will bring new friends and the elements of love and joy this weekend. Mercury will join in and make us very communicative. Much of your time will be spent organizing trips, or getting in touch with your past. This trend will be an interesting one, where friends and family members will all try to get in touch with you at the same time. This trio may drive you crazy and you will have your hands full of projects and not enough time to deal with them.

Love Affairs: Affairs of the heart will progress these days and the weekend could prove to be very interesting. Some teenagers need your attention; if you don't provide it, they could get themselves in trouble. Offer guidance and support to all in need, as they are not aware of the stars' impact on their lives. Some will be caught in love affairs of their past and may be deceiving themselves. Neptune will make you feel low of both mental and physical energy. If you are an air sign, expect much with love now.

Travel and Communication: The strength of Mars combined with the speed of Mercury may bring trouble on the road. Be safe; take the time to go places and give yourself plenty time to deal with everybody you care for. Use precautions and take your time if you have to travel far; don't let Mars or Neptune stop you. Most of all DON'T DRINK AND DRIVE! Neptune could get you into serious trouble. The past will become alive; deal with it and enjoy all the planning ahead.

Environment: Keep in mind that Mars is with us and many people will become aggressive, be patient with them. Uranus and Mars may decide to throw an earthquake or produce disturbing weather all around. Be patient with everyone.

Famous Personalities: This timing is ideal for meditation and renewing your faith in the universe. Pious rich and famous will prepare all sorts of activities to perform, and will give the checks to charitable organizations. Try your best to participate and provide for those in need.

Events: The last breath of the deceiving Pisces Age is in full action. Religions, dogmas, fears, man-made hells, and imaginative stories of the Apocalypse will be soon replaced by more healthy approaches to the future. With Uranus in its own sign, the new Age of Aquarius will completely transform man's cosmic consciousness within the next few years. Before this celestial transformation the worst of Pisces religious fanaticism must be experienced by the world at large by producing terrorist acts, wars and madness all over the world. Have faith in the future and the celestial order imposed by the stars' eternal motions. Man can only grow and eliminate any form of spiritual poisoning through spiritual research.

Shopping: Great deals will be found well before the upcoming festivities, in the most unexpected places. However, do not let all the advertisers run away with your pocketbook, as you will feel like buying all the best and most glamorous things right now. Be sure to treat yourself to something nice these days too. The Christmas spirit is already here, but people will be busy, short tempered and impatient. Make sure that you plan a leisurely day to do your shopping where the pull and hurry all around won't affect your mood. Remember, you know better than the others, so just smile and brighten a sad day. Many of you have realized the value of my work; Starguide is a perfect and valuable present to offer. Contribute a solid, true piece of the Universe to your loved ones with my books.

※

WED., THU., FRI., SAT. — OCTOBER 24, 25, 26, 27:
RULERS —Mars (Hostility/anger) and Venus (Highly valued/

caring):

Work, Career and Business: The New Moon will exert a revitalizing pull that will be felt in your business affairs. You may use this lunation to perhaps resolve conflicts in a difficult situation with a person of authority or a co-worker. Control Mars' opposing tendencies; don't let him affect your words, your attitude or your emotions. Practice patience during this Martian trend and use diplomacy; if you do so you'll make serious progress. You may also use the tough energy of Mars to do some needed tasks around the office, such as removing furniture; in any case, don't get hurt.

Partnerships: Even with the Waxing Moon, for a couple of days and learn to keep Mars' impatience under control and use Venus' diplomatic gifts to save difficult situations. Everyone is so intent on having their own way and there could be little cooperation around you. It's time to practice tact with the same dedication as a diplomat. Impatience could be detrimental to you and others, so use the knowledge found in this publication accordingly.

Family and Friends: With Venus' blessings upon us, you should try your creativity at home. Your fruitful Venusians imagination will lead you to creations of perfect interior designs. Realize your limits with troubled friends, and don't allow them to rely too heavily on you. As always, give spiritual support but avoid getting emotionally involved with their personal problems. You and your mate or family member can gain through financial endeavors, but discuss all possibilities before making any commitments. You might have an idea yourself that could be used; talk about it. Use what's left of the Waxing Moon and enjoy a gathering this weekend.

Love Affairs: Don't let your relationship becoming shaky because you sense that the person in question may be deceiving in some way. Do not fall for your own insecurity, false information or a wild imagination. Avoid guilt in any of your decisions, and if you feel a change is unavoidable, trust your future. Expect much from a night out on Friday or Saturday if you take a chance on someone. Enjoy social life but don't drink and drive. Mars (action) and Neptune (deception) are not great cohabiters. When alcohol and speed are mixed, it can produce serious accidents. If you are a Gemini, then Aquarius, Sagittarius and Libra will be strongly attracted to you. A friend born in April has a surprise for you.

Travel and Communication: Be vigilant if you must drive, and don't take chances on the road, as Mars' energy could make you careless. Don't let his aggressive nature make you complain about a person, and use your words cautiously. Venus has much more to offer, and it's your choice; so use your will and your knowledge. Someone from your past may call.

Environment: Some people will learn about fire or explosion the hard way. However, many thoughtful people will use Mars' power to further environmental knowledge on preventing fires in nature. As usual, Mars, the red and violent planet, doesn't seem to care much for the Waxing Moon. He may decide to pull a nasty trick with nature's devastating forces, where all the elements could be invited for a destructive dance. Explosions and fires are common during his reign, be aware. If you know someone in the Armed Forces, then request my 2007 Moon Power, so we can forward my forecast directly to them. You will save lives by doing so.

Famous Personalities: The oblivious rich and famous may be Mar's victims or make sad news involving accidents, drugs or alcohol. On a positive note, Venus will shine and induce love to those often-lonely famous souls.

Events: The Martian energy is tough and has in the past produced explosions and accidents of all sorts; be prudent. Venus will put up a serious fight against her destructive brother and may save many souls. Violent and dangerous sports will attract many people challenging their respective sides. Some unsuspecting souls may fall victim to Mars, and suffer head injuries.

Shopping: Invest in anything involving love, creativity or the arts. Show for whom you someone you care, the depth of your love. Under Mar's power, dangerous tools and machinery bought now will bring financial opportunities.

Full Moon — October 26, 2007 in Taurus: Disturbing news from financial corporations and the stock market are to be expected. Venus, the queen of security and love will suffer and bring serious setbacks to your security. Dramatic transformations in the world of finance and the banking industry are ahead. The impact will induce a form of financial death and rebirth for some large corporations, and others will have to merge to survive. Sad news from Switzerland and the arts are on the way. This Full Moon will also shed some light on the shameful manipulation, sexual and financial secrets of organized religions and some of their religious leaders.

Lunation impact on all signs:

Aries - Difficult news about your finances and a deal or a trip worries you.

Taurus - Trouble with a contract or corporation, be safe and don't sign anything now.

Gemini - Stress coming from your past and a business or emotional partner has to go.

Cancer - Don't worry about your friends or your kids and don't stress at work.

Leo - Career romance and new career or moving will get you worrying.
Virgo - A trip or a
 study is a problem, be patient and work diligently.

Libra - The mail or telephone may bring you sad news, be strong.

Scorpio - Expect a restructure of your self-esteem and partnerships soon.

Sagittarius - Don't take any chances with your health or at work, be patient.

Capricorn - Let go of your past, eliminate all guilt with love or children and no drinking.

Aquarius - Family matters or your home life will stress you for a while so deal with it.

Pisces - Your words can be destructive to you and others, no complaining, be positive.

※

SUN., MON., TUE., WED. — OCTOBER 28, 29, 30 31:
RULERS — Venus (Caring), Mercury (Siblings) the Moon (Endings).
Work, Career and Business: Your mind will wander about your position in this world and what to do to make it better. The deserving hard working may not benefit with well-earned bonuses or new opportunities and it might not be the time to promote their careers just now, be patient until the next lunation. Mercury will make you think fast, driving and running errands will have to be done. Be aware of the Full Moon's tension and be ready to change your schedule. Wait for the next New Moon to face important deals.

Partnerships: Some of the people you know will have to move away, or you yourself may decide to relocate to a better place within the next few days. Expect the beginning or ending of important phases of your life and others' too. Venus will endorse many gatherings with some colleagues you have not seen for a long time. Be ready to control your emotions during a Waning difficult Moon.

Family and Friends: Expect a brother or a sister to surprise you. A friend might show up uninvited and thus affect some of your plans too. You may receive an invitation to socialize with some faraway friends or family members; use this opportunity to grow closer to them if you can. Against all odds, endure patiently this Supernova Window, and enjoy these good old days. Don't forget that when the Moon becomes Full and is Waning, things may not go your way. A family member needs your advice. Be willing to consider the issue from his point of view; but avoid emotional involvement or forcing your opinion. Much time will be spent around the children talking about the upcoming Christmas trees. Prepare to enjoy the warmth of Mother and the good food of your friends and your family.

Love Affairs: Do not expect much progress if you are looking for that special person just now. Some of the people from your past may also become weighty; stand for yourself without guilt. Friends will bring good memories; have fun, but don't get caught up in the nostalgia. If you are a fire or water sign many will try to steal your heart. Have fun, but don't make any commitment if the person in question was met for the first time after the Full Moon.

Travel and Communication: You will have to run like mad to keep up with all the things you must accomplish. You will stay busy with all this activity and come in contact with interesting people. Combined with the Full Moon trend and a Supernova Window expect all sorts of delays, forcing you to think twice as fast. Slow down; be cautious and prudent in your driving, too. Watch for crazy drivers around the city; they might not have read "Moon Power," so don't let them hurt you (or your car). Many will fly to faraway places early and will get caught in bad weather or find themselves stuck in congested airports. Keep in mind that Mercury may decide to confuse some electronics and bring chaos. Chain-reaction accidents, bad weather and black outs are very high on the list; be careful out there.

Environment: Expect surprises and explosions soon. Be aware of fire and keep an eye on the children. Chances are that nature will go berserk soon, so you don't want to be a victim. She may demonstrate her power with shocking weather. Thousands of people may be forced to relocate, fleeing disasters, flooding or bad earthquakes.

Famous Personalities: A famous person (or his child) will make dramatic news. Expect news about famous or infamous people who have made history. The past will turn alive for a while.

Events: After the Full Moon, electronics may suffer or fail to function properly. This could produce another dramatic air crash. Not a time to take any risks in the air, unless you made reservations during a Waxing trend. Expect the beginning or ending of an important portion of your (and other) lives.

Shopping: Think about spending money on wisdom and on those, for whom you care, get your 2007 Moon Power. You can still find good deals on big-ticket items by comparison shopping. If you decide to visit Las Vegas' casinos after the Full Moon, you may encounter stress but you could get lucky. Yes, someone will hit the jackpot in a Waning Moon in Vegas, but the money will be spent on paying bills or taxes and little will be left. Better make all your important plans after the next New Moon for your own sake. Again, consider offering Moon Power Starguide to your loved ones for Christmas. It is affordable, valuable, and because it works for you, it will also work for them. They will probably love you for shedding some Light of the Universe upon their lives. Go to www.drturi.com to order your E-book or hard copy of "Moon Power".

Welcome to Your Day - to - Day Guidance
For November 2007

THU., FRI., SAT., SUN. — NOVEMBER 1, 2, 3, 4:
RULERS — The Moon (Big changes) and the Sun (Expectation).

Work, Career and business: The general mood will be depressive. You can expect the serious beginning and ending of important parts of your (and others) life. Be ready for those upcoming progressive variations. Keep in mind that life is a constant process of change and the stars are (even if you don't realize it) working for your benefit. Be patient with everyone around the office.

Partnerships: You will be forced to let go of negative people in your life and disturbing situations. You must take a chance on the new future with faith. Many will experience the closing of a destructive relationship and others may see the new beginning. Under these stars any new relationship will be loaded with challenge and karma. Further positive thoughts only and don't fall for the Waning Moon.

Family and friends: The Sun rules love, romance and children but we are still under a difficult trend so this energy won't bring you much good news. The Sun gives life to children but watch over them especially with fire and close to the water. On a more positive note, he will shine his undiscriminating light on many secrets. Friends will need spiritual support, so give love and attention and build good karma for yourself.

Love affairs: Be ready for new starts in love matters and provide a solid shoulder for the victims suffering a broken heart. The right partner might not be the one you were with, use the new found freedom to look (after the New Moon) for someone who really deserves your love. Under the Sun's command, the lucky ones will find great friends and happiness. A new arrival is to be expected by a young couple. If you are a Pisces, a Scorpio, a Virgo or a Taurus could induce serious stress in your life. A Capricorn friend has good advice for you; simply listen.

Travel and Communication: You may be asked to go home and see Mom. Be aware on the road, do not trust any driver and be ready for sudden action. Surprises are on the way and people from your past will come back into the picture soon.

Environment: There is nothing other to do than to accept the ultimate changes imposed by God, and nature will show her powers soon.

Famous personalities: Expect interesting but not necessarily positive surprises with the rich and famous. Be ready for the unexpected in their words and actions.

Events: Nature's forces may compel thousands of victims to relocate and rebuild new lives. Black outs and losses of power are on the way too. Tragedies and many volcanic eruptions have happened under this configuration and thousands of people were forced out of their homes because of nature's destructive forces. Be ready.

Shopping: What ever you do not invest in anything new or dangerous for the children. Get rid of the extra stuff clogging the house and a garage sale would make some lucky buyers happy. Anything to clean the house will also do well.

MON., TUE., WED., THU. - NOVEMBER 5, 6, 7, 8:

RULERS: Mercury (communication) Venus (Love)

Work, Career and business: Another week of stress but a new fresh breath of life will be offered to you after the next New Moon. Her blessings will make your life much easier. Wait for her upcoming green light, then go and ask the universe to make it happen. Do not try to push your business just now, instead plan and do some cleaning. Again advertisements, important calls, traveling, and meetings will pay off if you are patient. Use "Moon Power" wisely and respect the Universal Law.

Partnerships: Mercury rules the mail. Phone calls and communications in general could be a source of trouble with family members. A get-together after work could also bring stress; Mercury will have everyone sharing new ideas of how to get the job done better.

Family and friends: Don't let the Waning Moon get your spirit down. Many will need your support to help them clean up karmic relationships. Again do not let anyone exhaust your spirit and be patient with loved ones. Use Venus' generosity and show your love to everyone. Avoid spending too much time talking about a discouraged person.

Love affairs: Stay clear from someone who drinks too much and realize your limits if you are in a deceiving relationship. This is the perfect time to enjoy a great movie with the one you care for. With Venus around, the opportunity to show true love will be given to you. If you were born in January, someone born in September or May needs to talk to you. A friend born in November will share a secret with you.

Travel and Communication: Take this opportunity to do a check up on your car, as the stars will make your mechanic very detail oriented, thus helping him with detecting possible future trouble. Get your wheels in action, but prepare for traveling under the protection of the upcoming New Moon.

Environment: Recharge your spirits; a trip to the wild will do you so good. The energy gained from the earth will recharge your batteries and you could also appreciate the beauty of Mother Nature. Trouble may come from the sea or a plane crash.

Famous personalities: A notorious religious or scientist could make serious news soon.

Events: Be patient and relax while the Moon is still Waning, Mother Nature may decide to disturb us with bad weather. This is not a good time to fly, unless you made your reservation during the Waxing Moon.

Shopping: Some may decide to join the local gym or enroll in a weight loss program. Buy only things to improve the face of your home or cleaning products now.

New Moon — November 9, 2007 in Scorpio: This lunation in Scorpio promises to be very dramatic for many people. A New Moon is usually positive. Thus after any form of death, there is always a new life in store for all of us. Pluto, the planet of death and rebirth, rules this sign and all affairs related to finance, health, sex, secrets, death, war, drama and law enforcement will be on the rise. Expect tragedy of all sorts to take place this month, where all the devil's spirits will be invited to a macabre dance of horror. This will be one of the most difficult lunation this year where one must realize one's limits. The trend will play an important part in your life, where impartial judgment from above and below will take place. Watch for friends and family members too, the stars will force them into new sections of their lives. Expect serious restructuring to take place in your health, working life, relationships and the world at large will be affected. Many people and countries may be forced to realize the hard lessons of determination, cruelty, and death. The emphasis is on death and the potential for a rebirth in experiences, strength, and newfound wisdom to perform and live accordingly. Have faith and promote love, peace and respect for all. Never forget, the future is nothing other than the reincarnation of our common thoughts. Remember, knowledge is power and there is no room for ignorance with the stars.

Lunation impact on all signs:

Aries - This lunation will affect your corporate money, take chances but be wise.

Taurus - This New Moon will affect your emotional or business related partners.

Gemini - Improvement in your service to the world, health, good opportunities are ahead.

Cancer - Love, romance, and children; all will shine in these areas for you soon.

Leo - Great news from home and a solid opportunity to buy, sell, or move soon.

Virgo - Results of hard work will pay off, still another great study or a trip is ahead.

Libra - A contract or Legal endeavor will turn to your side. You're happy.

Scorpio - This lunation is on you, you cannot loose if you try hard enough. Go for it.

Sagittarius - Your intuition will become very clear, a deep study is ahead of you.

Capricorn - A younger or older friend will grant one of your dearest wishes. Get it.

Aquarius - Great progress, great changes, and your career, will improve your image.

Pisces - A trip to the past, a deep study, and foreign affairs shine on you.

※

Note: Attention, Pluto is back with us. Don't be a victim of the Lord of Hell and be aware of Pluto's destructive power. As always, use extreme caution in all you do. Better think twice before saying or acting on impulse. Anything you say or do under his power will follow you for the rest of your life. More than ever use diplomacy, as whatever you do now will have very serious repercussions. Expect secrets to be divulged, affairs of sex, and nature's devastating forces to be at work Killers, rapists, psychotics, and the worst of society will become active. While Pluto reigns, you'd better stay home and let the ignorant be killed. This is the time to really pay attention and make good use of my work. If you are a police officer, be very careful out there. As usual, if you know someone who is working for the police force or deals with a life and death situations, make this person aware of the power of the stars. You may save this person's life. Just point out Moon Power and the person won't be skeptical for long, once the drama unfolds. Time to think of investing and offering the real wisdom and true guidance found in Moon Power to someone for whom you care.

"He who reigns himself and rules his passion, desire, and fear, is more than a king."
— *Goethe*

FRI., SAT., SUN., MON., TUES — NOVEMBER 9 10, 11, 12, 13:
RULERS — Pluto (death/drama) and Jupiter (religion)

Work, Career and Business: You are now walking on fire! You'd better use all the "savoir faire" you know if you are to go through this lunation without trouble. A serious wake-up call will come to many abusers, as the heavy hand of karma will fall on them. Businesses or corporations will be forced into restructures, and those who don't fit the bill will have to go. The possibility to lose (and rebuild) it all will be a serious consideration for some karmic souls.

Partnerships: The offensive secret life of a person may surface; you may learn something valuable about a partner. Whatever you find out, do not divulge the secret. Stinky moneymaking schemes will play an important part of this trend; listen to your intuition in all you do. Stay clear of dark alleys; your life hangs upon your awareness. Many people will learn the hard way these days. The Moon is New; but even so, know your limitations, as nasty happenings can and will take place under Pluto's power.

Family and Friends: Do not expect relatives to be diplomatic during this trend, especially if the family is experiencing financial stress. Do not fall for Pluto's destructive or sarcastic remarks; words of love and support will pay off in the end. Be ready for dramatic news from someone close to you. Whatever happens, be strong; life must go on as Pluto has important work to do and he is part of a celestial design imposed by God. Time to further my work and offer knowledge to those you care for by letting them read Moon Power.

Love Affairs: Secret affairs of sex and passion may be divulged to the public, forcing people to take a stand in destroying and rebuilding relationships. This might happen to you too. In any case use tons of diplomacy to save unwanted trouble in your love life. If you are a water sign or have any planet in Scorpio, be ready for a wake-up call of some form. Stay clear of any new relationship and stick with the old one or refrain from social interaction until the Moon and you will be safe.

Travel and Communication: Expect news pertaining to secrets, sex, the police force, and medical discoveries. Be careful of what you do or say during this trend. Drive carefully; stay clear of strangers and strange places. Be ready for dramatic news to disturb the media.

Environment: Pluto will have fun destroying it all, remember he belongs to the divine celestial family and has a specific work to do. His dramatic impact on earth (and people) is needed. What Pluto demolishes he also gives the opportunity to rebuild even stronger and better. Be ready for dramatic news with the police and nature's forces soon.

From: ///@ix.netcom.com-Date: Thu, 1 May1997 23:43:29-0500(CDT)-
To: drturi@inetworld.net - Subject: Earthquakes — Dear Dr. Turi, I posted a note on alt.astrology that cited the 6.7 quake off the coast of Mexico in the Pacific Ocean. I included it under the rather "nasty" piece of mail that someone sent indicating that they believed your window of probability for April 30 to be invalid. Not that I think you need defending, as I have found your work very compelling. I just thought I'd let you know — in case you didn't — that you were "right again." On the late night of April 30, the 6.7 quakes took place. Mary.

Famous Personalities: Some famous people will be called back to God. Many famous spoiled children get involved with the wrong crowd and some are found shot to death along a road. Pluto doesn't care if he deals with the rich and famous or common folks.

Events: Hopefully knowledgeable Jupiter will slow Pluto's rampage and thirst for blood. Under his power many jealous souls lose control and kill or injure people.

Shopping: All water and earth signs will see important parts of their businesses or financial lives taking a specific direction within this lunation. In addition, Jupiter is with us too, so the worst might be avoided under his protection. A visit to your local church to pray for Pluto's victims will do you well. Do not invest in weapons; if you do, you might have to use them later. Anything bought now that can be used for metaphysics will bring unusual power to you. Take a chance on Astro-Psychology and help us to set up a crash course in your area. Get a good deal on all that I have to teach you too by calling 602-957-1617 or email us from www.drturi.com.

※

WED., THU., FRI., SAT. — NOVEMBER 14, 15, 16, 17:
RULERS — Uranus (surprises) and Saturn (rebuilding):

Work, Career and Business: With the good Moon upon us, expect to make some progress for a while; many of your plans should go forward. Listen to other people's stories; the stars affect everybody and they may come up with interesting deals or surprising news. Be ready to invest in some appliances or equipment. Saturn will help you to make some great adjustments after careful planning.

Partnerships: With Uranus in charge, anything unusual can happen. With a Waxing Moon (positive) upon us, those changes should be progressive. Changes should be accepted with faith in yourself and your new future. Be patient with everyone, as Uranus and Saturn may make people eccentric and depressed.

Family and Friends: An opportunity to meet with some family members or friends you have not seen for a while will be given to you by this lunation. The past will come alive again and a great time is offered to all. Make good use of these days and enjoy the food, security and love of your peers.

Love Affairs: Be ready for the incredible to happen; if you are in a karmic relationship changes may be forced upon you and are needed. Friends may fall in love with other friends or mistake love for friendship. An old love or a past friend will reappear in your life soon and with him the option to start fresh again. If you were born under one of the earth signs, expect good surprises and great changes. If you are a Sagittarius, a Leo friend needs to talk to you and someone born in April or February needs to go places with you. A friend born in June might fall for you.

Travel and Communication: A business trip or an invitation may lead you to many good contacts from the past. Be patient, as you will still have plenty of time to play and enjoy yourself with various and unusual people. For UFO investigators, now is the time to look for UFO's in secluded places. Don't forget your video camera; you may be sorry if you are not ready, as Uranus is now willing to display secrets of extraterrestrial intelligence. Expect things in the sky or NASA to make the news.

Environment: A nasty virus could produce an aeronautic disaster soon. Expect this type of news to happen: Australian wildlife officials made repeated attempts to prevent up to 300 long-finned pilot whales from beaching themselves on a remote part of Australia's west coast. Mammals, birds, and men's navigational systems get confused when Uranus is in charge, and many get lost. Tornadoes are high on the list. Go to www.drturi.com and register for my newsletter and get more information all year round. You may also join the Star-chat room at www.drturi.com and let me have your questions and comments.

Famous Personalities: Very surprising news will come from the rich and famous doing great things for the children of the world during this time.

Events: Uranus loves accidents and explosions; under his power expect surprising and original pieces of news to take place. Do not take chances with the children and be safe.

Shopping: Purchase new electronic equipment or plan a long voyage by air to a foreign land. As always, Uranus rules the future, and his psychic powers can be used through your trusted local psychic or astrologer. Invest in your own future and request a taped progressive reading for the upcoming year. You may also help us to set up a crash course in your city by contacting us at www.drturi.com.

SUN., MON., TUE, — NOVEMBER 18, 19,20:
RULERS — Neptune (religion), Mars (arguments) and Venus (affection)

Work, Career and Business: This trio will make life quite interesting. Neptune's blurring nature may affect your judgment. Be practical in all of your expectations. If a business is not doing well, you might be going the wrong way. Use all those above-mentioned planets to look for the right one for help. With the good Moon around, the opportunity might be in your local newspaper; take the time to cruise through it. Communicate your desires to whoever can help.

Partnerships: As always with Neptune, come clear with what you mean. Some people
could be deceiving; ask pertinent questions and watch their reactions. Be ready to help support depressed partners, but don't let their problems affect your judgment or feelings. A trip to Hawaii or an exotic place is in store for the lucky souls. A contract may be offered; sign it before the Full Moon.

Family and Friends: Expect tons of action around, and with Mars cruising above, use patience and diplomacy with others. Venus will bring an element of love and joy. Much of your time will be spent preparing for the future and the New Year. This trend will be an interesting one where friends and family members will try to get in touch with you all at the same time. This trio may drive you crazy with many projects.

Love Affairs: Affairs of the heart will progress these days and the weekend could prove to be very interesting. Some might be caught in a love affair from their past and may be deceiving themselves. Neptune will make you low in mental or physical energy. If you are a water sign you are lucky with love for a while.

Travel and Communication: The strength of Mars combined with the blurring vision of Neptune may bring trouble. Be cautious and take your time if you have to travel, don't let Neptune or Mars stop you.

Environment: Mars may decide to throw an earthquake or produce disturbing weather. Be patient with everyone.

Famous Personalities: This timing is ideal for meditation and renewing your faith in the universe. Try your best to participate and provide for those in need.

Events: The government needs to make lots of decisions about a disturbed area of the world. Let's hope for mankind's desire for peace in the Middle East.

Shopping: Great deals will be found in the most unexpected places. Treat yourself to something nice these days too. Make sure that you plan a leisurely day for yourself to relax your body and spirit. As the year comes to an end, many of you have realized the value of my work; Starguide is a perfect and valuable present to offer for any occasion: a birthday, a wedding, to a friend or child in trouble, for relocation, a comparison chart, etc. Contribute a legitimate piece of the Universe to those you really care for and tell them to visit www.drtrui.com for their free daily and monthly forecast.

※

WED., THU., FRI – NOVEMBER 21, 22, 23:
RULERS — Venus (sense of tact) and Mercury (communication):

Work, Career and Business: You need to reach out to new people and expand the various social networks in your life. The Moon is still Waxing positive, so promoting your business endeavors now is the right thing to do. Business encouraged now will have the potential for bringing financial security to all parties involved. Time to ask for a loan from your bank or a financial favor from a friend or family member. Money and security will play an important part of this trend and you might find yourself investing in a good deal. You should be confident of the outcome.

Partnerships: Candle light, soft music, courtship and social gatherings for the weekend are on the agenda. The soft Venus energy will tone down the aggressive tendencies of people around you. Time to make peace and to apologize for your mistakes. You need to reach out to new people and expand the various social networks in your life. Use finesse in all you do, you can't miss. Under Venus' blessings, you must keep in mind that what ever is offered with true love will bring luck to the giver. Abusing her kindness will bring back heavy karma and will be paid in full. Let your partner know about your deep feelings.

Family and Friends: If you are single do not turn down an invitation or a chance to socialize, as interesting people will be there, waiting for you. Communication is on the fore, don't hesitate to participate, everybody will listen to your comments. However avoid falling into useless gossip over the telephone, as only "Ma Bell" will benefit from that! You may hear good news about brothers or sisters or use Mercury's power of expression to write those long overdue letters.

Love Affairs: Some will happily give; some will gladly receive presents that will last forever in their hearts. Promote words of love and be aware of the feelings of others, lovely Venus will change uneasiness into love, attention and respect. You and a long-standing friend may discover that your relationship is growing towards romance and both are surprised. A dual situation may force some to make decisions, use your intuition, and keep a cool head. The lessons of the past should be remembered. If you were born in May then a Pisces or a Capricorn could be strongly attracted to you.

Travel and Communication: Interesting news is to be expected and your telephone might be full of messages. Now is the time for traveling, however avoid the impulsive Mercurial need for speed. You might have to deal with high winds and snow. Time to express yourself, write letters and/or start a book.

Environment: Nature may get out of hand with a bad earthquake, or a monetary scandal could make the news. A famous personality will have to pay a heavy price for something he could not keep secret.

Events: The broadcasting, transportation and educational industries will undergo some progressive changes. Idea of strikes will reach unhappy corporation workers.

Shopping: A camera purchased now will bring great joy to the family. Take care of your wheels and shop around for things for the office. If you decide to purchase a new car or strike a bargain for a used one, don't be afraid to barter aggressively. Mercury loves mental stimulation and your wit will help you to save money. Be happy and alert - don't be afraid to use your communication powers.

Full Moon in Gemini - November 24, 2007: Disturbing news about transportation and education and the possibility of strikes is to be expected. Mercury, "Lord of Communication and Transportation" will cause serious setbacks and disruptions to the possibility of traveling and communicating. Dramatic changes are ahead in the worlds of transportation, finance, traveling, and the postal industries. Sad news involving serious accidents, terrorism and devastating weather is on it's way. Many people will find themselves stranded in the airports. The impact of these events will bring on a form of death and rebirth to some large corporations who will merge to survive.

Lunation impact on all signs:

Aries - Difficult news from the mail and a deal or a trip gets you worried.

Taurus - Trouble with a contract or corporation, don't sign anything now.

Gemini - Stress coming from your past, a business or emotional partner is burdensome.

Cancer - Don't worry about your past. Stress at home is expected soon.

Leo - A friend and a new endeavor will worry you.

Virgo - A change of career or stress at home is a problem, be patient.
Libra - The mail or
telephone may bring you sad news from faraway.

Scorpio - Expect a restructure of your finances and a form of death soon.

Sagittarius - Don't take any chances with your partners or traveling.

Capricorn - Eliminate all guilt to bring about better work and health.

Aquarius - Love and children matters won't go well for a while, just be patient.

Pisces - Your home life brings stress, you may have to move soon.

✳

SAT., SUN., MON., TUE., WED. — NOVEMBER 24, 25, 26, 27, 28:
RULERS — Mercury (News) and the Moon (Important Changes):

Work, Career and Business: The blessings of a Waxing Moon are now gone; you should fight lethargy and depressions. Be confident, as much needed change is ahead for you and those you care. You may also consider using Mercury's mental agility to pass on new ideas to improve your business or communicate with the family. You could use these Waning days to re-write or plan new advertisements or publicity. The telephone will be particularly busy but the news could be depressive. Don't leave the office upset; you do not need to bring stress at home. Stay active and be mentally alert.

Partnerships: Dealing with others has and will always be a challenge for us all. Some of you have learnt hard lessons and the scars do take time to heal; don't re-open them again. Move on to better ground, the future always has better to offer. Keep a positive attitude in your conversations and promote only the great times of your past. Some karmic souls will have to experience a rebirth of their relationships. Whatever unfolds, accept the changes with confidence; the truth is that, life is a constant process of change and it always seems to be for the better. Enjoy time spent with those you care.

Family and Friends: Mercury is fast and rules communication, so expect family members to get in touch with you via mail or telephone. Some will be invited to enjoy great cooking at their friend's homes. "The Messenger of the Gods" loves to talk and throw jokes all over. Control Mercury's desire to exaggerate and do not fall for the negative things you may hear now. Keep in mind that your friends have the potential to fulfill all your wishes; get active in the social arena. As always, you might have a karmic debt with a long-standing friend; if so, you may have to experience annoyance. Try to clear it all up and you'll win the person back. The Full Moon will bring high emotions; avoid trouble from being too sensitive to idiot remarks.

Love Affairs: Be ready for the beginning or ending of important love phases of your love life. Keep your eyes and ears open on the people you know as the Moon affects everybody. If you were born in July, someone much older or younger than you born in March, November or January will be attracted to you. A friend may bring you sad news soon. You are missing some people you care about; be patient during the next 2 weeks.

Travel and Communication: Use Mercury's mental powers accordingly. Time to write those letters, as Mercury improves your mental faculties. He will reward you favorably if you decide to invest in your education or start a book after the upcoming New Moon. Control his strong desire to be a "chatterbox," and save money on your telephone bill. Mercury rules transportation and general motion; he also makes people restless on the road. Under his command you should be a defensive driver. It's time to plan for your future travels, or visit parts of the world via great books. Wait for the next New Moon to launch the trip. You'll be glad to know and respect God's Universal Laws.

Environment: We are into a Full Moon period and some will soon experience severe weather systems in some states. If you are into videotaping lightning, storms, volcanic eruptions, earthquakes, etc., be ready for those soon. Some will see the beginning or ending of dramatic times. This may force thousands of people to relocate. Be ready for disturbing news soon, where thousands of people will be forced to flee nature's destructive forces.

Famous Personalities: Full Moon; be aware, thus some famous artist or important political figure will experience shame with love, and their children will be directly affected. May see a lot of good done for the children.

Events: Prominent political personalities either from the Russia, US, France or Japan will make an important announcement. The government may come up with drastic news or decisions that could affect many families in the future. Let's hope for the best as terrorists will get active and disturb the holidays.

Shopping: Invest faithfully in anything to clean the house or the office. Equipment purchased now will bring trouble to its owner. This is a perfect time to take care of your car. Mercury also rules literature and great deals on old books will be available under its influence.

※

THU., FRI. – NOVEMBER 29, 30:
RULERS — The Sun (children/love), Venus (love), Mercury (traveling).

Work, Career and Business: Do not expect much progress these days. The Waning Moon (negative) will make sure to obstruct any business ventures. Don't take yourself too seriously; set a meeting with coworkers to discuss what could be done to improve the business. Why not forget about your responsibility for a while and smell the roses like everyone else? Enjoy the party after work and let your real feelings show.

Partnerships: Old and new friends will be happy to talk to you and will exchange ideas, hopes and wishes with you. Be aware of what your partner needs and offer him another surprise for the upcoming New Year.

Family and Friends: Don't let a gloomy feeling get to you, and learn to forget whatever dramatic experiences happened to you lately. We are on this earth to do specific work we set for ourselves. Take care of the young, life goes so fast; let them fully enjoy your love and your care. Don't let the Waning Moon bother you with guilt or your difficult past. Do something special that will help you fight the weary mood. The children have plenty of ideas; listen to them and enjoy life. Friends may request your help in some areas.

Love Affairs: With the Sun (love) in charge, an element of surprise is around. As usual in time of a Waning Moon (negative), don't expect long-lasting love if you fall for someone new. If you are an Aquarius, a Gemini or a Leo needs your spiritual help.

Travel and Communication: The police will begin to plan for the next holiday and may stop you if you drive insanely. Drinking heavily could seriously disturb your plans for the next year and should be completely out of the question. You do not want to ruin your or someone else's family because of depression (or a good time). Be safe and if you drink with friends on Sunday night, take a cab home.

Environment: Hopefully, lovely Venus and the magnanimous Sun will stop any drama imparted by the Waning Moon. The weather will be difficult so stay clear of lightning. An explosion or a fire could hurt some children; watch over them carefully.

Famous Personalities: Many famous people will shine, helping those born with difficult karmic stars. Great shows will be offered to the public. Don't fall for the promoters of the Apocalypse; they are after your money and their own successful future.

Events: We are still in a Waning period and some disasters are still happening; be aware and be careful in all you do.

Shopping: Use the light of the Sun to regenerate your spirit.

Invest in your favorite spiritual healer, psychic or astrologer; it will do you good. Visit your future with faith. Enjoy the fast-approaching festivities. Be wise: those three kings who followed a star to Bethlehem, the birthplace of Jesus Christ, were astrologers! Wait for the Next New Moon to launch important matters.

Welcome to Your Day – to – Day Guidance
For December 2007

December 1, 2007 — Mercury enters Sagittarius: A trend loaded with communication about legal activities, traveling, and foreign affairs. Much thought will be geared towards finding better ways of dealing with other countries. Souls born now will be gifted with natural abilities for learning and teaching and many will travel far. Many will also master foreign languages. The opportunity to acquire knowledge of man's laws and religions is offered to the soul. Many of them will be born with an aptitude for judicial investigation, philosophical values, and some will play important parts in passing their knowledge on to the world. Some will be attracted to the professions offering intellectual abilities such as the ministry, teaching and writing, and some will be investing in education for the well being of animals. Spiritual talents involving the new age will lead these souls towards positions of authority and respect. This position makes for either one of the most intellectually advanced or religious dogmatic signs of the Zodiac. The soul must avoid being righteous to others and must often endure the poisoning of an overly religious upbringing. Their challenge will be to take a critical approach to books and collected knowledge. An opportunity to reach cosmic consciousness and the teaching of the creator's celestial manifestation is offered to the advanced souls.

December 5, 2006 - Venus enters Scorpio: This trend will shed light on some secrets and may force you to rebuild your relationships. It will allow many souls to see clearly and do some serious cleanup in the near future. The lucky ones will start lifetime commitments that are blessed with love and happiness. If your natal Venus is in a good aspect to Pluto, your sensuality will be extreme, and sexual relationships will be for the better. Souls born now will be given the opportunity to experience love on an emotional level and much drama is to be experienced there. If Venus is badly afflicted, "La Femme Fatale" or the "Black Widow" will suffer many disturbing relationships. (Elizabeth Taylor is a good example). A full commitment is needed with this position and the soul will have to use its head in affairs of the heart. Blessed with such a powerful location, Venus in Scorpio will endow the soul with incredible magnetism. Some karmic souls will have to learn to be less emotional and more critical of their natural jealousy. This position makes for one of the most emotional but beautiful and loving partners. Usually artistic talent is present with this position. These souls are born to experience love on an emotional and dramatic level. Due to the emotional intensity of Scorpio, this is a top position for those in the arts.

※

SAT., SUN., MON., TUES., WED., THU., FRI., SAT. – DECEMBER 1, 2, 3, 4, 5, 6, 7, 8:
RULERS – Mercury (traveling/communication) Venus (love) Pluto (drama)

Work, Career and Business: With the Waning Moon and in charge, be ready for dramatic repercussions in your life towards the weekend. Let's hope this trend will not touch you directly, but if it does you will need to be strong and realize the harshness of life. You may also find out your real limits about your life's situation. Now is the time to review all your accomplishments and the reasons for your failures. Accept the upcoming changes with grace. You will be forced out of a situation where you do not belong and you should be thankful for your intuition. Meditate on improving your future.

Partnerships: Finances will play an important part in your life now. Be practical in all your expenses; you are advised not to overspend. The lucky souls will receive very expensive presents;

some good-hearted people will offer them. Just wait patiently for the next New Moon to invest in your future. Churches all over will be busy planning to accommodate many pious souls for fast approaching Xmas. Answering to Pluto in Sagittarius, the Christmas spirit is now getting stronger and the world will feel compassionate and loving for all his victims.

Family and Friends: Many will make plans to travel to visit friends and family members. Expect news from all over, as new plans must be set to accommodate visitors. Your family from afar will let you know how much they love and miss you. The circle of friends will be extremely busy as we are making early plans to enjoy the past. With Santa Claus in the mind, children get more excited and will be somehow be difficult to handle. Pluto will make everyone passionate and restless. Don't expect much diplomacy around, as people will become susceptible to your comments. Control emotions and watch the goings on in the house, especially if children are around. A great time is ahead of you if you listen to your intuition. As always, if a stranger is brought to your house, be aware of his motives. Drama is bound to strike a family somewhere, don't be one of Pluto's victims.

Love Affairs: The Moon is still Waning (negative); avoid trouble. If you are a or an earth sign, you may be experiencing some stress with love, be patient it will pass soon.

Travel and Communication: As you know, Pluto rules passion, the crooks and the police force. News pertaining to the police will always appear during his ruling days. It is my aspiration with my students and my books, to communicate this knowledge in the future to the police academies. Pluto's impact upon our courageous police officers is lethal; and in the name of ignorance from their superiors, many suffer early and wasteful deaths. In the future, when "ridicule" is cast aside, Police Executives will be forewarning their officers to the influence of the Plutonic impact upon their dangerous careers. Locating the destructive power of Pluto transpiring in the natal profile of a potential murderer can be identified with Astro-Psychology. Knowledge is power and there is no room for ignorance especially with the police force.

Environment: Pluto will induce drama and could disturb the earth's belly, producing a bad earthquake. As usual with Pluto in charge, be ready for many interesting secrets to surface and remember to keep quiet.

Famous Personalities: A famous personality will be called to God and many will miss the soul. A powerful reminder of our own mortality is ahead, this is the signature of Pluto's regular jurisdiction upon our lives. Note when a soul is born with a Dragon's Tail in Aries as was Mr. Kennedy, 39, son of the late U.S. Sen. Robert Kennedy. That soul is prone to experience a violent death. He died New Year's Eve (1997) in a skiing accident in Aspen, Colorado. You may order my book, "Power of the Dragon," from www.drturi.com to find the location of your own natal dragon.

Events: Under Pluto's explosive power, in 1988, at American Pacific's plant near Henderson -- Pacific Engineering & Production Co. of Nevada, or PEPCON -- a series of colossal explosions left two dead, injured 300 and caused $75 million in damage. Clark County fire investigators blamed the blasts on welders, cramped storage, messy conditions and wind. Company officials disputed those contentions. Shortly after that, the company moved the operation to Iron County, Utah, and renamed it Western Electrochemical. Pluto stirs man's animal tendencies and causes the infinite forces of good and evil to constantly tease each other. Don't trust anyone and be aware of the police. Fact: Controlled by Pluto, the planet of death and drama, the highest suicide rate is to be found within the police force. Expect this type of news soon: BALTIMORE (AP) -- Five women were found dead of multiple gunshot wounds in a home Sunday night, and police were searching for four suspects, officers said. The shootings capped an unusually violent weekend in the city, where 10 people were killed since Friday. FORT GIBSON, Oklahoma (CNN) -- A 13-year-old boy firing a 9 mm semiautomatic handgun wounded four classmates at their rural Oklahoma middle school before being subdued and taken into custody, police said. The victims were taken to hospitals; their injuries did not appear life threatening

Shopping: Only second-hand shopping or well advertised sales will give you the best deals in town. Better wait for the New Moon for super deals. Do not invest in dangerous toys for your children; with Pluto signature, they could get hurt. Give old toys to unfortunate children.

※

New Moon in Sagittarius — December 9, 2007: In Jupiter, the planet of codification of thought, rules this sign. Affairs of religions, foreigners and the formation of new laws will be on the rise. Expect news coming from foreign powers, forcing many governments to take secret drastic actions. This trend will play an important part on the religious front and could directly affect the Pope. Many people and countries may be forced to realize the hard lessons of religious freedom as dramatic changes are taking place. The emphasis is on abortion rights, foreigners, and religious values. The potential for rebirth is from newfound wisdom to perform and live accordingly with the rest of the world. Don't fall for the apocalyptic preachers' religious poisoning.

Lunation impact on all signs:

Aries - A far away trip or a foreigner will make you happy. Get published.

Taurus - Great financial news and rewards in investments. Study metaphysics.

Gemini - Project yourself to the world with a new partner. Learn photography.

Cancer - A secret will come to light, your siblings needs you. Communications improve.

Leo - An important wish will come true, a new friend brings luck. Run your show.

Virgo - Great opportunities for your career, you deserve it. Learn computers and write.

Libra - A study or a trip will bring you joy. You're a philosopher and a teacher.

Scorpio - A legacy or a business deal will pay off. You're a light worker, power to you.

Sagittarius - The business of a loving partner has good things for you. Don't be too tight.

Capricorn - Great opportunity and better service to the world. Master Astro-Psychology.

Aquarius - Love and light to you, write, talk, shine, be original. Learn metaphysics.

Pisces - An opportunity to do well from home or relocation soon. Be a teacher.

SUN., MON., TUES., WED. – DECEMBER 9, 10, 11, 12:
RULERS — Jupiter (religion) and Saturn (government):

Work, Career and Business: With the New Moon upon us opportunities to rebuild the damage inflicted by Pluto will be offered to the valiant. With Jupiter's protection, the finances, resources and expertise of others could provide support this week. All sorts of financial deals will be attainable, especially where foreigners are involved. Be ready for a restructure of a portion of your business, these changes could also affect your emotional life. Take chances, sign contracts, travel and promote your career while the Moon is on your side.

Partnerships: Saturn's gloomy attitude may make you feel insecure about life in general. Don't taint those close to you; put a smile on your face; caution in relationships is advised. You may find yourself forced to help someone; if you feel like saying no, don't feel guilty about it. This publication's purpose is to help and guide those who need help on a daily basis. If your partner becomes too heavy, mention my work and release yourself from guilt. Work towards your heart's desire with a practical mind. Saturn wants you to go and find all the answers yourself. Don't be too concerned about doing everything perfectly; you can only do your best. Use or learn computers to make life and your business easier and don't be afraid of technology.

Family and Friends: Share your feelings about a difficult situation with a family member or a trusted friend, but don't be pessimistic about the end. With benevolent Jupiter, a trip close to nature with the children will regenerate your soul. A trip to your local church on Sunday could give you a sense of faith in the creator and in yourself. Some juveniles may ask questions about life. Help them to think differently; inform them outside of religion and take chances on their spiritual natures, they will love it.

Love Affairs: Be particularly attentive to a fascinating foreigner. Being cautious in relationships is always a good thing; be sure to take your time before committing your heart. Expect a significant development with marriage or divorce unfolding with some karmic relationships close to you. If you happen to suffer one at the present time, don't stress yourself and be patient. Sooner or later it will all be gone and you will find a well-deserved peace of mind and true love with a suitable partner. If you were born under the sign of Leo, a Sagittarius or an Aries will be attracted to you.

Travel and Communication: This is the perfect time to make travel arrangements if you have to be away from home after the Full Moon. Be easy on a person who may be quite troublesome; use diplomacy, or the situation could turn nasty, even against you. Your presence may be requested for a gathering, and a wise person may play an important part in a critical decision. Enjoy the road and keep your eyes on the signs.

Environment: Sad news may come from foreign countries experiencing problems with terrorism and emigrations. With benevolent Jupiter with us these days, some "saviors" may become active in respect to their religious convictions or for nature.

Famous Personalities: Your management or some important government figures will impose some new rules. An old person will make his voice heard to the younger generation. The message will bring a new beginning for the children's education.

Events: Saturn always involves Government news such as the terrible explosion directed at an administrative building on April 19th, 1995. — Under the same celestial energy, in Oklahoma City, an explosion felt for miles around rocked a downtown federal office building, blowing away an entire 9-story wall and killing scores of people. Let's hope nothing of this sort will ever happen again. On the negative side, this lunation may activate destructive news pertaining to fanatic foreign groups.

Shopping: Use this trend to find great bargains just before the festivities or in garage sales. You could also enjoy shopping at your local antique store with an exuberant friend. If you have an Indian guide, invest in their works of art to channel spiritual information. Pets bought now will live long and happy lives and give you tons of love.

※

THU., FRI., SAT., SUN., MON. — DECEMBER 13, 14, 15, 16, 17: RULERS — RULERS: Neptune (religion) and Uranus (shocking news):

Work, Career and Business: The New Moon is here, making many of us much happier. Try to accomplish as much as you can, even though you may find it hard to concentrate on the tasks. It's time to socialize with co-workers and get to know them better. We are already half way through the month, and accompanying it, is a note of serious change and interesting developments. A business trip or an invitation may lead you to many good contacts. You will have time to play and mix business with pleasure.

Family and Friends: Many will be enjoying foreign places and the different cultures of these people. Expect brothers and sisters to contact you from afar and let yourself be immersed in the great Holiday season. Children are getting very excited and will be anticipating the upcoming festivities. With only a few weeks before Xmas, your friends and the family circle will be extremely busy making plans and at the same time enjoying the best of what life has to offer. People will plan to attend church services, responding to Neptune's religious power. Many of God's houses will be crowded and you should double check on your plans to get there on time. Combined with the New Moon and Neptune, the Christmas spirit of love and preparations will receive its full support from the stars. Many will participate in volunteer work to provide love and help to the needy.

Love Affairs: As usual with amazing Uranus in charge, avoid impatience and be ready for some surprises. With Neptune here, control your emotions and your imagination. The Moon is Waxing (positive), so any surprises ahead of you should be of a positive nature. Many will find love and this new relationship may lead you to a rewarding future.

Travel and Communication: Your telephone and your mail will bring you all sorts of news and invitations. The lucky ones will enjoy a trip close to those they love. Expect news from a brother or sister; get in touch with some of your friends for a good chat. Remember Neptune is also part of the early festivities and you must not overindulge in eating or drinking. A quiet walk by the sea will take your spirit high and stimulate your faith. Many lonely people will feel the depressing power of Neptune and some older souls may call on you for help. With Neptune's stressful imagination, many evangelists will stubbornly spew the gospel, and "Repent, Hell, and the End-Times" will be their favorite topics. The only change ahead is in our consciousness and in new faith; based upon the understanding of God's celestial tools.

Environment: The weather could prove to be very difficult in some places. Be especially aware around water. Tornadoes, hurricanes, typhoons, and volcanic activity is anticipated, especially close to the last Supernova window.

Famous Personalities: A fantastic time is to be expected by the efforts of many gifted artists to bring love, joy, and faith to the children of the world.

Events: Neptune may bring disturbing news from religion or the Middle East. Let's hope the New Moon will stop anything drastic from happening such as blowing up a church or synagogue somewhere killing innocent people. Some abortion activists will bring their convictions and trouble with them. Explosions and surprises are high on the list, watch for suspicious and suicidal people around you. The children could also be adversely affected, watch them closely.

Shopping: Those days belong to the children and all toys bought now will bring great joy to them on Xmas morning. You may now also invest safely in anything that can be used around water or any survival gear.

Jupiter enters Capricorn - December 18: Jupiter is higher education while Saturn is structure, so the opportunity is given to learn and teach all the affairs of public standing and career. These individuals tend to stay within the accepted norms of education and will reject any non-traditional proof. The real danger for mental snobbery is produced by a very strong desire for a position of power via traditional education. Capricorn rules engineering, architecture and all governmental and political endeavors, while Jupiter rules exploration. Hence, it induces traveling in the chosen careers. The soul will excel in foreign lands and with foreigners on many governmental projects that will force the soul to open up to a less rigid view of life. Honor and respect is deeply needed with this position and produces physicians, attorneys, city board of directors, political figures, etc. In some extreme cases, the soul's incapable to enter the spiritual or intuitive domain and appears to be very limited and judgmental to the more advanced souls. In reality, they are as stupid as they think they are educated and this is not to be confused with intelligence. Their reluctance to expand the mind in spiritual matters is simply a reflection of the deep-seated fear of ridicule in the eyes of society. With a more advanced soul, the ultimate structural power of Jupiter in Capricorn is applied to teach unconditionally, all areas of the human experience.

※

Mercury enters Capricorn - December 20: The souls born now are blessed with a scientific mind. They are the masters of practical detection and will excel in mathematics work, astronomy, geology, mechanics, computing and any science requiring an extreme attention to details. A top position involving the rational thought process, will lead the soul towards political activity and ability with architectural endeavors. By birth, many of them will miss the natural ingredient to assimilate the essence of any spiritual matter or enter into the intuitional domain of metaphysicians (or astrology). Fortunately, later on they will not only be able to see the trees, but the entire forest.

※

TUE., WED., THU., FRI. — DECEMBER 18, 19, 20, 21:
RULERS — Mars (action) Mercury (sales) and Venus (presents):

Work, Career and business: With the New Moon still here, don't miss opportunities that could be used to improve your business endeavors. The feeling of Xmas will make the general attitude positive and this trend will strengthen your chances of success in the near future. Trust your ability to communicate with Mercury and follow your intuition. The next few days will be vital for launching your business, and Venus' lucky touch will bring additional developments. Use the remaining positive days to maximize your promotions for business.

Partnerships: This timing is perfect for many to participate in all the Xmas festivities. But remember, Mars is around so you should use his strength instead of impatience when shopping. The future promises to bring encouraging results for next year's interviews, employment applications, promotions and other job opportunities. This week is a pivotal turning point for a key relationship. As always consider the long-term implications and respectability of the offer before making up your mind.

Family and friends: With Xmas approaching and with the "Lord" of communication, Mercury in charge these days, expect your telephone to be busy. Everybody will have something to share with you. Use Venus' loving touch in your verbal exchanges and avoid Mars' invective remarks towards an unlucky friend. Don't be shy and pass on your message. Be confident and direct in your approach; your impact on others will surprise you. Enjoy those days with the children but Mars will make them restless.

Love affairs: Currently, the New Moon and kind-hearted touch of Venus are upon us, and you will treat someone you truly love with your best intentions. The timing is perfect to discover what it is you can offer your loved ones. Early gatherings and great times are ahead. With them, your social life and romance is up; a trip is on the way for some. If you were born in June a Sagittarius, a Libra or an Aquarius may fall for you.

Travel and Communication: Anything related to Xmas and general communication will go particularly well and progress is imminent. This week promises to be worthwhile. For the more creative souls, your writing skills will improve dramatically. Under Mercury and Venus' auspices, especially in time of a New Moon, great gifts can be found. A trip to Vegas will pay off for some. Don't let Mars make you impatient or accident-prone on the road and be patient.

Environment: Let's hope that Mars' destructive temper will not produce tornadoes, explosions, high winds or flooding.

Famous personalities: Be ready for some good news about famous people's creativity, or great Xmas projects to come to the light.

Events: Do your shopping early; don't get caught in the madness. Remember Mars is around; don't take any chances with confrontations or the police. A positive attitude and diplomacy will keep you out of trouble. Impending breakthroughs with medicine or science is expected soon.

Shopping: The kids rule; Xmas is dedicated to them, to love, to joy and religious faith. This is a great time to buy interesting books, and electronics for your business. As Mercury rules transportation it would be a good idea for you to take care of your wheels or shop for a new car. Toys bought for kids now will bring great happiness later.

Full Moon — December 24, 2007 in Cancer: The Full Moon will mature in the loving family oriented sign of Cancer on Christmas Eve, so expect the US security to be touched directly and the dramatic impact will affect many families in the long run. Promote and appreciate the effects of co-operation, discipline and respect, so that you place high priority on working thru difficulties without alienating others. Expect important beginning or ending phases of your life, as some serious career or personal developments could take place that may represent a very important part of your destiny. Some will be starting new jobs and others will drop them, including business relationships. Promotion or deception; whichever happens to you (or others) will mark an important part of your life. Have faith in the future and be ready to offer a supportive shoulder to the victims. Nature will undoubtedly do some nasty tricks in some states promoting bad weather or earthquakes. The government will have to take serious steps to keep peace in some parts of the world. Disturbing news about dramatic change is ahead in the news; also involving possibility of serious accidents is on its way. Many people will find themselves having to react quickly to avoid danger. The impact of these events will bring on a form of transition that's needed to survive.

Lunation impact on all signs:

Aries – Relocation ahead and changes in your home life and career soon, accept those changes.

Taurus – An important letter or disturbing news. Uses your stamina and have faith..

Gemini – You will be forced to spend money for home or family. You will be glad you did it.

Cancer – Serious business or emotional stress is ahead of you. Changes are needed in your life.

Leo – Let go of your past, move on. Time to look for that position you deserve. Be ready.

Virgo –You will need to go out with your friends. New ones will bring you love and wishes soon.

Libra –Great career changes are ahead of you. You might have to go and look somewhere else.

Scorpio- A trip or someone far away will need you. Big business must be done.

Sagittarius – A legacy or a present is in store for you. Give if you want to receive some money.

Capricorn –You will have to work on yourself and your partner soon.

Aquarius –A great new opportunity to serve the world will be offered to you. Move on.

Pisces – A chance to find new love is offered to you, move on. A friend will need your help.

✳

SAT., SUN., MON., TUE. - DECEMBER 22, 23, 24, 25:
RULERS — Venus (caring), Mercury (contact) and the Moon (variation).

Work, Career and Business: Just before Xmas, you may find it difficult to concentrate on your duties. Your mind will wander about the anticipated good times ahead. Deserving hard-working souls will benefit with well-earned bonuses or new opportunities to promote their careers. Mercury will make you think fast, and action will be everywhere. Be aware of the Full Moon's tension and be ready to change your schedule. Wait for the next new Moon to face important deals.

Partnerships: Some of the people you know will have to move away, or you yourself may decide to relocate to a better place within the next few days. Expect the beginning or ending of important phases of your life and others' too. Venus will endorse many gatherings with colleagues you have not seen for a long time. Be ready to control your emotions during the Full Moon.

Family and Friends: Expect a brother or a sister to pleasantly surprise you. A friend might show up uninvited and thus affect some of your plans. You may receive an invitation to socialize with some faraway friends or family members; use this opportunity to grow closer to them if you can. Luckily for all of us, this Christmas season will take place in a positive sign (Aquarius) and we are due for some surprises and extraordinary events to celebrate. Against all odds, endure patiently this Supernova window, and enjoy these good old days. Don't forget that when the Moon becomes full and is waning, things may not go your way. A family member needs your advice. Be willing to consider the issue from his point of view; but avoid emotional involvement or forcing your opinion. Much time will be spent around the children enjoying their Christmas trees. Prepare to enjoy the warmth and the good food of your friends and your family.

Love Affairs: Expect much progress if you are looking for that special person. Some of the people from your past may also become weighty; stand for yourself without guilt. Friends will bring good memories; have fun but don't get caught up in the nostalgia. If you are a fire or water sign many will try to steal your heart. Have fun, but don't make any commitment if the person in question was met for the first time after the Full Moon.

Travel and Communication: You will have to run like mad to keep up with all the things you must accomplish. You will stay busy with all this activity and come in contact with interesting people. Combined with the Full Moon trend and a Supernova window expect all sorts of delays, forcing you to think twice as fast. Slow down; be cautious and prudent in your driving, too. Watch for crazy drivers around the city; they might not have read "Moon Power," so don't let them hurt you (or your car). Many will fly to faraway places early and will get caught in bad weather or find themselves stuck in congested airports. Keep in mind that Mercury may decide to confuse some electronics and bring chaos. Chain-reaction accidents are very high on the list; be careful out there.

Environment: Expect surprises and explosions soon. Be aware of fire and keep an eye on the children. Chances are that nature will go berserk soon, so you don't want to be a victim. She may demonstrate her power with shocking weather. Thousands of people may be forced to relocate, fleeing disasters, flooding or bad earthquakes.

Famous Personalities: A famous person (or his child) will make dramatic news. Expect news about famous or infamous people who have made history. The past will turn alive for a while.

Events: After the Full Moon, electronics may suffer or fail to function properly. This could produce another dramatic air crash. Not a time to take any risks in the air, unless you made reservations during a waxing trend. Expect the beginning or ending of an important portion of your (and other) lives.

Shopping: Use what's left of the New Moon to spend money on expensive gifts. You can still find good deals on big-ticket items by comparison shopping. If you decide to visit Las Vegas' casinos after the Full Moon, you may encounter stress but you could get lucky. Yes, someone will hit the jackpot in a waning Moon in Vegas, but the money will be spent on paying bills or tax and little will be left. Better make all your important plans after the next New Moon for your own sake. Consider offering *Starguide* to your loved ones for Christmas. It is affordable, valuable, and because it works for you, it will also work for them. They will probably love you for shedding some light of the universe upon their lives. Go to www.drturi.com to order your E-book or hard copy of *"Moon Power"*.

December 25, 2007 - Happy Holidays to all of my readers! Regardless, of what you had to go through in 2007 keep a positive attitude; 2008 has so much more to offer. Think of offering genuine guidance to your loved ones, visit my site www.drturi.com and let me take care of your future, you will be happy you did! Help me to pass on my important message to the world by helping us to set up a crash course in your area. Call the office (602) 957-1617 and get a super deal for yourself.
Good luck to all of you--
Dr. Turi

December 30, 2007 — Venus enters Sagittarius: With the planet of love in the independent sign of Sagittarius; an opportunity to find love with a beautiful stranger will be given to you. This trend will allow many souls to find philosophically oriented partners and will share the pleasures of traveling physically and mentally all over the world. Some lucky souls will be given enjoyable opportunities and they may end up with memorable moments to cherish for the rest of their lives. If Venus is badly affected, the soul will suffer many disturbing relationships with foreigners or loose a lot of money gambling. Souls born now will travel the world in their lifetimes and be given the opportunity to experience love and caring for animals, thus much joy is to be experienced. Blessed with such an intellectual nature, Venus in Sagittarius provides opportunity to love with mind and body. There is a need for freedom with this position and some will have to learn commitment. They will be attracted to beautiful, intellectually stimulating partners and will be inclined to marry foreigners.

✳

December 31, 2007 – Mars enters Gemini: This sign is ruled by the fastest planet orbiting around the Sun, Mercury. With dangerous Mars there, you are strongly advised to slow down for a while, if you want to keep your car and your life. Much of your desire for communication will be enhanced, but don't let yourself fall for verbal challenges. During this trend, people will have a bit of a problem listening and will display quite a lot of impatience. Some others will take things personally, so use "savoir faire" in all of your dealings. Souls born with this celestial signature could pursue a racing career or educate themselves to become fine attorneys. When well supported by other planets, a gift in communication and writing is usually present.

✳

WED., THU., FRI., SAT., SUN., MON. — DECEMBER 26, 27, 28, 29, 30, 31:
RULERS — The Sun (children/love), Mercury (traveling) and Venus (love).

Work, Career and Business: Do not expect much progress these days. The Waning Moon (negative) will obstruct any business venture. Don't take yourself too seriously and set a meeting with co-workers to discuss what could be done to improve the business. Why not forget about your responsibility for a while and smell the roses like everyone else? Enjoy a party after work and let your real feelings show.

Partnerships: Old and new friends will be happy to talk and will exchange ideas, hopes and wishes with you. The holiday season is getting close; make sure you don't get stuck at the last minute with heavy shopping yet to do. Be aware of what your partner needs and offer him another surprise for the upcoming New Year. A plan to travel close to the water will make some souls very happy.

Family and Friends: Don't be gloomy, and learn to forget whatever dramatic experiences you have had to experience lately. We are on this earth to do a specific work we set for ourselves. Take care of the young, life goes so fast; let them fully enjoy your love and your care. Don't let the Waning Moon bother you with guilt or your difficult past. Do something special that will help you fight the melancholic mood. The children have plenty of ideas; listen to them and enjoy life. Friends may request your help in some areas.

Love Affairs: With the Sun (love) in charge, an element of surprise is around. As usual in time of a Waning Moon (negative), don't expect long-lasting love if you fall for someone new. If you are an Aquarius, a Gemini or a Leo needs your spiritual help.

Travel and Communication: The police will begin to plan for the upcoming holidays and may stop you if you drive foolishly. Drinking heavily could disturb your plans for the next year and should be completely out of the question. You do not want to ruin your or someone else's family because of depression (or good time). Be safe and if you drink with friends at a gathering, take a cab home.

Environment: Hopefully lovely Venus and the magnanimous Sun will stop any dramas imposed by the Waning Moon. The weather will be difficult; stay clear of lightning. An explosion or a fire could hurt some children; watch over them carefully.

Famous Personalities: Many famous people will shine, helping those born with difficult karmic stars. Great shows will be offered to the public. Don't fall for the religious promoters of the Apocalypse; they are after your money and can only survive with your lack of awareness and your fears.

Events: We are still in a waning period and some disasters will be happening; be aware and careful in all you do.

Shopping: Use the light of the Sun to regenerate your spirit. Invest in your favorite spiritual healer, psychic or astrologer; this will do you good. Visit your future with faith. Enjoy the fast-approaching festivities. Be aware; those three kings who followed a star to Bethlehem, the birthplace of Jesus Christ, were astrologers! You can only follow a star when it is plotted in a map. Also remember that in the old days there were no astronomers, only astrologers! Wait for the Next New Moon to launch important matters.

The greatness of the Universe is unknown, but the magnetic forces that direct and move all the planets in our galaxy are known; this Divine source of power can be used to guide and bring man a life filled with happiness, peace and harmony.
— Dr. Turi

Closing Thoughts

Dear Clients and Friends:

I would like to sincerely thank you for your patronage and wish all of you a very successful New Year. It has been my privilege, with "Moon Power" to bring more cosmic consciousness to your life. Do you need any of my services or do you have a product or a service to offer my large clientele worldwide? If so visit www.drturi.com or call the offices at (602) 265-7667.

You may also find more information on my services and videos, and download my books at www.drturi.com. Being in the right place at the right time has a lot to do with your progress in terms of opportunities. My work will be a major contribution to success in your life.

Also, please help me promote the cosmic consciousness of everyone you care about. I need both your spiritual and financial help to build many Astro-Psychology schools for the children of tomorrow. Understand the importance of my mission and be a part of it in the unfolding world karma. Please help me, and invest in the future by promoting the true knowledge of the stars. Your contributions will allow me to spend more time on the air, writing, educating, and publishing my work to those in need. For centuries many resources have been used to discredit the stars and to advance wasteful and dangerous religious dogmas. Times have changed and the stars above do impose a "new consciousness" for mankind. Be a promoter of light and invest in the true light. The children of tomorrow need to gain cosmic consciousness and use the stars to live more productive and safer lives. Please communicate my work and help those in need to find guidance, comfort, direction and assistance in the celestial order. I hope in "Moon Power," you will find the pathway to the stars and the realization of God's Ultimate Will throughout the Universe. Walk in peace with your new knowledge of the stars and may God bless you all!

Dr. Turi

And God said, Let there be lights in the firmament of the heaven to divide the day from the night; and let them be for signs, and for seasons, and for days, and years:

And let them be for lights in the firmament of the heaven to give light upon the earth: and it was so.

And God made two great lights; the greater light to rule the day, and the lesser light to rule the night: he made the stars also.

And God set them in the firmament of the heaven to give light upon the earth,

And to rule over the day and over the night, and to divide the light from the darkness: and God saw that it was good. (Old Testament: Genesis 1:14-18)

A revival of Nostradamus Divine Astrology

I am not only offering you the golden keys of the Universe but a rewarding blissful career that will stay with you beyond your retirement days. With the entrance of the Dragon in Pisces more and more people are doing serious soul searching and using Nostradamus' methodology through Astropsychology you will offer them your most accurate guidance. Sedona is the ideal location to master Neptune's power productively! Meet with highly spiritual students and develop a relationship that will last a lifetime. Be a part of the Divine and further the wisdom of the Stars to the children of the future.

I can guarantee you that my Astropsychology course will change your perception of life and your entire destiny beyond your wildest expectations.

Learn the energies of the zodiac on this course and you will have a working understanding of the universal mind. No complicated math. This is a 'hands on' approach to astrology in which you will instantly begin to recognize the forces at work around you in your daily life and the world at large. There is a Diploma in Astropsychology to be awarded if the 75% pass mark is achieved.

You will be taught the basics of the great Seer, Nostradamus' method. With this foundation, you will also be able to see the world in a new light and be able to do accurate predictions. You will watch the moon in it's many fluctuations and be able to understand world events and why they take place when they do. It is the groundwork for all additional astrological methods. Dr. Turi will explain all the planets and their signs and symbols. He will show the results when certain planets fall in the different signs. One of the major techniques of Astropsychology is the understanding of the Dragon, which emphasizes the past life of the person and the opportunities offered in this lifetime. Also unique to this method is the housing system that is used.

Dr. Turi will lecture on the Dragon's incredible power involving its position by house and sign and its dramatic impact upon the human experience. He will also teach the medical aspect of Astrology and will reveal Universal Predictions for the current year. All along Dr. Turi will educate the students on the power of the subconscious and teach incredible Universal Laws. A 16X7 feet celestial artwork painting will be used at the workshop to illustrate. Once aware of the Dragon's phenomenal impact, one's power within increases dramatically. Your awareness and respect of your natal Dragon in your chart becomes a major contribution to establish your emotional, financial and spiritual stability.

Dr. Turi offers a practical and "street-wise" approach to astrology. He uses colorful stories and humor to illustrate the different energies, which makes them easy to remember. With the knowledge you will obtain in his class, you will be able to, within a few minutes of meeting a person and finding their month of birth, understand a great deal about that person's outlook to life. This can be very handy is many situations and can give you an upper edge in dealing with others, as you will have an instant understanding of their psychology. Dr. Turi class comes with a complete set of printed course material for future reference. Your decision to participate will bring a new "energy" to your emotional life and will attract a great career and many worthwhile opportunities. You are strongly advised to act fast as Dr. Turi is much too busy to teach his true powers soon again. We can only assure you to be directly touched by an Angelic Divine force and to completely and entirely change your life for the better. Call us anytime for information at (602) 265-7667 or email us at dr.turi@cox.net.

It is imperative that you understand that my teachings ARE UNIQUE.

1. This is **NOT** a course in Astrology, but Astropsychology, and well ahead of any and all forms of ordinary Astrology. Take it live or by mail for $550 - $850 or $1050.

Services

2. This course is **FREE** of mathematical jargon found in Modern astrology, and loaded with powerful symbolisms.

3. This course is **BASED** on Nostradamus' 16th century Divine Astrology methodology and the great Seer did not use a watch or a computer 500 years ago.

4. This course has **NOTHING** to do with all that you know, perceived, learned or taught about any forms of Astrology. This is the **MOTHER** of **ALL** Astrology.

5. This course is **HIGHLY** spiritual and involves metaphors and Chinese Astrology. The more spiritually inclined you are the better it will be for you to bring forth your cosmic consciousness.

6. This course is your **TICKET** to a new life, a new career and a brand new perception of your own reality.

7. This course will **GROUND** you, lead you and open the magical doors to the Divine Celestial Mechanics.

8. This course will be **USED** for the rest of your life in ALL areas of your life. You can use the knowledge for your family; guide your children, investments, traveling, planning and even to save your own life.

9. Any live tuition involves a huge **CELESTIAL** artwork that will help you to "fly" through the Universal Mind easily and build a reflex to perceive the Universal Mechanics in action. Visual and printed material are designed and carefully designed to make sure you graduate at the end of the course.

10. This course involves a **TREMENDEOUS** amount of unique teachings and vital information on the working of your subconscious.

11. This course involves also the teaching of the **ASTRO-TAROT** for those born natural psychics. Combining Astropsychology and the Tarot is simply phenomenal, and leaves nothing hidden about a person past or future.

12. Check my **UNARGUABLE** set of well-documented predictions on my site and think, why you would learn from anyone else?

13. Each one of my course is more advanced I will

also **INTENSIVELY** teach Nostradamus' Cabalistic Healing and do a slide presentation on the prophet

Note: This course is **NOT** a normal Astrology course you have taken with any other astrologers in the past or deal with Astrology as you know, read or practice. The worse thing that you can do for yourself is to do the **VERY SAME THINGS EVERY DAY** and expect different results. Call me ASAP at 602-265-7667 or email me at dr.turi@cox.net. **DO SOMETHING about it NOW.**

STARTHEME PUBLICATIONS
Publishers of True Celestial Knowledge and AstroPsychology
****

Dr. Turi
Astrological Services
Readings
Published by Startheme Publications
4411 N. 23rd St
Phoenix, AZ 85016
Tel: 602-265-7667 *Fax* 602-957-1678
E-mail: dr.turi@cox.net - Website – www.drturi.com

Dr. Turi's TOP SERVICE Satisfaction guaranteed -

Taped Full Life Reading
(Know all about your true mission and your fate in this world) 1-90MN audio tape and about 15 to 30 pages of printed materials, by mail or in person
Price: $300 plus $10 S&H

Dr. Turi's Platinum Package
1-90MN audio tape and about 15 to 30 pages of printed materials (Full Life and Progressive Reading)
- Moon Power 2007 (eBook)
- And God Created the Stars (eBook)
- I Know All About You (eBook)
- The Power of the Dragon (eBook)
- Fate of the World # 1 & 2 (2 DVD set)
- Divine Astrology and Astropsychology (2 DVD set)
- The Power Of Your Subconscious (2 CD set)
- 2 other 90 mn tape 2 of my best radio shows

- Career Path - Child Characterlogy and 12 months transits
Price: $799.00 plus $10 S&H

Taped Rising Reading
Many people are used to Modern Astrology methodology and this 90 mn taped reading is strongly recommended if you had both a Full Life and a Progressive Reading with Dr. Turi.
Price: $200 plus $10 S&H

Taped Progressive Reading
(Know all about the changes affecting your life right now and for the next 4 years)
1-60MN audio tape and 30 pages of printed materials, by mail or in person
Price $200 plus $10 S&H

Lucky Dragon Windows Dates
(Use with Universal Dragon dates)
Ride your Dragon's Head, get your best dates for the next twelve months. Be at the right time at the right place with the right people. Use them to travel, invest and promote your life.
Price: $100 (internet service only)

Cabalistic Healing and Deep Soul Cleansing
Find your health back, your inner peace, lose weight regain self-esteem, love and happiness and clear off all negative energy around you. Let me free your body mind and spirit of all blockages and be born again. Please call 602-265-7667 for your appointment - On location Phoenix AZ Healing Room. Please email DR.TURI@COX.NET AND REQUEST the Cabalistic form for you to fill up and Call 602-265-7667 to secure your appointment.
Price $1,000 for 3-4 hour session

Taped Comparison Chart
(Know all about your love or business relationship)
1-90MN audio tape and 30 pages printed materials, by mail or in person. Make sure to give us the name and information of the second person.
Price $400 ($200 per person) plus $10 S&H

SUPER Package Deal
90 mn taped Full Life Reading - (date and place of birth needed)- 12 months Astrological transits, another 90 MN Hypnotherapy tape, another 90 MN tape of George Noory and Dr. Turi Radio

show (Prediction of Katrina and Dr. Turi's 4 incredible UFO experiences).
Price $350 plus $10 S&H

Astro-Carto-Graphy
Find the best places for happiness in the world, don't relocate without it - 35 pages of printed materials, 5 maps (the World/USA/Europe/Asia and Australia) with Dr. Turi's translation, by mail or in person
Price $200 plus $10 S&H

Taped Hypnotherapy and DVD "Healing With Love"
Accomplish miracles by using the subtle forces of your Subconscious
1-90MN audio tape & DVD, by mail or in person
Price: $50 plus $10 S&H

Taped Children Characterology - Astropsychology used
(A must for any troubled children)
1-90MN audio tape and 30 pages of printed materials, by mail or in person
Price: $165 S&H included

Full Personal Report - 25/30 pages EMAIL
(Find all the strengths and weaknesses in your relationship)
Price: $25.95 (Internet)

Personal Yearly Transit Forecast 30/35 pages EMAIL
(What the Dragon and the stars have in store for you every day of the year)
Price: $25.95 (Internet)

Compatibility Chart 25/30 pages EMAIL
(Find out all about the good and bad areas of your relationship)
Price: $35.95 (Internet)

Career Path Interpretation 25/30 pages EMAIL
(What your best chances for wealth and happiness in a successful career)
Price: $35.95 (Internet)

New ➥**Astropsychology Album Course** by mail
(Master the secrets of the Universe)

Audio Tapes - TWO DVD'S (Cosmic Consciousness / Dragon Prophecies) - INTERNET FILES - EXAMS - THREE BOOKS "And God Created The Stars" "The Power Of The Dragon" and "I know All About You" and "Introduction to Hypnotherapy". Price: $850 - S&H included

Cabalistic Healing (filmed in Tucson, AZ) - DVD
This show is a live demonstration of Cabalistic Healing on two patients, along with an explanation of the power of the subconscious and healing values of stones and natural crystals. Dr. Turi also uses the Cabalistic tarot, and makes predictions for the Middle East and 2012.
If you are into natural healing this is your DVD.
Price: $19.

Fate of the World # 1 & 2 - DVD
This is Dr. Turi's lecture and television program, investigating the future of this planet and its inhabitants following the year 2012. An explanation of the dying and deceptive Age of Pisces giving its place for the next 2000 years to the advanced Age of Aquarius, and how this will also bring about the reality of extraterrestrials and will transform the entire Middle East region. Information on nuclear deals, religions, greedy oil and pharmaceutical corporations, and much more is dealt with the usual passion and directness involving Dr. Turi's advanced teachings. Dr. Turi also emphasizes how the Dragon's Head and Tail will affect each sign of the zodiac personally. Great sound and clear DVD indeed a great production of Dr. Turi's lecture and television show with famous Coast-To-Coast radio host George Noory.
Price: $39.95 + $10 S&H (2) DVDs, (2) hours 95 + $10 S&H

Celestial Mechanics DVD
More information on the Universal Mind interacting with the human psyche. This show explain in great detail how and why

Astrology unarguably works. This DVD is for anyone interested in the Divine and offers a deeper understanding on the effects produced by the celestial order upon mankind.
Price: $19.95 + $10 S&H

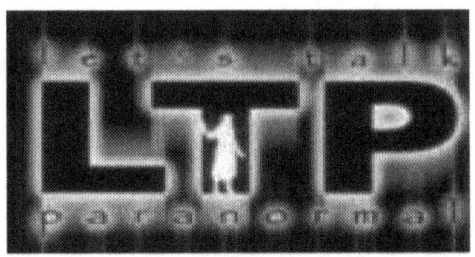

Divine Astrology and Astropsychology
DVD

Watch this incredible 2-part DVD of Dr. Turi on Let's Talk Paranormal. Dr Louis Turi is well known for the hundreds of accurate predictions that he makes. The hurricane Katrina, Rita, Elma, the Asia Tsunami, and 911 to name a few. See the "Modern day Nostradamus" at work and learn all about our relationship with the Universe. Dr. Turi educates the audience on the power of Universe and how its affect mankind's fate. World predictions and more incredible information from the Universal Mind! Enjoy those shows and bring forth your own cosmic consciousness.
2 DVDs, 2 hour presentation.
Price: $39.95 + $10 S&H

The Power Of Your Subconscious
2 CD set

These CD were produced while Dr. Turi was lecturing in England. Learn all about the incredible working and miraculous forces of your subconscious and make a good use of its creative forces to reach all your dreams. Your subconscious can and will

Services

bring you all that you really need: money, love, health and more. Take chance on those two CD and see the miracles unfold in your life.
Price: $24.95, S&H included

Dialogue with the Universal Mind with Dr. Turi DVD

Personal Dragon forecast for all, Universal predictions for the US, the Middle East and the world at large. Order this incredible DVD and see Dr. Turi channeling the stars on television.
Price: $19.95 + $10 S&H

Cosmic Consciousness - 60 MN show

DVD A perfect and full introduction to the Celestial design. Dr. Turi explains in great detail how the Universal Mind interacts with mankind and how to make the most of our celestial gifts. A very educational program in all aspects of Nostradamus' Divine Astrology as practiced by Dr. Turi
Price: $19.95 + $10 S&H

UFO Legacy - 60 MN show

DVD Since the tender age of 6 years, Dr. Turi has had encounters with extraterrestrial intelligences. Go with Dr. Turi on this incredible journey leading to four solid encounters in France and a trip in a flying saucer on August 11, 1991 in the US. See why extraordinary experiences breed incredible people that have mind-blowing UFO experiences to share. Lots of pictures in this show including X-ray of a Grey.
Price: $19.95 + $10 S&H

Healing With Love volumes 1 & 2 on DVD- Each 60 Min

Learn about Nostradamus' homeopathic methodology using all natural means. See Dr. Turi interacting and teaching the audience about the miraculous subconscious healing forces we

all possess. Learn and use this marvelous power to restore health to your body, mind and spirit contrary to what modern medicine pledges. Some of that vital information deals directly with the interaction of your subconscious and these practical teachings which can help you to heal a multitude of diseases, eliminate back problems, and unwanted weight. A must for anyone who does not trust drugs or modern medicine.
Price: $39.95 + $10 S&H

Dragon Prophecies - 60 MN show
DVD In this lively entertaining television show see Dr. Turi educating the audience on the power of the Dragon and how it will affect the world at large. Many interesting topics are approached but the focus is on predictions for the United Sates and the world at large and also for each sign of the Zodiac. This show was produced before President Bush was elected so hear the undeniable prediction and outcome of the presidential race.
Price: $19.95 + $10 S&H

2006 Dragon Predictions And Beyond - 60 MN show
DVD One of Dr. Turi's best show ever from 'The Cutting Edge' television. Be ready to hear some of the most dramatic predictions about the Middle East and so many others predicaments that will come to pass within the next two years. Jim Roger and his co-host carefully prepared all the questions. It's going to be an "Interesting Time" for all of us. As you know Dr. Turi was not shy in expressing himself in predictive astrology but he also gave the audience the option to join him through the Superconscious and mankind 's thoughts process that could alter the course of destiny.
Price: $19.95 + $10 S&H

Journey Into the Void - 60 MN show
DVD A great interview where all questions involving Dr. Turi's

methodology pertaining to the stars are approached in a logical way. The host is very rational and reflects what people who do not know Astrology think about the old science. This show is for both non-believers of Astrology, or skepticals willing to expand their minds on this interesting subject.
Price: $19.95 + $10 S&H

Astrology and Science - 60 MN show
DVD This show involves hard core scientists and psychologists. Their skepticism shows in debating the values of Astrology with the best astrologers in the the US. Dr. Turi unarguably made his point very clear that Astrology really works. See the reaction of his guests and other astrologers, and the scientist's feedback in this incredible show.
Price: $19.95 + $10 S&H

ORDER FORM FOR THOSE NOT USING CREDIT CARDS:

You must either mail this, fax or email it to Dr. Turi at the address below

Note: Hard copies of books will be sent to you via regular mail after reception of your payment. Ebooks will be sent to you via regular internet after reception of your payment. Use dr.turi@cox.net to confirm all orders.

PROCESSING INFORMATION

NAME: _____
ADDRESS: _____
CITY: _____ STATE: _____ ZIP: _____

D.O.B (month, day, year): _____ / _____ / _____ (EX: FEB. 26, 1950)
TIME OF BIRTH: _____ : _____ AM__ PM__

(Time is only needed for Astro-cartography)

PLACE OF BIRTH (City, State, Country): _____
_____

SECOND PERSON PROCESSING INFORMATION

NAME: _____
ADDRESS: _____
CITY: _____ STATE: ____ ZIP: ____
_____

D.O.B (month, day, year): _____ / _____ / _____ (EX: FEB. 26, 1950)
TIME OF BIRTH: _____ : _____ AM__ PM__
(Time is only needed for Astro-cartography)
PLACE OF BIRTH (City, State, Country): _____
_____

Credit Card Details-- Required credit card information

Total amount _____

Card number _____-_____-_____-_____

Expiration date _____-_____

Customer contact information:

Name _____

Phone number _____

Email address _____

Billing address:

Street address _____

City _____

State _____

Zip code _____

Product description: _____

MAIL YOUR ORDER AND PAYMENT PAYABLE TO:

Dr. Turi

4411 N. 23Rd St

Phoenix, AZ 85016

Tel: (602) 265-7667 - Fax (602) 265-8668

Email: Dr.turi@cox.net

Dear Prospective Star Student;

Often people ask me when I will be in their area to teach them the secret of the stars. Well let's be practical and in the process you will save precious time and a lot of money. There are many good reasons why you should take the course by mail, mostly because you do not need to be present for me to bring forth your cosmic consciousness. Taking the live course means taking off from work and flying to where I will be teaching. This is not only time consuming but very costly and often impossible for many of you. Thus I came up with the simple idea to always record my very last advanced class and make it available to students living far away or outside the US. Many of you may think, but I would rather be present at the class and I am sure I could learn faster and better.

Wrong! Again many of the questions you may have for me have already been asked by some of my smart students. Any student of the stars received my answers and you will learn much more by listening to the twelve ninety minute audio tapes in your own time. For those of you who are visual; the simple but elaborate astrological symbols in the printed material, books and videos are designed to help you to assimilate my teachings to the highest level. Taking the physical course is also much more expensive than the significant deal by mail and time is the essence for all of us. Also, if your natal Mercury (assimilation of information/ learning process) is in a slow sign, you will need much more time to assimilate the information and you can always play the tape back as many times as needed. Other advanced students are also there to give you a hand by email if needed. In the physical course, you will be left behind if you can not grasp something right away as time is the essence and mastering the Universal Mind in a few days could be stressing because it is quite a lot of study.

You can do all that in the privacy and security of your home and take all the time you need to learn at your own pace. Your exam questionnaire requires also a specific time and after a few hours that's it; you must remit the paper work for grading. At home you can take all the time you need and no one will rush you, you can also review your tapes if you are not sure of a question. The best part is that; I am constantly learning more and more as the months go by and with your help, you may be able to assist me to come to you. Note also that many of my best students want to keep up with my latest astrological information. Then in time, and with your assistance, I will be teaching in your area and you can still take the course again for a fraction of the price.

Thus you would get the famous two for one deal and you do not waste precious time. If you are serious about mastering the secret of the Universal time you do not want to waste away your inner drive and make a commitment to learn all about the divine as soon as possible. The stars naturally will induce a strong urge to do so and this is when the same stars will assist you to master the secret of the Universal clock. The quicker you start your study, the faster your new life and inner mission will take shape. Be a promoter of the future and help the children of tomorrow to live a more secure and productive life. Your contribution as a light worker will also bring an incredible karma for your next reincarnation. It an honor for me to teach you all that I know about the universal mind and point out the marvel of the stars' impact upon mankind on earth. I will also thank you for electing me to do so and lead the way to your new life and consciousness. Blessings to all --Dr. Turi

---

JOIN THE FAMILY OF STAR STUDENTS
Become a Astropsychology student

Call 602-265-7667

Services

You may read all about my courses and some of my students' feedback at the bottom of this page. You may call me personally for more information on any of the courses at (602) 265-7667.

- Live Introductory and Advanced Astropsychology Course: $1.500.00 (7 days)

- Live Introductory and Advanced Cabalistic Healing Course: $550.00 (2 days)

- Live Introductory and Advanced Astro - Tarot Course: $550.00 (2 days)

SPECIAL DEAL #1: Mail only **$1050.00** Advanced Latest Hawaii Astropsychology Course **ON 16 CD's**, Hypnotherapy, Cabalistic Healing and Astro-Tarot ~ This is the **TOP** one ~ S&H included.

SPECIAL DEAL #2: Mail only **$850.00** This is the same Advanced Latest Hawaii Astropsychology Course but it is home made on 20 - 60 mn tapes and the sound quality is **PERFECT!**, Hypnotherapy, Cabalistic Healing and Astro-Tarot ~ S&H included.

SPECIAL DEAL #3 : Mail only **$550.00** Astropsychology Course on **TAPE** - Hypnotherapy and Astro-Tarot ~ S&H included. This course is an old course but has all that you need to become a proficient Astropsychologist. This course is also home made and includes 12 - 90 MN tapes and all materials sent with any of my courses ~ S&H included.

IMPORTANT NOTE

You may order the Astropsychology course on TAPE for $550 (12 - 90 MN tapes) or the $850 course (20 - 60 MN tapes) or the LATEST Astropsychology Course (16 CD) for $1050. If you take the course on TAPE you may also qualify to take any of my live course with a serious discount. I want to help you to bring forth your own cosmic consciousness and offer you a new life and a rewarding career.

I understand also that any tuition on TAPES or CD's will provide the full album course package including 2 MORE Audio Tapes, 3 DVD (Cosmic Consciousness / Dragon Prophecies / Astrology and Science) - Internet Files - Exam of 150 questions -**3 HARD COVER Books** titled "And God Created The Stars" "The Power Of The Dragon" and "I know All About You" and also a 90 MN tape audio tape titled "Introduction to Hypnotherapy". **Email us if you need more information**

A 75% OF GOOD ANSWERS WILL QUALIFY ME AND GRADUATE ME AS AN ASTROPSYCHOLOGIST.

SOFTWARE

You may order the software anytime to start generate money from your website. (Total 7 programs 782.10 + $15 S&H) Please note that either Virtual PC or Soft Windows must be installed on your Mac to run these.

Use credit card form AND FAX TO 602- 265-8668 or send a check payable to:
Dr. Turi 4411 N. 23Rd St Phoenix, AZ 85016
~ E-Mail Dr. Turi@cox.net

PROCESSING INFORMATION

Credit Card Details-- Required credit card information
Total amount_____
Card number _____-_____-_____-_____
Expiration date _____-_____

Customer contact information:

Name_____
Email address _____

Billing address:

Street   address   _____
City_____
State_____
Zip code _____

Product description: _____

This will be one of the most rewarding experiences in your life!

TAKING THE COURSE PHYSICALLY

The celebrated French Astrologer Dr. Turi is offering a 5-day crash course in <u>YOUR CITY</u>. You will enjoy Nostradamus' 16th century Divine Astrology method and become an Astropsychologist in a single week. Master the golden key to the universe and congregate with spiritually advanced people. You will enjoy mental stimulation and meet exceptional new friends. Gain true cosmic consciousness, open your 3rd eye, and develop your celestial affiliation with infinity. Ultimately you will realize your direct relationship with God and the Universe. Start your own career, become financially independent while bringing the light to the children of tomorrow. No complicated math involved and a 98% graduation rate. Certainly the most advanced spiritual experience of your life.

****

GET THE COURSE FOR FREE!
ARE YOU PART OF A NEW AGE GROUP? DO YOU KNOW OR OWN A BOOKSTORE?

IF SO HELP US TO SET UP A LECTURE OR A COURSE IN YOUR AREA

Welcome to the Advanced Course on Astropsychology

Due to the time limit, the personal tuition is much more intense than the home study album course. There is no complicated math involved in Dr. Turi's class and the advanced or beginner students can take this course. In our live class, you will be taught the secrets of the Universal Mind, the Workings of the Subconscious, the Astro-Tarot, Astro-Carto-Graphy, Greek philosophy, Symbolism, Omens, Cabalistic candles rituals, the medical aspect of the stars, how to launch your new business get on the radio and television and so much more. You will assimilate quite a bit of information and slowly build solid cosmic consciousness. You will also refine your psychic powers and subconscious connections through the omens and symbols I will use in the class. For those of you who cannot afford or make the "live" class, you can take the initial introductory Astropsychology Course by mail. Payment options are available. This is an album of quality cassette tapes, books, videos, exams and all material needed to get started. The physical advanced Astropsychology tuition graduation ends up with a Party where other students and friends will also be invited to celebrate and welcome the new members of our star family.

Books, CD/DVD's, workbook, an exam of 150 questions are part of the advanced Astropsychology courses, while different software are also available upon your request. Those are the Personal Path Natal Interpretations, the Star Match Compatibility Interpretations, the Life Trends Transits interpretations, the Journey Interpretations, and the Career Path Interpretations. Two additional programs added are the Solar Return and child natal reports. You may use those programs immediately to generate an income from your home on your computer as you perfect your knowledge in your Astropsychology practice.

Days: Five days (includes 2 hours examination on the last day).

Examination: 150 questions (2 hours) 75% good answers to graduate.

Graduation: **Each student receives an Astropsychology Diploma, 3 Ebooks, and course materials. The taped course is offered to the entire class (optional), but each student must pay for its duplication and shipping charges if they want a copy.** Fee for 5 full day live class: $1.175.00 -

TRUE KNOWLEDGE IS PRICELESS

You must call the office at (602) 265-7667 or fax us your information at (602)265-8668 FOR YOUR SAFE CREDIT CARD TRANSACTION. **Graduation upon 75% of good answers.**

Software is available and is separate from the class fees

You may start with the discounted **basic program for $200**. The 10% discount price applies for the complete set of those **five** professional (cd's/disks) programs, which is **$ 602.10**, or add $180 more for the two new programs if interested. (Total **7** programs **782.10 + $15 S&H**) Please note that either Virtual PC or Soft Windows must be installed on your Mac to run these. The children of tomorrow will be able to regenerate and find in your newfound knowledge the golden keys of what it means to be human and attain peace of mind.

If you decide to take the Astropsychology class physically you need to confirm with us ASAP mailto: Dr.Turi@cox.net and send your payment to reserve a seat for you. Paid in full - Credit card or check accepted.

Payment options are available: We will work with you and get you started with the **DEAL Advanced Astropsychology Course #1 ONLY** with your fist down payment. Call (602) 265-7667 for information.

Double deal: When two people husband/wife - boyfriend/girlfriend attend the physical Advanced course together the second person's tuition is free. A small fee of $150 is required by the second person for the provided materials or books. **Previous students:** Those prices do not apply for previous students; if you already took the $850.00 deal course you can take the physical advanced Astropsychology Course for a small fee.

"Simply magical and extraordinarily rewarding" that's what students said about Dr. Turi's teachings!

Super deal: Bring any new student who pays the full price, and make $100.00 for each. Someone you know may dream of learning the secret of the Universal Mind, bring him/her with you and make some cash.

This will be the experience of your life; you will build a solid cosmic consciousness and congregate with highly spiritual people. Be there! ----Dr. Turi

<u>**Double deal:**</u> When two people husband/wife - boyfriend/girlfriend or two students attend the physical Advanced course together the second person's tuition is only $250.00. If you enjoyed the first course produced in July 1991, imagine what this

advanced course produced in July through December 2001, and the most recent Summer 2002 class is all about; simply magical and extraordinarily rewarding that's what students said!

<u>Super deal:</u> **Bring any new student to a course and save $100.00 each on your own tuition. Someone you know may dream of learning the secrets of the Universal Mind, bring him/her and save.** This will be the experience of your life; you will build a solid cosmic consciousness and congregate with highly spiritual people. Sincerely, --Dr. Turi

✳

Students Feedback:

UK Student - I found Dr. Turi's course very well presented and easy to understand. Even though I am an astrologer myself, I found the course useful for talking to people from an astrological point of view by just knowing their month of birth. Cheers, Gerald

Do this course and stop wasting your time, energy and money! Dr Turi has created a great, accurate, affordable new experience for any student of astrology whether you are a proficient or novice student of the ancient cosmology school. The course is audio, very clear and revelent. You are placed in the first day of a class where you are learning with those of simular interests, while being in the comfort of your own home, office or other enviornment.

This is discussion of great teaching, where ASTROLOGY is freely spoken. Dr. Turi a native of France discusses the divine astrology used by ancient seers to counsel the aristocracy and nobility of those times. Nostradamus the great prophet used a particular system of which Dr. Turi is the expert for our times, (he is also a son of Provence, France the birth place of Nostradamus.)

Learning by hearing, remembering, speaking the spiritual science of Divine Astrology, Astro Psychology, and the balance of the mystical path of the major and minor arcane known as tarot, Dr. Turi's students are being equipped with all the tools they will need to understand mysteries transformed into useful powers and practice.Sign by sign, house by house, relationship by relationship until the process of life, death and rebirth are well communicated, received and understood. You will find Dr. Turi ripping past the norm and opening your eyes to the reality that once looked only like a possibility.

Reincarnation is discussed and Dr. Louis Turi discusses what progress is all about how the soul journeys and how karmic debt is collected or repaid. Fascinating lectures, additionally speak of the beastly powers of organized crime, government, media, religion, military, education and medicine and what you and I can do to bring enlightenemt, balance and harmony in spite of the chaos so many are living through to our lives.There is follow up by email, newletters, forum that help support your studies. Dr. As you can tell I am a fan of this man and his work. The convincer for me came years ago as his observations and predictions came true as he spoke them for me at a program he did in Arizona back in 1991. C'est magnifique! Dr. Cheryl Golden.

What I liked best about this course is Dr. Turi's eagerness to share his knowledge. He has a generosity of spirit to get this information out into the world. To do that, he has had to develop a method using metaphor and symbolism that would enable ordinary folks to grasp the message quickly so as to be able to apply it accurately in a way to improve life. I suspect this has cost him more than people realize in terms of time, commitment, energy and perhaps even ridicule and danger. For that, I thank him. It's a great course...fun, exciting and very informative. For the rest of my life, I will see things in a new light. Thank you again, Carol Bucklew

Dr. Turi has several books out...that I have found to be very beneficial in understanding His Material & explains...very simply & in depth...how He arrives at His predictions. He is a "straight forward" type of Individual who has...through experience & hardship...been able to bring to light....a form of exact Astrology (from the Stars) termed... Astropsychology. Dr. Turi has been able to calibrate....an understanding of celestial bodies...their energies & effects...closely affiliated with a "Nostradamus" Style of accuracy!

I came across Dr. Turi's Astropsychology...while searching for more information on...Astrology & the planets effects on daily life. In My Life quest...to understand...more of what makes up individuality...I have studied many Sciences... including Graphology (the study of handwriting, doodles& scribbles, etc.) also Psychology & Social Sciences & Behavior modifications....along with Medical effects of medications verses herbal applications & genetics. My study of the "Advance Astropsychology by Dr. Turi" has enhanced My understanding of what makes up individual make up & some good reasons as to why We often do "what We do" in certain situations...due to certain aspects of planetary involvement & the energies that effect...at any given moment in time. His "Gift" of knowledge...transferred to the written word.... has simplified... (.a complicated format given in Main Stream Astrology)...with a more precise definition of "cause & effect."

I have always questioned everything that I have come in contact with...in My Life & Dr. Turi's Work ..is no exception! I have pulled apart...bits of information...& have searched on My own. Given My understanding of His work...through His advanced course...I have found His format to be "impeccable" in "accuracy!" The greatest advantage...to becoming a Student...is that this knowledge can be applied...on a day to day basis...not only for Your own personal use...but in every day interaction with the people around You! I have always had a belief that knowledge forms a protection... which helps in assessing the World around Me. The more informed You are of the dynamics of the people around You... the better the options...of making informed choices in Your Life. I wish You well in Your search for knowledge.
Marianne K

From: Mary
To: Dr.Turi@cox.net
Sent: Saturday, August 23, 2003 1:33 PM
Subject: book

Thank you, Dr. Turi. I was very fortunate in finding your book "The Power of the Dragon"! You have taught me so much, and I just wanted to write to say I am so grateful to you. I have been studying astrology for 18 years and have been toying with the idea of using the solar chart as well as the Placidus system and you confirmed my thoughts that it is correct but to use the zero point instead of the sun degree. I have seen it work with many charts correctly.

I also am thankful for your teachings of the nodes as most astrologers do not really understand them well and some do not even focus on them much going so far as not even putting the south node in the chart which I have never understood. You have given me so much and I am eternally thankful to you. Mary Kanz - Cedar Rapids, IA

Hello Dr. Turi,
Hi, this is Veronica (aka January) how are you, and your girls doing??? Hope fine, I had to write to you, because your class was one of the most intense and exciting experiences I ever had!!! Also, something amazing happened. After graduating, Laurent and I went to a restaurant to have lunch, and to celebrate our accomplishment. And you won't believe what happened. There was a lady talking on the phone (she seemed to know the people who worked there, or maybe she was one of the owners, because she was on the business phone). She was yelling like a crazy woman, and crying. Curiously, Laurent and I were the only two clients there at the time, and couldn't help but to get a bit irritated by that screaming crazy lady. I kept on looking back at her to see what the hell was going on. And suddenly, she was in front of us, calling us names for even doing eye contact. She asked if she could sit and I moved over offering her a seat right next to me. She sat, I could see without a doubt that she was in such pain, it hurt, and I could feel it too!!! I was just about to talk to her, when Laurent, who was afraid of her and what she could do, told her to get up and leave us alone. She did. Then Laurent and I guessed she must be a Pisces, and have some strong planets such as Mars and Mercury in her sun sign and first house. After a couple of minutes, she came back, and apologized for being rude. She explained that her husband was filing for divorce, and that he is getting the kids. She loves her kids and that she needed them in her life. I moved over once again and looked at Laurent. He offered her a seat, and we both decided to do her chart to help her out with her situation. Well, I just happened to have my ephemeris with me (we just picked it up after class- before going to the restaurant). So we pulled out her planets, and guess what??? She was a Pisces with Venus and Mercury in her 1st house; in addition to that she had Saturn!!! WOW!! I asked her if her ex-husband was a foreigner (because the tail of her dragon was in Sagittarius) and she said yes. We tried to explain to her that she shouldn't drink (she was soooooooooooooo drunk) because she had Neptune (deception) in her 9th house of foreigners in Scorpio!!! She also had Libra in

her 8th house of life and death!!! She also had Pluto (danger), Mars (aggressiveness), and Uranus (unusual way of expressing oneself) in her 7th house of marriage in Virgo. But unfortunately she being drunk, and having Taurus in her 3rd house of the mind didn't help us much because she would interrupt us constantly, and was soooo stubborn about letting go of her relationship, keeping sober, and fighting for her kids. Interesting enough the Moon was in Libra (contracts and relationships), the Moon will be in Scorpio today, which means her Neptune planet will keep her drinking her problems away, and Sunday the Full Moon will be in Sagittarius (her tail of the dragon). Laurent and I are completely sure she won't make it past this Sunday. She will probably kill herself. What a shame, she was a pretty girl, and looked pretty smart too (when sober). The amazing part is : 1-the universe asked us to get the ephemeris because this was going to happen, 2-we saw her problems as clear as water, 3-this was such a test of our abilities and our passion for helping people and bringing the light. Dr Turi, I am ready to start fulfilling my mission. and it is all thanks to you, Christy, and Madeline!!!! We are so excited; we can't wait to see what's in store for us!!! THANKS!!!!!!!!!!!!!!!!!
WITH LOVE, --VERONICA (JANUARY)

Hi Veronica,
Dr. Turi sent me your email. I want to add that this is the beauty of his work. It opens the intuitional domain. I have done that many times--guessed some planet in a sign, by the way a person behaved. When you think about how remarkable that is, to know what planet was in which constellation in the sky at the moment of a person's birth, is truly a signal that Astro-Psychology is absolutely real, and works. When Dr. Turi says this class will "open your third eye" and give you "cosmic consciousness", he is NOT KIDDING!!! What a great story --Madeline

Dear Dr. Turi,
I cannot express in enough words how I enjoyed your class. I did not want it to end. I could have gone on another week. I was not ready to leave. I had to leave right after the test to catch my plane at the airport. I looked for you to say good-bye, but you had gone. The only thing I regret is that I missed the Jordan Maxwell lecture Friday, because I got lost and could not find the conference hall. I learned more about astrology from your class, than I have learned over the last 35 years. I will never go back to conventional astrology. You are an excellent teacher. You made the class very

interesting, with your very witty, and funny personality, and sense of humor. I feel very comfortable around you. Your warm personality made me feel right at home. I feel like I could tell you all my troubles, and you would listen, and give sympathy. Also, Madeline and the other members of your staff were really great. They were warm, friendly and very helpful. I could listen to your talk all day. Your French accent is very soothing, and a joy to listen too. You'd also make a great hypnotist with your soothing voice. You showed up in my Astro-Card reading. It was my first reading, therefore, I don't know what it means, but I am happy to know that we will connect sometime again in the future, for whatever reason. Have a blessed day.
Love, --Theresa

Dear Dr. Turi,
I liked the mix of students on the tapes, especially Chief Sonne and Claudine! Dr. Turi you had an <u>excellent program structure,</u> so when you went through the signs, planets and houses you were <u>focused and exceptional</u> in imparting your knowledge. You are an awesome teacher! The hidden dragon in ones' chart was the icing on the cake - that really pulled everything together to show <u>the true essence and accuracy of Divine Astrology</u>. Finally, the opening Indian ceremony and closing session were especially memorable and made me feel like part of the class – being there in spirit! --Eileen

Dear Dr. Turi,
As you know I have been working in the field of Traditional Chinese Medicine for almost thirty years. At the time I was trained there were just the beginnings of schools in this art in this country. Dr. Turi's training reminds me of the roots and traditionalism of my original training. There are no recipes and no short cuts. There is no dogma or preaching. Dr. Turi expertly illustrates his teaching from a variety of angles until the facts become an unconscious aspect of the student's life. He is factual and vivid and addresses a current age with traditional concepts. This is the Astro-Psychology of today with roots in the past. One of the most outstanding aspects of the course is the many pragmatic uses I can envision. I can already see its usefulness in business planning, lifestyle decisions and health ramifications. Dr. Turi has developed a tool for anyone with emotions and a developing lifestyle. I find the information so practical that I cannot compare this course to other astrology philosophies that I am aware of.

I have been seeking this information for over thirty years and during the very first tape of Dr. Turi's course I gained more understanding than the other thirty years. I applaud Dr. Turi for making this fine tool available to those with the vision and understanding to "see" and only hope that I will prove a worthy student. Please feel comfortable sharing this letter with our teacher and anyone else who can benefit. Thank you for everything. Yours truly, --Tilottama Star, L.Ac.

Dr. Turi,
I wanted to let you know the Astro-Psychology class in Portland has changed my life! You are an amazing speaker and have incredible POWER. You are too generous to share 30 years of information in 5 days. I am happy you are apart of my life, to help me with my spiritual awareness and to help others learn the stars. Thank you for flying to Portland, and your time. I am forever grateful to you!

Love and Light, --Lisa

Hello Dr. Turi,
I have just returned from the July Astro-Psychology class. What a unique and enlightening experience! Besides the valuable knowledge given, Dr. Turi himself makes the class challenging and entertaining. By the end of the week, I could see the reflex action of intuition beginning to form in everyone who was there. I did not think such a thing could be possible. It is a life changing experience, and one can never view the world in quite the same way. When Dr. Turi says, "you will be given the keys to the Universal Mind", he really means it! I encourage anyone who is thinking of attending, to go, as I guarantee they will be raised in spirit. My blessings to all who attend this course in the future. -- Madeline

Dear Dr.Turi,

We are thankful for the profound blessing of enlightenment shared with our July Astro-Psychology class. With your guidance, we - reunited old souls in the Arizona desert - rededicated ourselves to the vision of sharing Astro-Psychology with the children of the world, who will carry it forward as the only practical spiritual philosophy of the emerging Aquarian cycle. The highest of spiritual world is now in our hands. Together we are changing the human world into a world of light and awareness.
With much love, --Chief Sonne and Claudine

Dear Dr. Turi,
Definitely Divine Astrology for me, I have never been exposed to any Astrology before hearing Dr. Turi on Jeff Rense's national program, but if modern Astrology is littered with mathematical jargon then it is more of a hand down Win for Divine Astrology. The favorite part for me was Dr. Turi's great humor through out the tapes, I of course need to practice the reflex and know it will get more interesting when I receive my computer program and plug in people I know birth dates to practice with the housing system. Thank you, -- Joyce

To Dr. Turi,
I have just return from the July Astro-Psychology class, and it was the greatest class I ever attended. Dr. Turi is the one of the best teachers I have ever known. I have learnt so much from this man. This class is a must for every one. If you want to soar with the eagles and be number one in your field as an astrologer and to help every one that will be in your life take the class. For it is truly enlightenment. Thank you once again Dr. Turi for all that you have taught me. Love & light, --Alice Brooks

Dr. Turi,
To all prospective Astro-Psychology students; It has now been one week since I have completed Dr. Turi's advanced astrology course in Phoenix AZ. It has been about five months since I passed his basic astrology class by mail. I am here to state that I absorbed so much more information and reflex in five days of hands on schooling, than I could ever imagine getting in months of home study. Don't get me wrong, the home course I hold very dearly, and It was an excellent prerequisite, and I highly recommend it, but it only put me on the runway, where as traveling to AZ. to get hands on schooling, placed me in the air. I guess it depends on what you want to do with the knowledge, and how fast you want to do it. Myself I planned to make a career out of it, and I knew that the home course would eventually produce those results. Now having completed the advanced course, I now face that reality. My new career has now sprouted, and I owe it all to one incredible man, Dr. Louis Turi. There are not enough kind words to describe this incredibly gifted, spiritual pioneer. To be taught by him is a great honor, and pure enlightenment. There is no doubt that you will notice that he has a little something different to offer, something you won't find anywhere else. With

that I leave it up to you, the prospective student to find that answer. Thank You, --Charles

Hi Dr. Turi,
There is a driving force of energy that moves and propels us in our quest for the truth, and the truth does not lie in any one area. This truth that the seeker seeks, lays scattered through out our planet. So we as we seek must be patient and discerning when we come across the path of others speaking the truth. And from my discernment and the trust of my heart, I feel very fortunate and blessed to have crossed paths with Dr. Turi in this time of life. Dr. Turi's wisdom and understanding is a vast as the stars he speaks of. I am thankful that we taped the seminar! Thank you, again for sharing your wisdom of the stars! Many Blessings, --James

Thanks Dr. Turi,
You are the greatest. Learning to do astrology the way you do it has made such a difference in my life. I use it all day long every day. My birthday is ///, I have the stars to teach astrology and that is what I want to do, I do it all day long for everyone around me I can't help myself, I see it in the news, the weather, everything everywhere, my cats and dogs, it's wonderful. It is nice to know who you are dealing with, where is Neptune? What will you lie about? Where is Pl. what part of your life do you rearrange all of the time. Where is Jupiter? What do you want to learn and teach, where will you expand and be lucky? I have Jupiter in the 1st house I want to teach. It is all so wonderful. One of these days I am going to call Jeff Rense when you are on the air and ask some general questions, so people can see how powerful it is. Wind heat and fires for the next two years. With the DT in Sagittarius and Pluto in Sagittarius the list is long for what this will bring. Thank you so much Dr. Turi. --Barbara

Dear Dr. Turi,
After finishing your Advanced Astro-Psychology class, my dream state has been enhanced. I've always journeyed my dreams, and I can see a change of consciousness in myself. The Universal Mind has certainly come to new life. It's exciting to meet new people and see the qualities that the stars have influenced in their lives. It helps one to have a more open mind to personality traits that would normally be unpleasant, to understanding what makes people tick. For me, it has made me

a more compassionate, understanding person. With the help of your teachings, I've learned the future is the reincarnation of thoughts today. I'm thinking and planning my future with light and love for a beautiful new life. It is just the beginning of great things to come. Thank you for all you've done for me. Thank you for being such a beautiful channel of light in this world. Your student, --Kiki

Please help me promote the cosmic consciousness of everyone you care about. Set up a class in your city and benefit from our deal. <u>You will get the full advanced Astro-Psychology course for free or you will save $100 per person you bring with you</u>. I need both your spiritual and financial help to build many Astro-Psychology schools for the children of tomorrow. Understand the importance of my mission and be a part of it in the unfolding world karma. Please help me and invest in the future in promoting the true knowledge of the stars. Your contributions will help me so that I can spend more time on the air, writing, educating and publishing my work to those in need. For centuries many resources have been wasted in discrediting the stars, and for dangerous religious dogmas. Times have changed and the stars above do impose a new consciousness for mankind. Be a promoter of light and invest in the true light. The children of tomorrow need to gain cosmic consciousness and use the stars to live a more productive and safe life. Please communicate my work and help those in need to find guidance, comfort, direction and assistance in the celestial order. You will find the pathway to the stars and the realization of God's ultimate will throughout the Universe.

LA Class Summer 2002

Portland December 2001 Class

Services

Phoenix July 2001 Class

U.K. Course April 2005 Class

Sedona Course August 2006 Class

Startheme Publications LTD
NEXT LIVE ASTROPSYCHOLGY COURSE IN SEDONA ARIZONA

Sunday August 19 through Friday August 24 2007
CALL 602-265-7667 for more information

Send your payment to:
Dr. Louis Turi – 4411 N. 23rd St. – Phoenix, AZ 85016
Tel: 602-957-1617 – Fax 602-957-1678

Check out my other websites at:

http://www.cherrytap.com/drturi

http://www.myspace.com/drturi

"When suffering is on all sides and man hungers for the unmanifested mystery in all phenomenon, He seeks reflection of the Divine. God's higher truths are cloaked in his creation and the message is in the stars."
-- Nostradamus

Contents © Dr. Louis Turi, 2006

AstroTarot

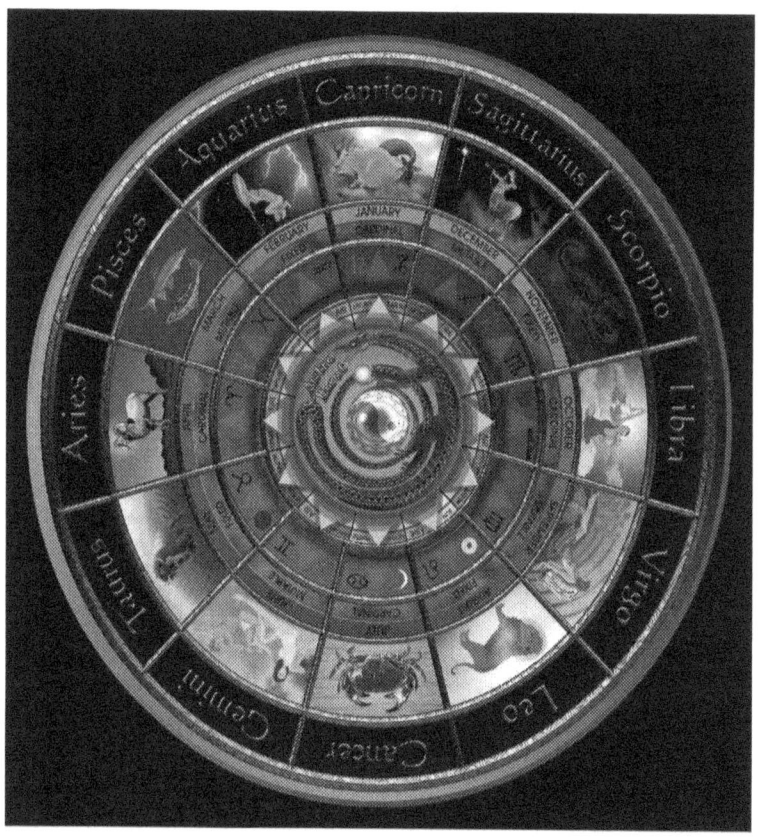

Tarot wheel was designed for Dr. Turi's astro-tarot and is available from Madeline Rosenstein.

www.madroseart.com

Astrology Chart designed by Madeline Rosenstein

This astrology chart is available as a poster. The Tarot table on the previous page is available as both a poster and a round board.

www.madroseart.com

www.ingramcontent.com/pod-product-compliance
Lightning Source LLC
Chambersburg PA
CBHW021828220426
43663CB00005B/173